TANGIER
• Tetouan
Larache
• Melilla
NORTHERN
ATLANTIC
COAST
MEDITERRANEAN
COAST & THE RIF
RABAT
FÈS
• Taza
ANCA
MEKNÈS &
VOLUBILIS
MIDDLE ATLAS
HIGH ATLAS
HERN
NTIC
AST
• Midelt
• Beni Mellal
Figuig
• Er-Rachidia
ARRAKECH
OUARZAZATE
& THE
SOUTHERN OASES
• Asni
• Ouarzazate
• Zagora
ute

Tangier
Pages 132–145

**Mediterranean Coast
& the Rif**
Pages 146–165

Meknès & Volubilis
Pages 188–209

Middle Atlas
Pages 210–225

Fès
Pages 166–187

High A...
Pages 24...

200

MOROCCO

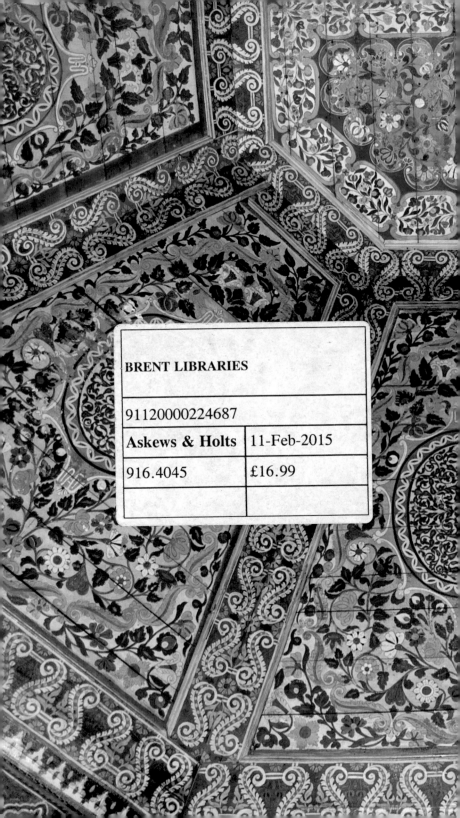

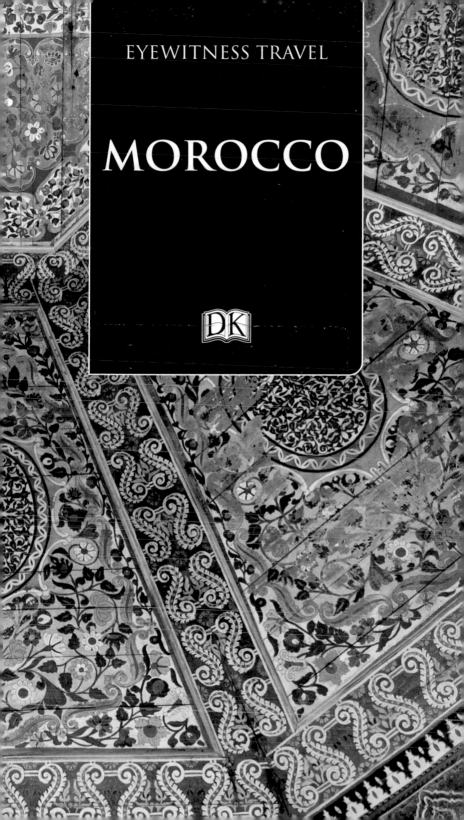

EYEWITNESS TRAVEL

MOROCCO

DK

LONDON, NEW YORK,
MELBOURNE, MUNICH AND DELHI
www.dk.com

Produced by Hachette Tourisme, Paris, France
Editorial Director Catherine Marquet
Project Editors Hélène Gédouin-Hines,
Catherine Laussucq, Paulina Nourissier
Art Director Guylaine Moi
Designers Maogani
Cartography Fabrice Le Goff

Contributors
Rachida Alaoui, Jean Brignon, Nathalie Campodonico,
Fabien Cazenave, Gaëtan Du Chatenet, Alain Chenal,
Carole French, Emmanuelle Honorin, Maati Kabbal,
Mohamed Métalsi, Marie-Pascale Rauzier, Richard Williams

Dorling Kindersley Limited
Publishing Manager Jane Ewart
Managing Editor Anna Streiffert
English Translation & Editor Lucilla Watson
Consultant Christine Osborne
DTP Jason Little, Conrad Van Dyk
Production Sarah Dodd

Printed In China By L. Rex Printing Co. Ltd.
First Published in the UK in 2002
By Dorling Kindersley Limited
80 Strand, London WC2R 0RL
14 15 16 17 10 9 8 7 6 5 4 3 2 1

Reprinted with revisions 2003, 2004, 2006, 2008, 2010, 2012, 2015

Copyright © 2002, 2015 Dorling Kindersley Limited, London
A Penguin Random House Company

All rights reserved. no part of this publication may be
reproduced, stored in a retrieval system, or transmitted
in any form or by any means, electronic, mechanical,
photocopying, recording or otherwise without the prior
written permission of the copyright owner.
A CIP catalogue record is available from the British Library.
ISBN 978-1-40932-977-0

MIX
Paper from
responsible sources
FSC www.fsc.org FSC™ C018179

**The information in this
DK Eyewitness Travel Guide is checked regularly.**
Every effort has been made to ensure that this book is as up-to-date as possible
at the time of going to press. Some details, however, such as telephone numbers,
opening hours, prices, gallery hanging arrangements and travel information are
liable to change. The publishers cannot accept responsibility for any consequences
arising from the use of this book, nor for any material on third party websites, and
cannot guarantee that any website address in this book will be a suitable source of
travel information. We value the views and suggestions of our readers very highly.
Please write to: Publisher, DK Eyewitness Travel Guides, Dorling Kindersley,
80 Strand, London, WC2R 0RL, UK, or email: travelguides@dk.com.

Front cover main image: The impressive Royal Palace Gate, Fès

 Painted wooden ceiling of the Bahia Palace in Marrakech

The village of Tamtattouchte, at the northern
end of the Todra gorge, with several fine *ksour*

Contents

A woman leaving the *zaouia* of
Sidi bel Abbès

A brassware and copperware shop in the Quartier Habbous, Casablanca

Survival Guide

Morocco Region by Region

Boundless expanses of desert near Laayoune

Olives from the Dadès valley

Travellers' Needs

Dish from the Fès region

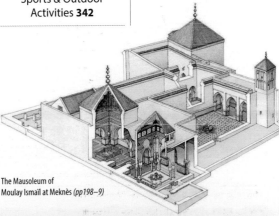

The Mausoleum of
Moulay Ismaïl at Meknès *(pp198–9)*

HOW TO USE THIS GUIDE

This guide helps you get the most from your visit to Morocco, providing expert recommendations and detailed practical information. *Introducing Morocco* maps the country and sets it in its historical and cultural context. The 13 sections comprising *Morocco Region by Region*, six of which focus on the country's major towns, describe important sights, using photographs, maps and illustrations. Restaurants and hotel recommendations, and information about hiking, trekking and other outdoor activities, can be found in *Travellers' Needs*. The *Survival Guide* contains practical tips on everything from visiting mosques to transport around the country.

Major Cities

In this guide, Morocco is described in 13 sections, three of which concentrate on Morocco's historic imperial cities – Fès, Meknès and Marrakech – and three on the country's major modern cities – Rabat, the capital, Casablanca and Tangier. A section is devoted to each city, except for Meknès. Each city's major sights are described in detail.

Coloured thumb tabs indentify the various regions of Morocco.

1 Introduction Each city's geographical setting and economic life are described, as well as its historical development and features of interest to the visitor.

A country map shows the city's location in Morocco.

2 City Map For easy reference, the sights are numbered and located on a map. The main streets, bus stations and railway stations and tourist offices are also shown.

A locator map shows the central area of each city in its context.

Sights at a Glance lists the chapter's sights by category: mosques and churches, historic buildings, museums, parks and historic districts.

3 Detailed Information All the sights in each city are described individually. Addresses, telephone numbers, opening hours, admission charges and information on how to get there are given for each sight. The key to symbols is shown on the back flap.

SOUTHERN ATLANTIC COAST

Each area of Morocco is identified by colour-coded thumb tabs.

1 Introduction

An overview of the history and characteristics of each region is given.

Country maps show the location and area of each region of Morocco.

Morocco Region by Region

In this book, the country is described in 13 chapters, six of which concentrate on Morocco's major cities and seven on the country's main regions. The map on the inside front cover shows this regional division. The most interesting places to visit are given on the *Regional Map* at the beginning of each chapter.

Exploring the Southern Atlantic Coast

2 Regional Map This shows
the main road network and gives an illustrated overview of the whole region. All interesting places to visit are numbered and there are useful tips on getting around.

Story boxes explore some of the region's historical and cultural subjects in detail.

3 Detailed Information All
the important towns and other places to visit are dealt with individually. They are listed in order, following the numbering given on the *Regional Map*. Each entry also contains practical information such as map references, addresses, telephone numbers and opening times.

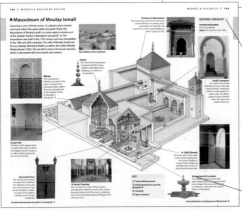

Mausoleum of Moulay Ismail

Practical information at the beginning of each entry includes a map reference relating to the road map on the inside back cover.

The Visitors' Checklist provides a summary of the practical information you need to plan your visit.

4 Morocco's Top Sights These
are given two or more full pages. Buildings are dissected to show their interiors.

Stars indicate the best sights and important features.

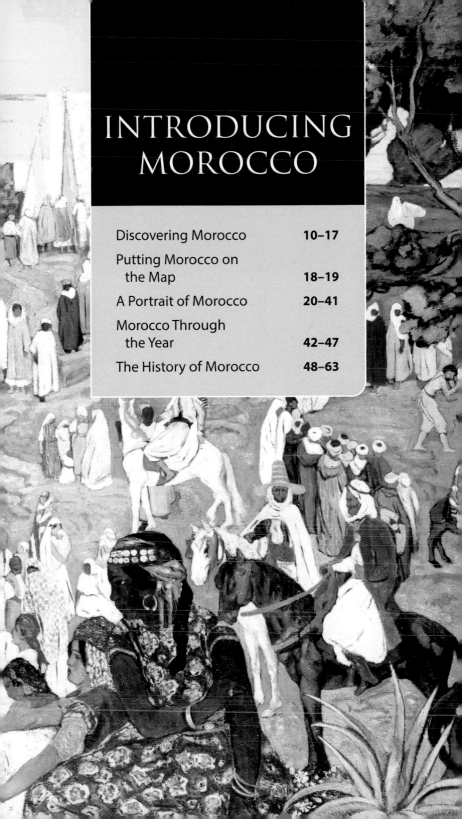

INTRODUCING MOROCCO

DISCOVERING MOROCCO

The following tours have been designed to take in as many of the country's highlights as possible, while keeping long-distance travel manageable. The first two itineraries outlined here take in the sights of Morocco's capital city Rabat and its commercial hub Casablanca. These itineraries can be followed separately or combined to form a longer trip. Next are two individual tours, which cover the fascinating cities of Meknès, Fès and Volubilis over four days, and Tangier and the alluring Mediterranean Coast over seven days. The 14-day itinerary encompasses the attractions of Marrakech and the South, a region that offers so much to experience. Choose and combine tours or dip in and out and be inspired.

Place Jemaa el-Fna
A UNESCO World Heritage Site, this iconic square comes alive in the evening with throngs of locals and visitors savouring grilled meats and watching musicians and jugglers or listening to storytellers.

14 Days in Marrakech and the South

- Take a horse-drawn carriage ride from outside Marrakech's towering **Koutoubia Mosque** for a circular tour of the city.

- Savour the atmosphere of the bustling **Place Jemaa el-Fna** before heading off to haggle in the souks.

- Join locals and artists along the Sqalas on a visit to the pretty fishing village of **Essaouira**.

- Follow the picturesque but tortuously snaking road through the western Atlas Mountains to experience the **Tizi-n-Test Pass**.

- Walk in the footsteps of Hollywood stars at **Ouarzazate** and **Aït-Benhaddou**.

- Go on a camel trek near **Mhamid** to see the first sand dunes of the vast Sahara.

Key

— 14 Days in Marrakech and the South

— 7 Days in Tangier and the Mediterranean Coast

— 4 Days in Meknès, Volubilis and Fès

◄ *Moroccan Festival*, a painting by André Suréda (1872–1930)

7 Days in Tangier and the Mediterranean Coast

- Wander the mesmerizing labyrinth of alleyways that open onto dusty squares in Tangier's ancient medina.

- Learn about local history in Tangier's Dar el Makhzen, which houses the **Musée Archéologique**.

- Admire the panoramic view of Tangier from atop the **Colline du Charf**.

- Be captivated by **Chefchaouen**, one of Morocco's prettiest towns, famous for its medina and weavers producing *jellabas*.

- Trek through the **Zegzel Gorge**, between the towns of Saïdia and Oujda.

4 Days in Meknès, Volubilis and Fès

- Survey the imperial city of Meknès from atop the beautiful **Bou Inania Medersa**.

- Examine displays that include a traditional Moroccan-style room at Meknès's **Musée Dar Jamaï**.

- Spend some time away from the bustle of the city at the **Bassin de l'Aguedal**.

- Explore the remains of the once magnificent town of **Volubilis** in the foothills of the Zerhoun Mountains.

- Wander around the historic medina of Fès and stop by the city's most famous landmark, the **Karaouiyine Mosque**.

- Tuck into a succulent chicken tagine in one of the elegant restaurants in **Fès el-Jedid**.

Musée Dar Jamaï
Set in a former palace, this museum houses an absorbing collection of traditional ceramics, carpets, jewellery and exquisite examples of woodwork among other exhibits. The museum's leafy Andalusian garden offers a tranquil spot.

View of the majestic Mausoleum of Mohammed V, Rabat

2 Days in Rabat

- **Arriving** Rabat is served by the modern Rabat-Salé International Airport, located about 8 km (5 miles) from the city centre. An express shuttle bus service runs between the terminal and the Rabat Ville Train Station, located in Place Mohammed V.

- **Moving on** Casablanca is 86 km (53 miles) away from Rabat and easy to reach by road or rail from the city's train station.

Day 1

Morning Start the day with a visit to Rabat's bustling medina. Dozens of shops line the medina's arterial road, the **Rue Souïka** *(see p78)*, which throngs with people going about their everyday lives. Continue along the **Rue Souk es-Sebat** *(see p78)*, then turn left into **Rue des Consuls** *(see p75)* to reach the famous Wool Market, where a carpet auction is held every Thursday. Up ahead is the **Bab Oudaïa** *(see p74)*, a monumental gate leading to the **Oudaïa Kasbah** *(see pp72–3)*. A walk through the kasbah will reveal architecture from the Almohad period (1147–1248), and from the 17th century when Moulay Ismail transformed it into a formidable

fortress. Look out for the oldest mosque in Rabat, the El-Atika Mosque, on Rue Jamaa. Round up the morning spending an hour or so in the **Musée des Oudaïa** *(see p74)*, admiring its collection of Berber jewellery and traditional costumes.

Afternoon From the Oudaïa Kasbah, follow the scenic Wadi Bou Regreg, a road that runs alongside the river, past the Jewish district, to the El-Alaouiyine boulevard. Located at a little distance from here is the **Mausoleum of Muhammad V** *(see pp80–81)*, a massive white Italian marble structure, which contains the tombs of members of the royal

Exterior of a typical house decorated with potted plants in the Oudaia Kasbah, Rabat

family, and the elaborately decorated **Hassan Tower** *(see p78)*. These majestic buildings are considered Rabat's most prominent landmarks. The mausoleum's twelve-sided dome with *muqarnas* (stalactites), and the intricate motifs on Hassan Tower's topmost level deserve particular attention.

Day 2

Morning Get a feel for modern-day Rabat by spending the morning in the attractive **Ville Nouvelle** *(see p79)*. Wide tree-lined boulevards, such as the Avenue Mohammed V, and vast areas of parkland provide the backdrop to Hispano-Maghrebi-style residential buildings and office blocks. Amble through the town's green spaces to reach the contemporary Musée de la Monnaie, which occupies the Bank of Morocco building and tells the history of the country's currency. Afterwards, take the Rue Abou Inan, which leads to the Art Deco Cathédral Saint-Pierre, dating from the 1930s.

Afternoon Arrive at the **Musée Archéologique** *(see pp82–3)*, which contains the largest collection of archaeological treasures in Morocco. Most of the artifacts displayed have been recovered from the town of Volubilis. The museum is extensive, and could easily take up the entire afternoon. However, leave time to visit the **Chellah Necropolis** *(see p84)*, a burial place and site of the Roman city Sala Colonia. Follow the Avenue Yacoub el-Mansour, past the walls of the **Dar el-Makhzen** *(see p84)*, the seat of the Moroccan government, to get here.

> **To extend your trip...**
> Take a leisurely drive through the foothills of the **Middle Atlas** *(see pp211–25)* to see rural villages or travel along the coast to **Moulay Bousselham** *(see p95)*, famous for its lagoon that attracts migrating birds.

2 Days in Casablanca and the Coast

- **Arriving** Located 30 km (19 miles) south of the city centre, the Mohammed V International Airport serves Casablanca and links it to Morocco's major cities. Taxis and car hire companies can be found outside or within its three terminals.

- **Moving on** Casablanca has a good road network linking it to the Southern Atlantic Coast. Domestic flights, trains from Casa-Port station and the N1/N6 highways provide easy options for onward travel to Meknès.

Day 1

Morning The monumental **Hassan II Mosque** (see pp106–107), as it stands silhouetted against the sky, is the perfect place to start this itinerary. The mosque is situated on a promontory with the Atlantic Ocean waves crashing against the shore behind it. Take a tour of the fabulously ornate interior crafted by master artisans; soak in the spectacular views of the ocean bed through the glass floor of the Prayer Hall. Later, pause awhile outside to contemplate the scale of this architectural marvel and the minaret, which is the tallest in the world. Then, drive or walk along one of the boulevards signposted to the port.

Afternoon Arrive at the **Old Medina** (see p104) that lies off the Boulevard des Almohades. The area has changed little in the past century, even as Casablanca continued to expand around it. Market stalls covered in copper pots and old jewellery line the medina walls daily; join the locals in search of a bargain. Next, head to the **Place des Nations Unies** (see p102), south of the medina, where major thoroughfares, such as the **Boulevard Mohammed V** (see p102), converge. The arcaded buildings here house trendy restaurants and designer fashion centres. End the day with a screening at the Rialto cinema.

Day 2

Morning Take a leisurely morning stroll through the **Parc de la Ligue Arabe** (see p104), Casablanca's largest park. Admire the tall palm trees vying for attention amid lavishly planted flowers beds and lawns designed to a formal French layout. The splendid Art Deco houses that surround the park are also worth a look. Next, head northwest to reach the Villa des Arts gallery and spend the afternoon appreciating contemporary Moroccan painting.

A seafront café along the Corniche d'Aïn Diab, Casablanca

Evening Head out of the city centre via the Boulevard Zerktouni, past the **Casablanca Twin Center** (see p110), to the elegant, elevated coastal suburb of **Anfa** (see p111). There are wonderful panoramic views of the city to be enjoyed from here. Go for a drive along the **Corniche d'Aïn Diab** (see p111), an avenue lined with tidal swimming pools, beaches and hotels, before heading to one of the many upmarket restaurants for a last sumptuous dinner in Casablanca.

> **To extend your trip...**
> Drive 180 km (112 miles) south-west from Casablanca to **Oualidia** (see p119), an unassuming town near a gorgeous lagoon and beach. It is famous throughout Morocco for the succulent oysters that thrive here.

Opulent interiors of the Prayer Hall in Hassan II Mosque, Casablanca

Exquisitely carved courtyard with a pool in the centre in Bou Inania Medersa, Meknès

4 Days in Meknès, Volubilis and Fès

- **Arriving** The international Fès-Saïss Airport serves the city of Fès and Meknès. While buses ferry visitors into central Fès, trains run from the terminal to the Ville Nouvelle in Meknès. Car hire companies have offices in the airport.

- **Transport** A car and driver are ideal for this itinerary. However, the medinas in both Fès and Meknès can only be explored on foot.

- **Moving on** Flights and trains can be taken from Meknès, and buses run from Fès to Tangier.

Days 1 and 2: Meknès

No visit to Meknès would be complete without exploring the medina with its massive **Ramparts** and bustling **souks** (see p192). Spend time at the **Grand Mosque** (see p192), the most important place of worship in the city, and admire the sweeping view of Meknès from the top of the **Bou Inania Medersa** (see p193). While away the afternoon at the **Musée dar Jamaï** (see p194) where displays include a Moroccan-style room with lavishly decorated walls and furnishings.

Start the next day at the **Koubba el-Khayatine and Habs Qara** imperial pavilion (see p196), and then head for the

Mausoleum of Moulay Ismaïl (see pp198–9) nearby, which is famous for its elaborate stuccowork. Later, drive past the **Dar el-Makhzen** (see p196) to the **Dar el-Ma** (see p197), a grand water house that lies along side the tranquil **Bassin de l'Aguedal** (see p197). Be sure to stop by the **Heri es-Souani** (see p197), a monumental building once used to store grain.

Day 3: Volubilis

Spread over a vast plateau in the foothills of the Zerhoun Mountains, the ruins of the ancient city of **Volubilis** (see pp206–209) easily warrant a day of exploration. Dating from around the 3rd century BC, Volubilis was one of the wealthiest cities of the Roman Empire's Kingdom of Mauretania. Take time out to see the well-preserved basilica

Elaborately decorated gate leading to the Mausoleum of Moulay Ismail, Meknès

and the triumphal arch, which affords wonderful vistas of the site. A café provides refreshment during the day.

Day 4: Fès

Wander around the medina in **Fès el-Bali** (see p169) and see the **Andalusian Quarter** (see p179), with its towering mosque, and the **Tanners' Quarter** (see p179), where locals work on the hides that are processed to make leather slippers sold in the souks. Visit Fès' most famous landmark, the **Karaouiyine Mosque** (see pp180–81), then head to the **Fondouk el-Nejjarine** (see p171), a splendid former cara-vanserai. The coppersmiths' workshops around here are worth checking out. Spend an hour or more exploring the **Souks** (see p171), including the El-Attarine Souk with its heavenly aroma of spices. The Bou Inania Medersa, which houses the **Musée Dar el-Batha** (see pp172–3), offers an afternoon learning about local history. End the day with a drive to the **Fès el-Jedid** district (see pp184–88) to dine on a tasty chicken tagine.

> #### To extend your trip...
> Visit **Ifrane** (see p216), which lies around 63 km (39 miles) south of Fès high in the Middle Atlas mountains. In summer, it offers a respite from the heat; in winter, blanketed by snow, it becomes a ski centre.

7 Days in Tangier and the Mediterranean Coast

- **Arriving** The Ibn Batouta International Airport is located 15 km (9 miles) south-west of Tangier and, along with the smaller airports at Oujda, Nador and Al-Hoceima, serves Morocco's northern coast. Visitors can also arrive and depart by ferry.

- **Transport** A car and driver is essential for visiting the Bay of Tangier as well as for touring the Mediterranean Coast.

- **Moving on** Domestic flights from Angads Airport in Oujda fly to Marrakech.

Day 1: Tangier

Tangier's medina is a mesmerizing place, with alleyways opening onto dusty squares and the minaret of the **Kasbah Mosque** dominating the scene *(see p136)*. Soak up history in the Dar el Makhzen, which houses the **Musée Archéologique** *(see p136)*. Wander through the medina to the **Rue Es-Siaghine** *(see p138)*. Lined with cafés and souks, this street is always fun. Turn right for the **Grand Socco**, otherwise known as the **Place du 9 Avril 1947** *(see p142)*, and stay until evening when the square turns into a colourful, open-air bazaar.

Day 2: Tangier

Start the day in Rue d'Angleterre, from where exhibits in the **Galerie d'Art Contemporain Mohammed Drissi** beckon *(see p142)*, then drive on to admire the architecture of the **Anglican Church of St Andrew** *(see p142)*. Enjoy lunch in the Café de Paris, located on the corner of **Place de France** *(see p143)*. The café is Tangier's most famous eatery and the primary haunt of its legendary literati. The afternoon can be spent exploring the Art Deco Ville Nouvelle. Its main thoroughfare, **Avenue Pasteur** *(see p143)*, is where locals amble each evening.

Day 3: Tangier

Head out of the city to the **Bay of Tangier** *(see p145)* – the cragged coastline here has some of Morocco's best beaches. The **Colline du Charf** *(see p145)*, a hill rising to a height of 100 m (328 ft), provides a backdrop to the beaches and is a popular drive for Tangier locals. Almost the whole city can be seen from a vantage point at the summit.

Day 4: Ceuta and Tétouan

Begin at one of **Ceuta**'s *(see p151)* two top museums, the Museo de la Legión that elaborates the role of the Spanish Foreign Legion in Morocco, before heading to the Museo Municipal. Then, explore the plazas and cobbled streets of this picturesque Spanish enclave. From here, follow the coast road or take the highway to **Tétouan** *(see p153)* and wonder at its centuries-old "living museum" medina. In contrast is Tétouan's Ville Nouvelle, a place of elegant Hispano-Mauresque architecture and boulevards.

Day 5: Chefchaouen

Allow a day to appreciate **Chefchaouen** *(see p154–5)* – one of the prettiest towns in Morocco. The town is famous for its 500-year-old blue-and-white medina dotted with weavers' workshops producing *jellabas*. Be sure to visit the kasbah and the Musée Ethnographique that occupies a traditional galleried house in its grounds.

Day 6: Al-Hoceima to Cap des Trois Fourches

A fishing harbour and resort, **Al-Hoceima** *(see p157)* is one of the most beautiful coastal spots

The town of Chefchaouen, with the ech-Chaoua rising in the background

in Morocco. Relax awhile here, then head for **Nador** *(see p162)*, and on through the Spanish town of **Melilla** *(see p162)* until the dramatic landscape at **Cap des Trois Fourches** *(see p163)* comes into view. The rock formations and beaches offer excellent photo opportunities.

Day 7: Moulouya Estuary to Oujda

See oystercatchers, flamingos and terns on a visit to the **Moulouya Estuary** *(see p163)*, a nature reserve located just outside **Saïdia** *(see p164)*. The **Zegzel Gorge** *(see pp164–5)* nearby offers a challenging trek to **Oujda** *(see pp164–5)* – there is a road from Saïdia for the less adventurous.

To extend your trip…

Check out the tourist board's suggested itineraries and routes for hikers that take in the best of the **Rif Mountain** region *(see pp154–5)*, including the scenic Talassemtane National Park.

Spectacular view of a zigzag road leading to Al-Hoceima

14 Days in Marrakech and the South

- **Arriving** International flights, and those from Moroccan cities, arrive and depart from the modern Marrakech-Menara Airport in Marrakech.

- **Transport** Marrakech is a large city and a car and driver is necessary to see its outlying sights. Domestic flights are available between Marrakech and Agadir's Al Massira Airport, the Plage Blanche Airport in Tan Tan and the Mogador Airport in Essaouira. Smaller airports serve Zagora, Taroudannt and Ouarzazate.

Day 1: Marrakech

Start at **Koutoubia Mosque** (see pp240–41) with its stunning minaret and restored pink-coloured brickwork. Hop aboard a horse-drawn carriage from outside the mosque for a circular tour of Marrakech. Once back, head to **Place Jemaa el-Fna** (see p238) and take the time to soak in the festive atmosphere created by dancers, musicians and snake-charmers who throng the place. Reserve plenty of time to navigate the network of tiny streets in the souks. Don't miss the **Ben Youssef Medersa** (see p232), one of the finest Koranic schools in Morocco.

Day 2: Marrakech

On the second day in town, revel in the splendour of Marrakech's palaces. Start with the Moorish-style Dar Menebhi, which houses the **Musée de Marrakech** (see p232), displaying a collection of contemporary art and Orientalist paintings. Proceed by car to the **Dar Si Saïd** (see p244) palace to see its exquisite museum exhibits. End the day with a visit to the grand 19th-century **Palais Bahia** (see p238) and the sprawling remains of the 16th-century **Palais el-Badi** (see p239).

Day 3: Marrakech

Explore the bustling streets of Marrakech's kasbah district where even everyday life is a spectacle. Look up at the **Kasbah Mosque**'s fine minaret (see p242) before heading out to the magnificent and ornate **Saadian Tombs** (see p242). The quiet garden here offers a respite from the busy kasbah.

Day 4: Marrakech

Flora is the theme of the day, with visits by car to the city's historic **Aguedal Gardens** (see p246), the vast **Menara** (see p246) where locals take a daily walk around the pool, and the beautiful **Majorelle Garden** (see p247) in the heart of Ville Nouvelle. On the outskirts is the **La Palmeraie** (see p247), said to contain 150,000 trees. Camel rides are available around the garden.

Fishing boats moored at the port, Essaouira

Day 5: Essaouira

A three-hour drive from Marrakech, **Essaouira** (see p124) is a delightful fishing village, popular with artists. Join locals in strolling along the *sqalas* or bastions built to protect the town from the sea. Spend time on the beach and explore the busy port and brilliant whitewashed medina.

Days 6 and 7: Agadir

Drive or fly to the growing metropolis of **Agadir** (see pp290–91), whose mild climate draws holidaymakers to its beaches. Take time to admire Berber exhibits in the Musée Municipal du Patrimoine Amazighe, and visit the Jardin Olhao museum to see how Agadir was rebuilt after an earthquake. Around 10 km (6 miles) away is Polizzi Medina, a relatively new medina built in the traditional style.

Day 8: Tan Tan or Souss Massa National Park

For a taste of unspoiled Morocco, complete with camel markets and nomads, go out to **Tan Tan** (see p298) – take an early morning flight from Agadir as it is nearly 350 km (217 miles) south. Alternatively, take a road trip over a couple of days to see the **Souss Massa National Park** (see p296), which hosts hundreds of migratory birds from southern Spain and France. A little further south is **Tiznit** (see p296), where craftsmen produce Berber jewellery and other items in silver.

The Art Deco museum surrounded with cacti and palms in Majorelle Garden, Marrakech

Ruins of the Tamnougalt kasbah in the midst of palm groves near Draa Valley

Day 9: Taroudannt

Return by air to Agadir and head 80 km (50 miles) east to spend the afternoon in **Taroudannt** *(see p292)*. Behind the mighty red-ochre ramparts are scenes of traditional Berber life, including craftspeople making jewellery and creating carvings of white stone. Pick up exquisitely crafted souvenirs at one of the souks here.

Day 10: Tizi-n-Test Pass and Asni

Devote this day to getting a taste of rural and mountainlife. The plains heading out of Taroudannt towards the western Atlas Mountains are pristine and dotted with argan trees before the ascent to the mountains begins. A picturesque but serpentine, and at times narrow road, leads through the **Tizi-n-Test Pass** *(see p256)* and on to the scenic village of **Asni** *(see p256)*, with its red-walled kasbah and surrounding orchards.

Day 11: Ouarzazate to Aït-Benhaddou

Drive to the beautiful **Ouarzazate** *(see p268)*, where the mountains meet the desert. An amble around this delightful town will reveal small red-pink kasbahs standing in an orderly fashion along wide streets. About 6 km (4 miles) out of town is the Atlas Film Studios where hundreds of Hollywood films have been shot, while in the opposite direction the **Taourirt Kasbah**

(see p268) is the dramatic focal point of a Berber village. Drive 30 km (19 miles) to **Aït-Benhaddou** *(see p269)*, a UNESCO World Heritage Site that has also had a starring role in many films. Return to Ouarzazate for the night.

Day 12: Skoura to Dadès Gorge

See some of the most splendid kasbahs in Southern Morocco in **Skoura** *(see p276)*, a pretty town surrounded by palm groves in the Wadi Dadès. Drive on to the town of **Boumalne du Dadès** *(see p277)*, which marks the beginning of the **Dadès Gorge** *(see p277)*. Join a guided trek or simply admire the panoramic views for which the region is famous.

Day 13: Draa Valley to Tamegroute

After a leisurely drive through the scenic **Draa Valley** *(see p272)*, allow a few hours to mingle with the Berber residents of **Zagora** *(see p272)*. Take time to sit and think about the camel caravans that once passed through here into the Sahara – a famous road sign in the town reads "Timbuctu 52 Days by Camel", referring to the number of days it might take to reach Timbuktu in Mali. The lovely village of Amazraou nearby is known for its intricately fashioned silver jewellery. Further on is **Tamegroute** *(see p273)*, an important educational and religious centre. The library

containing a priceless collection of manuscripts is a must see.

Day 14: Camel trek into the dunes

No visit to Southern Morocco would be complete without a camel trek into the dunes. Short guided trips into the Tinfou Dunes and the Chigaga Dunes, which lie south of the border post town of Mhamid, are available from **Zagora** *(see p272)* or **Tamegroute** *(see p273)*.

To extend your trip...
The fishing port of **Tarfaya**, along with **Laayoune** and **Dakhla** in the deep south *(see p298)*, are beautifully unspoiled and reward travellers making the long journey with breathtaking desert scenery.

Typical desert landscape surrounding the town of Zagora

Putting Morocco on the Map

Morocco has many faces. It is situated on the African continent and has traces of African heritage. But its climate and varied topography, its historical association with Andalusian Spain, and its wish to join the European Union give it a European facet. In the distant past it belonged to the indigenous Berbers. To the Arabs and Muslims who have held Morocco since the 7th century, it is known as Maghreb el-Aqsa – the westernmost country of the Muslim world. Morocco has 33,750,000 inhabitants, almost 40 per cent of whom are under 15 years old. The population is unevenly distributed over the country's 710,850 sq km (274,388 sq miles), being concentrated along the Atlantic coast and in the Rif and the High Atlas mountains.

Key

━━ Motorway
═ ═ Motorway under construction
━━ Major road
⋯⋯ Minor road
─── Railway line
─ ─ ─ Ferry route
━━ National border
▪ ▪ Disputed territory border

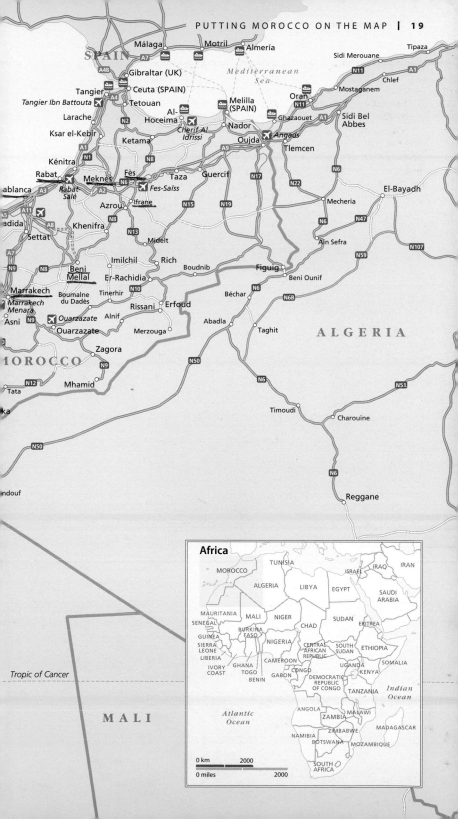

A PORTRAIT OF MOROCCO

Morocco is like a tree whose roots lie in Africa but whose leaves breathe in European air. This is the metaphor that King Hassan II (1929–99) used to describe a country that is both profoundly traditional and strongly drawn to the modern world. It is this double-sided, seemingly contradictory disposition that gives Morocco its cultural richness.

Morocco is a country that is unique in the Muslim world. Its richly diverse culture has been shaped by 3,000 years of history, by ethnic groups whose roots go far back in time, and also by its geographical location, with the Atlantic Ocean to the west, sub-Saharan Africa to the south, Europe to the north and the Mediterranean countries to the northeast.

The Moroccan people are torn between the lure of modernity on the one hand and a profound desire for Islamic reform on the other. With events such as the death in 1999 of Morocco's king, Hassan II, and the enthronement of his son,

Mohammed VI, as well as the establishment of a left-wing coalition government and the problems that the government faces regarding the economy and the proposal of a new constitution by Mohammed VI, Morocco today stands on the threshold of a challenging new phase in its history.

An Evolving Society

Since the 1950s, Morocco has undergone profound social change. Traditional tribal cohesion has been replaced by the European-style nuclear family, polygamy has become distinctly rare, a money-based economy is now the norm, and

Au Petit Poucet, an historic bar in Casablanca

◀ Beautiful interior of the Moulay Idriss II Mosque in Fès

Members of a Gnaoua brotherhood

has made attempts to tackle three major scourges: illiteracy, unemployment and poverty. The government has increased spending on education at all levels and education is compulsory, but many children – particularly girls in rural areas – do not attend school. Country-wide literacy rates are estimated at 67.1 per cent among the adult population, but the female literacy rate in rural areas is as low as 10 per cent.

Berber Culture

the notion of individuality has emerged. These changes have been accompanied by a growth in the urban population and by the rise of a bi-cultural elite, with a traditional background and a European outlook. With an unusually large percentage of young people, Moroccan society is unmistakably breaking away from the past. However, Morocco still faces the challenge of resolving the difficulties that sharp contradictions in its social, political and economic life present. Since gaining independence from France in 1956, Morocco

Water-seller in Marrakech

With its mixed Berber and Arab population, Morocco has, however, successfully maintained ethnic and cultural stability and equality between the Berber and Arabic languages. Although Tamazight, one of the major variants of the Berber language, is not spoken or taught in schools, it is heard on Moroccan radio and television. The movement to promote Berber language and culture through the medium of newspapers, concerts and other cultural events is dynamic, as are efforts to encourage the wider use of the language and to nurture respect for the rich Berber culture. Pilot

Filming at the Atlas Studios at Ouarzazate

Traditional agricultural labour in the Ourika valley

in March 1999 were met by opposition and incited the wrath of the Minister of Religious Affairs, the *ulemas* (councils) and Parliament's Islamic deputies. In 2005, following years of resistance from religious bodies, Morocco's king introduced a new *mudawwana*, which has improved the status of women.

Political Change

Until the death of Hassan II in 1999, Morocco was ruled by a distant and autocratic king. The effect of the attempted coups d'état of 1971 and 1972 was to encourage the Moroccan authorities to control the wheels

Westernized young girls in Casablanca

of government even more tightly. Driss Basri, then Minister of the Interior, was responsible for this clamp down.

At the end of his reign, Hassan II began to relax his authoritarian grip on power by involving the left wing in the country's government. In February 1998, a government of national unity, led by

projects, such as the construction of mosques, wells, roads and schools, have been undertaken in the southern Souss region, funded by money sent back by Berbers of southern Morocco working abroad.

The Status of Women

Women today work in all sectors – as political delegates and ambassadors, airline pilots, company directors and royal advisers; they are also Olympic champions, writers, publishers, active militants and journalists. Thus they have a secure place in Moroccan society.

In the space of 30 years, the status and position of women has radically changed. The constitution of 10 March 1972, which granted women the right to vote and to be elected, was the first of these changes. In 1994, 77 women were elected to the Chamber of Representatives. However, the highly militant feminist associations were still not entirely satisfied. They demanded the abolition of the *mudawwana* – a statute of 1957 that dominates the lives of Moroccans and prevented women from being treated as fully fledged adults. Moves to raise the status of women made

Berber women in the traditional costume of the Rif

The Rose Festival in El-Kelaa M'Gouna

the Socialist leader Abderrahmane Youssoufi, was formed, although in the years since, its success is deemed to have been limited.

Since 1999, Mohammed VI has ushered in a different style of government. Underlying his political approach are a willingness to listen more closely to his people and a commitment to countering Islamic radicals. He also won popular support for sacking Driss Basri, Minister of the Interior. Brushing aside protocol, he publicly presented his wife and ordered the setting-up of royal commissions to look into economic development, the problem of the Western Sahara, employment and education.

For the September 2002 parliamentary election, Morocco had more than 20

Berber cameraman

parties, many of which had been specially formed. This led to the success of the Islamic Party of Justice and Development (PJD), the third political party in the country after the Socialist Party (USFP) and the Istiqual Party, the principal opposition party to the coalition government.

The terrorist bombs of May 2003 in Casablanca, which killed 43 people, brought instability to the country, halting the progress of democratization started by Mohammed VI. However, parliamentary elections were again held in 2007.

A Varied Economy

Morocco's geographical location, at the nexus between Africa and Europe, brings it considerable economic advantage, especially in the fields of tourism, agriculture and the textile industry. The discovery of extensive oil-fields has also been a boost for the country's economy. Fishing and hydroelectric power are Morocco's other two natural resources. The economy also benefits from the influx of funds sent back by Moroccans working abroad. Some US $2,000 million are sent back to Morocco each year.

The arrival of multinational companies has transformed telecommunications

Schoolchildren in the Dadès valley

and has led to an explosion in the use of mobile phones. The number of computers has also risen.

Nevertheless, the Moroccan economy is handicapped in several ways: agriculture is dependent on rainfall, the education system is inadequate, energy costs are prohibitively high, and sparse investment is made in the population. In 2014, the number of people living on or below the international poverty line stood at 6.3 million. Every year, around 500,000 rural emigrants swell the poor ghettos in the towns and cities. For a number of reasons, the economic reforms introduced by the government of national unity have not had the anticipated effect. Morocco is being encouraged by the World Bank to develop a business environment that is more competitive, achieve sustainable job creation and boost exports.

The country has a positive image in Europe, and relations are being consolidated. In March 2013, negotiations for free trade status between Morocco and the EU were formally launched. The arrangement depends on Morocco putting in place a solid financial and technological

A spice and medicinal plant seller in one of the souks of Marrakech

infrastructure. The country is in need of modernization, although the evolution of true democracy is likely to be slow. This is a key policy since the slow progress of reforms is encouraging young people to emigrate. Under Mohammed VI there has been economic liberalization but time will tell whether he will succeed in significantly reducing poverty and unemployment, controlling Islamic radicals and abolishing illiteracy.

The picturesque Jemaa el-Fna in Marrakech

The Landscape and Wildlife of Morocco

With a mountain range exceeding a height of 4,000 m (13,130 ft) and a coastline stretching from the Mediterranean to the Atlantic, Morocco has a varied topography. In environments ranging from arid scrublands to cedar forests and high mountains, plant life comprises over 4,000 species adapted to extreme conditions. The coast is visited by migratory birds while the mountains are the habitat of Barbary sheep and birds of prey, including the lammergeier *(see p223)*.

The argan, a tree growing only in southwestern Morocco *(see p131)*

Mountain Forests and High Steppes

Forests grow in the Rif, the Middle Atlas and the western High Atlas, at altitudes of 1,400–2,500 m (4,600–8,200 ft), where annual rainfall is 650 mm–2,000 mm (25–78 in). The varied vegetation here includes Atlas cedar, maritime pine and holm-oak. The high steppes, covered with low, thorny vegetation, are found at altitudes over 2,700 m (8,860 ft) in the High Atlas *(see pp222–3)*.

Arid Coastal Regions and Desert

The rocky coastal lowlands between Safi and Agadir has an annual rainfall ranging from 40–150 mm (1.5–6 in). Vegetation, which is adapted to saline conditions, consists of sparse shrubs, mostly acacia. Further south is the desert with *ergs* (sand dunes) and the stony *hammada*.

The bald ibis, almost extinct, is found in the Souss Massa National Park *(see p296)*, a fertile exception to the arid littoral.

The golden eagle is seen mostly in the mountains, where it preys on jackals, bustards and small mammals.

The Barbary squirrel, whose favourite food is argan nuts, inhabits the arid lowlands of southwestern Morocco.

The lammergeier builds its nest on rocky outcrops. It is a scavenger but sometimes also kills its prey by knocking it off high rocks with a strong flap of its wing.

The great cormorant nests on sea cliffs between Agadir, in the north, and the Arguin sand banks of Mauritania.

The Macaque or Barbary Ape

The macaque is North Africa's only monkey. Three-quarters of the population lives in the cedar forests of the Middle Atlas, up to an altitude of 2,000 m (6,565 ft). Macaques are also found in the Rif, the High Atlas and on the Rock of Gibraltar. The animals live in colonies of 10 to 30 individuals, consisting of adults and young monkeys of both sexes. In summer, they feed on caterpillars, acorns, mushrooms and asphodel bulbs. In winter, their diet consists of grasses, cedar leaves and sometimes bark.

The macaque, a tail-less monkey of North Africa

Scrub and Steppe

Southeastern Morocco consists of steppes covered in esparto grass and artemisia. On the high plateaux, on the southern slopes of the High Atlas and on part of the Anti-Atlas annual rainfall ranges from 100 mm–300 mm (4 in–12 in) and snow is rare. Trees include Atlas pistachio, juniper and ash.

Dry Woodland

Almost all the low-lying and middle-altitude regions on the northern side of the Atlas are covered by dry woodland. Annual rainfall here ranges from 350 mm–800 mm (14 in–31 in) and snowfall is occasional. Trees include holm-oak, cork oak (pictured above) and kermes oak, olive, Barbary thuya, and Aleppo and maritime pine.

The Numidian crane nests on Morocco's high plateaux in summer.

The Houbara bustard lives in the semi-desert plains of the south.

Dorca's gazelle inhabits the semi-desert regions of the south and east. It feeds on grasses and acacia shoots.

The golden jackal is found throughout North Africa and in the Sahara. It can survive for long periods without water.

The booted eagle lives in the forests of the north and the Atlas Mountains. It makes its nests in tall trees.

The Urban Architecture of Morocco

The history of urban architecture in Morocco goes back more than 1,000 years. The Karaouiyine Mosque in Fès was built in 857 by the first Idrissid rulers of Morocco *(see p50)*, who founded the city. From the age of the Idrissids until the 20th century, a succession of many different architectural styles has produced a rich architectural heritage. The artistic conventions and styles of each period shed light on the secular and religious life of the rulers and people who lived in those times.

Karaouiyine Mosque *(see pp180–81)*, the earliest Idrissid building

The Almoravids (11th–12th C.)

It was under the Almoravids that the Moorish style developed in Morocco, which was then the centre of an Ibero-Maghrebian empire. Andalusian elements included the horseshoe arch and the lobed arch, Kufic script, which was often used in conjunction with floral decoration, the scrolling acanthus-leaf motif and the use of decorative plasterwork.

The exterior of the 12th-century Koubba Ba'Adiyn dome

The interior of the Koubba Ba'Adiyn *(see p233)* is made up of interlaced pointed arches and radiating rosettes.

The Almohads (12th–13th C.)

The Almohads, under whom the Ibero-Maghrebian empire reached its apogee, established an architectural style that later dynasties were to emulate. The Koutoubia Mosque in Marrakech, the Hassan II Mosque in Casablanca and grand monumental gateways each exemplify this style.

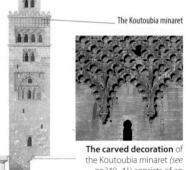

The Koutoubia minaret

The carved decoration of the Koutoubia minaret *(see pp240–41)* consists of an interlacing geometric pattern.

The Merinids (13th–15th C.)

The Merinids used the same building techniques and mostly the same architectural forms as those of the preceding period. They were, however, the greatest builders of *medersas* *(see pp176–7)*, those peculiarly Moroccan masterpieces of architecture. They also displayed a remarkable aptitude for exquisite architectural ornamentation.

The inner façade of the Bou Inania Medersa displays a wide range of techniques, ornamental styles and materials.

Pyramidal roof of green tiles

Carved wooden corbels

Carved or incised plaster

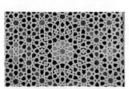

Zellij **tilework** of coloured terracotta squares in the Bou Inania Medersa in Fès depicts complex geometric patterns.

Carved wooden double doors

The Saadians (16th–17th C.)

Morocco's Saadian rulers gave the country two masterpieces: the Palais el-Badi (*see p239*) and the Saadian Tombs (*see p238*), both in Marrakech. These embody the Andalusian traditions that had taken root in Morocco.

Carved wooden corbels

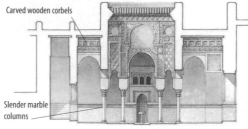

Slender marble columns

Decorative plasterwork, with a lattice of floral and geometric motifs, covers the upper walls of the mausoleum.

The royal mausoleum, in Marrakech, is a magnificent building. It was completed in the 16th century by the sultan Ahmed el-Mansour.

The Alaouites (17th C.–Present Day)

The two great builders of the Alaouite period were Moulay Ismaïl, who made Meknès the royal city, and Sidi Mohammed ben Abdellah, who founded Essaouira (*see pp124–9*).

The Mausoleum of Moulay Ismaïl (*see pp198–9*) is designed in a style similar to that of the Saadian Tombs.

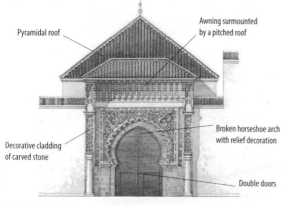

Pyramidal roof

Awning surmounted by a pitched roof

Decorative cladding of carved stone

Broken horseshoe arch with relief decoration

Double doors

The Mausoleum of Mohammed V (*see pp80–81*), built in the 1960s, continues the Moorish tradition.

The Modern Era

During the French Protectorate, in the early 20th century, Nouvelles Villes (modern towns) were built outside the medinas, whose traditional layout (*see pp30–31*) thus was spared from development. A Neo-Moorish style evolved in many towns, while Art Deco was predominant in the city of Casablanca (*see p105*).

The Casablanca Post Office (1918–20) has a loggia decorated with *zellij* tilework. The interior is in Art Deco style.

Tile-covered roof

Modern *zellij* tilework

Arched entrance in the Moorish style

Medinas

Almost all Morocco's medinas have the same layout. The typical medina (meaning "town" in Arabic) consists of a densely packed urban conglomeration enclosed within defensive walls set with lookout towers. The tangle of narrow winding streets and countless alleyways turns the layout of a medina into a labyrinth. The centre of the medina is cut through by wide avenues running between the main gateways and by other main streets, which, as a defensive measure, are either angled or closed off by houses or projecting walls.

Hundreds of narrow streets wind through the medina. Some are no more than 50 cm (20 in) wide.

The monumental gateway, a fortified entrance flanked by projecting crenellated towers, leads into the medina. Bab el-Chorfa in Fès is a particularly splendid example.

Roof-terrace

The Layout of a Medina

Despite their apparent chaos, medinas are laid out according to certain set considerations. The mosque is always located at the heart. Other features include the separation of different religious and ethnic groups, the distinction between home and the workplace, and the location of activities according to a social and commercial hierarchy. Every medina is laid out according to these factors.

Street partly blocked by a house

Lookout tower

Open-air souks, like the basket souk in Marrakech, are markets where specialist crafts and other products are sold. Souks are also the regular meeting places of city people and visiting country-dwellers.

Quarters

The quarters of a medina are no more than loosely defined areas. A quarter, or *hawma*, is really just a communal space consisting of several small streets and alleyways, and it is the focus of the inhabitants' material and spiritual life. Each quarter has a communal oven, a hammam (steam bath), a Koranic school, and a grocer's shop, which is always located in one of the smaller streets. The shop sells such basic necessities as vegetables, fruit, oil, coal, sugar, spices and other foods. There are no shops selling luxury goods in quarters like these.

A grocer's shop in a quarter of Fès

The patio, or *riad*, like this one in Essaouira, is the focal point of a building. The rooms are arranged around the courtyard, which often contains a fountain.

The grand mosque is the central point of the city.

Sturdy defensive walls protect the medina.

Craftsmen, like the tanners of Fès, work together in parts of the medina known as souk, *kissaria* or *fondouk*. Their location, from the centre to the periphery, depends on the craft's rarity and its pollution level.

The souk for valuable items is located next to the mosque.

Workshops in the souks, like the dyers' souk in Marrakech, shown here, are often tiny. The craftsman has only just enough space to make and sell his products.

Moroccan Crafts

The custom of producing utilitarian objects that are visually pleasing and enlivened with decoration is a deeply rooted tradition among Moroccan artisans. They inject beauty into the humblest of materials, from leather, wood and clay, to copper and wool. The importance given to decoration is often so great that it sometimes takes precedence over the object to which it is applied. The endless interplay of arabesques, interlacing patterns, beguiling floral motifs and intricate inscriptions are an integral part of traditional Moroccan life.

Perfume bottle

Sheepskin binding for the Koran, with geometric decoration

Leatherwork

Leatherworking has always been a major industry in Morocco, particularly in Fès, Meknès, Rabat, Salé and Marrakech. The leather-workers and tanners of Marrakech and Fès, whose numerous workshops fill the picturesque quarters of the medina, are those with the most illustrious reputation. Tanners first clean the hide – either sheepskin or goatskin – and then dye it red, yellow or orange. Gold-leaf decoration may also be applied. The leatherworkers then fashion the material into utilitarian or decorative objects such as pouffes, handbags, *babouches* (slippers) and desk sets.

Sheepskin binding for the Koran with gold-leaf decoration

Woodwork

The traditional craft of woodworking is centred mostly in Essaouira, Fès, Meknès, Salé, Marrakech and Tetouan. The many different kinds of wood used by Moroccan woodworkers and cabinet-makers come from the forests of the Atlas and the Rif. Cedar and walnut are used mostly by cabinet-makers, who are highly skilled makers of carved or studded doors, and also in the construction of wooden ceilings. Ebony and citrus wood are used for marquetry and veneering. Thuya, with its beautiful rosewood hue, can be made into elegant furniture and decorative objects.

Painted wooden bread box from Meknès (early 19th century)

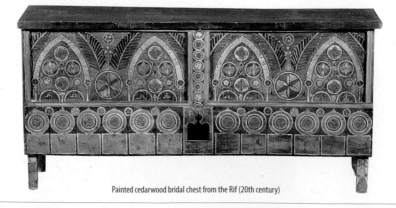

Painted cedarwood bridal chest from the Rif (20th century)

Carpets

Carpets are a ubiquitous part of the furnishings of the Moroccan home *(see p336)*. City-made carpets, woven mostly in Rabat and Médiouna, are characterized by bright colours and a pattern consisting of a rectangular field on a red background, framed by bands of edging and with geometric motifs. Symmetry is a central feature of carpets made in Rabat. Village carpets, which are either woven or knotted, are produced in the Middle and High Atlas, in Marrakech and in Haouz. They have more imaginative patterns, such as animal, plant and architectural motifs, which the weavers (mostly women) themselves devise. Weaving and knotting techniques vary according to region, and the various types of village carpets are referred to by their place of origin, such as Middle Atlas, High Atlas, Haouz or Marrakech.

Sahraoui woman weaving a carpet

A knotted carpet from Rabat

Pottery

Glazed pottery dish from Fès (19th century)

Decorated pottery is an integral part of everyday domestic life. Jugs, dishes and bowls are seen in every Moroccan kitchen and living room. Fès, one of the most important centres of pottery production, is renowned for its pottery – blue and white and multicoloured on a white base. Safi, whose pottery industry is more recent, produces pieces characterized by shimmering colours. Local tradition dictates shape, colour, glaze and type of decoration. Meknès and Salé are two other important centres of pottery manufacture.

Pottery oil jar

Ceramic honey jar with floral decoration

Copper and Brass

Brass door with geometric and other decorative motifs

Copper and brass are metals that lend themselves to being cut, hammered, embossed, inlaid and engraved. The repertoire of the Moroccan coppersmith ranges from the humblest domestic objects to the most ostentatious, such as inlaid or panelled doors, trays and chandeliers. This craft reveals a highly developed skill and a love of intricate detail, and follows an ancient tradition.

Copper jug from Meknès (19th century)

The Islamic Faith in Morocco

Morocco's official religion is the orthodox, or Sunni, sect of Islam. It is based on the Koran and the Sunna, in which the words and deeds of the Prophet Mohammed are recorded. It is this religion, which was introduced to Morocco in the 7th century, that underpins both the country's law and its faith. Islam is also the unifying force in the daily life of every Moroccan, whose duty it is to respect the Five Pillars of Islam. These are *chahada* (profession of faith), *salat* (prayer), *zakat* (ritual almsgiving), Ramadan (fasting) and *hadj* (the pilgrimage to Mecca). The king of Morocco is both the country's secular and spiritual leader. On his accession to the throne in 1999, Mohammed VI strongly reaffirmed this double prerogative.

Mohammed VI, King of Morocco, at prayer. For 1,000 years, each Moroccan sovereign has borne the title "leader of the faithful".

Ritual ablutions must be performed before prayers. The courtyards of mosques always contain fountains and basins, with hammams (steam-baths) nearby. The Islamic faith places great importance on personal cleanliness.

Maghrebi calligraphy, characteristic of North Africa, is derived from the more austere Kufic script.

Ceramic tiles painted with religious motifs, carved plaster and carved wood are the three main elements in the decoration not only of mosques and medersas but also of traditional Muslim homes.

Koran in Maghrebi Script

The Koran, the holy pronouncements of Allah dictated to the Prophet Mohammed, is central to Islamic faith. Islamic calligraphy, a major art form in the Muslim world, is highly stylized and combines perfect legibility with visual harmony and colourful illumination.

Dish with three mihrabs (niches)
Calligraphy and religious symbols are two prominent themes in the traditional decorative arts of the Muslim world.

Friday Prayers

The five daily prayers *(salat)* form part of the five obligations, or "pillars", of Islam that are incumbent on Muslims. The faithful are required to come to the mosque for the midday prayers that are said every Friday. On this day devoted to Allah they also hear a sermon delivered by the *khotba*, or preacher. The gathering at Friday prayers also reinforces the sense of belonging that Muslims have in their community.

Muslims leaving a mosque

Muslim prayer beads consist of a string of 33 or 99 beads separated by markers. Muslims use the beads to recite the 99 names or attributes of Allah.

The chapters, or suras, of the Koran are separated by illuminations.

Daily prayer consists of a series of recitations and prostrations. Kneeling in rows, on a strictly egalitarian basis, the faithful face the direction of Mecca. This direction is called *qibla*, and it is symbolized by the mihrab, a niche in the wall of the mosque. The imam, who leads the prayers, kneels in front.

Islamic Festivals

The Muslim calendar is based on the lunar year, which is a little shorter than the solar year *(see p45)*. The ninth month, Ramadan, is a time of fasting. Aïd el-Fitr, or Aïd es-Seghir, marks the end of Ramadan, and at Aïd el-Adha, or Aïd el-Kebir, a sheep is sacrificed in memory of the sacrifice of Abraham. Mouloud commemorates the birth of the Prophet Mohammed.

Cakes baked for Ramadan

Sacrificial sheep

The Berbers

Two out of every three Moroccans are, in cultural and linguistic terms, Berber. Thought to be the descendants of people of mixed origins – including Oriental, Saharan and European – the Berbers settled in Morocco at different times, and they do not make up a homogeneous race. By finding refuge in mountainous regions, they survived several successive invasions – those of the civilizations of the Mediterranean basin, of the Arabs, then, much later, those of the French and the Spaniards. The Berbers still speak several dialects and maintain distinct cultural traditions. They are renowned for their trading activities and for the strength of their tribal and family ties.

The *fouta* is a rectangular piece of fabric with red and white stripes. It is worn with a conical straw hat by women of the Rif.

Young Berber girls dress in bright colours and from an early age wear a headscarf knotted at the top of the head, as their mothers do.

Veils of many colours cover the women of the Tiznit region.

Young girls do not wear veils. Only when they reach adulthood do girls cover their face.

Henna patterns, which Berber women paint on themselves, give protection against supernatural forces. Besides keeping evil spirits away, they are supposed to purify and beautify the wearer. On feast days, women decorate their hands and their feet.

The grand souk at the *moussem* of Imilchil is both a social and a commercial gathering. It is an opportunity for Berbers from all over the Atlas Mountains to buy all that they need for the year ahead.

The *hendira*, a striped cape woven on a simple loom, is the typical overgarment worn by Berber women.

The *jellaba*, an ankle-length robe with long sleeves and a hood, is worn over a wide-sleeved shirt by Berber men of the Atlas mountains. The turban is also part of Berber men's traditional attire.

Berber Tribes

Berber woman in feast-day dress

Although Berber tribal structure is complex, three groups, each with their own histories, can be identified. The Sanhaja, nomadic herdsmen originating from the south, inhabit the central and eastern High Atlas, the Middle Atlas and the Rif. They speak the dialects of the Tamazight group. The Masmouda, settled farmers, live mostly in the western High Atlas and the Anti-Atlas, and they speak the Chleuh dialect. It was a Masmoudian tribe that founded the Almohad empire in the 12th century.

The Zenets are hunters and herdsmen who came from the East and settled in eastern Morocco. They speak the dialect of the Znatiya group. They founded the Merinid dynasty in the 13th century.

The *situla*, a copper vessel of distinctive shape, is used by the women of the Igherm region in the Anti-Atlas to fetch water.

Religious *Moussems*

For Berber women, religious moussems (see pp42–5) are occasions when they sometimes travel far from home. This is an opportunity for them to meet other women, to sing and dance, and to get away from their everyday chores.

This amber and silver necklace, from the Taliouine region of the Anti-Atlas, is part of the attire traditionally worn on feast days.

A mule is a prized possession among the Berbers. It is used as a beast of burden, to carry such heavy loads as fodder, sacks of grain and containers of water.

Horses of Morocco

Two thousand years ago, at the time of the Phoenician, Carthaginian and Roman invasions, the first horses to be used in Morocco were cross-bred with Mongolian stock. The Arab horse was introduced to Morocco by the Arab conquest in the 7th century and, used in war, it played an important part in the establishment of Islam here. Today, owning horses is considered to be a sign of wealth in rural areas. Horses are shown off at festivals, especially in the performance of fantasias (displays of horsemanship), and are also used in daily life.

Tall embroidered leather boots and loose white short breeches are worn by riders in a fantasia.

Mokahlas, long ceremonial guns, have engraved butts inlaid with mother-of-pearl and ivory.

Horse's harnesses, brightly coloured and made of sumptuous materials are made by skilled and specialized craftsmen. The severe bit allows the rider to stop abruptly and steer his mount deftly. The blinkers protect the horses' eyes from sand and smoke.

Studs

There are national studs in Meknès, El-Jadida, Marrakech, Oujda and Bouznika. Their purpose is to promote the breeding of horses and to produce horses for racing, for equestrian sports and for fantasias. In Morocco today there are 180,000 horses, 550,000 mules and 1 million donkeys. To encourage horse-breeding, stallions are made available to breeders free of charge to cover their mares. On average, 15,000 mares are put to a stallion and 5,000 foals are registered every year.

Thoroughbreds are used for racing. The racing season runs from September to May.

The Barb, a type of horse used by the Berbers before the arrival of the Arabs, is strong, compact and capable of covering long distances.

The fantasia saddle, with typically elaborate decoration, consists of a wooden framework sheathed in goatskin. It is covered in embroidered silk and rests on several layers of woven saddlecloths decorated with pompoms. The high pommel and back restraint keep the rider securely in place.

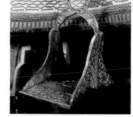

Large stirrups made of sheet metal or leather are attached to the saddle by stirrup-leathers.

Fantasias

Fantasias are displays of horsemanship that are performed according to precise rules. Galloping at full speed down a course 200 m (650 ft) long, the riders whirl their guns in the air and, at a signal from their leader, fire them in unison.

The mule, a robust beast of burden, is more widely used than the horse. Here, its owner perches on a pack-saddle made out of thick blankets.

Fantasia horses, which are at least four years old, are Barb or Arabian Barb stallions.

At the *moussem* of Sidi Abdallah Amghar, in El-Jadida, horses are bathed in the sea at dawn. Later in the day, in the fierce August heat, they will perform the galloping charges of the fantasia.

The Arabian Barb, an agile and robust horse, was produced by crossbreeding Arabs and Barbs in the 7th century. It is a saddle horse particularly well suited to the fantasia.

The pure-bred Arab was introduced to Morocco in the 7th century. Its elegance and beauty, as well as its capacity for endurance, make it one of the world's best-loved horses.

Moroccan Dress and Jewellery

Traditional dress indicates the wearer's geographical origin and social status. Berber women wrap themselves in rectangular pieces of fabric, secured by a brooch and a belt, while the men wear a *jellaba* and a burnous against the cold. In towns, the elegant kaftan, a long garment with buttons down the front, has become standard formal wear for women, who increasingly often dress in the Western style. Jewellery has long been made by Jewish craftsmen. Berber jewellery is made of silver, sometimes with the addition of coral and amber; necklaces, bracelets and brooches may simply be decorative, or may be a status symbol or an heirloom. Gold, sometimes inlaid with precious stones, is the material of city-made jewellery.

Zemmour women of the Middle Atlas wear a belt in the form of a long plaited and twisted cord decorated with pompoms.

Hoodless collar

The shape of the **sleeves** and of the neck-opening varies from one kaftan to the next.

In oases bordering the Sahara, women cover their head with a large black or white cotton shawl. On feast days, they bedeck themselves with all their jewellery.

Berber women, on feast days, don more elaborate headwear. The shape often indicates the wearer's status, either as a married woman or as an unmarried girl.

Silk brocade kaftan made in Fès in the 18th–19th century.

This golden diadem from Fès consists of hinged plates that are decoratively pierced and set with many precious stones.

In the High Atlas, capes worn by women identify their belonging to a particular tribe. Aït Haddiddou women are recognizable by their *hendira*, a cloak made of woollen cloth with blue, white, black and red stripes.

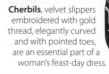

Cherbils, velvet slippers embroidered with gold thread, elegantly curved and with pointed toes, are an essential part of a woman's feast-day dress.

For special occasions, women may wear a gold or silver belt. Silver is most usually worked by being liquefied and poured into a mould, but it may also be beaten into sheets, cut to shape, and then incised or engraved.

In rural areas, older men still wear a voluminous *jellaba* with pointed hood. The garment is made of handwoven woollen cloth, which is either of one colour or with patterned stripes.

These musicians and dancers from the Rif are wearing their festival costume. On their head they wear the traditional orange and white *rezza*.

Gold lace

Kaftans

The women's kaftan, an ankle-length, tunic-like garment, collarless and with wide sleeves, is always made of such fine fabric as silk, satin, velvet or brocade. It is often worn with a mansourya, *a light, transparent overgarment made of silk that sets off the kaftan. The garments are secured at the waist by a wide belt embroidered with silk and gold thread.*

Tiny buttons made of silk or gold thread are sewn down the front of the kaftan.

Cotton, silk and velvet kaftan, made in Salé in the 19th century.

This young bride wears a kaftan and, over it, a luxuriant veil, which is traditional in Fès.

Embroidery, decorating kaftans, belts and *jellabas,* is an integral part of women's clothing. The patterns, such as geometric, floral and animal motifs, the colours and the materials used are different in every city.

Coral, amber and shells, combined with silver, are strung together to make attractive necklaces, which are worn proudly by Berber women.

MOROCCO THROUGH THE YEAR

Muslim feast days, agricultural festivals and *moussems* (pilgrimage-festivals) punctuate the Moroccan year. Because the Muslim calendar is lunar, the dates of religious festivals are never fixed. After the harvests of early summer and during the autumn, lively festivals at which the local produce is fêted are held in every region of the country.

More than 600 *moussems* take place each year in Morocco; besides the pilgrimage to the tomb of a saint, there is a large regional souk, singing and dancing, and sometimes a fantasia. The month of Ramadan is a major religious occasion; then, the inactivity of the daylight hours, when fasting is required, is followed by joyful night-time festivities.

Spring

If rainfall is not scarce, spring in Morocco is a remarkable season. In the space of a few days, the dry ochre earth becomes carpeted in flowers of every hue and the mountainsides are flushed with the pale green of new barley. The high peaks, however, are still covered in snow. In the Saharan south, spring is much like summer. It is already warm enough to swim in the Mediterranean and off the southern Atlantic coast.

March

Amateur Theatre Festival, Casablanca.
Cotton Festival, Beni Mellal *(after the harvest)*.
Classic Car Rally *(10 days)*. The itinerary of this international rally for cars dating from 1939 crosses part of Morocco.
***Moussem* of Moulay Aissa ben Driss**, Aït-Attab (in the Beni Mellal region). Pilgrimage to the holy man's tomb.
Aïcha Gazelles' Trophy *(1 week)*. An international event for women rally drivers, along tracks in the desert regions.

April

Candle Festival, Salé. At Achoura, 10 days after the Muslim New Year, boatmen place candelabras full of flaming candles at the Marabout of Sidi Abdallah ben Hassoun.
Marathon des Sables *(8 days)*. Foot race run over 200 km (124 miles) in the Saharan south of Morocco.
***Moussem* of the Regraga** *(40 days)*. Pilgrimage that takes place in 44 stages, passing through the provinces of Essaouira and Safi, in honour of the Regraga – descendants of the Seven Holy Men of Berber history.

May

Rose Festival *(after the rose harvest)*, El-Kelaa M'Gouna

Rose Festival at El-Kelaa M'Gouna, near Ouarzazate

(near Ouarzazate). Held in the town that is the capital of rose cultivation *(see p276)*, this festival features folk music and dance.
International Festival of Sacred Music *(1 week)*, Fès. Concerts every day. Jewish, Christian and Sufi religious music, gospel singing and Senegalese songs.
Harley-Davidson Raid *(15 days)*. Harley-Davidson motorbike rally through Spain and Morocco.
Crafts Festival, Ouarzazate.
***Moussem* of Moulay Abdallah ben Brahim**, Ouezzane. Pilgrimage held in honour of the holy man who came to the town in 1727 and then converted it into a religious centre.
***Moussem* of Sidi Mohammed Ma al-Aïnin**, Tan Tan. This commercial and religious festival is held in honour of the founder of the town of Smara, who was a great

The Candle Festival at Salé, which takes place at Achoura

Cherry Festival in Sefrou, at the foot of the Middle Atlas

hero of the French Resistance. Events include a performance of the *guedra*, the famous dance of the Guelmim region.
Oudaïa Jazz Festival *(4 days)*, Rabat. This popular jazz festival is named after the loyal Oudaïa, a well-known tribe of Arab descent whom Moulay Ismail entrusted with watching over the town. (see p72).

Summer

In summer the only parts of the country that are spared high temperatures are the coasts, which are cooled by sea breezes, and the Atlas mountains. This is not the best time to tour the inner country-side or visit inland towns and cities. In the Saharan south, the sky becomes leaden with the heat, and elsewhere the medinas are stifling. Despite this, the start of summer is marked by many festivals.

June

National Folklore Festival *(10 days)*, Marrakech. At this festival, in the Palais El-Badia, troupes of dancers and musicians from Morocco and elsewhere bring Moroccan folk traditions to life.
Gnaoua Festival *(4 days)*, Essaouira. Gnaoua musicians perform their distinctive music at this event. There is also other traditional Moroccan

music, as well as visiting American and European jazz groups.
Cherry Festival *(2 days, after the cherry harvest)*, Sefrou. Folk performers take part in this festival, which is held in honour of Sefrou's famous cherries.
Fig Festival *(after the fig harvest)*, Bouhouda, near Taounate.
Moussem of Sidi el-Ghazi *(last Wednesday in June)*, Guelmim. Sahraouis gather to attend a major camel market. A fantasia is also performed.
Sahraoui Festival, Agadir. Camel races, dancing and music.
Moussem of Moulay Bousselham. Religious festival, with music and festivities.

July

Moussem of Moulay Abdessalam ben Mchich, Tetouan. Thousands of people, most of them from local tribes, take part in this great pilgrimage to the holy man's tomb.
Throne Day *(30 July)*. Major celebrations marking the anniversary of the accession to power of Mohammed VI in 1999 take place throughout the country.
Music Festival, Tangier.
Moussem of Sidi Mohammed Laghdal, Tan Tan. Religious pilgrimage.

August
Honey Festival *(between 15 and 20 August)*, Imouzzer des Ida Outanane (north of Agadir). Celebrations marking the end of the honey harvest, with folk performances and an exhibition showcasing different kinds of honey, one of the region's major products.
Moussem of Moulay Abdallah Amghar *(1 week)*, El-Jadida. Major pilgrimage with renowned fantasias and other entertainments.
International Cultural Festival, Asilah *(2 weeks)*. Music, poetry and painting competitions, discussions with artists, and other events, including street performances.
Festival of Folk Music, Al-Hoceima.
Moussem of Setti Fatma. Pilgrimage and souk in the Ourika valley, southeast of Marrakech.
Moussem of Dar Zhiroun, Rabat. Religious festival.
Moussem of Sidi Ahmed (or Sidi Moussa), east of Tiznit. Religious festival in honour of the holy man and Acrobats' Festival.
Apple Festival, Imouzzer du Kandar, 38 km (24 miles) south of Fès.
Moussem of Sidi Daoud, Ouarzazate. Religious pilgrimage.
Moussem of Sidi Lahcen ben Ahmed, Sefrou. Festival in honour of the town's patron saint, who lived during the 18th century.
Moussem of Sidi Yahya ben Younes, Oujda. Religious festival in honour of St John the Baptist, the town's principal saint, to whom Muslims, Jews and Christians all pray.

Performer at the Gnaoua Festival

Camel race at the Sahraoui Festival in Agadir

Moussem of Moulay Idriss II in Fès

Autumn

September and October are very pleasant months in which to explore the Atlas mountains, visit the imperial cities, or experience the vastness of the Moroccan desert, where the heat is then bearable. In November, heavy rains can sometimes make the *wadis* burst their banks and render tracks impassable.

September
Festival of Fantasia *(early September, 4 days)*, Meknès.

Thousands of horsemen gather to demonstrate their skills in fantasias. Traditional dances are also performed.
Marriage Fair *(towards end of September, 3 days)*, Imilchil. Tribal gathering of the Aït Haddidou at which betrothals are made. Performances of folk song and dancing take place at this colourful event.
***Moussem* of Moulay Idriss Zerhoun**. Pilgrimage to the tomb of Moulay Idriss, founder of the first dynasty, marked by major festivities.
***Moussem* of Moulay Idriss II** *(1 week)*, Fès. Processions of craftsmen's guilds and of brotherhoods to the mausoleum of the city's founder.
***Moussem* of Sidi Alla el-Hadj**, Chefchaouen. Religious festival held in the hills around the city.
Festival of Volubilis *(1 week)*, Meknès. Performances by musicians and dancers from Morocco and the Arab world, but also from Europe and the United States.
***Moussem* of Sidi Ahmed ben Mansour**, Moulay Bousselham. Religious festival.

***Moussem* of Dar Zhira**, Tangier. Religious festival.
Jazz Festival, Tangier.

October
Date Festival *(3 days after the date harvest in the groves of the Tafilalt)*, Erfoud. Many tribes from the Tafilalt gather, and several varieties of dates are sold in the souks. Folk dancers and musicians perform in the streets of Erfoud.
Apple Festival *(after the harvest)*, Midelt.
Horse Festival *(1 week)*, Tissa. Various breeds of horses

Date Festival in Erfoud, taking place after the harvest

Charging horsemen at a fantasia performed at the Horse Festival in Tissa

Almond trees in blossom in the Tafraoute region

December
Olive Tree Festival, Rhafsaï
(north of Fès). Agricultural festival.

January
Go-Kart 24-Hour Race, Marrakech.

February
Almond Blossom Festival,
Tafraoute *(south of Agadir)*.
Agricultural festival marking the
short-lived but spectacular pink
and white almond blossom.
Marrakech Biennale, Marrakech.
Month-long cultural festival.

compete and take part in
several shows, and many
fantasias are performed.
Walnut Festival, Al Haouz.
**Festival of Andalusian
Music**, Rabat.

November
Moussem **of Mohammed
Bou Nasri**, Tamegroute. This
religious festival is held in
memory of the great saint,
Mohammed Bou Nasri
(see p273).
**International Music
Festival**, Ouarzazate.

Winter

The best time to explore
Morocco's Saharan region is
in the winter. The days are
sunny and the sky is a deep
blue but the nights are cold.
On the coasts, the temperature
remains mild. By contrast, the
valleys of the High Atlas can
receive heavy snowfalls and
may be inaccessible. In
February, the almond trees
of the Tafraoute valley are
covered in blossom. Few
festivals take place in winter.

Public Holidays

Year's Day (1 Jan).
**Manifesto of Independence
Day** (11 January).
Labour Day (1 May).
Throne Day (30 July).
Allegience Day (14 August).
**King Mohammed VI's
Birthday and Youth
Day** (21 August).
Day of Green March
(6 November)
Independence Day,
return from exile of King
Mohammed V (18 November)

Religious Festivals

The dates of Muslim festivals are set according to the lunar calendar of the Hegira (the beginning of the Muslim
era in 622). The Muslim year is 10 or 11 days shorter than that of the Gregorian calendar. Religious festivals also
take place 11 days earlier each year in relation to the Western calendar. Guided by the phases of the moon, the
religious authorities wait until the last moment before deciding on the exact date of each festival.
Moharem: Muslim New Year.
Achoura: traditional almsgiving *(zakat)* to the poor; presents are also given to children.
Mouloud (Aïd al-Wawlid): anniversary of the birth of the Prophet Mohammed. Many *moussems* also
take place at the same time as Mouloud, and their dates are therefore different each year. Among the
most important are the *moussem* of Moulay Brahim, near Marrakech, that of Moulay Abdessalam ben
Mchich, in the north, the *moussem* of Sidi Mohammed ben Aïssa, of Sidi Ali ben Hamdouch, the Candle
Festival in Salé and the *moussem* of
Moulay Abdelkader Jilali.
Ramadan: practising Muslims fast for a
month, eating only after sunset.
Aïd es-Seghir ("the small festival"), also
known as Aïd el-Fitr: festival marking the
end of the 30-day fast of Ramadan.
Aïd el-Kebir ("the grand festival"), also
known as Aïd el-Adha: this festival, taking
place 68 days after Aïd es-Seghir,
commemorates the day when, by divine
order, Abraham prepared to sacrifice his
son Isaac, when Allah interceded by
providing a ram in place of the child.
Every household sacrifices a sheep and
shares the meat at a family meal.

Souk in the High Atlas with sheep for sale just before Aïd el-Kebir

The Climate of Morocco

Bordered by the Atlantic and the Mediterranean, joined to the African continent by the Sahara, and diagonally bisected by the long mountain chain of the High and Middle Atlas, Morocco does not have a uniform climate. It is cooled by moist northwesterly winds and seared by hot, dry southeasterlies such as the *chergui*. In summer, conditions are those of a hot arid zone. In winter, which is very mild except in the mountains, conditions switch to those of a temperate coastal zone. Water is in relatively short supply everywhere and agriculture, involving about 40 per cent of the economically active population, is acutely dependent on adequate rainfall.

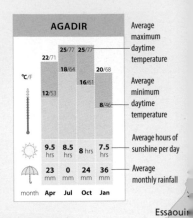

AGADIR

°C/F	Apr	Jul	Oct	Jan
Average maximum daytime temperature	22/71	25/77	25/77	20/68
Average minimum daytime temperature	12/53	18/64	16/61	8/46
Average hours of sunshine per day	9.5 hrs	8.5 hrs	8 hrs	7.5 hrs
Average monthly rainfall	23 mm	0 mm	24 mm	36 mm

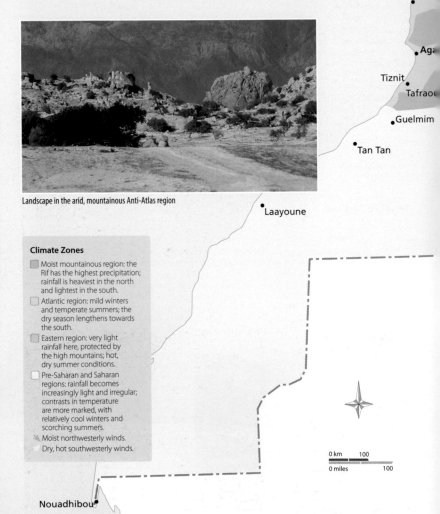

Landscape in the arid, mountainous Anti-Atlas region

Essaouir

Ag

Tiznit

Tafraou

Guelmim

Tan Tan

Laayoune

Climate Zones

- Moist mountainous region: the Rif has the highest precipitation; rainfall is heaviest in the north and lightest in the south.
- Atlantic region: mild winters and temperate summers; the dry season lengthens towards the south.
- Eastern region: very light rainfall here, protected by the high mountains; hot, dry summer conditions.
- Pre-Saharan and Saharan regions: rainfall becomes increasingly light and irregular; contrasts in temperature are more marked, with relatively cool winters and scorching summers.
- Moist northwesterly winds.
- Dry, hot southwesterly winds.

Nouadhibou

0 km   100

0 miles   100

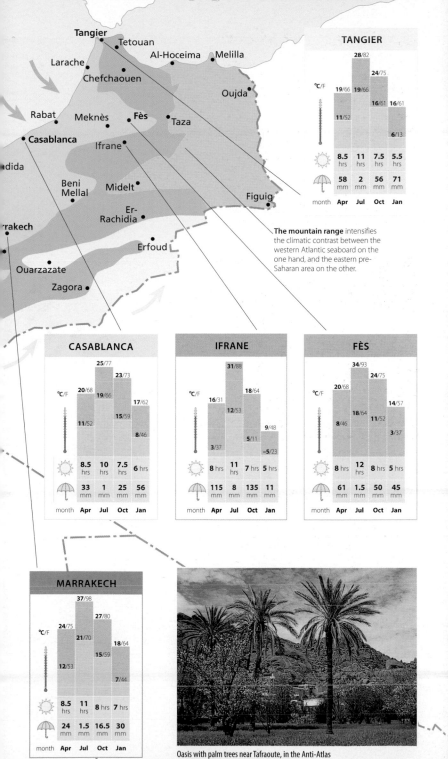

TANGIER

°C/F	Apr	Jul	Oct	Jan
	19/66	28/82	24/75	16/61
	11/52	19/66	16/61	6/13
☀	8.5 hrs	11 hrs	7.5 hrs	5.5 hrs
☂	58 mm	2 mm	56 mm	71 mm
month	Apr	Jul	Oct	Jan

The mountain range intensifies the climatic contrast between the western Atlantic seaboard on the one hand, and the eastern pre-Saharan area on the other.

CASABLANCA

°C/F	Apr	Jul	Oct	Jan
	20/68	25/77	23/73	17/62
	11/52	19/66	15/59	8/46
☀	8.5 hrs	10 hrs	7.5 hrs	6 hrs
☂	33 mm	1 mm	25 mm	56 mm
month	Apr	Jul	Oct	Jan

IFRANE

°C/F	Apr	Jul	Oct	Jan
	16/31	31/88	18/64	9/48
	3/37	12/53	5/11	−5/23
☀	8 hrs	11 hrs	7 hrs	5 hrs
☂	115 mm	8 mm	135 mm	11 mm
month	Apr	Jul	Oct	Jan

FÈS

°C/F	Apr	Jul	Oct	Jan
	20/68	34/93	24/75	14/57
	8/46	18/64	11/52	3/37
☀	8 hrs	12 hrs	8 hrs	5 hrs
☂	61 mm	1.5 mm	50 mm	45 mm
month	Apr	Jul	Oct	Jan

MARRAKECH

°C/F	Apr	Jul	Oct	Jan
	24/75	37/98	27/80	18/64
	12/53	21/70	15/59	7/44
☀	8.5 hrs	11 hrs	8 hrs	7 hrs
☂	24 mm	1.5 mm	16.5 mm	30 mm
month	Apr	Jul	Oct	Jan

Oasis with palm trees near Tafraoute, in the Anti-Atlas

THE HISTORY OF MOROCCO

Morocco is an ancient kingdom. It came under the influence of Carthage and Rome, but its origins are Berber, Arab and African. Since the arrival of Islam in the 7th century, the country has been an independent power, and at times an empire. The only Arab country not to have fallen to the Ottomans, it entered the modern era under the Alaouite dynasty at the end of the colonial period.

For 40,000 years Morocco has been a bridge between the East, Africa and Europe. Archaeological finds and rock engravings prove that it was settled in the remote past. but little is known of the first Berbers, who may have come from the east.

The Phoenicians, fearless navigators, established trading posts – such as Russaddir (Melilla) and Lixus (Larache) – along the Moroccan coast. They also introduced iron-working and the cultivation of vines.

In the 5th century BC, Hanno, a naval commander from Carthage (in modern Tunisia), set out to explore the Atlantic coast westwards, and soon the trading posts were taken over and developed by Carthage. Under their influence, the Berber tribes eventually joined forces and established the kingdom of Mauretania.

In 146 BC, having destroyed Carthage, the Romans extended their control westwards over the northern half of Morocco. Emperor Augustus made Tingis (Tangier) a Roman city.

In 25 BC, the kingdom of Mauretania was entrusted to Juba II, king of Numidia. A Berber ruler who had been Romanized and educated, he married the daughter of Antony and Cleopatra. Ptolemy, Juba's son and heir, was murdered in AD 40 on the orders of Emperor Caligula. Emperor Claudius later annexed the kingdom, dividing it into Mauretania Caesariensis (west Algeria) and Mauretania Tingitana (Morocco). The Romans established few new towns here, but developed the existing ones, among them Tangier, Volubilis, Lixus, Banasa, Sala and Thamusida. The southern frontier lay at the level of Rabat. In the 3rd century, however, Christianity began to spread and Roman domination was severely diminished.

The Vandals, whose king Genseric (428–77) conquered North Africa, followed by the Byzantines, maintained a lasting presence only at a few points along the Mediterranean coast. Religious unrest and local uprisings gradually extinguished the hold of all the ancient civilizations.

		c.400 BC Berber tribes unite to establish the kingdom of Mauretania	**46 BC** Numidia becomes a Roman province	**430–533** Vandals conquer North Africa	**6th century** Byzantine domination
	c.1000 BC Arrival of the Phoenicians				
8000 BC		**4000 BC**		**AD 1**	
8000–7000 BC Ancestors of the Berbers arrive from the east. They domesticate the horse and use iron		**c.800 BC** Foundation of Carthage	**201 BC** End of the Second Punic War. Rome destroys Carthage in 146 BC		

A Moor and a Christian in combat

◀ *The Sultan Moulay Abderrahman Leaving Meknès, by Eugène Delacroix*

Pages from the Koran in the Maghrebi Kufic script of North Africa

Arrival of Islam

From the end of the 7th century, a new set of invaders, and with them a new religion, began to make its mark on Morocco. The Arabs had started to expand their rule westwards, and in 681 there was a first attempt into Morocco. But the true conqueror of Morocco was Moussa ibn Nosaïr, who, active from 705, brought the territory from Tangier to the Draa valley under the control of the Umayyad caliph in Damascus. With some resistance, Islam was introduced to the Berber population. Quickly rallying a mainly Berber army, Moussa then turned his attention to Europe, initiating the conquest of Spain in 711.

Reacting against their haughty Arab overlords, the Berbers of the Maghreb rebelled against them and, usually but not always, against Islam. Battles with troops sent from the East continued for more than 30 years, from 739 to 772. Petty kingdoms were formed and the western Maghreb kept the power of the caliphs at bay.

The Idrissid Dynasty (789–926)

Meanwhile, Islam divided itself into two main sects: Sunni and Shia. In 786, the Sunnite Umayyad caliph crushed the Shi'ite Muslims. One of them, Idriss ibn Abdallah, escaped the massacre and was received in Morocco as a prestigious religious leader. In 789, the Aouraba, a Berber tribe in Volubilis, made him their leader. Idriss I carved out a small kingdom, and set about building a new city, Fès. He died soon afterwards, probably poisoned by an envoy of the caliph. His son, Idriss II (793–828), succeeded him and made Fès the Idrissid capital. The Idrissids are considered to be the founding dynasty and the first of Morocco's seven ruling dynasties.

Fès soon became densely populated and a prestigious religious centre. At the death of Idriss II, the kingdom was divided between his two sons, then between their descendants. They were unable to prevent the simultaneous attacks of the two powerful rivals of the Abbassid caliph, the Shi'ites of Tunisia and Egypt, and the Umayyad caliphs of Córdoba in Andalusia – Sunnis who for long fought over Fès and the allegiance of the Berber tribes.

The Almoravids (1062–1147)

An unexpected push came from the south. A tribe of nomadic Sanhadja Berbers, based in present-day Mauritania and converts to Islam in the 9th century, were to give rise to a powerful new empire. The tribe's headman, Yahia

Fountain in the 9th-century Karaouiyine Mosque in Fès

Remains of the Koubba Ba'Adiyn in Marrakech *(see p233)*

ibn Ibrahim, invited a holy man to preach the Islamic faith to his people. A fortified camp, or *ribat*, was built on the estuary of the Senegal river. In 1054, "the people of the *ribat*" (the al Mourabitoun, or Almoravids), fighters for a pure Islamic state, launched a holy war northward as far as the Atlas. The founder of the Almoravid empire was Youssef ibn Tachfin (1061–1107), who proclaimed himself Leader

of the Faithful. Having founded Marrakech, which became Morocco's second capital, in 1062, he conquered the country as far north as Tangier and in 1082 as far east as Algiers.

In Al-Andalus (Andalusia), the fall of the Umayyad caliphate of Córdoba in 1031 led to the creation of *taifas*, small Muslim principalities. Alfonso VI, King of Castile and León, led the Christian Reconquest, taking Toledo in 1085. In response to a call for aid from the *taifas*, Youssef ibn Tachfin crossed the strait and routed Alfonso VI's forces at the Battle of Badajoz in 1086. He soon extended his empire as far north as Barcelona. In the south, Almoravid influence stretched to the Senegal and the Niger (1076).

The empire was unified by the orthodox, Sunni branch of Islam. On the death of Youssef ben Tachfine, his son Ali, whose mother was an Andalusian Christian, succeeded him. During his long reign (1107–43) the refined culture of Andalusia took hold in Morocco, although the empire itself was in decline. More Andalusian than Moroccan, the last Almoravids fled to Spain to escape a new rebellion from the south, that of the Almohads.

Carved wooden lintel from a mosque in Marrakech, dating from the 9th century

929 Abderrahman III establishes an independent caliphate in Córdoba

1062 Youssef ibn Tachfin founds Marrakech and starts to expand his Almoravid empire

1086 Spanish king Alfonso VI is defeated at Badajoz. The Reconquest is temporarily halted

960

1030

1100

1010 Berbers sack Abderrahman's palace at Medina Azahara, Córdoba

Zellij *tilework in the Palais du Glaoui, Marrakech*

1107–43 Andalusian culture takes root during the reign of Ali ben Youssef

Morocco and Al-Andalus

For almost eight centuries – from 711, when Tariq ibn Ziyad and his Berber forces crossed the Straits of Gibraltar to reach Spain, to the fall of the Nasrid kingdom of Granada in 1492 – the Iberian peninsula was partly under Muslim control. Muslim territory, known as Al-Andalus (the Land of the Vandals), was at times a melting pot of Muslims, Jews and Mozarabs (Christians adopting an Islamic lifestyle), philosophers, traders, scientists and poets. This gave birth to the most illustrious civilization of the late Middle Ages.

A love of gardens was one aspect of the cultured civilization of Al-Andalus

The Giralda, the clocktower of Seville Cathedral, added in the 16th century.

The minaret of the Great Mosque in Seville, transformed after the Christian Reconquest into the famous Giralda.

Irrigation
Under the Umayyad caliphs and their Berber successors, irrigation in Andalusia underwent a dramatic advance. The introduction of the *noria*, a waterwheel for the mechanical extraction of water – shown here in a 13th-century manuscript – was to change, permanently, the method of water distribution in Spain.

The minaret of the Koutoubia Mosque, in Marrakech, which was begun in 1162, was the model for those that the Almohads built later in Andalusia.

c.1184   1172–1198

Averroës
One of the greatest Islamic thinkers, and a protégé of the Almohad rulers, Averroës was born in Córdoba in 1126 and died in Marrakech in 1198 *(see p233)*.

Judaism in Morocco

Inscriptions in Hebrew dating from the Roman period show that there has been a Jewish community in Morocco since antiquity. It was involved chiefly in agriculture, stock-farming and trade. Judaism flourished thanks to the conversion of the Berber tribes and to the immigration of Jews fleeing from the east and from Spain. When Fès was founded, a Jewish community settled there, and scholars and rabbis travelled throughout the country. Although strictures imposed by the Almoravids and Almohads caused some Jews to emigrate, they flourished once again under the Merinids and Wattasids, who welcomed thousands of Jews expelled from Spain after 1492. The Alaouite sultans also protected them. Although their numbers are reduced, Jews hold certain influential positions in Morocco today.

Bronze Hanukkah lamp, 19th century

Minarets

After the end of the independant Cordoban caliphate, Almoravids and Almohads directly controlled Al-Andalus, where their monumental architecture flourished. The architectural heritage of Al-Andalus, above all of religious architecture, is a clear expression of Andalusian culture. The striking similarity between the minarets of the three mosques built by the Almohads in Marrakech, Rabat and Seville demonstrates the unity of the Almohad architectural style.

The Battle of Higueruela
This 15th-century fresco depicts an episode in the Reconquest, a centuries-long struggle between Muslim rulers and Christians for control of Spain.

Reconstruction of the unfinished part of the Hassan Tower.

c. 1195

The Hassan Tower in Rabat, a colossal project and an over-ambitious undertaking, was never completed.

King Boabdil's Farewell
Painted by the Orientalist Alfred Dehodencq (1822–82), this famous scene from Spanish history is redolent with nostalgia but is probably spurious. It depicts the fall of the last Moorish kingdom in Andalusia, that of the Nasrids of Granada, in 1492. Al-Andalus was to acquire a mythical aura in the minds of the Moorish communities who fled the Iberian peninsula during the Reconquest. In architecture, daily life, cuisine, music and vocabulary, Andalusian culture lives on in Moroccan towns and cities to this day.

The Almohads and the Apogee of the Western Muslim Empire

In 1125, after a life devoted to study and to travelling in the Muslim world, Ibn Toumart, a Berber man of letters, settled in Tin Mal, a narrow valley in the High Atlas. A religious puritan driven by the doctrine of unity, he declared himself the *mahdi* (messiah) and,

in opposition to the increasingly decadent Almoravids, began preaching moral reform. On his death, his successor Abd el-Moumen assumed the title of Leader of the Faithful. In 1146–7 he took control of the main cities of the Almoravid empire,

Mihrab of the mosque at Tin Mal, birthplace of the Almohads

including Marrakech, Fès and the great cities of Al-Andalus. Now the leader of the greatest empire that ever existed in the Muslim west, he went about centralizing it and reorganizing its army, administration and economy. He imposed taxes and land surveys, created a navy, founded universities and enlisted the support of the great Arab

Tiled panel depicting the Battle of Las Navas de Tolosa of 1212

dynasties. With such thinkers as Ibn Tufaïl and Averroës *(see p233)*, intellectual life flourished. In 1162, Abd el-Moumen, founder of the Almohad dynasty, proclaimed himself caliph. The dynasty was at its peak during his reign, and that of his grandson Yacoub el-Mansour ("the Victorious", 1184–99).

But over the following decades the dynasty declined. The combined forces of the Spanish Christian princes inflicted a heavy defeat on Mohammed el-Nasser at the Battle of Las Navas de Tolosa. With the fall of Córdoba in 1236 and of Seville in 1248, the Muslims lost Spain, with only the small Nasrid kingdom of Granada surviving until 1492. The last Almohad sultans, who were reduced to the Maghreb, were challenged by dissidents: the Hafsids – Almohads who established their own dynasty (1228–1574) in Tunisia and western Algeria – and the Abdelwadid Berbers in Tlemcen in 1236.

In the south, the Almohads lost control of Saharan trade routes, while at the very heart of the kingdom, the Merinids,

Carved wooden Merinid chest

the Almohads' Berber allies of the high plateaus, defied their authority. The cycle is described by the great Maghrebi historian Ibn Khaldoun *(see p185)*, in which over the centuries simple nomads wrench power from corrupt city-dwellers, who are themselves overthrown, and it begins again.

The age of the Almohads, a period of unequalled splendour, has left a lasting impression on Morocco: a form of Islam that is both spiritual and precisely defined, a *makhzen* (central power) to control tribal

1130–63 Abd el-Moumen, the first Almohad caliph, conquers the Maghreb as far as Tripoli	**1212** Alfonso VIII of Castile defeats Mohammed el-Nasser at Las Navas de Tolosa		**1248–86** Abou Yahia, followed by Abou Youssef Yacoub, establishes the Merinid dynasty

1120   **1180**   **1240**   **1300**

1125 The *mahdi* Ibn Toumart settles in Tin Mal	**1195** Yacoub el-Mansour defeats the Castilians at Alarcos	**1212–69** Decline of the Almohad dynasty; gradual loss of territories in Al-Andalus	*Standard captured from the Muslims at the Battle of Las Navas de Tolosa*

self-determination, and a great urban Moorish civilization that is still in evidence.

The Merinids (1248–1465)

Under the Merinids, Morocco was gradually reduced to the territory that it covers today. Unsuccessful on the battlefield, the Merinids were, however, inspired builders, and during their rule a brilliant urban civilization came into being. Led by Abou Yahia, these Zenet Berber nomads took control of the major cities and fertile plains from 1248, although it was not until 1269 that they conquered Marrakech, thus putting an end to the Almohad dynasty. Fès, which had been made capital by Abou Yacoub Youssef, experienced a new phase of expansion.

Despite some minor victories, the Merinids were unsuccessful in their attempts to reconquer territory on the Iberian peninsula. In 1415, the Portuguese, led by Henry the Navigator, took Ceuta. However, Abou el-Hassan (the "Black Sultan") managed to re-establish temporary order and unity in the Maghreb. He and his successor, Abou Inan, were great rulers and great builders. But crises of succession gradually undermined

Geography

Geography was a favourite discipline with Arabs in the early Middle Ages. Ibn Battuta (c.1300–c.1370), who was born in Tangier and studied in Damascus, took the art of the *rihla* – encyclopedic travel writing –

Map by the cartographer Al Idrissi (1099–1166), born in Ceuta, who put together one of the first geographic accounts of the known world

to its height. Towards the end of his life he dictated an entertaining account of his travels over almost 30 years. He visited the holy cities of Arabia, was a minister in the Maldives, a merchant in India and China, and explored Indonesia and the Persian Gulf. Having returned to the Maghreb, he travelled through the kingdoms of sub-Saharan Africa.

their authority, and the Wattasids, another Zenet Berber dynasty, started taking over power from 1420 and ruled solely from 1465–1549. With the 15th century began the slow decline of Moroccan power: fortune now favoured the Europeans.

Tapestry depicting the fall of Ceuta to the Portuguese in 1415

1331–49 The Merinid period reaches its peak under Abou el-Hassan

1415 Henry the Navigator wins Ceuta for Portugal

Tiled panel depicting the conquest of Ceuta

1360

1420

1480

1349–58 Reign of Abou Inan, a great builder

1420 The Merinids come under the control of the Wattasids

1465 The Wattasids oust the Merinids permanently

1497–1508 After the fall of Granada to the Christians, the Spanish move into northern Morocco

The Two Shorfa Dynasties

Since the time of Idriss I, the *shorfa* (the plural form of sherif) – Arabs of high social standing who are descendants of the Prophet Mohammed – have always played an important part in the social and political life of Morocco. Putting an end to Berber rule, they emerged from the south and governed Morocco from the 16th century to the present day. Because of their social origins, these two final dynasties, the Saadians and the Alaouites, are known as the Shorfa dynasties.

Saadian Prosperity (1525–1659)

At the beginning of the 16th century, the encroachment of Christian armies on Moroccan soil stimulated a vigorous renewal of religious fervour. From 1509, supporters of the movement of resistance against the Europeans found a leader in El-Kaïm, sherif of the Beni Saad, an Arab tribe from the Draa valley. Boldly leading the campaign for the reconquest of the Portuguese enclaves and for the seizure of power, they took control of the Souss, of Marrakech (1525), which was to become their capital, and of Fès (1548), ousting the last Wattasid sultans.

The Saadians stepped onto the stage of international relations; in 1577, France even appointed a Moroccan consul. To help counter the threat of the Turks, who had settled in Algiers, Mohammed ech-Cheikh requested the support of Madrid, whose attention was then focused on the Americas

A gold dinar, proof of Saadian prosperity

Dom Sebastião, the young king killed in battle in Morocco in 1578

rather than the Maghreb. The Ottomans had Mohammed assassinated in 1557, but did not conquer Morocco.

The Saadians traded with Europe and drew up treaties with England and the Netherlands. From the Moriscos, the last Spanish Muslims, they received the final heritage of Al-Andalus.

Once the Saadians had retaken Agadir (1541), only Mazagan (El-Jadida), Tangier and Ceuta remained in Portuguese hands. Portugal's "Moroccan dream" was extinguished at the Battle of the Three Kings in 1578, when two rival Saadian sultans and Dom Sebastião, the young king of Portugal, all died at Ksar el-Kebir (*see p96*). His uncle, Philip II of Spain, swiftly annexed the Portuguese kingdom.

Saadian prosperity culminated with Ahmed el-Mansour, (1578–1603) whose conquests secured control of Saharan trade, and who set up the *makhzen* (a central administration). Gold from Mali and slaves reached Marrakech. Political and religious links with western Africa, and the presence of African folk culture brought here by slaves, made a mark on Morocco that can still be seen today.

Like their preceding dynasties, the Saadians declined as the result of ambition and disputed succession. In the distant Tafilalt, the ascetic *shorfa*, descendants of Ali, cousin of the Prophet, revolted against the decadence of Saadian rule under Moulay Sherif, and seized control of the region, which they held until 1664.

1525 The Saadians take Marrakech, which becomes their capital

1578–1603 Reign of Ahmed el-Mansour, "the Golden One"

1631–36 Moulay Sherif, in the Tafilalt, rebels against Saadian decadence

1664–72 Reign of Moulay Rachid, founder of the Alaouite dynasty

1500

1570

1640

1509 The Saadians begin their campaign to expel the Europeans

Portal of the Saadian Tombs

1578 Battle of the Three Kings

1636–64 Reign of Moulay Mohammed

Moulay Ismaïl

1672–1727 The Alaouites reach the peak of their power under Moulay Ismaïl

Alaouite Greatness and External Threats

The Alaouite dynasty, the seventh and present ruling dynasty, has given the country some rulers of great stature. During its long reign, each ruler concentrated on bringing stability to the country and on countering the threat of imperialist powers. It

Trade agreement of 1767. During his reign Sidi Mohammed signed treaties with France, Denmark, Sweden, England, Venice, Spain and the newly created United States

took ten years for Moulay Rachid (1664–72), founder of the dynasty, to bring the country under his control. The long and glorious reign of his younger brother, Moulay Ismaïl (1672–1727), marked Morocco's final apogee *(see pp58–9)*. He transferred the capital from Fès to Meknès, imposed central authority in the remotest corners of the country, recaptured Mehdya, Tangier and Larache from the Europeans, and maintained relations with the courts of Europe.

After a period of instability, his grandson, Sidi Mohammed ben Abdallah, restored order, expelled the Portuguese from Mazagan and founded Mogador (Essaouira) to facilitate trade with Europe. Under Moulay Yazid and Moulay Sliman, epidemics, uprisings and diplomatic isolation caused the country to withdraw into itself. Moulay Abderrahman, another great ruler, attempted to modernize the country, but was frustrated by European colonial expansion. He was defeated by the French at Isly in 1844.

Moulay Abderrahman and his successors, Mohammed IV and Hassan I, were forced to concede commercial and consular privileges to Britain, France and Spain. In 1860, Spain took control of Tetouan. Hassan I, a dynamic ruler, attempted to balance the influence of these rivals, but the Conference of Madrid of 1880 sanctioned the intervention of foreign powers in Morocco. On his death, the country was stable and the dynasty's prestige intact, but Morocco was weakened.

French victory at the Battle of Isly, near Oujda, in 1844, depicted by the French painter Horace Vernet

1728–57 Reign of Moulay Abdallah	**1792–1822** Reign of Moulay Sliman, the Pious		**1873–93** Moulay Hassan I attempts to repulse the French	**1894–1908** Reign of Moulay Abdelaziz and regency of Ba Ahmed
	1780		**1850**	
1757–90 Rule of Sidi Mohammed ben Abdallah who establishes his capital in Rabat		**1822–59** Reign of Moulay Abderrahman	**1859–73** Reign of Moulay Mohammed IV	**1907–12** Reign of Moulay Hafidh

Sultan Moulay Hafidh

The Great Age of Moulay Ismaïl

Moulay Ismaïl, of partial Saharan parentage and a man of phenomenal vitality, stamped his authority on Morocco during a long and brilliant reign. Ruling for 55 years (1672–1727), he was a contemporary of Louis XIV. He made Meknès his capital and maintained a powerful army, recruited tens of thousands of men for the Black Guard, and modernized the artillery. With these forces, he was able to overcome rebellious tribes and bring temporary peace to the country. He wrenched from European control several fortresses, including Tangier and Larache. He also exchanged ambassadors with the French court.

Sultan Moulay Ismaïl
He was the greatest, most ruthless ruler of the Alaouite dynasty.

The capital of Moulay Ismaïl in 1693.

Morocco's Ambassador in Paris (1682)
In conflict with Spain, Moulay Ismaïl sought an alliance with France in order to vanquish the fortresses that Spain held in Morocco. Once in France, the sultan's ambassador, Hadj Tenim, concluded a treaty of Franco-Moroccan friendship in 1682. Morocco then became an important trading partner for European countries.

Moulay Ismaïl's retinue

Black Guard
Moulay Ismaïl greatly expanded the army, which consisted of three contingents: units provided by the tribes, Christian renegades and *abid*, black slaves and mercenaries, whose exclusive duty was to protect the sultan. This latter regiment led to the formation of the famous Black Guard, which still exists.

Anne Marie de Bourbon
So as to strengthen his links with Europe, Moulay Ismaïl sent a request to Louis XIV for the hand of the princess, the French king's cousin, in marriage. His request was not granted.

The Architectural Heritage of Moulay Ismaïl

Moulay Ismaïl's achievements as a builder are most clearly seen in Meknès. This was formerly a small town overshadowed by the prestigious city of Fès, but the sultan transformed it into Morocco's fourth imperial city. It was enclosed by a double line of defensive walls and was described by some as the Versailles of Morocco. Next to the medina, the sultan built a kasbah, an extensive architectural complex enclosed within its own walls. This was the seat of power and of administration, consisting of several palaces, mosques, garrisons and studs, cisterns and stores for water. It was the ideal imperial city.

Chevalier de Saint-Olon

Large-scale building projects undertaken by Moulay Ismaïl, such as the Dar el-Ma, shown here *(see p197)*, called for an army of craftsmen. These were recruited from other tribes, Christian prisoners and slaves. Contemporary writers record that the cruel sultan supervised the work himself, passing a death sentence on the slowest workers.

Bab el- Berdaïne, the Gate of the Pack-Saddle-Makers *(see p192)*, takes its name from the pack-saddle market held nearby. In the 17th century, Meknès was enclosed by triple walls with imposing gates.

Audience Given by Moulay Ismaïl
As depicted in this painting in the Palace of Versailles by M. P. Denis (1663–1742), Louis XIV, the Sun King, sent an ambassador to Meknès in 1689. The ambassador, the Chevalier François Pidou de Saint-Olon, was received with full honours. For 20 years, Louis XIV and Moulay Ismaïl exchanged embassies, but relations between them soured when France declined to engage in conflict with Spain.

The Sultan's Mausoleum
(see pp198–9), which was built in the 17th century, was completely restored by Mohammed V in 1959. The clocks in the burial chamber were presented as gifts by Louis XIV.

Marshal Lyautey, Morocco's first resident-general, with Moulay Youssef

European Domination

When Moulay Abdel Aziz, a weak ruler, ascended the throne in 1894, France already had an imperial presence in Algeria and Tunisia. The French now aimed to secure a free hand in Morocco, parallel with Britain's designs in Egypt and those of Italy in Libya. After controversial fiscal reform, Moulay Abdel Aziz entered into heavy debt with France. Meanwhile, the French military administration in Algeria gradually pushed back the frontier with Morocco, which was to lead to a long drawn-out conflict. When Kaiser Wilhelm II of Germany arrived in Tangier in March 1905 to claim his share, the "Moroccan question" took on another dimension. The Conference of Algeciras of 1906, in which all the interested powers took part, forcibly opened Morocco to international trade, and assigned France and Spain as administrators.

In 1907, various incidents provided the French forces with the pretext to move into Oujda and Casablanca. In the same

year, Abdel Aziz was deposed by his brother Moulay Hafidh, who attempted to resist but was forced to yield. Numerous uprisings led the French to impose a protectorate, through the Treaty of Fès in 1912. Moulay Hafidh was then replaced by his half-brother, Moulay Youssef.

What was called "pacification" at the time continued until 1934: it took French forces 22 years to bring the whole country under control. In the Rif, a state of war persisted up until 1926. Abd el-Krim Khattabi, a brilliant strategist and organizer, defeated the Spanish at Anoual in 1921, proclaimed a republic in 1922, and long held out against the forces of the Spanish and French colonial powers, led by Francisco Franco and Philippe Pétain respectively. He left the country and died in exile in Cairo in 1963.

Marshal Hubert Lyautey, an exceptional man who was made France's first resident-general in Morocco in 1912, played a decisive role in the imposition of French rule. He installed the capital in Rabat, and worked to promote the country's economic development, but firmly refused to consider assimilation, a process by which colonies were modelled on the mother country. The country's traditional infrastructure was left intact and town planners safeguarded the imperial cities.

Abd el-Krim Khattabi, heroic leader of an ephemeral Rifian republic

On the death of Moulay Youssef in 1927, his third son, Sidi Mohammed ben Youssef, who was then 18, succeeded him, taking the name Mohammed V. He was to restore the country's independence.

1912 Protectorate agreement is signed at the Treaty of Fès

Sultan Moulay Youssef

1921–26 Revolt in the Rif

1930 France imposes the Berber *dahir*

1910

1920

1930

1911 French troops enter Fès

1912–27 Reign of Moulay Youssef, who deposed his half-brother

Marshal Pétain received by Marshal Lyautey in Rabat in 1925

1927 Start of the reign of the sultan Mohammed ben Youssef, the future Mohammed V

The Fight for Istiqlal

Morocco was divided into two zones: a French zone, covering the largest part of the country, and a Spanish zone, in the north and south. Tangier was an international free city.

The French Protectorate was both beneficial and detrimental to Morocco. The country's infrastructure was modernized, its mineral resources were exploited

1930s building, Casablanca, dating from the Protectorate

and the most fertile land turned over to agriculture. The population of Casablanca, the economic capital, doubled every ten years, and the city became a major port.

The administration of Lyautey's 13 successors, however, was increasingly direct, so that the role of the local *makhzen* became redundant. Colonial ideology triumphed in the 1930s. When France imposed a Berber *dahir*, giving Berber areas a separate legal system, the effect was to divide the country.

World War II justified the Moroccan people's desire for freedom. In 1942, the Allies arrived in Morocco and President Roosevelt pledged the sultan his support. Showing a progressively higher profile, Mohammed V drew a following of young nationalists, who set up the Istiqlal (Independence) Party. The Manifesto of Independence called on the sultan to head a movement for independence, a challenge that he formally accepted in a speech in Tangier in 1947. The power struggle with Paris lasted almost a decade. In 1951, the French authorities supported

the rebellion of El-Glaoui, the pasha of Marrakech *(see p257)*. The sultan refused to abdicate but the French deposed him in 1953, replacing him with the elderly Ben Arafa. The royal family were forced into exile but the fight for independence gained momentum.

International opinion no longer supported the colonial powers, and the United Nations took over the Moroccan question.

After negotiations with France, the deposed sultan made his triumphant return from exile as King Mohammed V, with Hassan, the heir apparent, at his side. The Protectorate ended in 1956, and in 1958 Tangier and the Spanish enclave of Tarfaya were restored to the kingdom. Independence had been won, although national unity was still to be achieved.

Mohammed V and his son, the future king, Hassan II, in 1955

The Glaoui kasbah at Telouet

1943 The sultan meets US President Roosevelt at the Anfa Conference

1951 France supports the rebellion of El-Glaoui, pasha of Marrakech

1955 The royal family returns from exile

1940

1950

[19]34 Allal el-Fassi [set]s up the [M]oroccan Action [Co]mmittee

1944 Publication of the Manifesto of Independence

1953 France deposes Sultan Mohammed V, who goes into exile in Madagascar

1958 Tangier and the Spanish enclave of Tarfaya are returned to Morocco

The future Hassan II, in 1957, with Allal el-Fassi, the founder of Istiqlal

Political and Social Change in Contemporary Morocco

In the rest of the Arab world monarchies were replaced by authoritarian republican regimes (as in Iraq, Egypt, Yemen and Tunisia). In Morocco, however, Mohammed V's patriotic sentiment united the country behind a monarchy that has long-established roots and that ensures its unity and stability. A pious and outward-looking Muslim, the king encouraged the emancipation of women, the education of his people, and agrarian reform. During this period, Morocco, unlike neighbouring countries, embraced political pluralism (albeit in a tightly controlled form) and relative economic liberalism, choices that were decisive for its future. In 1958, having broken away from Istiqlal, the progressive wing of the nationalist movement founded a left-wing party – the Union Nationale des Forces Populaires, the future USFP – with Abderrahim Bouabid and Mehdi Ben Barka.

The king also had to contend with the impatience of nationalist sentiment, which believed that the country should engage in armed conflict to regain all Saharan territory and that it should give military aid to Algeria, which was still fighting its war for independence.

Mohammed V died suddenly, after an operation, in 1961. His eldest son, Moulay Hassan, who had been closely associated with power for many years, succeeded him as Hassan II. A skilled politician, he was to witness political as well as social change in his country, in the course of a reign lasting 38 years. It was, however, often marked by unrest and mixed success.

On the international front, Hassan II steered Morocco in the direction of the Western world and even spoke of the

The National Question

The question of the reintegration of Moroccan territory is a long-standing theme in contemporary Moroccan politics. At issue is the western Sahara, an area of 266,000 sq km (102,700 sq miles), from which Spain withdrew in 1975. In November that year Hassan II launched a Green March to win back this mineral-rich territory. The Polisario Front, an armed movement supported by Algeria, meanwhile fought for the territory's independence. Open conflict raged until 1988, when both sides accepted a plan drawn up by the United Nations, with consideration for the area's Sahraoui population. Since 1991, a referendum on the issue has been continually postponed because of lack of agreement on voters' lists.

Green March, keeping the national question at the top of Morocco's political agenda

		1965 Mehdi Ben Barka is murdered in Paris, where he lived		**1985** Pope John Paul II visits Casablanca
	1963 Outbreak of war with Algeria	in exile after being accused of plotting against the king	**1975** Start of the Green March	**1981** (Jun) Unrest in Casablanca
1956 The Protectorate formally ends				

| **1950** | **1960** | **1970** | **1980** |

| *Hassan II* | **1961** Death of Mohammed V. Hassan II is crowned king | **1962** First constitution is adopted through a referendum | **1971** Attempted coup d'état in Skhirat | **1972** Second attempted coup d'état | **1970s** Morocco is a focus of the hippy trail |

The ceremony marking Throne Day in Marrakech

country joining the European Union. He pursued policies that were distinctive in the Muslim world, leading the Al Qods Committee in Jerusalem and encouraging reconciliation between Israel and the Palestinians. By contrast, deep-seated caution marked his relations with neighbouring Algeria, which had gained independence in 1962. Disputes over the border between the two countries led to war in 1963.

On the domestic front, supported by General Oufkir, Dlimi then Driss Basri, Hassan II alternated liberalizing policies with repression. The first constitution, drawn up in 1962 and followed by parliamentary elections in 1963, failed to unify the country. A new constitution was drawn up in 1970. Social unrest caused by poverty marked the following years, as public life returned to normal. When a new constitution was drawn up in 1996, the time had come for a less autocratic style of government.

After parliamentary elections in 1997, Hassan II opened the doors to political change. Abderrahmane Youssoufi, a political opponent. was instructed to form a broad coalition government around the Socialist Union, and wisely

brought in thoroughgoing reforms to modernize the country.

The king died in 1999, and was succeeded by his eldest son, Mohammed VI. He has addressed human rights issues, has allowed remaining exiles to return and takes a close interest in the northern provinces that were neglected by his father. Fundamental problems such as under-development, illiteracy and poverty still remain. After the terrorist bombs of 2003, the king proclaimed "the end of the era of indulgence", and limited human rights and freedom of the press. In 2011 young Moroccans began demonstrating for democracy and social change; this became known as the 20th February Movement. The king and his government created a new constitution and held a referendum on 1 July 2011. Parlimentary elections were held in November with the Justice and Development Party leader, Abdelilah Benkirane becoming the Prime Minister. In October 2013, the king appointed a new government.

Mohammed VI, who came to the throne in 1999

	Hassan II attends the first Maghrebi Union Treaty	2003 Birth of Prince Moulay Hassan	2011 Months of demonstrations begin on 20th February in Rabat, with thousands of Moroccans calling for constitutional reform
	1994 (Feb) Islamic riots on the campus in Fès	2007 Birth of Princess Lalla Khadija	2013 (October) The king appoints a new government.

1990	2000	2010	2020
1988 First Maghrebi Union Treaty in Algiers	1991 (6 Sep) Ceasefire agreed with the Polisario Front	1999 Death of King Hassan II. His son Mohammed VI is enthroned	2004 Morocco's parliament approves a free-trade agreement with the US	2011 (1 Jul) A referendum is held for constitutional reforms. Parlimentary elections held in November
	1998 Abderrahmane Youssoufi forms a new government			

MOROCCO REGION BY REGION

Morocco at a Glance

From the Mediterranean coast to the High Atlas, beyond which the country stretches out into the boundless expanses of the Sahara Desert, Morocco forms a gigantic semicircle facing onto the Atlantic. Its major towns and cities, the focus of the country's economic and political activity, are located along the Atlantic seaboard from Tangier to Agadir and from Fès to Rabat. Topography, climate and history have together created a multifaceted country which offers everything from beaches, high mountain valleys and fertile agricultural land with almond and peach trees to majestic mountains and an extensive desert dotted with oases and palm groves. In secret medinas, in labyrinthine souks, or at the foot of Almohad and Merinid minarets, traders and artisans can be seen continuing ancient artistic traditions.

Casablanca is renowned for its Art Deco architecture. It also boasts the richly decorated Hassan II Mosque *(see pp106–107)*.

Essaouira

Agadir

Essaouira, a strikingly white town that appears to rise up out of the water, is also a surfer's dream location *(see pp124–9)*.

Laayoune

El-Mahb

SOUTHERN MOROCCO & WESTERN SAHARA

Agadir is the place to go for sun, sand and relaxation. An attractive medina has been built in the south of the town *(see pp290–91)*.

Dakhla

The South is a varied region of deserts, oases, mountains and coastline. The architecture and the colours of the houses in Tafraoute, in the Anti-Atlas, are highly distinctive *(see p297)*.

◄ Aerial view of the delightful town of Chefchaouen in the Rif region

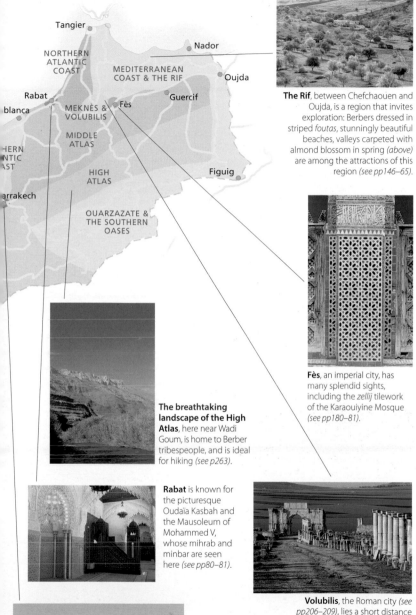

Tangier

Nador

NORTHERN
ATLANTIC
COAST

MEDITERRANEAN
COAST & THE RIF

Oujda

Rabat

Guercif

blanca

MEKNÈS &
VOLUBILIS

Fès

MIDDLE
ATLAS

HERN
NTIC
AST

HIGH
ATLAS

Figuig

arrakech

OUARZAZATE &
THE SOUTHERN
OASES

The Rif, between Chefchaouen and Oujda, is a region that invites exploration: Berbers dressed in striped *foutas*, stunningly beautiful beaches, valleys carpeted with almond blossom in spring *(above)* are among the attractions of this region *(see pp146–65)*.

Fès, an imperial city, has many splendid sights, including the *zellij* tilework of the Karaouiyine Mosque *(see pp180–81)*.

The breathtaking landscape of the High Atlas, here near Wadi Goum, is home to Berber tribespeople, and is ideal for hiking *(see p263)*.

Rabat is known for the picturesque Oudaïa Kasbah and the Mausoleum of Mohammed V, whose mihrab and minbar are seen here *(see pp80–81)*.

Volubilis, the Roman city *(see pp206–209)*, lies a short distance from Meknès, one of Morocco's imperial cities.

Marrakech, a city enclosed within its ochre ramparts *(see p231)*, stands in the shadow of the snowy Atlas.

0 km   100

0 miles   100

RABAT

Facing onto the Atlantic Ocean, Rabat is an attractive city of domes and minarets, sweeping terraces, wide avenues and green spaces. It is markedly more pleasant than some other Moroccan cities and is also undergoing fundamental change. Facing Salé, its ancient rival, across Wadi Bou Regreg, Rabat is the political, administrative and financial capital of Morocco, the country's main university town and its second-largest metropolis after Casablanca.

Archaeological excavations of the Merinid necropolis at Chellah *(see pp84–5)* have shown that this area was occupied by the Romans, and even earlier too. Much later, around 1150, Abd el-Moumen, the first ruler of the Almohad dynasty, chose to establish a permanent camp here and ordered a small imperial residence to be built on the site of a former *ribat* (fortified monastery).

The caliph Yacoub el-Mansour then embarked on the construction of a great and splendid city that was to be known as Ribat el-Fath (Camp of Victory), in celebration of his victory over Alfonso VIII of Castile at the Battle of Alarcos in 1195. On the death of the caliph in 1199, work on this ambitious project ceased: although the city gates and walls had been completed, the Hassan Mosque and its minaret *(see p53)* were unfinished. The Almohads' defeat at the Battle of Las Navas de Tolosa in 1212 weakened their power and led to the city's decline.

In 1610, Philip III of Spain expelled from his kingdom the remaining Moors, who fled to the cities of the Maghreb. Among them were a large colony of emigrants from Andalusia who settled in Rabat.

Rabat became the capital of a minor and relatively autonomous coastal republic. Funds brought by the Andalusian refugees were put to equipping a flotilla of privateers that preyed on European shipping. The "Republic of Bou Regreg", as it was known, was then annexed to the sherif's kingdom in 1666, although piracy was not brought to an end until the mid-19th century.

In 1912 Marshal Lyautey *(see p60)* made Rabat the political and administrative capital of Morocco. Its population now exceeds 1.77 million.

The majestic Mausoleum of Mohammed V

◀ Fishing boats moored with the Kasbah des Oudaias in the background

Exploring Rabat

Rabat has four main areas of interest. In the north is the picturesque Oudaïa Kasbah, which is partly enclosed by ramparts dating from the Almohad period. The medina, which contains the city's souks, is bounded to the west by Almohad ramparts and to the south by the 17th-century Andalusian Wall, which runs parallel to Boulevard Hassan II. Avenue Mohammed V is the new town's busy central north- south axis, with residential blocks dating from the Protectorate (1912–56). In the northeast stands the Hassan Tower and Mausoleum of Mohammed V. In the Merinid necropolis at Chellah, to the south, are vestiges of the Roman town of Sala.

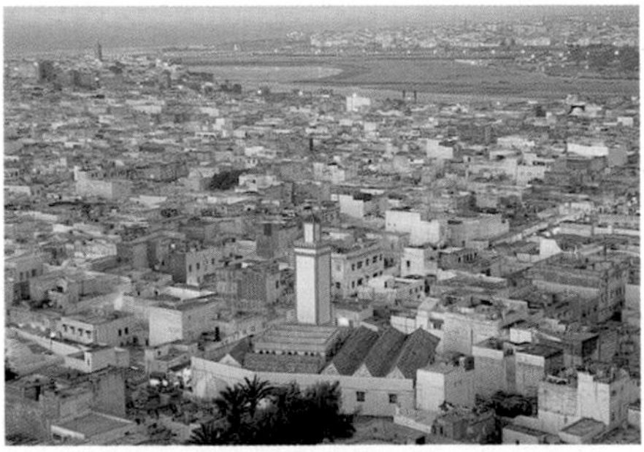

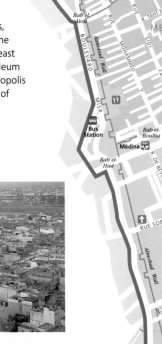

The Sliman Mosque and the medina in Rabat

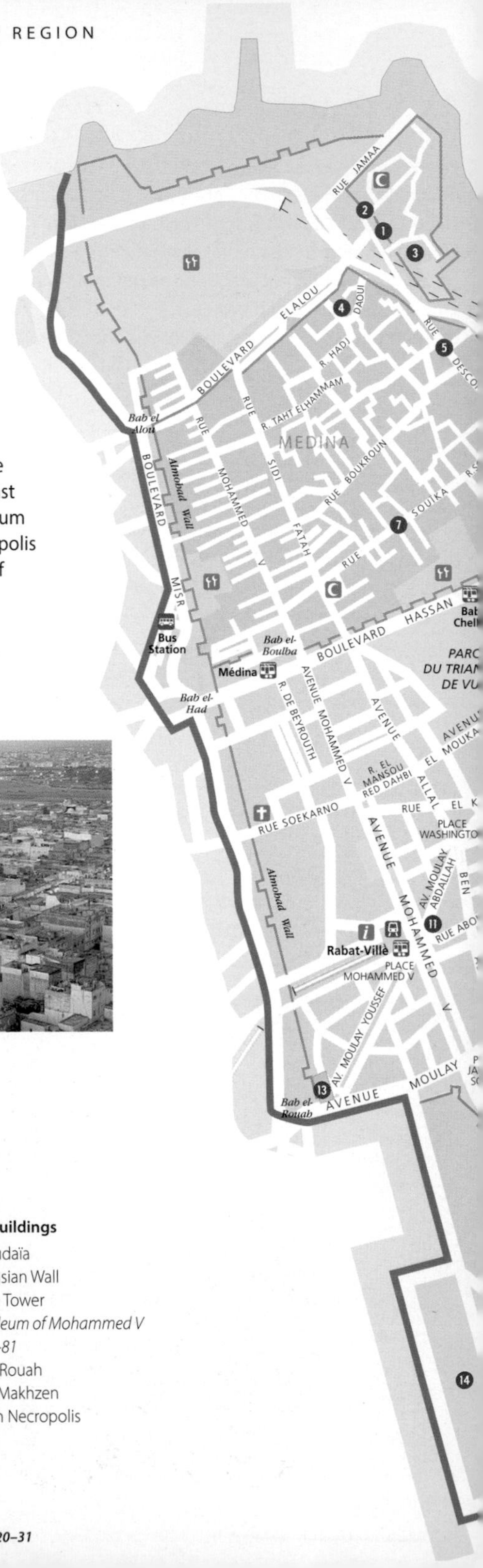

Sights at a Glance

Districts, Streets & Squares

- 1 City Walls
- 4 Place Souk el-Ghezel and Rue Hadj Daoui
- 5 Rue des Consuls
- 6 Rue Souk es-Sebat
- 7 Rue Souïka
- 11 Ville Nouvelle

Museums

- 3 Musée des Oudaïa (Museum of Moroccan Crafts)
- 12 *Musée Archéologique pp82–3*

Historic Buildings

- 2 Bab Oudaïa
- 8 Andalusian Wall
- 9 Hassan Tower
- 10 *Mausoleum of Mohammed V pp80–81*
- 13 Bab el-Rouah
- 14 Dar el-Makhzen
- 15 Chellah Necropolis

For hotels and restaurants see pp306–313 and pp320–31

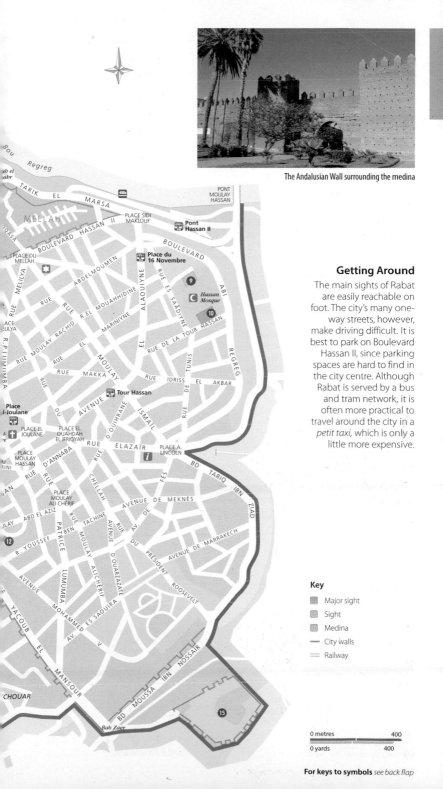

The Andalusian Wall surrounding the medina

Getting Around

The main sights of Rabat are easily reachable on foot. The city's many one-way streets, however, make driving difficult. It is best to park on Boulevard Hassan II, since parking spaces are hard to find in the city centre. Although Rabat is served by a bus and tram network, it is often more practical to travel around the city in a *petit taxi*, which is only a little more expensive.

Key

- Major sight
- Sight
- Medina
- City walls
- Railway

0 metres   400
0 yards   400

For keys to symbols *see back flap*

Street-by-Street: the Oudaïa Kasbah

The kasbah takes its name from the Oudaïas, an Arab tribe with a warrior past that was settled here by Moulay Ismaïl (1672–1727) to protect the city from the threat of rebel tribes. Part of the city walls that surround this "fortress", built on the top of a cliff, and Bab Oudaïa, the gate that pierces it, date from the Almohad period (1147–1248). On Rue Jamaa, the main thoroughfare of this picturesque district, stands the El-Atika Mosque, built in the 12th century and the oldest mosque in Rabat.

❷ ★ Bab Oudaïa
An archetypal example of Almohad military architecture, this monumental gate was built by Yacoub el-Mansour in the 12th century.

❶ City Walls
The western ramparts were built by Yacoub el-Mansour in 1195, after his victory over Alfonso III.

El-Alou cemetery

❸ ★ Musée des Oudaïa
Since 1915 the historic palace of Moulay Ismaïl (see pp58–9) has housed a museum with a rich collection of Moroccan folk art and crafts.

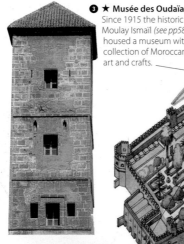

RUE BAZZO

★ Andalusian Garden
This pleasant garden, laid out in the Moorish style at the beginning of the 20th century, features a traditional Arabic *noria* (waterwheel for irrigation).

Café Maure
This is where Rabatis come to relax and pass the time. From here there are views of Salé's medina, of the Bou Regreg and of the Atlantic Ocean. A doorway leads through to the Andalusian Garden.

Locator Map
See Rabat Map pp70–71

Narrow Kasbah Street
Although some elements date back to the 12th century, the houses in the kasbah, lime-washed in blue or white, were built in the late 17th to early 18th centuries, at the time of the first Alaouite rulers.

Prayer Hall of the El-Atika Mosque
Founded in about 1150 by Abd el-Moumen, this place of worship is Rabat's oldest monument. The mosque was remodelled in the 18th century, and again under the Alaouites.

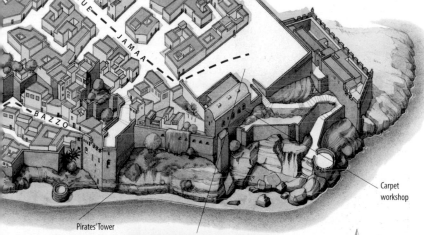

Fountain

Almohad walls

Carpet workshop

Pirates' Tower

Platform of the Former Oudaïa Signal Station
Built in the 18th century by Sultan Sidi Mohammed ben Abdallah, this signal station defended the Bou Regreg estuary. The warehouse to its right contains a carpet workshop.

0 metres 50

0 yards 50

Key

— Suggested route

Walls of the Andalusian Garden, built in the reign of Moulay Rachid

❶ City Walls

In the north of the city. Accessible via Place du Souk el-Ghezel and Place de l'Ancien Sémaphore.

Separated from the medina by the Place du Souk el-Ghezel, the Oudaïa Kasbah is defended by thick ramparts. These were built mostly by the Almohads in the 12th century, and were restored and remodelled in the 17th and 18th centuries by the Moriscos and the Alaouite kings.

Most of the Almohad walls that face onto the sea and run inland survive. The walls surrounding the Andalusian Garden date from the reign of Moulay Rachid (founder of the Alaouite dynasty). The Hornacheros (Andalusian emigrants) who occupied the kasbah and rebuffed attacks from both sea and land rebuilt the curtain wall in several places and constructed the Pirates' Tower, whose inner stairway leads down to the river. They also pierced the walls of the old Almohad towers with embrasures to hold cannons. A complex system of underground passages leading from within the kasbah to the exterior beyond the walls was also dug.

The city walls are built of rough-hewn stone covered with a thick coating of ochre plaster. They are set with imposing towers and bastions, which are more numerous along the stretch of the walls facing the sea and the river. Standing 8 to 10 m (26 to 33 ft) high, and having an average thickness of 2.50 m (8 ft), the walls are surmounted by a rampart walk bordered by a low parapet; part of the rampart walk survives.

This sturdy building and sophisticated military construction defended the pirates' nest and withstood almost all attacks from European forces.

❷ Bab Oudaïa

Oudaïa Kasbah. The gate leads to the kasbah from Place du Souk el-Ghezel.

Towering above the cliffs that line the Bou Regreg, and dominating Rabat's medina is Bab Oudaïa, which is the main entrance into the kasbah. This monumental city gate, built in dressed stone of red ochre, is considered to be one of the finest examples of Almohad architecture. But the particular design and conception of this gateway, built by Yacoub el-Mansour in 1195, make it more of a decorative feature than a piece of military defence work. Flanked by two towers, it is crowned by a horseshoe arch. The inner and outer façades are decorated with rich ornamentation carved in relief into the stone, starting at the opening of the arch and continuing in several tiers as far up as the base of the parapet. Above the arch, two bands with interlacing lozenges are outlined with floral decoration. Both sides of the gate are crowned by a band of calligraphy.

As in all Moorish palaces, the gatehouse of the former

Stylized seashell on Bab Oudaïa

Oudaïa Palace was also a defensive feature and a tribunal. Today, the gatehouse serves as an exhibition hall.

❸ Musée des Oudaïa

Oudaïa Kasbah. Accessible via a gateway in the southwestern walls. **Tel** (0537) 73 15 37. **Open** 9am–4:30pm Wed–Mon. **Closed** Tue and public holidays.

In the 17th century, Moulay Ismaïl built a small palace within the kasbah. This became the residence of the first Alaouite sultans while they were based in Rabat, as an inscription on the wooden lintels of the central patio indicates: "Unfailing fortune and brilliant victory to our lord Smaïl, leader of the faithful." The palace was completely restored and slightly altered in 1917, during the Protectorate, and has undergone further phases of restoration, as well as a renovation since then.

The palace as it is today consists of a main building arranged around an arcaded courtyard. The four sides of the courtyard lead off into large rectangular rooms with marble floors and geometrically coffered ceilings. The surrounding buildings include a prayer room for private workship, a hammam (steam bath) and a tower. A beautiful garden laid out in the

The Musée des Oudaïa, laid out in a 17th-century palace

Andalusian style gives the palace the status of a princely residence.

Since 1915, the palace has housed the Musée des Oudaïa. On display here is an extensive collection of jewellery, including traditional pieces fashioned by Berber families. There are also displays of woodcarvings, carpets and copperwork, astrolabes (for measuring the altitude of stars) dating from the 14th and 17th centuries, and collections of ceramics and of musical instruments. One room in the museum is laid out as a traditional Moroccan interior, with sofas covered in sumptuous gold-embroidered silk fabrics made in Fès. Another room is devoted to the traditional dress of the region between the Rif and the Sahara.

A small shop in the Souk el-Ghezel district of Rabat

❹ Place Souk el-Ghezel and Rue Hadj Daoui

A convenient place to start exploring Rabat's medina is the Place Souk el-Ghezel, (Wool Market Square), so named because of the market that once took place here. This was also the place where Christian prisoners were once sold as slaves. Today, it is the fine carpets made in the city that are auctioned here every Thursday morning.

Rue Hadj Daoui, just southwest of Place Souk el-Ghezel, leads into the residential area of the medina, where the streets are quieter and where houses built by the Moriscos are still visible.

The unmistakable mark that the Moriscos made on the architecture of Rabat can be seen in certain styles of building: for example, those involving the use of semicircular

arches and ornamental motifs such as the pilasters consisting of vertically arranged mouldings that decorate the upper parts of doors. The smaller houses are of simple design, most of them built of stone rendered with limewashed plaster. Most of the richer houses tucked away in the different quarters of Rabat are built around a central courtyard, like those in other Moroccan medinas, and have a refined elegance.

Walking west along Rue Hadj Daoui leads to Dar el-Mrini, a fine private house built in 1920, which today has been transformed into an exhibition and conference centre.

❺ Rue des Consuls

Eastern part of the medina.

Running through the medina, Rue des Consuls begins at the Wool Market in the north and leads down towards the Andalusian Wall in the south. Up to the time of the Protectorate, this street was where all foreign consuls in Rabat were obliged to live. Covered with rushes and a glass roof, the street

Shops selling leather goods, in the eastern part of the medina

is lined with the shops of craftsmen and traders, making it the most lively quarter in the medina. The two former *fondouks* at No. 109 and No. 137 are now the workshops of leatherworkers and woodworkers.

South of Rue Souk es-Sebat *(see p78)* the street changes name to Rue Ouqqasa, which borders the mellah (Jewish quarter). In Rue Tariq el-Marsa is the Ensemble Artisanal, selling Moroccan crafts, and, a little further on, is a restored 18th-century naval depot.

Rue des Consuls, one of the lively thoroughfares in the medina

Decorative interior of the Mausoleum of Mohammed V in Rabat ▶

❻ Rue Souk es-Sebat

In the medina.

This thoroughfare, which begins at the Great Mosque and ends at Bab el-Bhar (Gate of the Sea) crosses the Rue des Consuls.

Covered by a rush trellis, this lively street is filled with the shops of leatherworkers, jewellers and fabric merchants and of traders in all sorts of other goods.

❼ Rue Souïka

In the medina. Great Mosque: **Closed** to non-Muslims.

Running southwest from Rue Souk es-Sebat, Rue Souïka (Little Souk Street) is the main artery through the medina and also its most lively thoroughfare. Lined with all manner of small shops selling clothes, shoes, food, radios and DVDs, with restaurants and with spice merchants, the street throngs with people most of the day.

At the intersection with Rue de Bab Chellah stands the Great Mosque, built probably between the 13th and the 16th centuries and remodelled and restored on several occasions during the Alaouite period. The mosque's most prominent feature is the minaret, rising to a height of 33 m (109 ft) and completed in 1939. It is built of ashlars (blocks of hewn stone), decorated with dressed stone, and pierced with openings in the shape of lobed or intersecting arches.

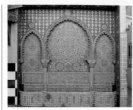

Merinid fountain in the Great Mosque district

Opposite the mosque is a fountain with a pediment of intersecting arches, built in the 14th century, during the reign of the Merinid sultan Abou Fares Abdelaziz. Further along the street, on the corner of Rue Sidi Fatah, is the Moulay Sliman Mosque, or Jamaa el-Souika. It was built in about 1812 on the orders of Moulay Sliman, on the site of an earlier place of worship.

❽ Andalusian Wall

Between Bab el-Had and Place Sidi Makhlouf.

In the 17th century, the Moriscos – Muslim refugees from Andalusia – found the medina undefended and so encircled it with a defensive wall. Named after its builders, the Andalusian Wall stands about 5 m (16 ft) high and runs in a straight line for more than 1,400 m (4,595 ft) from Bab el-Had (Sunday Gate) in the west to the *borj* (small fort) of Sidi Makhlouf in the east. Boulevard Hassan II runs parallel to it. During the Protectorate, a stretch of the walls about 100 m (328 ft) long, and including Bab el-Tben, was destroyed to allow easier access to a market.

The walls are set with towers placed at intervals of some 35 m (115 ft) and are topped by a rampart walk. This is protected by a parapet that the Andalusians pierced with numerous narrow slits known as loopholes.

To the east of the walls they built the Bastion Sidi Makhlouf, a small, irregular fort which consists of a platform resting on solid foundations, with a tower close by. They also built embrasures over two of the Almohad gates, Bab el-Alou and Bab el-Had.

Bab el-Had was once the main gateway into the medina. Dating from the Almohad period (1147–1248), it was rebuilt by Moulay Sliman in 1814. On the side facing Boulevard Misr, one of gate's two pentagonal towers stands close to the Almohad walls, which probably date from 1197.

Moulay Sliman Mosque

Bab el-Had contains several small chambers which were intended to accommodate the soldiers who were in charge of the guard, the armouries and the billetting of the troops.

❾ Hassan Tower

Rue de la Tour Hassan. **Closed** to the public.

For more than eight centuries, the Hassan Tower has stood on the hill overlooking Wadi Bou Regreg. Best seen as one approaches Rabat by the bridge from Salé, it is one of the city's most prestigious monuments and a great emblem of Rabat.

It is the unfinished minaret of the Hassan Mosque, built by Yacoub el-Mansour in about 1196. The construction of this gigantic mosque, of dimensions quite out of proportion to the population of Rabat at the time, suggests that the Almohad ruler intended to make Rabat his new imperial capital.

Bab el-Had, the "Sunday Gate", built in the 17th century

For hotels and restaurants see pp306–313 and pp320–31

The Hassan Tower and remains of the Hassan Mosque's prayer hall

An alternative interpretation is that the Almohads were attempting to rival the magnificent Great Mosque of Córdoba, the former capital of the Islamic kingdom in the West *(see pp52–3)*. Either way, after the death of Yacoub el-Mansour in 1199, the unfinished mosque fell into disrepair. All but the mosque's minaret was destroyed by an earthquake in 1755.

The Hassan Mosque was built to a huge rectangular plan 183 m (600 ft) by 139 m (456 ft); the Great Mosque of Córdoba was just 175 m (574 ft) by 128 m (420 ft). It was the largest religious building in the Muslim West, in size inferior only to the mosque of Samarra in Iraq. A great courtyard lay at the foot of the tower, while the huge columned prayer hall was divided into 21 avenues separated by lines of gigantic columns crowned with capitals. Remains of these imposing stone columns survive and still convey an impression of infinite grandeur.

The minaret, a square-sided tower about 16 m (52 ft) wide and 44 m (144 ft) high, was to have surpassed the height of the Koutoubia Mosque *(see pp240–41)* and the Giralda in Seville *(see pp52–3)*, but it was never completed. According to Almohad custom, it would have reached 80 m (262 ft), including the lantern. Even unfinished it seems huge. Each of its four sides is decorated with blind lobed arches. On

the topmost level of the minaret extended interlacing arches form a *sebkha* motif (lozenge-shaped blind fretwork) as on the Giralda of Seville. The interior is divided into six levels, each of which consists of a domed room. The levels are linked and accessed by a continuous ramp.

It was from the Hassan Tower that Mohammed V conducted the first Friday prayers after independence was declared.

⑩ Mausoleum of Mohammed V

See pp80–81.

⑪ Ville Nouvelle

During the 44 years of the Protectorate, Marshal Lyautey and the architects Prost and Ecochard built a new town in the empty part of the extensive area enclosed by the Almohad walls.

Laying out wide boulevards and green spaces, they created a relatively pleasant town. Avenue Mohammed V, the main avenue, runs from the medina to the El-Souna Mosque, or Great Mosque, which was built by Sidi Mohammed in the 18th century. The avenue is lined with residential blocks in the Hispano-Maghrebi style. They were built by the administration of the Protectorate, as were the Bank of Morocco, the post office, the parliament building and the railway station. The Bank of Morocco also houses the **Musée de la Monnaie** (Coin Museum).

Rue Abou Inan leads to the **Cathédrale Saint-Pierre**, a pure white building dating from the 1930s.

Musée de la Monnaie
Bank of Morocco, Rue du Caire. **Tel** (0537) 26 90 96. **Open** 9am–5:30pm Tue–Fri, 9am–noon & 3–6pm Sat, 9am–1pm Sun. **Closed** Mon.

Cathédrale Saint-Pierre
Place du Golan. **Tel** (0537) 72 23 01. **Open** 3–6pm Sat, 9am–1pm Sun.

The dazzling white Cathédrale Saint-Pierre, built in the 1930s

⑩ Mausoleum of Mohammed V

Raised in memory of Mohammed V, the father of Moroccan independence, this majestic building was commissioned by his son, Hassan II. It was designed by the Vietnamese architect Vo Toan and built with the help of 400 Moroccan craftsmen. The group of buildings that make up the mausoleum of Mohammed V include a mosque and a museum devoted to the history of the Alaouite dynasty. The mausoleum itself, in white Italian marble, stands on a platform 3.5 m (11.5 ft) high. Entry is through a wrought-iron door that opens onto a stairway leading to the dome, beneath which lies the sarcophagus of Mohammed V.

★ **Dome with Muqarnas**
This twelve-sided dome, with painted mahogany *muqarnas* (stalactites), crowns the burial chamber.

★ **Sarcophagus**
Carved from a single block of marble, the sarcophagus rests on a slab of granite, facing a *qibla* (symbolizing Mecca).

Guard
The traditional attire of the royal guard is white in summer and red in winter.

Fountain
Embellished with polychrome *zellij* tilework and framed by a horseshoe arch of Salé sandstone, this fountain is in the Moorish style.

Stained-Glass Windows
The stained-glass windows in the dome were made in France, in the workshops of the factory at St-Gobain.

Calligraphy
This marble frieze features a song of holy praise carved in Maghrebi script.

Doorways
The doorways on the four sides of the mausoleum are fronted by slender columns of Carrara marble.

Candelabra
These large candelabra, with slender vertical shafts, are made of pierced and engraved copper.

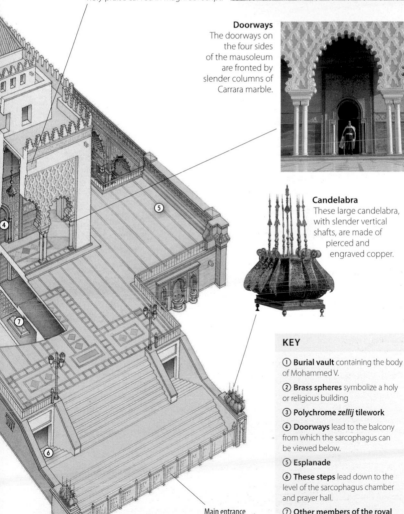

KEY

① **Burial vault** containing the body of Mohammed V.

② **Brass spheres** symbolize a holy or religious building

③ **Polychrome *zellij* tilework**

④ **Doorways** lead to the balcony from which the sarcophagus can be viewed below.

⑤ **Esplanade**

⑥ **These steps** lead down to the level of the sarcophagus chamber and prayer hall.

⑦ **Other members of the royal family**, lie in the mausoleum.

Main entrance

⑫ Musée Archéologique

The most extensive collection of archaeological artifacts in the country is housed in the Musée Archéologique. The museum building was constructed in the 1930s, to house the Antiquities Services. The initial prehistoric and pre-Islamic collections, consisting of objects discovered by archaeologists working in Volubilis, Banasa and Thamusida, were put on public display for the first time in 1930–32. The addition of further material from Volubilis in 1957 considerably enlarged the museum's collections, raising it to the status of a national museum. The displays present the collections according to historical period. These range from the prehistoric period up to the findings of recent archaeological excavations.

Roman pitcher of the 1st to 2nd centuries, with strainer and spout

Abderrahmane and Daya el-Hamra; the Mousterian culture; and, finally, the Aterian culture of around 40,000–20,000 BC. The latter, specific to North Africa, is illustrated by the only human remains to have been discovered at Dar al-Soltane and el-Harhoura.

The House of the Ephebe, Volubilis *(see pp208–209)*

Temporary Exhibitions

The space on the ground floor reserved for temporary exhibitions illustrates the results of archaeological investigations in Morocco, using photographs, graphics, models, sculpture and various other objects.

A map of Morocco in the lobby shows the various archaeological sites that have been discovered to date, and the methods used to excavate them are explained. The reconstruction of a mosaic from Volubilis is laid out on the floor of the room opposite. The marble statue in the centre of the room, dating from AD 25–40, is that of **Ptolemy**, king of Mauretania Tingitana and the son and successor of Juba II

and Cleopatra Selene, who was assassinated by the Roman emperor Caligula.

Prehistoric Cultures

Also on the ground floor is a collection of stone artifacts relating to the earliest cultures and civilizations. Exhibits include altars and stelae carved with inscriptions, sarcophagi, stone arrowheads, pebble tools, pottery, polished stones, axes and swords, fragments of tombs and mouldings, as well as rock carvings. Among the cultures highlighted here are the Pebble Culture, known from sites at Arbaoua, Douar Doum and Casablanca; the Acheulian culture, known at sites in Sidi

Roman bone and ivory carving

Sala-Chellah and Islamic Archaeology

The site of **Sala-Chellah** *(see pp84–5)* is that of a Mauretanian and Roman town which flourished up to the 4th century AD and which in the 13th century became a royal necropolis under the Merinids.

The collection of implements and other objects (including pottery and oil lamps)

Head of a Berber youth

displayed on the upper floor of the museum traces the history of the site. Particularly striking exhibits include the bronze bust of Juba II (52 BC–AD 23) which was discovered in Volubilis and probably came from Egypt. An Early Christian altar, a Byzantine censer and an ivory figure of the Good Shepherd show the presence of Christianity in Morocco from the 3rd to the 8th centuries.

The section on Islamic archaeology highlights the principal sites that have been excavated. The displays of objects that have been unearthed include coins, pottery made in Sijilmassa and other ceramics, notably a 14th-century dish from Belyounech, as well as fragments of carved plaster and sugar-loaf moulds from Chichaoua.

Pre-Islamic Civilizations

Artifacts uncovered during excavations at Volubilis, Banasa, Thamusida, Sala and Mogador are arranged by theme, illustrating in an informative fashion the most salient aspects of both pre-Roman Morocco (Mauretanian civilization) and Roman Morocco (Mauretania Tingitana). A range of objects show the extent of trade relations between Morocco and the Mediterranean world, particularly Carthage; and public and private life is illustrated through everyday objects, including the taps that were used in public baths, fragments of terracotta piping, and cooking utensils such as plates, dishes, glasses and knives. A section on the Roman army includes a military diploma from Banasa, certificates of good conduct engraved on bronze plaques and military decorations.

The collection of white marble sculpture includes the

Head of Oceanus (1st century BC)

Head of a Berber Youth from Volubilis carved during the reign of Augustus, a *Sphinx* from a votive throne, and a *Sleeping Silenus* from Volubilis. There are also figures of Roman gods such as Venus, Bacchus and Mars, and of Egyptian deities such as Isis and Anubis.

A particularly impressive part of the museum's displays is the collection of antique bronzes which come mainly from Volubilis and which demonstrate the wealth enjoyed by Morocco's Roman towns. A well-preserved bust of *Cato the Younger*; this 1st-century sculpture discovered in the House of Venus was imported into Morocco. *Ephebe Crowned with Ivy* is, without a doubt, the star piece in the collection. The naked *ephebe* (young soldier in training) wears a crown of delicate ivy and is depicted in a standing position. The stance suggests that in his left hand he held a torch; this type of representation, known as a "lampadophore", together with the classicism of the statue, are typical of sculpture of the 1st century. The *Dog of Volubilis*, found on the site in 1916 in the vicinity of the triumphal arch, dates from the reign of Hadrian (early 2nd century) and was also made outside Morocco. The position

of the dog, which is clearly designed to be accompanied by a human figure (undoubtedly Diana), suggests that it was made to decorate a fountain in public baths. The *Lustral Ephebe*, also discovered in Volubilis in 1929, brings to mind the *Lustral Dionysus* of Praxiteles, preserved in a museum in Dresden, in Germany, and known through numerous copies. Finally, the bust of Juba II which dates from 25 BC was probably imported from Egypt.

Roman votive stele from Volubilis, 1st–2nd century AD

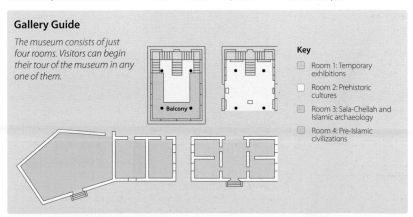

Gallery Guide

The museum consists of just four rooms. Visitors can begin their tour of the museum in any one of them.

Balcony

Key

- ☐ Room 1: Temporary exhibitions
- ☐ Room 2: Prehistoric cultures
- ☐ Room 3: Sala-Chellah and Islamic archaeology
- ☐ Room 4: Pre-Islamic civilizations

⓭ Bab el-Rouah

Place an-Nasr. Gallery: **Open** daily during exhibitions.

A sturdy and imposing Almohad gateway, Bab el-Rouah, the Gate of the Winds, dates from the same period as Bab Oudaïa *(see p72)*.

The entrance is decorated with the outline of two horseshoe arches carved into the stone and surrounded by a band of Kufic calligraphy.

The interior of the gate contains four rooms with elegant domes. These rooms are now used for exhibitions.

Rabat's Dar el-Makhzen (royal palace), where 2,000 people live and work

Bab el-Rouah, a fine Almohad gate with arches set into the stonework

⓮ Dar el-Makhzen

In the northwest of the city. **Closed** to the public. The exterior of the palace complex is of interest in its own right. The méchouar (assembly place) and the gardens are open to the public.

An extensive complex enclosed within its own walls, the Dar el-Makhzen (royal palace) is inhabited by about 2,000 people. Built on the site of an 18th-century royal residence, the current palace was completed in 1864, but was constantly enlarged thereafter; today, it even includes a racecourse.

The palace now houses the offices of the Moroccan government, the Supreme Court, the prime minister's offices, the ministry of the Habous (responsible for religious organizations), and the El-Fas Mosque. The *méchouar*, a place of public assembly, is the venue for major and important gatherings, including the *bayaa*, a ceremony at which senior

government ministers swear their allegiance to the king. Traditionally, the king would reside in the former harem though Mohammed VI stays in his own private residence.

Besides private buildings, the palace also includes an extensive garden, immaculately kept and planted with various species of trees and with flowers in formal beds.

⓯ Chellah Necropolis

In the southeast of the city.
Open 9am–6pm daily. Access via Bab Zaer but best reached by taxi.

Access to the Chellah Necropolis is via Bab Zaer. This gate, named after a local tribe, was the only one on the southern side of the ramparts built by Yacoub el-Mansour. The necropolis is nearby.

Detail of the Gate of Ambassadors at the Royal Palace

The entrance to the necropolis itself is marked by an imposing Almohad gate with a horseshoe arch flanked by two towers. Above the arch is a band of Kufic calligraphy with the name of its builder, Abou el-Hassan, and the date 1339. On the left, inside a former guardhouse, there is a café. Through the gate, a stepped walkway leads to a terrace offering spectacular views of the Bou Regreg valley, the Merinid necropolis and the remains of the Roman town of Sala Colonia, which are surrounded by lush vegetation.

It was Abou Yacoub Youssef, the first Merinid caliph, who chose this as the site of a mosque and the burial place of his wife, Oum el-Izz, in 1284. Abou Yacoub Youssef died in Algeciras in 1286, and his body was brought back to the necropolis. His two successors, Abou Yacoub, who died in 1307, and Abou Thabit, who died in 1308, were also laid to rest here. The burial complex was completed by the sultan Abou Saïd (1310–31) and his son Abou el-Hassan (1331–51), and was later embellished by Abou Inan. The walls around the necropolis, which have the ochre tones typical of the earth stone of Rabat, were built by Abou el-Hassan, who probably recon-structed the existing Roman walls. In 1500, Leo Africanus recorded the existence of 30 Merinid tombs.

Situated within the walls of the necropolis are the ruins of the mosque built by Abou Youssef and of the buildings that surrounded it. To the right

Storks nesting on the minaret of the former *zaouia* at Chellah

behind the mihrab is the *koubba* (shrine) of Abou Yacoub Youssef.

Opposite the *koubba*, the Mausoleum of Abou el-Hassan, the Black Sultan and the last Merinid ruler to be buried here, in 1351, lies alongside the walls. His funerary stele is still in place. Also to be seen here is the *koubba* of his wife, who died in 1349. Named Chams el-Doha (which can be translated as "light of the dawn"), she was a Christian who converted to Islam. She was the mother of Abou Inan *(see p55)*, one of the most illustrious Merinid rulers. Her accomplishments include the building of the Bou Inania

Medersa in Fès *(see pp176–7)*.

Also within the walls of the necropolis was a *zaouia*, a religious institution that functioned simultaneously as a mosque, a centre of learning and a hostel for pilgrims and students (some of the cells can still be made out). Built by Abou el-Hassan, the *zaouia* is designed and decorated like the medersas in Fès, and it is thought that it may have been even more luxuriously appointed. Abou el-Hassan covered the upper part of the minaret with a decorative design of white, black, green and blue *zellij* tilework, which is still visible today.

The necropolis at Chellah was abandoned at the end of the Merinid dynasty, and in the course of the following centuries was ransacked several times. It was largely destroyed by the earthquake of 1755. Vegetation invaded the stonework and colonies of storks built their nests in the trees and on the minarets, giving the place a supernatural atmosphere, particularly at sunset.

The necropolis has become the subject of much folklore and many legends, as can be seen from the large number of *marabouts* (shrines) of holy

men that are scattered about the garden. The sacred eels in the fountain (once the ablutions fountain for the mosque) are also believed to bring good fortune to barren women. These supplicants feed them eggs, symbols of fertility, which are offered for sale by young boys in the square.

The interior of the mosque built by Abou Youssef

Environs

Archaeological excavations at Chellah have uncovered the remains of the major buildings of **Sala Colonia**. Once a prosperous Roman city, Sala Colonia later declined and by the 10th century had fallen into ruin. Still visible today is the *decumanus maximus*, the main thoroughfare that crossed all Roman cities from east to west. It led out from Sala Colonia to the port, built in the 1st century BC and now buried in sand.

From the forum, a road to the right leads towards the Merinid necropolis.

The walls around the Chellah Necropolis, raised by Abou el-Hassan in the 14th century

NORTHERN ATLANTIC COAST

Morocco's Northern Atlantic coast offers extensive beaches of soft fine sand, lagoons, winter havens for migratory birds, and forests that are highly prized by hunters. But to explore it is also to travel back in time, since the heritage of the Phoenicians and the Romans, the corsairs, the Portuguese and the Spanish, as well as of the colonial period is present alongside the modern prosperity brought by agriculture, port activity, trade and tourism.

Although it attracts far fewer tourists than the interior or the imperial cities, the Moroccan coastline from Rabat to Tangier has much to offer visitors. It has not undergone the high level of development that has transformed the coastal area from Rabat to Casablanca and the south. Nevertheless, this region is no less characteristic of the modern, vibrant and outward-looking country that Morocco has become. For 250 km (155 miles), the ocean seems omnipresent, as roads and motorways often skirt the coastline and the beaches. For motorists following the coastal roads, the ocean may suddenly come into sight at an estuary or over a dune. The road follows roughly the course of a Roman road linking Sala Colonia (known today as Chellah, *see pp84–5)* and Banasa, Lixus and Tangier. This is the heart of one of earliest regions of Morocco in which towns and cities were established.

The ocean has shaped the history of the coastal towns: occupied from Phoenician times and into the Roman period, they have attracted pirates, invaders and Andalusian, Spanish and French occupiers, each of whom left their mark. It is also the ocean that gives the region its gentle, moist climate (strawberries, bananas and tomatoes are grown in greenhouses) and that drives industry and port activity from Kenitra to Tangier, where a port has been built to handle cargo bound for Europe.

Roman temple ruins at the ancient site of Lixus

◀ Asilah, a small Andalusian-style town, facing the Atlantic

Exploring the Northern Atlantic Coast

Travelling along Morocco's Atlantic coast between Salé and Tangier reveals a natural paradise of sea, forests, lagoons, hunting and fishing within sight of beaches that appear to stretch to infinity. The coast is punctuated by ancient sites: Thamusida, nestling in a bend of Wadi Sebou; Banasa, set a little way back from the sea, in the fertile plain of the Rharb; and Lixus, standing on a promontory opposite Larache, on the estuary of the Loukkos. From Salé to Tangier, a succession of small walled towns with interesting monuments bears witness to a rich history: Mehdya, whose kasbah dominates the final meanders of Wadi Sebou; Moulay Bousselham, with its attractive lagoon and beach protected by the tomb of the eponymous saint, which draws numerous pilgrims; Asilah, where walls pierced by mysteriously screened windows enclose narrow, secretive streets; Larache, a charmingly Andalusian town; and Tangier, which looks over the Straits of Gibraltar towards Spain and Europe.

Agriculture in the region of Kenitra

0 kilometres 20

0 miles 20

Sights at a Glance

1. Salé
2. Sidi Bouknadel
3. Mehdya
4. Forest of Mamora
5. Kenitra
6. Thamusida
7. Moulay Bousselham
8. Larache
9. Lixus
10. Asilah
11. M'Soura Stone Circle
12. Ksar el-Kebir
13. Souk el-Arba du Rharb
14. Banasa

For hotels and restaurants see pp306–313 and pp320–31

Migratory birds in the lagoon at Moulay Bousselham

Getting Around

A motorway (with toll) provides a direct
link between Rabat and Tangier. Even
when driving on a motorway, care
should be taken: animals or people may
try to cross unexpectedly. The N1 goes
further inland, reaching the coast at
Asilah. A bus service running from Rabat
and Tangier provides transport to and
from most places.

Key

- Motorway
- Major road
- Minor road
- --- Track
- Railway

Colourfully painted doors in the medina at Asilah

For keys to symbols *see back flap*

The tropical gardens in Sidi Bouknadel

❶ Salé

Road Map C2. West of Rabat, on the right bank of Wadi Bou Regreg. 710,000. Rabat-Salé,10 km (6 miles) on the Meknès road. Route de Casablanca. Rabat; (0537) 66 06 63. Festival and night-time Candle Procession (on the eve of Mouloud). Thu.

Founded in about the 11th century, Salé was fortified and embellished at the end of the 13th century by the Merinids. They built a medersa, a mosque, a medical school and a magnificent aqueduct, which can still be seen from the road to Kenitra. During the Middle Ages, Salé was a busy port, used by traders from the northern Mediterranean, and in 1609 it provided sanctuary for refugees from Andalusia. Salé shared the lucrative business of privateering with its neighbour and rival Rabat *(see pp68–85)*, with which it came into conflict. When piracy was brought to an end in the 18th century, the town went into decline.

In the 20th century, however, Salé found prosperity once more, as a major centre of the crafts industry.

At the entrance to the town (from the direction of Rabat) stands the 13th-century **Bab el-Mrisa** (Gate of the Sea). This was the entrance to the maritime arsenal built by Yacoub el-Mansour, and a canal linking Wadi Bou Regreg to the harbour passed through it.

Within the town, near Rue Bab el-Khebbaz, the main street through the medina, are the Kissaria and souks, both filled with artisans and traders.

Chest, Musée Dar Belghazi

Nearby are the **Grand Mosque** and the medersa. A doorway framed by a horseshoe arch and covered with a carved wooden porch leads into the medersa. Built during the reign of the Merinid ruler Abou el-Hassan, it is notable for its central tower surrounded by a colonnaded gallery covered in *zellij* tilework and carved plaster and wood. The mihrab has a decorated wooden ceiling.

The **Seamen's Cemetery**, in the northeast of the town, is dotted with the *marabouts* (shrines) of such holy men as Sidi ben Achir. In the 16th century, he was credited with the power to calm the waves so as to allow vessels to enter the harbour safely. The *marabout*

The walls of Salé, near Bab el-Mrisa

of Sidi Abdallah ben Hassoun (patron of Salé, of boatmen and of travellers) has an unusual dome that abuts the Grand Mosque. Further north along the coast the *marabout* of Sidi Moussa overlooks the sea.

❷ Sidi Bouknadel

Road Map C2. 10 km (6 miles) north of Salé on the N1 to Kenitra. 6,900. Rabat. Sun.

The tropical gardens (**Jardins Exotiques**) just outside Sidi Bouknadel were laid out in 1951 by the horticulturist Marcel François and are today owned by the State. Some 1,500 species native to the Antilles, South America and Asia grow in the garden.

Jardins Exotiques
Open 9am–6:30pm daily.

Environs
Two kilometres (1.25 miles) to the north is the **Musée Dar Belghazi**, with its collection of fine objects, including jewellery, kaftans, marriage belts, carved wooden doors, minbars, pottery and musical instruments. This privately run museum was established by a master woodcarver, with bequests from artists and collectors.

Musée Dar Belghazi
Km 47, Route de Kenitra. **Tel** (0537) 82 21 78. **Open** 10am–6pm daily.

❸ Mehdya

Road Map C2. 39 km (24 miles) from Salé on the N1 to Kenitra, at km 29 turning onto the Mehdya-Plage road. 5,800. Kenitra, then by taxi.

This small coastal resort is much frequented by the inhabitants of Rabat and Kenitra. On the estuary of Wadi Sebou, it stands on the site of what may have been a Carthagenian trading post in the 5th century BC, and then an Almohad naval base, which was known at the time as El Mamora ("the populous one"). Later, the town was occupied by the Portuguese, the Spanish and the Dutch, and was finally captured by Moulay Ismaïl *(see p57)* at the end of the 17th century.

The kasbah which stands on the plateau, dominating the estuary, still has its original walls, which were built by the Spanish, and its moated bastions. The monumental gate, built by Moulay Ismaïl, leads to the governor's palace, which has a central courtyard, rooms, outbuildings, hammam and mosque.

Environs
The **Sidi Bourhaba Lake**, 27 km (17 miles) along the Mehdya-Plage road, is a large bird sanctuary: thousands of birds, such as teal and coot, rest here during their migration between Europe and sub-Saharan Africa.

⊠ Sidi Bourhaba Lake
Tel (0537) 74 72 09. Exhibition centre and marked walks: **Open** noon–4pm Sat, Sun and public holidays.

❹ Forest of Mamora

Road Map C2. East of Rabat on the N1 to Kenitra or the N6 to Meknès.

The Forest of Mamora, between Wadi Sebou and Wadi Bou Regreg, covers an area 60 km (37 miles) long and 30 km (19 miles) wide. Although the forest is now planted mostly with eucalyptus, which grows much faster than other species, large tracts of it are still covered with cork-oak, which is grown for its bark. At a factory in Sidi Yahia

Pieces of bark stripped from the cork-oak

eucalyptus wood is turned into a pulp that is used in paper-making and the manufacture of artificial silk.

Being intensively exploited and degraded by the grazing of cattle, sheep and goats, the forest is becoming increasingly bare. However, enough cover remains to allow a refreshingly cool walk in summer, when wood pigeons, kites, rollers and spotted flycatchers can be seen.

❺ Kenitra

Road Map C2. ⚑ 300,000. ⊟ ⊞ Rabat. ⊟ Mon & Sat.

Established in 1913 in the early days of the French Protectorate, from 1933 to 1955 this town was known as Port-Lyautey. Nowadays, Kenitra consists of distinct districts: residential areas with villas, a European-style town centre and poorer suburbs.

In the harbour, on the right bank of Wadi Sebou, regional produce from the Rharb (such as citrus fruit, cork, cotton, cereals and pulp for papermaking) are unloaded for use in local industries. Once a marshy area where malaria was rife (but still used for extensive stock-farming), the alluvial plain of the Rharb has been transformed by

irrigation. It is now one of Morocco's major agricultural areas, specializing in rice, sugar beet, cotton and citrus fruits.

The Roman baths at Thamusida, on the banks of Wadi Sebou

❻ Thamusida

Road Map D2. 55 km (34 miles) northeast of Rabat, 17 km (10.5 miles) northeast of Kenitra. Motorway exit: Kenitra N.

On the N1, at the milestone reading "Kenitra 14 km, Sidi Allal Tazi 28 km", a track heading westwards leads to this ancient site on Wadi Sebou. It was inhabited by the Romans from the 2nd century BC to the 3rd century AD.

Part of the walls can still be seen, along with the outline of the Roman army camp (with streets intersecting at right angles) and the site's major feature, the *praetorium* (headquarters), with columns and pilasters. To the northeast the remains of baths and a temple with three chambers, or *cellae*, can be made out. North of Wadi Sebou are vestiges of the harbour docks.

Fishing harbour at Mehdya, on Wadi Sebou

A horse-drawn carriage in Plaza Zelaka, Asilah ▶

❼ Moulay Bousselham

Road Map D2. 48 km (30 miles) south of Larache. 🏛 900. 🚌 Boat trips: available from Café Milano. 🎭 Moussem (early summer).

The small town of Moulay Bousselham is a coastal resort that is very popular with Moroccans. The mosque and the tomb of Moulay Bousselham tower above the ocean and the Merja Zerga lagoon. As the burial place of Moulay Bousselham, the 10th-century holy man, it is also a major place of pilgrimage, attracting many followers in late June and early July.

The life of the holy man is wreathed in legends associated with the ocean and its perils. The Moulay Bousselham sandbar is, indeed, highly dangerous: the waves come crashing in over the reefs and onto the beach. The waters of the lagoon are calmer; boat trips are organized to see the thousands of birds – herons, pink flamingoes, gannets and sheldrake – that come to the lagoon on their migrations in December and January. Boat trips around the lagoon depart from the small fishing harbour.

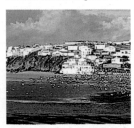
The town of Moulay Bousselham and the Merja Zerga lagoon

❽ Larache

Road Map D1. 🏛 95,000. 🚌 from Tangier, Rabat. 🛒 Sun.

Set a little way back from major roads, Larache is both an Andalusian and an Arab town. The modern part bears obvious signs of the Spanish Protectorate.

Established in the 7th century by Arab conquerors, by the 11th century Larache was

Andalusian-style fountain on Place de la Libération, Larache

an important centre of trade on the left bank of Wadi Loukkos. In the 16th century it was used as a base by corsairs from Algiers and Turkey, and was subject to reprisals by Portuguese forces from Asilah. The town passed to Spain in 1610, and was then taken by Moulay Ismaïl at the end of the 17th century. During the Spanish Protectorate (1911–56) Larache was held by Spain.

The medina is reached from Place de la Libération, a very Spanish plaza, and through Bab el-Khemis, a brick-built gate roofed with glazed tiles. In the fabrics souk – the *kissaria (socco de la alcaicería)* – a market, offers a wide range of goods. Narrow streets lined with houses with floral decoration lead down towards the harbour. Bab el-Kasba separates the southern edge of the fabrics souk from Rue Moulay el-Mehdi, a street covered with overhead arches that leads to an octagonal minaret and a terrace overlooking the meandering Wadi Loukkos, salt-marshes and the Lixus promontory.

Not far from Lixus is the Château de la Cigogne (Stork's Castle), a fortress that was built in 1578 by the Saadian rulers and then remodelled by the Spanish in the 17th century. It is closed to the public.

It is pleasant to stroll along the seafront – the "balcony of the Atlantic". Nearby is the Moorish market. Finally, in the **Catholic Cemetery**, the tomb of the French writer Jean Genet (1910–86) can be found, lying facing the ocean.

❾ Lixus

Road Map D1. 5 km (3 miles) northeast of Larache on the N1. 🚌 from Larache.

This ancient site, which commands a view of the ocean, of Wadi Loukkos and of Larache, is a UNESCO's World Heritage Site. According to legend, this is where one of the Labours of Hercules – picking the golden apples in the Garden of the Hesperides – took place. The ancient Roman writer Plinius, writing in the 7th century BC, described Lixus as the most ancient Phoenician colony in the western Mediterranean.

In the 7th century BC the Phoenicians established a trading post here, serving as a stage on the Gold Route. After it had been taken by the Romans between 40 and 45 AD, Lixus became a colony and a centre of the manufacture of *garum*, sauce made with scraps of fish marinaded in brine from salting vats. The Romans abandoned Lixus at the end of the 3rd century AD. The wall built around

The Roman ruins of Lixus, set on a magnificent promontory

the city at that time reduced its inhabited area by half.

The vats in which meat and fish were salted and *garum* was made – Morocco's major industry in Roman times – can be seen around the edges of the site. In the amphitheatre, with its circular arena, public games took place.

The **Acropolis** above the town has its own walls; only on the western side, where there is a sheer drop, do they coincide with the town walls. An apsidal building, preceded by an atrium with a cistern, has been excavated. The Great Temple (1st century BC– 1st century AD), to the south, features an arcaded *area* (courtyard). The *cella*, where the god dwelt, on the axis of the peristyle, backs onto an apsidal wall; opposite is a large semicircular apse with a mosaic floor.

Colourful display of fruit on a stall in the market at Asilah

❿ Asilah

Road Map D1. 🚹 25,000. 🚉 2 km (1.5 miles) north of town. 🚌 from Tangier or Rabat. 🎭 Cultural Festival (Aug). 🛍 Thu.

Established by the Phoenicians, Asilah was an important town in Mauretania's pre-Roman period (when coins were minted here), and also under the Romans. It was captured by the Portuguese in 1471 and became a centre of trade with connections to the Mediterranean countries. The town came under Moroccan control in 1691, during the reign of Moulay Ismaïl.

At the end of the 19th century, Raissouli, a pretender to power and a brigand, extortioner and kidnapper, made Asilah his base. In 1906, taking advantage of the intrigues that surrounded the sovereign, Abdul Aziz, he assumed the mantle of pasha then that of governor of the Jebala. He built himself a palace facing the sea, from which he was expelled by the Spanish in 1924.

This small Andalusian-style town is enclosed within ramparts. The narrow streets are paved or limed, and lined with houses fronted by balconies with restrained *mashrabiyya* (wooden latticework panel used as a screen), and with blue-or green-painted woodwork.

The Criquia jetty, northwest of the town, overlooks a tiny cemetery with tombstones covered in glazed tiles. At the foot of the square tower on Place Ibn Khaldoun stands Bab el- Bahr (Gate of the Sea). On the opposite side of the square, Bab Homar (Gate of the Land), with the Portuguese royal coat of arms, leads out from the ramparts and into the new town.

In summer, the **Centre Hassan II des Rencontres Internationales**, in Rue de la Kasbah, within the walls, hosts cultural events and exhibitions. Asilah is also frequented by painters, who are fond of marking the walls with signs of their passing.

⓫ M'Soura Stone Circle

Road Map D1. El-Utad to Chouahed. 27 km (17 miles) southeast of Asilah on the N1, then R417 towards Tetouan.

This Neolithic site is reached via a 7-km (4-mile) track running from Sidi el-Yamani towards Souk et-Tnine. Perhaps the burial place of an important local ruler, it consists of 200 monolithic standing stones ranging in height from 50 cm (20 inches) to 5 m (16 ft) and surrounding a burial area about 55 m (180 ft) in circumference. Unique in the Maghreb and the Sahara, by its sheer size, this monument is reminiscent of those seen in Spain. The type of pottery decorated with impressions of *cardium* shells and bronze weapons, which excavations have brought to light, are also identical to Spanish examples.

One of the 200 standing stones at the M'Soura Neolithic stone circle

Sugarcane plantation in the fertile region around Ksar el-Kebir

⑫ Ksar el-Kebir

Road Map D1. 🏘 107,000. 🚉 Moulay el-Mehdi (approx. 3 km/ 2 miles). 🚌 from Tangier. 🛍 Sun.

The town takes its name from a great fortress which, during the Almoravid and Almohad periods, controlled the road leading to the ports along the Straits of Gibraltar.

It was at Wadi el-Makhazin nearby that the Battle of the Three Kings took place in 1578. The conflict has been described as the "last crusade undertaken by the Christians of the Mediterranean". It was instigated by the Saadian sultan El-Mutawakkil, who, having been driven from Morocco, was zealous for a crusade. In alliance with Sebastião I, king of Portugal, he made a bid to win back his kingdom. Sebastião, El-Mutawakkil and their opponent, the Saadian sultan Abd el-Malik (who was victorious over the invaders), all died in the battle. Moulay Ahmed, brother of Abd el-Malik, succeeded him, becoming known not only as Ahmed el-Mansour ("the Victorious") but also as Ahmed el-Dhebi ("the Golden"), because of the ransom that he exacted.

Ksar el-Kebir is, today, a sizeable country town. A particularly large souk is held here on Sundays: goods on offer include the produce of local market gardens, as well as that of the area's olive plantations and citrus groves.

⑬ Souk el-Arba du Rharb

Road Map D2. 🏘 38,000. 🚉 🚌 Rabat, Tangier. 🛍 Wed.

A major agricultural centre on the northwest border of the Rharb, Souk el-Arba du Rharb is especially busy on Wednesdays, when the souk is held. The town's position on the intersection of roads leading to Tangier, Rabat, Meknès and the coastal town of Moulay Bousselham has made it a key staging post.

⑭ Banasa

Road Map D2. 103 km (64 miles) northeast of Rabat on the N1 or Rabat-Tangier freeway (Kenitra North exit).

This ancient town, an inland port on Wadi Sebou and the most developed in Mauretania Tingitana, was a centre of ceramic production from the 3rd century and during the 1st century BC. A Roman colony from 33 to 25 BC, Banasa was a prosperous and bustling commercial town until the end of the 3rd century AD.

The entrance to the town, through a vaulted gateway, leads to the basilica and the paved and arcaded forum. South of the forum rises the capitol, where several altars stand before the temple's five *cellae* (chambers). In the public baths to the west, the various rooms for the Roman ritual of bathing – robing rooms, a *caldarium* and *tepidarium* (hot and warm rooms) with underfloor heating, and *frigidarium* (cold room) can be distinguished. Wall paintings and a brick floor paved in a herringbone pattern can be made out in another bathhouse at a lower level.

A famous document engraved on bronze was discovered at Banasa. Known as the *Banasa Table*, it was an edict by which Caracalla granted the province relief from taxes in return for lions, elephants and other animals that the emperor desired for public spectacles in Rome.

From the N1 or freeway, Banasa is reached by taking the R413, then, 3 km (2 miles) before Souk Tleta du Rharb, by turning off onto the P4234. As it approaches the site, the road is reduced to a track.

Stele with an inscription in Latin, standing in the ruins of Banasa

Roman Towns in Morocco

Towns were established in Morocco during the reigns of Juba II and Ptolemy, kings of Mauretania who ruled under the aegis of Rome. Under Roman control, they developed either into *coloniae* (colonies such as Lixus and Banasa) or *municipiae* (free towns such as Sala and Volubilis). The inhabitants, who grew prosperous through the cultivation of the land, endowed their towns with such civic features as forums, basilicas, capitols and triumphal arches. Adapting to the Roman way of life, they built houses with columned courtyards and mosaic floors in the Roman style, and imported bronze sculptures from Egypt and Italy and pottery from Etruria. Public and private baths fulfilled the desire for personal cleanliness and also acted as places in which to socialize. The arcades along the *decumanus maximus* (main thoroughfares) were filled with shops, while cottage industries were established around the edges of the towns.

Juba II (52 BC–AD 23), who married the daughter of Cleopatra and Mark Antony, turned Mauretania into a highly prosperous country.

Ptolemy, who succeeded Juba II, was murdered in Rome in AD 40. Under him, Mauretania became completely romanized.

Roman Rule

Juba II was made king of Mauretania by Augustus. After Ptolemy's death, the province was administered by Rome under Claudius. Triumphal arches were built during the reigns of Commodius and Caracalla. In the late 3rd century, under Diocletian, the country was administered with the province of Spain.

Mauretania's cities were centres of trade and administration, as well as garrison towns. As in Rome, the focal point was the forum (a market place and public area) and the basilica, simultaneously a monetary exchange, law court and meeting place. The capitol was the city's religious centre.

The basilica and the columns of the capitol at Volubilis

Art

As Rome imposed political unity, so Roman artistic influence spread throughout the Maghreb.

Roman funerary art can be seen in Morocco. Many stelae (free-standing stone columns) take the shape of a pointed rectangle carved with a figure dressed in a full-length tunic.

Head of the young Bacchus, with soft, rounded features and an effeminate appearance, in the artistic style that prevailed at the time in Rome.

Mosaic depicting Aeolus, Roman god of wind, whose breath restores nature to life. It comes from the floor of the house in Volubilis.

CASABLANCA

Straddling east and west, Casablanca, the commercial and financial capital of Morocco, is a baffling metropolis where tradition and modernity co-exist. A city where skyscrapers stand in stark contrast to the small shops of the medina, with its narrow, winding streets, this is where the prosperous rub shoulders with paupers.

In the 7th century, Casablanca was no more than a small Berber settlement clinging to the slopes of the Anfa hills. However, for strategic and commercial reasons, it was already attracting the attention of foreign powers. In 1468, the town was sacked by the Portuguese, who wrought wholesale destruction on the city's privateer ships. Then, in the 18th century, with the sultanate of Sidi Mohammed ben Abdallah, Dar el-Beïda (meaning "White House" – "Casa Blanca" in Spanish) acquired a new significance. This was thanks to its harbour, which played a pivotal role in the sugar, tea, wool and corn markets of the Western world. But it was in the 20th century, under the French Protectorate (see pp60–61), that Casablanca underwent the most profound change. Against expert advice, Marshal Lyautey, the first resident-governor, proceeded with plans to make Casablanca the country's economic hub. To realize this vision, he hired the services of town planners and modernized the port. For almost 40 years, the most innovative architects worked on this huge building project. Casablanca continued to expand even after independence. Futuristic high-rise buildings and a colossal mosque sending its laser beams towards Mecca once again expressed the city's forward-looking spirit. With about 4 million inhabitants, and a further 5 million in the perfecture, Casablanca is, today, one of the four largest metropolises on the African continent, and its port is the busiest in Morocco.

Moroccans relaxing on the terrace of a café in the Parc de la Ligue Arabe

◀ Interior of Hassan II Mosque, the second-largest religious structure in the world

Exploring Casablanca

The centre of the new town (Ville Nouvelle) revolves around two focal points: the Place des Nations Unies and the Place Mohammed V, squares that are lined with fine 1930s buildings. To the north, the old medina is still enclosed within ramparts, while the Parc de la Ligue Arabe, Casablanca's green lung, extends to the southeast. Further out, towards the west, is the residential district of Anfa and the coastal resort of Aïn Diab. The Boulevard de la Corniche leads to the monumental Hassan II Mosque. The Quartier Habous, a modern medina built in the 1920s, also features some interesting architecture.

Sights at a Glance

Avenues and Boulevards

② Avenue des Forces Armées Royales
③ Boulevard Mohammed V

Squares

① Place des Nations Unies
④ Place Mohammed V

Districts

⑥ Old Medina
⑦ Port
⑨ Quartier Habous (New Medina)
⑫ Anfa
⑬ Corniche d'Aïn Diab

Park

⑤ Parc de la Ligue Arabe

Building

⑩ Casablanca Twin Center

Mosque

⑧ *Hassan II Mosque pp106–107*

Museum

⑪ Musée du Judaïsme Marocain

Environs

⑭ Mohammedia

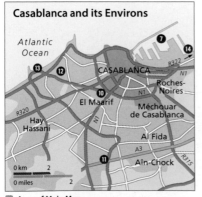

Area of Main Map

Detail of a 1930s façade in Casablanca

For hotels and restaurants see pp306–313 and pp320–31

Getting Around

Allow at least one day to explore Casablanca. The old medina and the new town, with their fine architectural heritage, are best seen on foot. By contrast, the Quartier Habous and the Hassan II Mosque can be reached only by motorized transport. Parking is not a problem as there are many car parks. It is also possible to travel around Casablanca by bus or *petit taxi*. Bus and tram routes serve both the city centre and outlying districts.

Stained-glass window in the Church of Notre-Dame-de-Lourdes

Key

■ Major sight
■ Sight
■ Medina
— Ramparts
= Railway

0 metres 400
0 yards 400

For keys to symbols *see back flap*

The Moretti Milone apartment block, one of the highest in 1934

and is one of the square's finest buildings. In 1934, the 11-storey **Moretti Milone** apartment block, at the corner of Boulevard Houphouët Boigny, was the first high-rise building in central Casablanca. **Boulevard Houphouët Boigny**, lined with shops and restaurants, runs from the square to the port. At the end, on the right, the *marabout* of Sidi Belyout, patron saint and protector of Casablanca, stands in stark contrast to the neighbouring residential buildings.

No. 208 Boulevard Mohammed V, faced with friezes and balconies

❶ Place des Nations Unies

South of the old medina.

At the beginning of the 20th century, this was still no more than a market square, a place which, by evening, would become the haunt of story-tellers and snake charmers. Today, it is the heart of the new town, a hub where major thorough-fares converge.

When the square was laid out in 1920, it was known as Place de France, but was later renamed. Beneath the arcades of 1930s apartment blocks are rows of brasserie terraces and souvenir shops. In the northeast corner of the square, the **clocktower**, which dates from 1910, was demolished in 1940 and then rebuilt to an identical design. At the time that it was built, the clock symbolized colonial rule, indicating to the population that it should now keep in time with an industrial society.

At the **Hyatt Regency Hotel** memories of Humphrey Bogart and Ingrid Bergman, stars of the famous film *Casablanca*, made in 1943 by Michael Curtiz, hang on the walls. In the southeast corner of the square is the **Excelsior Hotel** (1914–16), with Moorish friezes and balconies, which was the first of Morocco's Art Deco hotels

Window of the Excelsior hotel

❷ Avenue des Forces Armées Royales

South of the old medina, running between Place Oued el-Makhazine and Place Zellaga.

Lined with high-rise buildings, major hotels such as the **Sheraton** and **Royal Mansour**, with airline offices and travel agents and the towering, futuristic glass building of **Omnium Nord Africain** (ONA), this avenue marks the boundary of the commercial district. Further development is planned for its continuation towards the Mosque of Hassan II.

❸ Boulevard Mohammed V

Running from Place des Nations Unies to Boulevard Hassan Seghir.

Running through the city like a spine, this boulevard links Place des Nations Unies with the railway station in the east of the city. When it was built in 1915, it was intended to be the major artery through the commercial heart of Casablanca. On both sides, covered arcades house shops and restaurants.

A raised strip sections off traffic and widens into a square level with the **Central Market**. The high-rise buildings here are notable for their façades, which feature loggias, columns, *zellij* tilework and geometric carvings. Peculiar to the

The Glaoui residential block, built in 1922 by M. Boyer

The Palais de Justice, built in the Moorish style in 1922

buildings of this period is the mixture of styles – Art Deco, on the one hand, seen in white façades of simple design, and the typically Moroccan, more decorative style on the other. Among the finest of these buildings are three residential blocks: the **Glaoui** (designed by M. Boyer, 1922), on the corner of Rue El-Amraoui Brahim; the **Bessonneau** (H. Bride, 1917), opposite the market; and the **Asayag** (M. Boyer, 1932), at the corner of Boulevard Hassan Seghir. The latter, very innovative at the time it was built, is five storeys high and has three towers set around a central hub. From the fourth storey upwards, terraces extend the studio apartments. Buildings at numbers 47, 67 and 73 are also fine examples, with overhanging loggias and rounded balconies.

Another particular feature of Boulevard Mohammed V is its covered arcades, which are similar to the shopping arcades built during the same period (the 1920s) along the Champs-Élysées in Paris. Among the most interesting of these arcades is the **Passage du Glaoui**, which links Boulevard Mohammed V to Rue Allal ben-Abdallah. Lit by prismatic lamps, the arcade is punctuated by glass rotundas. **Passage Sumica**, opposite Passage du Glaoui, is closer to the Art Deco style. This runs through to **Rue du Prince Moulay Abdallah**, which also contains some notable 1930s

apartment blocks. This pedestrianized street is very popular with shoppers.

In Rue Mohammed el-Quori, off Boulevard Mohammed V, stands the **Rialto**. This renovated cinema is renowned for its fine ornamentation, stained-glass windows and Art Deco lighting.

🏛 **Central Market**
Boulevard Mohammed V.
Open 7am–2pm daily.

❹ Place Mohammed V

North of the Parc de la Ligue Arabe.

Exemplifying the architecture of the Protectorate, this square, the administrative heart of Casablanca, combines the monumentality of French architecture with Moorish sobriety. This is the location of the Préfecture, the law courts, the central post office, banks and cultural organizations.

Zellij decoration on the façade of the Post Office

The **Préfecture** (by M. Boyer, 1937), over which towers a Tuscan-style campanile 50 m (164 ft) high, stands on the southeastern side of the square. Its buildings are set around three courtyards, each with a tropical garden. The central stairway is framed by two huge paintings by Jacques Majorelle *(see p247)* depicting the festivities of a

moussem and the performance of the *ahwach*, a Berber dance.

Behind stands the **Palais de Justice** (law courts, designed by J. Marrast and completed in 1922). The strong verticality of the Moorish doorway, with its awning of green tiles, contrasts with the horizontal lines of the arcaded gallery, which are emphasized by a carved frieze running the length of the building.

Two buildings set slightly back abut the façade of the law courts on either side. On the right is the **Consulat de France** (French Consulate, by A. Laprade, 1916), whose gardens contain an equestrian statue of Marshal Lyautey, by Cogné (1938), which stood in the centre of the square until Moroccan independence. On the left, in the northeastern corner, is the **Cercle Militaire** (by M. Boyer). To the north is the **Post Office** (A. Laforgue, 1920), fronted by an open arcade decorated with *zellij* tilework and semicircular arches, which leads through to an Art Deco central hall within.

Opposite, along Rue de Paris, a small area of greenery where people like to stroll gives a more picturesque feel to the square, in the centre of which is a monumental **fountain** dating from 1976. At certain times of day, the fountain plays music and gives light displays.

A long, straight walkway in the Parc de la Ligue Arabe

❺ Parc de la Ligue Arabe

South of Place Mohammed V (between Boulevard Rachidi and Boulevard Mohammed Zerktouni).

Laid out by the architect A. Laprade in 1919, this huge garden incorporates café terraces and is a popular place for a stroll. Avenues lined with impressively tall palm trees, ficus, arcades and pergolas frame some stunning formal flowerbeds. The streets surrounding the park, including Rue d'Alger, Rue du Parc and Boulevard Moulay-Youssef, contain Art Nouveau and Art Deco houses.

Northwest of the park stands the **Église du Sacré-Cœur**, built in 1930–52 by Paul Tournon. A white concrete twin-towered building with an Art Deco flavour to its façade, it is now deconsecrated and used for cultural events.

To the southeast stands the **Église Notre-Dame-de-Lourdes** (1956). Its stained-glass windows depict scenes from the life of the Virgin against motifs taken from Moroccan carpets. They are the work of G. Loire,

a master-craftsman from Chartres. To the southwest is the **Villa des Arts** displaying contemporary Moroccan paintings.

🏛 **Église du Sacré-Cœur**
Rond-point de l'Europe. **Open** only for concerts and other events.

🏛 **Villa des Arts**
30 Bd Brahim Roudani. **Tel** (0522) 29 50 87. **Open** 9:30am–7pm Tue–Sun.

❻ Old Medina

Between Boulevard des Almohades and Place des Nations Unies.

At the beginning of the 20th century, Casablanca consisted only of the old medina, which itself comprised no more than a few thousand inhabitants. The walls around the old town were originally pierced by four gates, two of which survive today. **Bab Marrakech** and **Bab el-Jedid**, on the western side, face onto Boulevard Tahar el-Alaoui. A daily **market**, with jewellers, barbers, public letter-writers and so on, stretches out along the length of the walls.

Opposite the fishing harbour is the *sqala*, a fortified bastion built in the 18th century, during the reign of Sidi Mohammed ben Abdallah. Behind the

A cannon in the *sqala*, facing the port and onto the ocean

bastion, the *marabout* (shrine) with a double crown of merlons contains the **Tomb of Sidi Allal el-Kairouani**, who became Casablanca's first patron saint in 1350. **Bab el-Marsa** (Gate of the Sea), which opens onto Boulevard des Almohades, also dates from the 18th century. It was at this spot that the French disembarked in July 1907.

❼ Port

East of the old medina.

Casablanca is Morocco's principal port. Covering an area of 1.8 sq km (0.70 sq miles), the port was built during the Protectorate and is one of the largest artificial ports in the world. A groyne protects it from the pounding of the ocean that destroyed several earlier constructions. The port is equipped with ultra-modern commercial, fishing and leisure facilities.

Access to the port complex is via the fishing harbour. On the seafront in the port itself, as well as along the avenue leading down to it, some excellent fish restaurants are to be found *(see pp321–2)*.

A multi-million dirham development of towering hotels, restaurants, shops, offices and apartments, together with a marina, is changing the shoreline between the port and the Hassan II Mosque. The first phase is due to be completed by 2015.

A fish auction on the quay, where fishing boats land their catch

Architecture of the 1920s and 1930s

In 1907, when innovative architects set to work to create buildings in a range of contemporary styles, Casablanca began to look like a huge building site. In the early 1920s, numerous teams of architects were working in the city. Whatever the style, avant-garde tendencies were often counterbalanced by the traditional Moroccan style.

Thus, as the architects drew on the repertoire of Neo-Classicism, Art Nouveau and Art Deco, which were fashionable at the time, they also took inspiration from the Moorish style that Europeans found so fascinating. Towards the end of the 1920s and into the early 1930s, a new taste for simplicity became apparent. Emphasizing shape and outline at the expense of decoration, this gave prominence to the interplay of convex and concave shapes, and to balconies and bow windows. Another significant factor was the expectations of the colonial population and of European speculators: lifts, bathrooms, kitchens and parking areas appeared.

Façades

The façades of residential blocks were encrusted with putti, fruit, flowers and pilasters and featured roofs covered in green tiles, stucco and zellij tilework. Colonial houses, in the suburbs, were built in a style that was a cross between a grand Parisian town house and a Moroccan-style seaside residence.

Wrought-iron balconies, like this one from the Darius Boyer House, are typical of the Art Nouveau ironwork that often graced French windows and balconies.

The dome is an example of the Western use of a Moorish architectural element.

Balconies are an adaptation to the sunny climate and bright light.

Mosaic decoration

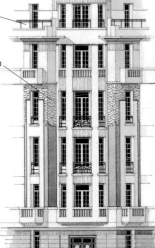

Mosaic decoration on the law courts consists of multicoloured *zellij* tilework in geometric shapes overlying a frieze of stucco carved with inscriptions.

Casablanca's main post office has a loggia of semicircular arches and *zellij* tilework.

1930s architecture features traditional Moorish elements, including semicircular arches and decoration in the form of pretty carved stucco.

This building has an elegantly classical appearance, with decoration consisting of columns, belvederes and a dome with Art Nouveau motifs.

❽ Hassan II Mosque

With a prayer hall that can accommodate 25,000, the Hassan II Mosque is the second-largest religious building in the world after the mosque in Mecca. The complex covers 9 hectares (968,774 sq ft), two-thirds of it built over the sea. The minaret, the lighthouse of Islam, is 200 m (656 ft) high, and two laser beams reaching over a distance of 30 km (18.5 miles) shine in the direction of Mecca. The building was designed by Michel Pinseau, 35,000 craftsmen worked on it, and it opened in 1993. With carved stucco, *zellij* tilework, a painted cedar ceiling and marble, onyx and travertine cladding, it is a monument to Moroccan architectural virtuosity and craftsmanship.

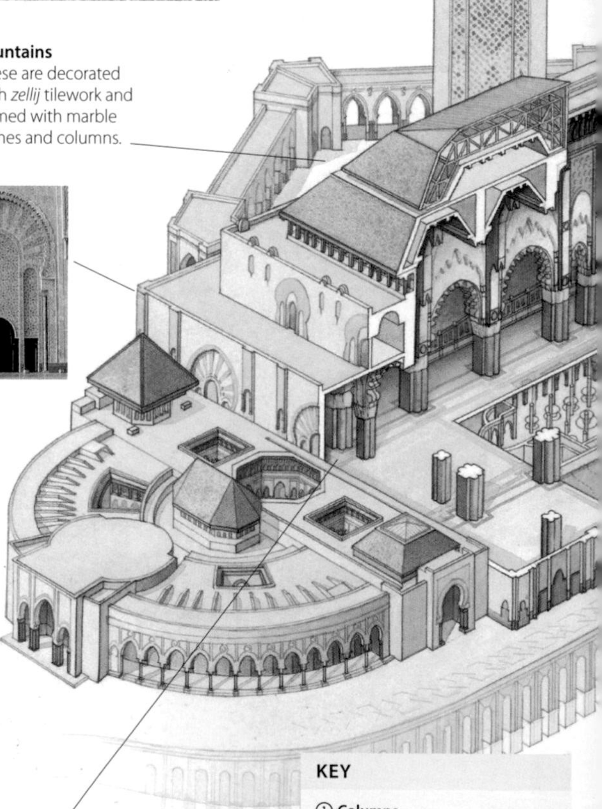

★ The Minaret
Its size – 25 m (82 ft) wide and 200 m (656 ft) high – and its decoration make this an exceptional building.

Fountains
These are decorated with *zellij* tilework and framed with marble arches and columns.

Marble
Covering the columns of the prayer hall and seen on doorways, fountains and stairs, marble is ubiquitous, sometimes used in combination with granite and onyx.

Minbar
The minbar, or pulpit, located at the western end of the prayer hall, is particularly ornate. It is decorated with verses from the Koran.

KEY

① **Columns**

② **Mashrabiyya**, screenwork at the windows protects those within from prying eyes.

③ **Hammam**

Women's Gallery
Above two mezzanines and hidden from view, this gallery extends over 5,300 sq m (57,000 sq ft) and can hold up to 5,000 women.

VISITORS' CHECKLIST

Practical Information
Accessible from the port, southwards along the seafront.
Tel (0522) 48 28 89/86.
📷 9am, 10am, 11am & 2pm
Sat–Thu. 🅿

Dome
The cedar-panelled interior of the dome over the prayer hall glistens with carved and painted decoration.

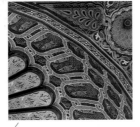

Royal Door
This is decorated with traditional motifs engraved on brass and titanium.

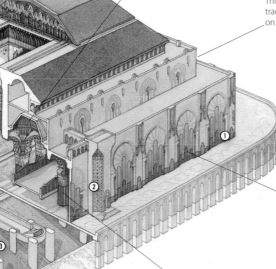

Doors
Seen from the exterior, these are double doors in the shape of pointed arches framed by columns. Many are clad in incised bronze.

Stairway to the Women's Gallery
The stairway features decorative woodcarving, multiple arches and marble, granite and onyx columns, arranged in a harmonious ensemble.

★ Prayer Hall
Able to hold 25,000 faithful, the prayer hall measures 200 m (656 ft) by 100 m (328 ft). The central part of the roof can be opened to the sky.

The copper and brass souk in the Quartier Habous

❾ Quartier Habous (New Medina)

In the southeast of the city centre, near Boulevard Victor Hugo.

In the 1930s, in order to address the problem of an expanding urban population and to prevent Casablanca's underprivileged citizens from being forced to settle in insalubrious quarters, French town planners laid out a new medina (Nouvelle Medina). Land to the south of the existing city centre earmarked for this development was given over to the Habous, the administration of religious foundations, hence the new town's name.

This new town – which did not, however, forestall the later development of shanty towns – was built in the traditional Arab style at the same time as obeying modern town planning and public health regulations. It contains public areas, such as a market, shops, mosques, a *kissaria* and baths, as well as private dwellings (arranged around a courtyard separated from the street by a solid wall).

The new medina is another facet of colonial town planning during the Protectorate, and its flower-filled, arcaded streets offer the opportunity for a stroll in a scenic quarter of the city. While the most modest houses are located around the market, the finest are set around the mosque.

Northeast of the medina are the copper and brass Souk and **Chez Bennis**, Casablanca's most famous patisserie, which sells pastries known as *cornes de gazelle* (gazelles' horns), fritters and *pastilla*. There are also shops specializing in curios and collectors' items, and they can be good places to find Art Deco objects. A wide range of Moroccan rugs and carpets is also on sale at the weekly auction in the carpet souk.

Northwest of the Quartier Habous is the **Mahakma du Pacha**, a formal tribunal and today one of the city's eight *préfectures* (administrative headquarters). The building (by A. Cadet, 1952), which centres around a tall tower and two courtyards, is a fine example of the adaptation of traditional Arab architecture to modern needs. The traditional Arabic decoration of its 64 rooms is the work of Moroccan craftsmen: it consists of carved stucco and *zellij* tilework on the walls, carved cedarwood panels on the ceiling and wrought iron on the doors.

The **Royal Palace**, on the fringes of the Quartier des Habous and set in extensive Mediterranean gardens, was built in the 1920s by the Pertuzio brothers, whose aim was to create a luxuriously appointed yet modern dwelling.

🏛 **Mahakma du Pacha**
Boulevard Victor Hugo.

🏰 **Royal Palace**
Between Boulevard Victor Hugo and Rue Ahmed el-Figuigui. **Closed** to the public.

Carpets displayed for sale in the Quartier Habous

The Twin Center, shaped like the hull of a ship, and its two towers

❿ Casablanca Twin Center

At the intersection of Boulevard Zerktouni and Boulevard El-Massira.

Dominated by its two towers, which rise to a height of 100 m (328 ft), this extensive complex is proof and symbol of the city's economic importance. Built by Ricardo Bofill and Elie Mouyal, it comprises offices, shopping malls and a hotel. By its outward appearance no less than in its infrastructure, the building signals the economic role that Casablanca plays on both the national and international stage.

⓫ Musée du Judaïsme Marocain

81 Rue Chasseur Jules Gros, Quartier de l'Oasis. **Tel** (0522) 99 49 40. **Open** 9am–5pm Mon–Fri.

The modernized Museum of Moroccan Judaism contains displays of scarves, kaftans, prayer shawls and other religious objects, and a reconstructed synagogue.

From Roman times up to independence in 1956, Morocco had a sizeable Jewish community. Today numbering some 5,000, Morocco's Jews occupy prominent positions in the spheres of politics, economics and culture.

The Anfa quarter occupies a hill overlooking the city

pools, hotels, restaurants, fashionable nightclubs and an institute of thalassotherapy.

The earliest establishments to be built here – with the needs of a wealthy clientèle in mind – opened in the 1930s. A string of public beach clubs, each one rivalling its neighbour, lines the Corniche, offering a variety of pools and restaurants. The most modern and fashionable is the **Tahiti Beach Club**.

At the foot of the hill of Anfa, near the **Palais Ibn Séoud**, the foundation of the same name houses a mosque and one of the most comprehensive libraries on the African continent. At the western end of the Corniche, 3 km (2 miles) further on, the **Marabout of Sidi Abderrahman**, perched on a rock, is accessible only at low tide. It attracts Muslim pilgrims suffering from nervous disorders and those who have had evil spells cast on them.

⓮ Mohammedia

28 km (17 miles) northeast of Casablanca. 🚊 🚙

At the beginning of the 20th century, Mohammedia (formerly called Fedala) was nothing more than a kasbah. This changed in the 1930s, when its port began to receive oil tankers. Today, petroleum accounts for 16 per cent of all Moroccan port traffic. Although the flaming chimneys of the refineries blight the landscape, this town of over 300,000 inhabitants, now part of greater Casablanca, is still residential. It has a golf course and a yacht club. Its fine beaches and friendly atmosphere have helped to turn Mohammedia also into an upmarket coastal resort for wealthy Moroccans. A visit to the kasbah and the fish market can be followed by a stroll along the seafront. From the port, the clifftop walk offers fine views of the sea and Mohammedia.

El-Hank lighthouse

⓬ Anfa

Northwest of the city.

Occupying a hill that overlooks Casablanca from the northwest, Anfa is a residential quarter with wide flower-lined avenues where luxurious homes with terraces, swimming pools and lush gardens bring to mind Beverly Hills. Since the 1930s, villas in a great variety of styles have been built here, and they constitute a catalogue of successive architectural styles and fashions.

It was at the Hôtel d'Anfa, now demolished, that the historic meeting between US president Franklin D. Roosevelt and British prime minister Winston Churchill took place in January 1943, during World War II, at which the date of the Allied landings in Normandy was decided. Although they got wind of the meeting, the Germans were misled by the literal translation of "Casablanca". Under the impression that the location was to be the White House in Washington, they failed to prevent it from going ahead.

During the meeting, President Roosevelt also formally pledged his support to Sultan Mohammed V in his aim to obtain independence from France, thus opening new avenues for Morocco in the postwar period.

⓭ Corniche d'Aïn Diab

West of the Mosque of Hassan II.

The Corniche d'Aïn Diab has been an upmarket part of Casablanca since the 1920s. Running from the **El-Hank Lighthouse** (built in 1916) in the east, to the *marabout* of Sidi Abderrahman in the west, this coastal avenue is lined with a succession of tidal swimming

SOUTHERN ATLANTIC COAST

Like the whole of Morocco's Atlantic coastline, the area south of Casablanca is of variable interest to visitors. It is, however, worth the detour, as much for the architecture of the fortified towns built by the Portuguese, such as El-Jadida and Essaouira, as for the breathtaking coastal scenery. In addition, there is also the coastal resort of Oualidia, which has a very safe beach.

Morocco's southern Atlantic coastal area contains many smaller towns and resorts, which are especially attractive to those who wish to escape the frenetic activity of the imperial cities.

This region, more than almost any other part of Morocco, has always had contact with the outside world. The Phoenicians, then the Romans, established trading posts here. The Portuguese and the Spanish built military strongholds and centres of trade along the coast, whose topography also made it a haven for pirates. Fortified towns like El-Jadida, Safi and, most especially, Essaouira bear witness to the Spanish and Portuguese contribution to Morocco's history. Under the French Protectorate, the region became the country's economic and administrative centre. Today, this stretch of coastline is industrial and visibly oriented toward the modern world: most of the country's phosphate is produced here, the industry attracting a large workforce from the interior.

The entire coastline, punctuated by scenic viewpoints over the ocean, is ideal for bird-watching and palaeontology. Gourmets will also enjoy Oualidia's famous oysters.

The road, excellent from Casablanca to Essaouira, passes stunningly beautiful deserted beaches that are ideal for surfing. It winds on to Agadir, the great sardine-processing port and Morocco's most popular coastal destination. The wild landscape is dominated by the argan tree. Goats can often be seen climbing its branches to feed on its fruit. The tree *(see p131)* produces the highly prized argan oil.

Fishing boats in the harbour at Imessouane, south of Cap Tafelney

◀ The old Portuguese water cistern in El-Jadida

Exploring the Southern Atlantic Coast

This part of Morocco's Atlantic coastline is punctuated by the fortified towns of Azemmour, El-Jadida, Safi and Essaouira, which were established by the Portuguese in the 15th and 16th centuries. The road running inland from Settat to Boulaouane crosses a stunningly beautiful plateau, carved out of the landscape by Wadi Oum er-Rbia (Mother of Spring), where all the colours of the splendid Doukkala region can be seen. Further south, the road leading to Agadir offers interesting tours up into the lower foothills of the High Atlas. In the 1970s, the most accessible part of the foothills was given the name Paradise Valley. The well-marked road that winds between luxuriant cascades provides points of departure for hikes in the mountains, and it eventually leads to Imouzzer des Ida Outanane, a quiet summer resort.

Getting Around

A motorway runs between Casablanca and El-Jadida, which is a distance of 99 km (62 miles). From here, the N1 goes to Agadir. This major road goes inland from El-Jadida as far as Essaouira, 360 km (224 miles) from Casablanca, and runs near or actually on the coast for the 165 km (103 miles) between Essaouira and Agadir. However, the quickest route to Agadir is by motorway via Marrakech. A dual carriage-way runs between Marrakech and Essaouira. The R301 is a minor road that follows the coast between El-Jadida and Essaouira, passing through Oualidia and Safi, 241 km (150 miles) from Casablanca. A motorway and the N9 run inland from Casablanca towards Settat (and Marrakech). From Settat, the R316 leads to Kasbah Boulaouane, from where it is easy to rejoin the coast road.

Azemmour, on Wadi Oum er-Rbia

For hotels and restaurants see pp306–313 and pp320–31

Rabat

CASABLANCA

Dar Bouazza

R320 N1

Sidi Boubeker Lighthouse

Bir-Jdid

ADIDA

④ AZEMMOUR

Berrechid

③

OULAY DALLAH

R318

Souk-Khemls-des-Gdana

N11

Khourigba

A8

N1

R316

Oulad-Saïd

SETTAT **①**

N9

Boulaouane

② KASBAH BOULAOUANE

R202

Sidi Smaïl

N7

Arba-Aounate

Sidi Bennour

Mechra-Benâbbou

Skhour-des-Rehamna

Arba-Amrane

A7

Youssoufia

R206

Ben Guerir

Bahira

N9

maïa

Ej-Jemaâ

R204

El-Arba

Sidi-Bou-Othmane

N7

Jbilet

d Tensift

MARRAKECH

Beni Mellal

N8

R212

Ouarzazate

Sights at a Glance

① Settat
② Kasbah Boulaouane
③ Azemmour
④ El-Jadida
⑤ Moulay Abdallah
⑥ Oualidia
⑦ Safi
⑧ Kasbah Hamidouch
⑨ Chiadma Region
⑩ *Essaouira pp124–9*
⑪ Tamanar
⑫ Tamri

Tour

⑬ Imouzzer des Ida Outanane

The *sqala* (bastion) in the harbour at Essaouira

Key

━━━ Motorway

═══ Motorway under construction

━━━ Major road

⋯⋯ Minor road

--- Track

∿∿ Railway

△ Summit

A potter adding finishing touches to a tagine in Safi

0 km   20
0 miles   20

For keys to symbols *see back flap*

A village near Settat, on the fertile coastal plain of Chaouia

❶ Settat

Road Map C3. 🏛 100,000.
🚌 🚉 ℹ Avenue Hassan II,
El-Haram building; (0523) 40 58 05.
🎭 Moussem of the Chaouia (first
week in July or in Sept), Chaouia Folk
Art Festival (final week in Nov).
🛍 daily; livestock market Sat.

A crossroads between north
and south, Settat is the capital
of a province with some 850,000
inhabitants. It is the economic
hub of the Chaouia, a coastal
plain that is known as Morocco's
grainstore. While the north
of the region is famous for its
fertile agricultural land, the
southern part is given over
to livestock (*chaoui* means
"breeder of sheep").

When Moulay Ismaïl built the
Kasbah Ismaïla, at the end of the
17th century, the security and
stability of the region – which
was traversed by major caravan
routes – was strengthened. The
sultan would stay in the kasbah
on his travels between Fès
and Marrakech. Vestiges of the
building can still be seen in
the modern town.

Today, Settat offers little of
interest to tourists. However,
under the aegis of Driss Basri, a
native of the region and Minister
of the Interior for almost 20 years,
it stood as a model of urban
development in the 1990s. The
merits of this distinction can be
seen from Place Hassan II, in the
town centre, in the arrangement
of open spaces and of pedestrian
and shopping areas, and in
buildings combining Art Deco
and Moorish styles.

Environs
The tiny village of **Boulaouane**
can be reached by road from
Settat. The journey there gives
a foretaste of the semi-arid
southern landscapes. The roads
are lined with Barbary fig trees,
and donkeys can be seen
carrying barrels of the local
rosé wine.

❷ Kasbah Boulaouane

Road Map C3.

Located in a meander of Wadi
Oum er-Rbia, this stunning
kasbah stands on a promontory
in the heart of a forested area
covering 3,000 hectares (7,400
acres). It was apparently built
by the Almohads, who made it
an imperial stopping place on
the road running along the
coast and inland to Fès. At
the beginning of the 16th

century, it was the scene of a
battle that halted the advance
of the Portuguese towards the
interior. Moulay Ismaïl revitalized
the village by choosing to build
a kasbah here in 1710 – in an
attempt to pacify and control
the region.

The stone-built fortress is
encircled by a crenellated
wall set with bastions and
pierced by an angled gate
with three pointed arches.
Above the gate is an inscription with the name of Moulay
Ismaïl and the date of the
kasbah's foundation.

This gate, which
accommodated sentries, is
the only point of entry into the
fortress. It leads through to
the sultan's palace, which is built
around a central courtyard with
elaborate mosaic decoration.
Beside the palace, a square
tower about 10 m (33 ft) high,
and now disfigured by cracks,
afforded a vantage point over
the surrounding territory.
Disused vaulted armouries were
used for storing food supplies.
The mosque, with five aisles, is
in a very bad state of preservation.
Next to it is the tomb of a saint
named Sidi Mancar, whom the
region's inhabitants still revere
today, since he is believed to
have the power to cure paralysis
and sterility.

Ceaselessly battered by
the elements, the kasbah
has suffered a great deal of
deterioration over the centuries.
It was declared a historic
monument in 1922. The

Kasbah Boulaouane, built in the 18th century

Boulaouane Wine

Extensive vineyards near Boulaouane

Connoisseurs consider that the wine known as Gris de Boulaouane, a rosé with an orange tint, is one of the best Moroccan wines. Although the Romans successfully exploited the soil and climate of Mauretania Tingitana to grow vines, the establishment of Islam in the Maghreb did not further the upkeep of the vineyards. Under the French Protectorate, the vineyards were revived, and in 1956 wine production passed into state control. The state-owned company that marketed Gris de Boulaouane collapsed, however, and the quality of the wine deteriorated. The French company Castel retook control of Moroccan wine production in the 1990s: the old vines were dug up and new stock planted, this time Cabernet-Sauvignon, Merlot, Cinsault, Syrah and Grenache gris. Today, Moroccan vineyards cover 350 hectares (865 acres) in the district of Boulaouane, the Doukkala region, the foothills of the Atlas and along the Atlantic coast. The vines are planted in sand, the heat of which prevents the development of phylloxera. The grapes are hand-harvested at the end of August and the wine, bottled in France, is exported mostly to Europe.

A bottle of Gris de Boulaouane

mosque and city walls are undergoing restoration work.

The region is also famous for its tradition of falconry, a sport still practised today by falconers from several important local families.

❸ Azemmour

Road Map B2. 🏔 32,800. 🚌
ℹ Avenue Mohammed V.
🎭 Moussem (Aug). 🛒 Tue.

An ancient Almohad town located on the left bank of the Wadi Oum er-Rbia estuary, Azemmour is also known by the name of Moulay Bouchaïb – the town's patron saint, who, in the 12th century, was also patron saint of the trade that then flourished between the town and Málaga, in Spain.

In 1513, the Portuguese took control of the town. The fort that they built became the kasbah that can be seen today.

A typical Portuguese-style door in the medina, Azemmour

They abandoned the town when Agadir fell in 1541.

Despite its year-round gentle climate and coastal location, Azemmour has few hotels and not many tourists come here. The narrow white streets of the medina are peppered with architectural features recalling the former Portuguese presence – the style of the doors being particularly prominent in this respect. The town also has a tradition of Portuguese-style embroidery, which features dragons and lions depicted face to face, an exclusively Moroccan motif. The mellah (Jewish quarter), once within walls, is now derelict. The synagogue, however, has a notable pediment with an inscription in Hebrew.

Environs

Eight kilometres (5 miles) north on the coast road, the **Sidi Boubeker lighthouse** offers a view of the town's Portuguese defences. **Haouzia** beach, starting 2 km (1.5 miles) southeast of Azemmour, stretches for 15 km (9 miles) from the Oum er-Rbia estuary to El-Jadida. Along the way it passes a forest of eucalyptus, pine and mimosa with flowering cacti.

Embroidery with dragon motifs, of Portuguese inspiration and typical of Azemmour

❹ El-Jadida

The Portuguese settled here in 1502 and built a fort that they named Mazagan. In time, the town became a major centre of trade, and ships from Europe and the East anchored here to take on provisions. In 1769, the sultan Sidi Mohammed expelled the Portuguese, who dynamited it as they fled. It was resettled by local Arab tribes and a large Jewish community from Azemmour at the beginning of the 19th century. The town was then known as El-Jadida (The New One), but temporarily reassumed its original name – Mazagan – under the French Protectorate.

🔲 Ramparts
Entry into the old town is through a gateway that leads to Place Mohammed ben-Abdallah. The walls were originally fortified with five bastions but only four of these were rebuilt after the Portuguese had destroyed the town as they escaped Sidi Mohammed in 1769. The rampart walk leads to the Bastion de l'Ange, which commands a panoramic view over the old town. The Bastion de St Sébastien was once the seat of the Inquisition's tribunal and the prison.

Bastion de l'Ange, commanding a fine view of El-Jadida's harbour

🔲 Medina
The main street leads to the sea gate (Porta do Mar), from where there is access to the rampart walk. This gate, now blocked in, once linked the town to the seashore. Halfway along the main street is the entrance to the Citerne Portugaise, originally an underground arsenal, which is one of El-Jadida's most interesting sights and should not be missed.

The mellah has a deserted air: most of the Jewish community emigrated to Israel in the early 1950s.

The old town of El-Jadida, built by the Portuguese

Citerne Portugaise (Portuguese Cistern)

The Portuguese built this underground "cistern" in 1514. First an arsenal, then an armoury, it came to be used as a cistern only in 1541. The reflection of the columns and the vaulting on the water is an atmospheric and mysterious sight.

A well, 3.5 m (11.5 ft) across, was sunk through the central span, allowing daylight to enter.

The vaults rest on five lines of columns.

The cistern takes the form of a square 34 m by 33 m (111 ft by 108 ft).

The 25 pillars are reflected in the stagnant water.

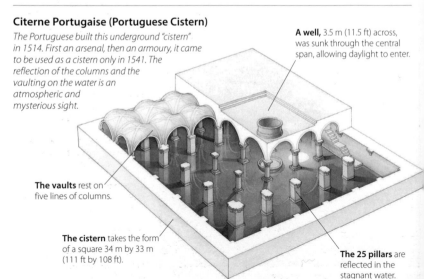

Oualidia Oysters

Lovers of seafood hold Oualidia oysters in especially high esteem. The species of edible oyster that is raised in the local oyster farms is related to those from the Marennes-Oléron region of France, which were imported in the 1950s. Oyster Farm No. 7, which was set up in 1992 in the lagoon here, is one of the most modern in Morocco. The oysters and other shellfish that are farmed here are raised according to stringent European health and hygiene regulations.

Oualidia oysters

🎬 Citerne Portugaise

Open 9am–1pm & 3–6pm daily. 🎬

This former armoury, in the Manueline Gothic style, was converted into a cistern after the citadel was enlarged in 1541. It was then constantly fed by fresh water so as to guarantee the town's water supply in the event of a prolonged siege. Rediscovered by chance in 1916 when a shopkeeper was knocking down a wall to enlarge his shop, it has fascinated many artists as well as visitors. Orson Welles used it as a location for certain scenes of his film *Othello*, released in 1952.

Environs

El-Jadida is a short bus ride away from the very popular **Sidi Bouzid** beach, which is about 5 km (3 miles) further south.

---

❺ Moulay Abdallah

Road Map B3. 11 km (7 miles) south of El-Jadida and 82 km (51 miles) north of Oualidia. 🎬 Moussem (Aug).

The origins of this fishing village lie in a 12th-century Almohad settlement which was then known as Tit. The old site's impressive ruins can still be seen today, together with a minaret dating from the same period as that of the Koutoubia Mosque in Marrakech *(see pp240–41)*. The settlement was, at that time, a *ribat*, or fortified monastery, built around the cult of the saint Moulay Abdallah, whose purpose was to guard the coast. It became a busy port, but was destroyed in the early 16th century to prevent the Portuguese, who were at Azemmour, from taking it. The fishing industry revived the village, which then assumed the name of the saint in whose

---

honour it was established. The *moussem* held here in August is renowned for its fantasias *(see p39)*.

Environs

From the coast road leading south from Moulay Abdallah you can see the huge installations of the mineral **Port de Jorf Lasfar**, the largest port in Africa. Built in the 1980s, it has a chemical complex and petrol refinery.

---

❻ Oualidia

Road Map B3. 🗺 3,000. 🚌 🚗 Sat.

This small coastal resort takes its name from the sultan El-Oualid, who built a kasbah here in 1634. The rather unattractive town centre leads through to a stunningly beautiful beach on the edge of a lagoon. Swimming is safe here but on either side, the sea is rough and foaming. This is one of the beaches on the Atlantic coast that is good for surfing, particularly for beginners. Among the summer villas here is the residence built for Mohammed V.

The town is an important centre of the oyster industry. A visit to the oyster farms *(parcs à huitres)*, particularly **Oyster Farm N° 7** – including the opportunity to sample some oysters – is a pleasant way to pass some time. The **Ostrea** restaurant and hotel is also located here.

Oyster Farm N° 7 (and Ostrea)
On the El-Jadida road. **Tel** (0523) 36 64 51/(0664) 49 12 76.

Environs

The coast road running southwards along the clifftop leads to **Cap Beddouza**, and on to Safi.

Heaps of phosphate in the mineral port of Jorf Lasfar

❼ Safi

Road Map B3. 260,000. tourist office, Rue Imam-Malek & main market, Ave de la Liberté; (0524) 62 24 96. Moussem of the Seven Saints (mid-Aug), Moussem of Lalla Fatna (mid-Nov). Mon.

An important Moroccan port since the 16th century, the town of Safi is today an industrial centre and a major sardine-processing port. It owes its importance to the growth of the fishing industry and to the processing and export of phosphates, as well as to its pottery. A rapidly expanding town, Safi has an interesting medina as well as traces of its Portuguese history.

Medina

The area covered by the medina takes the form of a triangle whose widest side faces onto the coast. Rue du Souk, lined with shops and workshops, leads to Bab Chaaba (Gate of the Valley). Near the Grand Mosque, south of the medina, is the **Portuguese Chapel**, originally the choir of Safi's cathedral, built by the Portuguese in 1519.

Dar el-Bahr

Open 8:30am–noon & 2:30–5:30pm Wed–Mon.

This small fortress, also known as the Château de la Mer, overlooks the sea. It was built by the Portuguese at the beginning of the 16th century, and served as a residence for the governor, then for the sultans in the 17th century. On the esplanade are cannons cast in Spain, Portugal and Holland.

Kasbah Hamidouch, built by Moulay Ismaïl

Musée National de la Céramique

Kechla. **Open** 8:30am–noon & 2–6pm Wed–Mon.

Built by the Portuguese in the 16th century, the citadel, known as the Kechla, encloses a mosque and garden dating from the 18th and 19th centuries. Since 1990 the Kechla has housed the Musée National de la Céramique, which contains displays of traditional and modern ceramics, including blue-on-white wares made in Safi, pottery from Fès and Meknès, and pieces by Boujmaa Lamali (1890–1971).

Safi candlestick, 20th century

Colline des Potiers

In the Bab Chaaba district, craftsmen can be seen making the ceramic wares that have made Safi famous. Finished pieces are displayed and offered for sale in commercial showrooms and visitors can follow the various stages of pottery production at the training school.

A potter at work in Safi, where a particularly high-quality clay is used

❽ Kasbah Hamidouch

Road Map B3. 29 km (18 miles) south of Safi on the coast road.

This kasbah forms part of a system of fortified outposts that Moulay Ismaïl *(see pp58–9)* established along the main routes of communication so as to control the region and accommodate travellers.

The kasbah is encircled by an outer wall, within which stand a mosque and various buildings, now in ruins. An inner wall, set with square towers and reinforced by a dry moat, surrounds a courtyard that is lined with shops, various houses and a chapel.

❾ Chiadma Region

Road Map B3–4.

The territory of the Chiadma, in the provinces of Safi and Essaouira, is inhabited by Regraga Berbers. They are descended from seven saint apostles of Islam, who, during a journey to Mecca, were directed by the Prophet Mohammed to convert the Maghreb to Islam. In spring, a commemorative pilgrimage is made, ending at the small village of **Ha Dra**.

A souk, one of the most authentic markets in the area, takes place in Ha Dra on Sunday mornings. Grain, spices, animals and a wide range of goods, mostly food, are offered for sale.

◀ View of the delightful town of Essaouira from the North Bastion

Sea Fishing in Morocco

The Moroccan coastline, which is more than 3,500 km (2,175 miles) long, faces both the Atlantic Ocean and the Mediterranean Sea, and gives the country access to some of the richest fishing grounds in the world – with some 240 species of fish. Morocco brings in the largest catches of fish in the whole of Africa. Its pre-eminence is due especially to sardines, of which Morocco is the largest processor and exporter in the world. Coastal fishing has created a major canning industry, too. The Moroccan sea fishing industry employs some 200,000 people and exports bring in US $600 million per year. Modern fishing methods, however, have not completely replaced traditional ways.

Small trawlers, many of them made of wood, as well as motorized dinghies, ply the coastal waters as far out to sea as the edge of the Continental Shelf. Their catches consist of many different species of fish.

Sardine fishing in Essaouira uses swivel nets. In spite of their expert knowledge of the sea bed, the fishermen often have to repair damaged nets when they return to harbour every day.

The eateries in Essaouira's harbour invite customers to select a plateful of fish and eat it on the spot. Many such establishments are to be found in the port, at the exit from the *sqala*.

The fish market at Agadir is one of the largest sardine ports in the world. An auction, which sells almost 250 different kinds of fish, takes place here every day.

Crates of fish are packed ready for sale. Sardines are the most important catch, but other fish, including hake and grey mullet, are also on offer.

Conservor, the canning company, is one of Safi's major industries. It revitalized the local economy in the 1920s.

⑩ Essaouira

With the brilliant whiteness of its lime-washed walls and the sight of women enveloped in voluminous *haiks*, Essaouira, formerly Mogador, is a quintessentially Moroccan town and one of the most enchanting places in the country. By virtue of its location on this stretch of the Atlantic coast, where trade winds prevail almost all year-round, the town enjoys a particularly pleasant climate. It is a prime location for surfing, but has managed to escape mass tourism. A mecca for hippies during the 1970s, it is still an artists' town and is very fashionable with independent travellers.

The Porte de la Marine, built by Sidi Mohammed ben Abdallah

Women in Essaouira wearing the characteristic *haik*

Exploring Essaouira

In the 7th century BC, the Phoenicians founded a base on the site where Essaouira now stands, and in the 1st century BC Juba II made it a centre of the manufacture of purple dye. The Portuguese established a trading and military bridgehead here in the 15th century, and named it Mogador. The town itself, however, was not built until around 1760, by the Alaouite sultan Sidi Mohammed ben Abdallah (Mohammed III), who had decided to set up a naval base here. The town, the harbour and the fortifications, in the style of European fortresses, were designed and built by Théodore Cornut, a renowned French architect who had worked for Louis XV.

🏠 Ramparts

On the side facing the sea, the outer walls, which have bevelled crenellations, were designed to give protection from naval attack and are thus typical of European fortifications. By contrast, the inner walls, which have square crenellations and are similar to the fortifications around Marrakech, are Islamic in style. These are built in stone and roughcast with a facing of earth. The walls are pierced by gates – Bab Sebaa on the southern side, Bab Marrakech on the eastern side and Bab Doukkala on the northeastern side – that lead into the medina.

🏠 Sqalas

Two *sqalas* (sea bastions) were built to protect the town: the **Sqala de la Ville**, in the northwest, and the **Sqala du Port**, in the south.

The Sqala de la Ville consists of a crenellated platform featuring a row of Spanish cannons and defended at its northern end by the North Bastion. This was built by Théodore Cornut on the site of the Castello Real, a citadel constructed by the Portuguese in about 1505. The esplanade (where scenes from Orson Welles' film *Othello* were shot in 1949) commands a view of the ocean and the Îles Purpuraires. A covered passage leads from the bastion to the former munitions stores, which now house marquetry workshops.

Port

Sqala du Port. **Open** daily. 🎫

The Porte de la Marine, leading to the docks, is crowned by a classical triangular pediment and dominated by two imposing towers flanked by four turrets. The rectangular Sqala du Port is surmounted by battlements.

From the 18th century, 40 per cent of Atlantic sea traffic passed through Essaouira. It became known as the Port of Timbuctu, being the destination of caravans from sub-Saharan Africa bringing goods for export to Europe. Once one of Morocco's largest sardine ports,

Sqala de la Ville, a favourite place for strolls at sunset

View of the Sqala du Port, at the southern entrance to the town

Essaouira now provides a living for no more than 500 to 600 families. But it still has its traditional shipyard, where vessels are made out of wood. Visitors can also watch the fish auction and sample freshly grilled sardines.

🏠 Medina

The layout of Essaouira is unusual because it was planned before the town was developed. It was laid out by the French architect Cornut, who, between 1760 and 1764, built the Sqala de la Ville and the Sqala du Port, endowing them with fortifications and outer and inner walls.

As elsewhere in Morocco, the medina in Essaouira is a labyrinth of narrow streets; the town itself, by contrast, has straight, wide streets laid out at right angles to one another and cut by gateways. The **Grand Mosque** is situated in the heart of the medina. Further north, the market, **Souk Jdid**, is divided into four by the intersection of two thoroughfares: there is a daily souk for fish, spices and grains, and a souk for second-hand and collectable items, known as *joutia*.

The daily spice souk, laid out next to the fish souk

Essaouira Town Centre

① Ramparts
② Sqala de la Ville
③ Sqala du Port
④ Port
⑤ Medina
⑥ Grand Mosque
⑦ Souq Jdid
⑧ Former Mellah
⑨ Église Notre-Dame
⑩ Beach
⑪ Galerie Damgaard
⑫ Musée Sidi-
Mohammed-
ben-Abdallah

Working with Thuya

Thuya, a highly prized wood with a delicious perfume, grows abundantly in the region of Agadir and Essaouira, and has been the source of that latter's prosperity. Thuya is a very dense hardwood, and almost every part of the tree apart from the branches can be used: the trunk, with its relatively light-coloured wood; the stump, used for making small objects; and the gnarl, a rare excrescence streaked with brown and pink. The gnarl is polished, inlaid with decorative motifs in citron wood, mother-of-pearl or ebony and sometimes with threads of silver or copper, or slivers of camel bone. It is used to make such items as coffee tables, caskets, small statues, boxes in all shapes and sizes, trays and jewellery. The country's best marquetry craftsmen can be seen working at this traditional craft in the former munitions stores beneath Essaouira's ramparts.

Marquetry

Essaouira's cabinet-makers were already renowned in antiquity, and the town has remained the capital of marquetry ever since. Tradition dictates that the artistically skilled part of the work (from the construction of a piece to its decoration) be done by men. Women and children are given the task of polishing the finished items.

The high sheen of this bread box is produced by polishing the surface with methylated spirit and gum arabic. Linseed oil feeds the wood and prevents it from developing cracks.

The decoration of this dish is based on a geometric scheme. The border pattern consists of an inlay of alternating pieces of ebony and citron wood.

The Thuya Gnarl

This excrescence, which grows on certain trees, particularly the thuya, is highly sought after by cabinet-makers for its veined and speckled appearance.

Artisans apply all their ingenuity and imagination to produce novel shapes.

The thuya gnarl is separated from the trunk.

The old part of the Jewish cemetery at Essaouira

🏚 Former Mellah

From Bab Doukkala, accessible via Rue Mohammed Zerktouni. 🔄 Controlled access.

Having risen to prominence and prosperity in the 18th and 19th centuries, the Jewish community in Essaouira came to hold an important economic position in the town, and Jewish jewellers acquired wide renown.

The town's former Jewish quarter is no longer inhabited by Jews, but on Rue Darb Laalouj the former houses of Jewish businessmen can still be seen; they are now converted into shops. In contrast to Muslim houses, they are fronted by balconies opening onto the street and some have lintels with inscriptions in Hebrew.

Rue Mohammed Zerktouni, the main street in the quarter, has a very lively market. Leaving by Bab Doukkala, you will pass the austere Jewish cemetery, which is worth a visit. (The keys are available on request from the caretaker.)

🏛 Église Notre-Dame

Avenue El-Moukaouama, south of the post office. 🕘 9am Mon–Sat, 10am Sun. **Tel** (0524) 47 58 95.

This Catholic church stands outside the walls of the medina, on the road leading to the beach. It is the only church in the country where the bells are rung on Sundays to summon the faithful to mass at 11am.

Most of the church furnishings are made of thuya wood. On an alternating basis, the services here are said in one of four languages: French, English, Dutch or German.

🏖 Beach

Essaouira's beach, to the south of the town centre, is known as one of the finest in Morocco. All through the summer, the trade winds keep this part of the coast surprisingly cool. At times, however, the gusty winds are so strong that they drive people to seek shelter in the medina.

At the estuary of Wadi Qsob, on the far side of the beach, vestiges of the system of defences built on a rocky promontory by the sultan Sidi Mohammed are visible. Although they have crumbled, thick walls can still be made out.

Surfer

By following the *wadi* upstream, after a tumbled-down bridge, you reach the village of Diabet. It is also accessible via the road to Agadir, turning off to the right after 7 km (4 miles). An interesting sight here

are the ruins of **Dar Soltane Mahdounia**, a palace built by Sidi Mohammed ben Abdallah in the 18th century and now almost completely engulfed in sand. It inspired Jimi Hendrix (who lived in Diabet for several years) to write the song *Castles in the Sand*.

Surfers will particularly enjoy the many beaches each side of Essaouira. Thanks to the enterprise of dynamic local associations, Morocco is about to become one of the top destinations for surfers and windsurfers. (The Océan Vagabond café is a good place to hire surfing equipment.) The windiest time of year in the Essaouira area, and therefore the best time for surfing and windsurfing here, is from April to September. However, while the air, at 20–30 °C (68–86 °F), is always pleasantly warm, the water is always a very cool 16–18 °C (61–64 °F).

South of Essaouira, at **Cap Sim** (beyond Diabet) and at **Sidi Kaouki**, and to the north, at **Moulay Bouzerktoun**, the waves are very strong, and safe only for experienced surfers.

Also to the south, at **Tafelney** (beyond the village of Smimou), there is a magnificent bay where the water is warmer. In spite of the constant gusty wind, it is easier to get into the water on the beach at Essaouira, as the waves are much gentler.

Essaouira beach, swept by strong gusts of wind all year round

🏛 Galerie Damgaard

Avenue Oqba Ibn Nafia. **Tel** (0524) 78 44 46. **Fax** (0524) 47 58 57.
Open 9am–1pm & 3–7pm daily.

For about a quarter of a century, a generation of painters and sculptors has made Essaouira an important centre of artistic activity. Many talented artists have been brought to public attention by the Dane Frederic Damgaard.

Formerly an antique dealer in Nice, since 1988, Damgaard devoted his energies to the art produced in Essaouira, opening his own art gallery in the medina until he retired in 2006. On display is the work of artists from the humblest walks of life. Among the best known are Mohammed Tabal, a Gnaoua painter who has become known as "the trance painter", Zouzaf, Ali Maïmoune, Rachid Amarlouch and Fatima Ettalbi. Others to be discovered include the expressionist Ali, whose style is mid-way between naive and Brutalist. All of them draw their inspiration from Essaouira's cultural variety, and reflect the traditions of different schools. Many exhibitions and other projects, in Morocco and throughout the world, have been devoted to the painters of Essaouira.

🏛 Musée Sidi-Mohammed-ben-Abdallah

Rue Darb Laalouj. **Open** 9am–6pm daily. 🖼

This small ethnographic museum is laid out in a 19th-century house that was a

Art gallery of Frederic Damgaard, the great discoverer of artistic talent

former pasha's residence and the town hall during the Protectorate. It contains fine displays of ancient crafts and of weapons and jewellery. There are also instruments and accessories used by religious brotherhoods, Moorish musical instruments and some stunning examples of Berber and Jewish costumes in silk, velvet and flannel. Carpets illustrating the traditional weaving of local tribes are also exhibited.

Rbab, in the Musée Sidi-Mohammed

Environs

On the **Îles Purpuraires**, visible across the bay from Essaouira, is a bird sanctuary where gulls and the rare Eleonora's falcon, a threatened species, and other birds can be seen.

Phoenician, Attic and Ionian amphorae discovered on the Île de Mogador, the main island, and now in the Musée Archéologique in

Rabat (*see pp82–3*), prove that trade was taking place here from the 7th century BC. In the 1st century BC, Juba II (*see p49*), founder of Volubilis, set up a centre for the production of purple dye, from which the islands take their name. Purple dye, highly prized by the Romans, was obtained from the murex, a mollusc. The ruins of a prison, built in the 19th century by the sultan Moulay el-Hassan, are also visible.

Some 12 km (7.5 miles) south of Essaouira, the splendid beach at **Sidi Kaouki** is very popular with surfers. A mausoleum, which appears to rise up out of the water, contains the tomb of a *marabout* (holy man) who, according to legend, had the power to cure barren women. An annual pilgrimage, with many devotees, takes place here in mid-August.

🏛 Îles Purpuraires

Controlled access (information available from the tourist office).

Mausoleum of Sidi Kaouki, at the far end of a spectacularly extensive beach south of Essaouira

The Painters of Essaouira

Essaouira, a town imbued with art and culture, is home to a group of painters known as "free artists", each of whom has his or her own unique style. Their talents have won recognition abroad and their work has been shown in many European art galleries. Using bright colours, their naive or "tribal" art is inspired by the myths, Arab-Berber history and African origins of Moroccan popular culture. These self-taught painters are also woodcarvers, sailors and builders, and they have in common an unconditional love of their town. Arabesques, geometric designs, dots, stippling and a swarm of objects, animals and human figures populate their poetic world.

Mohammed Tabal

A leading figure in Essaouira's artistic circles, Mohammed Tabal draws inspiration from his Gnaoui ancestry – from the ritual of spiritual possession and from the trances that form part of the rites of this popular brotherhood of African origin. His paintings are splashed with bright, contrasting colours and feature a multitude of tiny details, such as naive motifs rich in symbolism.

Mohammed Tabal's paintings are imbued with mysticism.

Abdallah Elatrach is inspired by scenes of daily life in the souks and by the traditions of various brotherhoods whose rituals involve trance.

Ali Maïmoune paints tree-filled worlds that are populated by terrifying monsters, animals and fantastic warriors.

⑬ Imouzzer des Ida Outanane

This tour follows a very scenic river valley with many natural swimming pools surrounded by palm trees. From Agadir, a winding road leads to the village of Imouzzer, set on a hilltop in the foothills of the High Atlas. It is the heart of the territory of the Ida Outanane, a confederation of Berbers whose traditional speciality is gathering honey. Despite the exodus from the country into the towns, many women – dressed in brightly coloured robes – can still be seen at work on the hillsides.

① Win t'mdoum Caves
Located 35 km (22 miles) from Imouzzer, these caves are the most extensive in North Africa. Work is under way to make them accessible to the public.

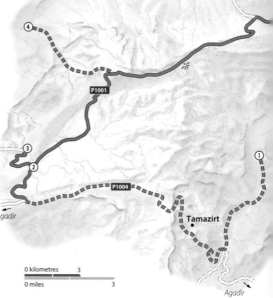

② Imouzzer
This village of white houses is famous for its waterfalls, which flow in winter and spring. It is the starting point for many excursions, on foot or by donkey, organized by the Hôtel des Cascades.

0 kilometres 3
0 miles 3

Agadir

Tamazirt

Agadir

---

⑪ Tamanar

Road Map B4. 🚌 Thu in Tamanar, Fri in Arba des Ida Outrhouma, 10 km (6 km) south of Tamanar.

The small town of Tamanar, which extends along its one main street, is a regional administrative centre and, effectively, the capital of the argan industry. It is at the heart of Haha territory, home to a settled yet dynamic Berber population which was self-governing in the 15th century.

On the way out of the village, near Café Argane, is a store selling locally produced argan oil. The highly organized women who run it show the fruits of their labour in a friendly atmosphere and sell their products in a cooperative.

Pretty landscape near the town of Tamanar

Environs
Between Smimou (where there is a picturesque souk on Sundays) and Tamanar, a small sign saying "Tafadna" indicates

the route to **Tafelney**. Two-thirds along this road, the landscape takes on a majestic beauty. The road comes to a sudden stop at a magnificent bay, where fishermen can often be seen mending their nets on the beach.

To the left, a huddle of identical shanty houses are home to thousands of birds. To those with a taste for remote spots, the strange beauty of this place will have a strong appeal.

⑫ Tamri

Road Map B4. 🗺️

This village is located on the estuary of a river that in winter is fed partly by the waterfall at Imouzzer *(see above)*. There is an extensive

③ Tamaroute

The waterfalls in this attractive village are known as "The Bridal Veil". They are the southernmost waterfalls above the Sahara. Flowing from several levels, the waters are abundant when the snow begins to melt in spring.

④ Assif el-Had

The natural bridge at Assif el-Had was created by water flowing down from the mountains and eroding the rock beneath.

⑤ Imi Irhzer

In February, the red-ochre houses of the villages almost disappear in a sea of almond blossom. A sheepfold has been converted into a gîte.

Argana, Marrakech

Biramane •

Tasguint

P1001

N8

⑥

Agadir ↓

Key

— Itinerary (road)
•• Itinerary (track)
= Other roads
= Other tracks

⑥ Bigoudine

The road to Bigoudine offers a succession of panoramic views. This is where the argan forests begin. When it is completed, a new road crossing the N8 and passing through Bigoudine will provide a link to Imouzzer.

Tips for Travellers

Departure : Imouzzer des Ida Outanane, at Hôtel des Cascades.
How to get there: From Agadir, northwards on the N1 turning off after 12 km (7.5 miles) onto a track. From the north, turn left onto the road 20 km (12 miles) after Cap Rhir. From Agadir, a bus departs from next door to the bus station at about 12:30pm daily (allow three and a half hours), returning from Imouzzer at 8am the next day.
Stopping-off point: Hôtel des Cascades at Imouzzer has relaxing gardens and a restaurant.

banana plantation. On the left, as you approach Tamri from the north, an inland road leads to a major bird-watching area, where Audouin's gulls, Barbary falcons, Lamier's falcons, sparrows and various other species can be seen.

Environs

About 19 km (12 miles) north of Agadir is **Taghazoute**, a fishing village that is popular with surfers. It was also colonized by the hippie movement, and, on the way out of Taghazoute, you can see curious signs saying "Banana Village" and "Paradise Valley" – names that were originally given by those who followed in the footsteps of Jimi Hendrix in the 1970s.

The Argan Tree

Bottle of argan oil

The argan (*Argania sideroxylon*) is North Africa's weirdest tree. It is interesting not only in its own right, but it is also ecologically and economically important. This tenacious, twisted tree, which never grows higher than 6 m (19.5 ft), has a multitude of uses. Being a very hard wood, it is ideal for making charcoal. It is also used to feed animals (camels and goats find the leaves and fruit delectable), and to make argan oil, which is extracted from the kernel. The vitamin-rich oil has a wide range of applications, according to the degree

to which it is refined. It is used in cosmetics for what are thought to be its hydrating and anti-ageing properties, and in medicine to combat arteriosclerosis, chicken pox and rheumatism. Argan oil also has culinary uses – a few drops are enough to bring out the flavour of salads and *tajines* – and it is used as fuel for lamps.

Goat perched in an argan tree, feeding on its fruit

TANGIER

Once an international city, Tangier has a special character that sets it apart from other Moroccan cities. It has drawn artists and writers, from Henri Matisse to Paul Bowles and writers of the Beat generation. Tangier's port, dominated by the medina, is the main link between Africa and Europe. With a road now linking Tangier to Rabat and the construction of a port, the city continues to expand.

The history of Tangier has been shaped by the sea and by its strategic location on the Straits of Gibraltar. The Phoenicians established a port here in the 8th century, and it was later settled by the Carthaginians. In 146 BC, Tangier, known as Tingis, became a Roman town and the capital of Mauretania, to which it gave the name Tingitana. In 711, Arab and Berber forces gathered here to conquer Spain. By the 14th century, the town was trading with Marseilles, Genoa, Venice and Barcelona. Tangier was captured by the Portuguese in 1471, by the Spanish (1578–1640) and then the English, who were expelled from the city by Moulay Ismaïl in 1684. In the 19th century, Morocco was the object of dispute between European nations. When, in 1905, Kaiser Wilhelm II denounced the *entente cordiale* between France and Britain, the stage was set for Tangier's transformation into an international city. This was sealed by the Treaty of Algeciras (1906), after which the diplomatic corps in Tangier took over Morocco's political, financial and fiscal affairs. When colonial rule was established in 1912, Spain took control of the northern part of the country. Tangier, however, remained under international administration. This was the city's heyday; its image as a romantic and sensuously exotic place was made in literature and on the big screen.

After independence in 1956, Tangier was returned to Morocco. Mohammed VI now includes it in his royal visits. In March 2014, he launched a 130 million dirham project for an arts compound in downtown Tangier as part of the Tangier-Metropolis programme.

Rooftop view of the city and Grand Socco, Tangier

◀ Musicians playing at Marhaba Palace, a luxurious palace restaurant in the old town, Tangier

Exploring Tangier

The best overview of the city is from the vantage point of the Colline du Charf or Colline de Bella-Vista, to the southeast. While the historic heart of Tangier is the medina, the soul of the city is the kasbah, which has a palace-museum, narrow streets, gateways and a seafront promenade. In the evening, when it is wise not to linger in the medina, visitors who explore Ville Nouvelle (New Town), along Avenue Pasteur and Avenue Mohammed V, will come across the Spanish custom of the *paseo* (evening promenade). Alternatively, the cafés on Place de France and Place de Faro offer relaxing views of the port and the Straits of Gibraltar, and, in clear conditions, a sight of the lights along the coast of Spain.

Sights at a Glance

Avenues, Streets and Squares
6 Rue Es-Siaghine
12 Rue de la Liberté
13 Place de France & Place de Faro
14 Avenue Pasteur

Quarters and Promenades
1 Kasbah
3 Ramparts
4 Petit Socco
8 Grand Socco (Place du 9 Avril 1947)
17 Quartier du Marshan
18 Colline du Charf
19 Bay of Tangier

Mosque and Church
5 Grand Mosque
9 Anglican Church of St Andrew

Historic Buildings
11 Fondouk Chejra
15 Ancien Palais du Mendoub
16 Café Hafa

Museums
2 Musée Archéologique
7 American Legation
10 Galerie d'Art Contemporain Mohammed Drissi

0 metres	200
0 yards	200

For hotels and restaurants see pp306–313 and pp320–31

Getting Around

Parking is available in Ville Nouvelle, on Place du 9 Avril 1947 (Grand Socco) or on the Plateau du Marshan. The medina and kasbah must be explored on foot. The only practical use for cars and taxis is for reaching the Colline du Charf and Colline de Bella-Vista, the Plateau du Marshan and La Montagne, or for a trip along the bay, from the port to the edge of the wooded hills before Cap Malabata.

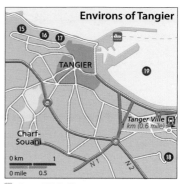

Area of Main Map

Key

- Sight
- Medina
- Ramparts
- Railway

Bab el-Assa, leading through to Place de la Kasbah

For keys to symbols see back flap

Fountain at Bab el-Assa, with mosaic decoration and ornamental stuccowork and woodcarving

❶ Kasbah

From the Marshan, accessible via Bab el-Kasbah; from the medina, via Rue Ben Raissouli and Bab el-Assa; from the Grand Socco, via Rue d'Italie and Rue de la Kasbah.

The kasbah was built on the site of the Roman settlement. Its present appearance dates from the Portuguese period and that of Moulay Ismaïl *(see pp58–9)*. With its quiet streets and friendly inhabitants, it has a special character, and its walls and gates command stunning views over the strait, the bay and the city.

Place de la Kasbah was once the *méchouar* where the sultan or his pashas held public audiences. It is also the location of the Dar El-Makhzen, the former palace that is now a museum *(see below)* and of the **Kasbah Mosque**, whose octagonal minaret is clad in coloured tiles. Its present form dates from the 19th century;

the *mendoub* led Friday prayers here. Also on the square is the Dar ech-Chera, the former tribunal, fronted by an arcade of three white marble columns. The large fig tree growing against the wall of an elegant house is supposed to be the place where Samuel Pepys wrote about Tangier in his diary in the 17th century.

Bab el-Assa (Gate of Bastinado) leads from the square to the medina. It was set at an angle so as to make it more difficult to attack. The gate gets its name from the *bastinado* (caning the soles of the feet) that was once the punishment of criminals. In the lobby, between the two porches, stands a fountain decorated with mosaics, stuccowork and woodcarving. Gnaouas, distantly related to those of Marrakech and Essaouira, regularly perform music and dance here. In the evening, audiences can talk

with them about their musical traditions and their repertoire. From the lobby, a narrow passage allows sight of a small *derb* (alleyway) lined with very fine houses, while beyond the gate is a view over the city. The **Musée d'Art Contemporain**, located in the former British Consulate building, which dates from 1890, houses collections of modern Moroccan art and temporary exhibitions featuring the works of foreign artists.

🏛 **Musée d'Art Contemporain**
52 Rue d'Angleterre, Tanger. 🛈 (0539) 94 99 72. **Open** 9am–12:30pm and 3–6:30pm Wed–Mon. **Closed** Tue.

Central courtyard of the interesting Musée Archéologique

❷ Musée Archéologique

Place de la Kasbah. 🛈 (0539) 93 20 97. **Open** 9am–6pm Wed–Mon. 🖼

The Museum of Archaeology is laid out in the Dar el Makhzen, a former sultans' palace built in the 17th century by Ahmed ben Ali, whose father Ali ben Abdellah al Hamani Errifi liberated Tangier from the British settlers in 1664. The palace was remodelled and enlarged several times in the 17th and 19th centuries. Bit el-Mal, the treasury – a separate room with a magnificent painted cedar ceiling – contains large 18th-century coffers with a complex system of locks.

A gallery leads to the palace itself. It is built around a central

The octagonal minaret on the Kasbah Mosque

courtyard paved with *zellij* tilework and surrounded by a gallery supported by white marble columns with Corinthian capitals. The seven exhibition rooms opening onto the patio display artifacts evoking the material history of Tangier from prehistoric times to the 19th century. These include sets of bone and stone tools, ceramics, terracotta figurines and Phoenician silver jewellery.

The Petit Socco, or Souk Dakhli

The Voyage of Venus, a Roman mosaic from Volubilis *(see pp206–209)*, is displayed in the museum's courtyard. Reproductions of several famous bronzes from the Musée Archéologique in Rabat *(see pp82–3)* are also on display. One room is devoted to Morocco's major archaeological sites. On the upper floor, the prehistory and history of Tangier and its environs, from the Neolithic period to its occupation by foreign powers, are presented through displays of grave goods, pottery and coins.

Adjacent to the palace is the Andalusian Garden.

❸ Ramparts

Place de la Kasbah. Accessible via Bab el-Bahar.

On the side of the square facing the sea, opposite Bab el-Assa, stands Bab el-Bahar (Gate of the Sea), which was built in the walls in 1920. From the terrace there is a breathtaking view of the port, the straits and, in clear conditions, the Spanish coast.

The walkway, which starts on the left, follows the outside of the ramparts and leads to the impressive **Borj en Naam**, a fort. Continuing along the seafront and through residential districts, the route leads to Hafa.

▦ Borj en Naam
Closed to the public.

❹ Petit Socco

Accessible via Rue Es-Siaghine or Rue Jma el-Bahir.

Known today as the Souk Dakhli, the Petit Socco probably corresponds to the area on which the forum of Roman Tingis once stood. It was a country souk, where people would come to buy food, and with the arrival of the Europeans at the end of the 19th century it became the pulsing heart of the medina. This was where business was done; diplomats, businessmen and bankers, whose offices were located around the square or in the close vicinity,

Doorway of the Grand Mosque

could be seen in the cafés, hotels, casinos and cabarets of the Petit Socco. The Fuentes, a café-restaurant and hotel, now gives but a faint impression of these halcyon days. From the 1950s, the hub of city life shifted to Ville Nouvelle, leaving the Petit Socco to a few writers, and to idlers, smokers of kif and shady traffickers.

❺ Grand Mosque

Rue Jma el-Kbir.
Closed to non-Muslims.

The Grand Mosque, built on the site of a Portuguese cathedral, probably also overlies a former Roman temple dedicated to Hercules. Dating from the reign of Moulay Ismaïl, it was enlarged in 1815 by Moulay Sliman. Mohammed V led Friday prayers here on 11 April 1947, during a visit to Tangier, when he also made a historic speech in the Mendoubia grounds *(see p142)*. Opposite the mosque, the state primary school (established by nationalists during the French Protectorate) is a former Merinid medersa that was remodelled in the 18th century.

Nearby, the Borj el-Hadjoui commands a view of the port and a pair of Armstrong cannons, each weighing 20 tonnes. They were purchased from the British in Gibraltar, but were never used.

From the *borj*, Rue Dar el-Baroud leads to the **Hôtel Continental**, located opposite the port and one of Tangier's oldest hotels. The building's architectural style, its Andalusian-style lounges and its open terraces give this establishment great appeal. Its patrons have included writers and painters – among them Edgar Degas – and film producers.

▦ Hôtel Continental
36 Rue Dar el-Baroud. **Tel** (0539) 93 10 24. **Open** daily.

The Hôtel Continental, one of the oldest hotels in Tangier

A jeweller's shop near Rue Es-Siaghine

❻ Rue Es-Siaghine

Running from the Petit Socco to the Grand Socco.

This street was once the *decumanus maximus*, the main axis and busiest thoroughfare of the Roman town. It led from the harbour out through the southern gate, marked today by Bab Fahs. Lined with cafés and bazaars, the street is as lively now as it must have been in antiquity.

The small administrative building at No. 47, with a courtyard planted with orange trees, was from 1860 to 1923 the residence of the *naib*, the Moroccan high official who served as intermediary between the sultan and foreign ambassadors. The Spanish **Church of the Immaculate Conception** (La Purísima), at

No. 51, was built by the Spanish government, work beginning in 1880. It was used by the whole city's Christian community, as well as by foreign diplomats. It is now used for social activities.

Further up the street, on the left, is Rue Touahine, which is lined with jewellers' shops and which leads to the **Fondation Lorin**, an arts centre in a disused synagogue. On display here are newspapers, photographs, posters and plans relating to the political, sporting, musical and social history of Tangier since the 1930s. Temporary exhibitions of paintings also take place here.

▥ Fondation Lorin
44 Rue Touahine. **ℹ** (0539) 93 91 03.
Open 11am–1pm & 3:30–7:30pm
Sun–Fri. **Closed** Sat.

❼ American Legation

8 Rue d'Amérique. **Tel** (0539) 93 53 17.
Open 10am–1pm & 3–5pm Mon–Thu,
10am–noon & 3–5pm Fri, by appt on
Sat & Sun.

The American Legation consists of a suite of rooms that originally formed part of the residence that Moulay Sliman presented to the United States in 1821, and which served as the US Consulate for the next 140 years. Another suite, on several floors looking out onto a garden, was presented by a Jewish family: the doors, windows and ceilings were decorated by craftsmen from Fès.

The rooms contain engravings of Gibraltar and Tangier, old maps, and paintings (by Brayer, Mohammed ben Ali Rbati, James McBey, Claudio Bravo and others), which were given to the legation by Margarite McBey, wife of James McBey and a resident of Tangier. Through photographs, early editions and recordings, a room devoted to Paul Bowles gives an overview of the writer's life and work during the years that he lived in Tangier. A reference library is also available for the use of scholars and specialists on North Africa.

The elegant interior courtyard of the American Legation

Artists and Writers in Tangier

At the beginning of the 20th century, many writers from Europe and the United States came to Tangier, most of them settling here more or less permanently. Drawn not only by the climate, they also came in search of stimulation and spiritual wellbeing, and in particular sought the atmosphere, freedom and sense of adventure that the city seemed to project. Tangier's exotic reputation as a den of traffickers and spies, and of drugs, sex and dissipation was also a powerful draw.

Painters

The light, architecture and inhabitants of Tangier have inspired many European and American painters. Discovered by Eugène Delacroix at the end of the 19th century, the city later became the subject of paintings by Georges Clairin, Jacques Majorelle, James Wilson Morrice, Kees Van Dongen, Claudio Bravo and the Expressionist painter Henri Matisse.

Eugène Delacroix (1798–1863) discovered Morocco in 1832. The experience of visiting the country marked a turning point in his career. Orientalism was then to inspire his work for the rest of his life.

Henri Matisse (1869–1954) was one of the greatest Fauvist painters. His *Odalisque à la Culotte Grise* is typical of his work.

Writers

In the wake of Paul Bowles came writers and musicians of the Beat, Rock and Hippie generations. Tennessee Williams arrived in 1949, followed by Truman Capote, who came to Tangier "to escape from himself". William Burroughs lived here for longer than all other foreign writers, finding Tangier a city where "throbbed the heartbeat of the world".

Paul Bowles, who came to Tangier for the first time in 1931 on the advice of Gertrude Stein, settled there permanently in 1947. He died in 1999.

Mohammed Choukri, born in the Rif in 1935, was a friend of Jean Genet and Tennessee Williams. Discovered by Paul Bowles, he came to fame in the 1980s with *For Bread Alone*.

Paul Morand, a diplomat and writer, and also a great traveller, wrote *Hécate et ses chiens* in Tangier in 1955. A unique atmosphere pervades this short novel on the subject of couples: "In Africa, the first thing you learn is to live life as it comes."

❽ Grand Socco (Place du 9 Avril 1947)

The link between the medina and Ville Nouvelle, Place du Grand Socco was renamed Place du 9 Avril 1947 in memory of the speech that Mohammed V made in support of independence. The square comes to life in the evenings, when vendors spread out their wares on the ground – extensive displays of a huge variety of second-hand goods. A colourful market, where peasant women in striped *foutas* and wide-brimmed straw hats come to sell fruit and fowl, takes place above the square, near the Anglican Church of St Andrew, at the far end of Rue d'Angleterre.

The minaret of the **Mosque of Sidi Bou Abib** (1917), decorated with polychrome tiles, overlooks the square from the southwest. Near Bab Fahs, a double gateway leading into the medina, are the grounds of the Mendoubia. This was the residence of the *mendoub* when Tangier was under international administration (1923–56).

❾ Anglican Church of St Andrew

Rue d'Angleterre. **Open** 9:30am–12:30pm & 2:30–6pm. Keys obtainable from the caretaker. 🕆 11am Sun.

Built on land that Moulay Hassan donated to fulfil the needs of an increasingly large British population in Tangier,

Church of St Andrew, with a belltower in the shape of a minaret

the church of St Andrew was completed in 1894. The interior is a curious mixture of styles, in which the Moorish style predominates.

The lobed arch at the entrance to the choir, and the ceiling above the altar, which is decorated with a quotation from the Gospel in Arabic, are of particular interest. The belltower, in the shape of a minaret, overlooks the cemetery. Among those buried here are Walter Harris, a journalist and correspondent for *The Times*, and Sir Harry McLean, a military adviser to the sultans.

A plaque at the west end of the church commemorates Emily Kean: she came to Tangier in the 19th century, married the Cherif of Ouezzane and devoted her life to the welfare of the people of northern Morocco.

❿ Galerie d'Art Contemporain Mohammed Drissi

Rue d'Angleterre.
ℹ️ (0539) 93 60 73. **Open** 9am–6pm Tue–Sun. 🎨

This contemporary art gallery, named in homage to the Moroccan artist Mohammed Drissi (1946–2003), hosts regular exhibitions by Moroccan and international artists.

⓫ Fondouk Chejra

Rue de la Liberté. Accessible via the steps below the level of the Hôtel el-Minzah. ℹ️ (0539) 94 80 50.

The buzzing atmosphere in Fondouk Chejra, known as the Poor People's Souk or Weavers' Souk, is that of an Oriental bazaar. Above the shops on the ground floor, the rooms that were once used by travellers and passing tradesmen have been converted into weavers' workshops, where the white and red fabric that is typical of the Rif is produced. The original layout of the former *fondouk*, or caravanserai, is difficult to make out, the central courtyard having been much altered.

⓬ Rue de la Liberté

This street runs from Place du 9 Avril 1947 (or Grand Socco) to Ville Nouvelle. It was formerly known as Rue de Fès, then as Rue du Statut, its current name dating from the beginning of Moroccan independence. The French Consulate, which is set in the centre of a pleasant and attractive park, dates from 1929; the classical arcade of the façade is offset by decoration in the Moorish style.

In the **Galerie Delacroix**, housed in the French Cultural Institute next door, temporary exhibitions are organized by the Institut Français. The Hôtel el-Minzah, dating from 1930, is one of the most illustrious hotels in Morocco, with an Andalusian-style courtyard and gardens, comfortable lounges

The Grand Socco, also known as Place du 9 Avril 1947

◀ Fishing harbour with the medina in the background

The dilapidated Art Deco façade of the Gran Teatro Cervantes

and bars. Winston Churchill, Paul and Jane Bowles, Jean Genet and Hollywood stars from Rita Hayworth to Errol Flynn stayed in this magical place.

🏛 Galerie Delacroix

86 Rue de la Liberté. **Tel** (0539) 93 21 34. **Open** 11am–1pm, 4–8pm Tue–Sun.

⑬ Place de France & Place de Faro

Place de France is a major meeting place for the inhabitants of Tangier. The **Café de Paris**, which opened in 1920, was the first establishment to open outside the medina. Among its regular customers were Paul Bowles, Tennessee Williams and Jean Genet, as well as foreign diplomats. The café has remained a hub of city life.

Very near Place de France, on Avenue Pasteur, is Place de Faro (named after the Portuguese town twinned with Tangier in 1984), complete with cannons. It is one of the few places to have escaped the attentions of the developers. It offers a view of the medina and of ferry traffic in the harbour and the strait.

⑭ Avenue Pasteur

Together with Avenue Mohammed V, which extends eastwards from it, Avenue Pasteur is Ville Nouvelle's main artery and its economic centre. In the evening, the avenue is

given over to the Spanish custom of the *paseo*, a leisurely evening stroll. The Moroccan tourist office, at No. 29, occupies the first building to be constructed on the avenue, while the villa at No. 27 houses the **Great Synagogue**. The **Librairie des Colonnes**, the bookshop at No. 54, has lost some of its former prestige and importance. All the writers in Tangier, whether visitors or residents, regularly patronized this bookshop, which stocks most available books on Tangier. Lectures and signing sessions are still held here.

The **Gran Teatro Cervantes** (accessible from Avenue Pasteur, which is reached along Rue du Prince Moulay Abdallah and via steps continuing from it) opened in 1913. One of North Africa's major theatres, it was here that the greatest singers and dancers of the age

performed. The building, with an Art Deco façade, is in a bad state of repair. Restoration has been delayed by disputes between the city and the Spanish state, which had undertaken to finance its upkeep.

✪ Great Synagogue

27 Avenue Pasteur.

📖 Librairie des Colonnes

54 Avenue Pasteur.

⑮ Ancien Palais du Mendoub

Avenue Mohammed Tazi (in the northwest of Ville Nouvelle). **Closed** to the public.

The Mendoub was the sultan's representative during the international administration of Tangier. While his main residence was the Mendoubia, near the Grand Socco, this palace, built in 1929, was used mostly for receptions. It was acquired in 1970 by Malcolm Forbes (1919–90), the American multimillionaire who founded *Fortune* magazine. It became a luxury residence where Forbes threw lavish parties and where such international stars as Elizabeth Taylor were guests. The house also contained a display of Forbes' 120,000 piece collection of toy soldiers. The Palace is now state-owned and will be used as a residence for important visitors from abroad.

The elegant Ancien Palais du Mendoub

For hotels and restaurants see pp306–313 and pp320–31

⑯ Café Hafa

Rue Mohammed Tazi (in a narrow street opposite the football stadium, leading towards the sea).

The café opened in 1921, and neither the furniture nor the décor seem to have changed since then. Assorted tables and rush matting are laid out on terraces rising in tiers from the edge of the cliff, offering a breathtaking view of the strait. Writers and singers, from Paul Bowles to William Burroughs and from the Beatles to the Rolling Stones, have come here, seeking out Tangier's young generation or the company of local fishermen. People come here to smoke and drink mint tea, which is probably brewed exactly as it was in 1921.

⑰ Quartier du Marshan

Rue Mohammed Tazi, Rue Assad Ibn Farrat, Avenue Hassan II (western part of the kasbah).

Located west of the kasbah, the Quartier du Marshan was developed from the late 19th to the early 20th century. Being removed from the bustle of the medina and of Ville Nouvelle, it was an attractive

residential location, and high officals and the *shorfa* of Ouezzane built their palaces and grand villas here in the late 19th century. The Italian Consulate (Rue Assad Ibn Farrat), rebuilt in 1916 and with walls covered in *zellij* tilework, housed Garibaldi in 1849–50. The former palace of the sultan Moulay Hafid, in Moorish style, became the Palais des Institutions Italiennes in 1926. On the edge of the strait, the

An elegant villa in the Quartier du Marshan

Beaches Around Tangier

The Bay of Tangier, a grand crescent that is sometimes likened to the Baie des Anges in Nice or to Copacabana in Rio de Janeiro, stretches for almost 4 km (2.5 miles) from the edge of the port round to the residential districts and resort areas and to the first spurs of land that mark its eastern extremity. The proximity of the city and the rivers that flow into it unfortunately make this the most polluted beach in Morocco. For swimming and sunbathing, it is better to make for the beaches between Cap Spartel and the Grottes d'Hercule and beyond, or for the coves of Cap Malabata, or, further east, the beaches at Sidi Khankroucht and Ksar es-Seghir.

③ **The Bay of Tangier** forms a splendid and extensive sweep, but is unfortunately very polluted.

② **Between Tangier** and Cap Spartel, small coves are reachable on foot from the Perdicaris Belvedere. The walk down passes through mimosa and woods of umbrella pine.

① **Between Cap Spartel** and the Grottes d'Hercule are many attractive little bays separated by rocky outcrops.

Cap Spartel

Grottes d'Hercule •

Asilah ←

S701

S702

P2

0 km   2
0 miles   2

Marshan ends at the limits of Hafa, a poorer residential district with a great deal of local colour, up on the sea cliff.

⑱ Colline du Charf

In the southeast of the city.

A hill rising to a height of about 100 m (328 ft), the Colline du Charf commands the most impressive and most complete view of Tangier.

The panorama stretches from Cap Malabata in the east to La Montagne, which rises over the old town to the west. From here the beach appears as a strip lining the bay, and the white, densely packed medina seems to cling to the hillside as it slopes down towards the port, while the high-rise blocks of Ville Nouvelle stand along its wide avenues. Poorer residential districts stretch out southwards:

in among them, at the foot of the hill, can be seen Plaza Toro, whose bullrings are now used for public functions. Further north is the Syrian Mosque, with a style of minaret rarely seen in the Maghreb.

The mosque-like building on the hill was a café during Tangier's international period. A favourite form of relaxation for the inhabitants of Tangier is to stroll on the hill or sit and gaze out over the strait.

⑲ Bay of Tangier

Between the port and Cap Malabata, the bay forms a beach-lined semicircle. Avenue d'Espagne, which runs along the bay, is lined with hotels, from small guesthouses to large modern establishments. Dotted with the blues, reds and whites of the boats and the ochre,

Tangier's fishing harbour, at the foot of the medina

green and orange of the nets, the small fishing harbour is a colourful sight, and the freshly caught fish that is offered makes a delicious meal.

It was on Avenue d'Espagne that Bernardo Bertolucci shot scenes for his 1990 film *The Sheltering Sky*. Many literary works, by William Burroughs and others, took shape in the small guesthouses here. The French philosopher Michel Foucault would stay at the Hôtel Cecil, while Samuel Beckett preferred the Solazur.

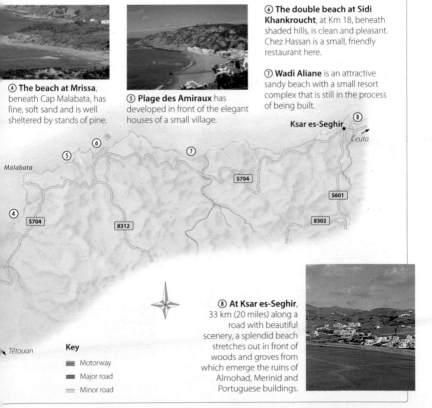

④ **The beach at Mrissa**, beneath Cap Malabata, has fine, soft sand and is well sheltered by stands of pine.

⑤ **Plage des Amiraux** has developed in front of the elegant houses of a small village.

⑥ **The double beach at Sidi Khankroucht**, at Km 18, beneath shaded hills, is clean and pleasant. Chez Hassan is a small, friendly restaurant here.

⑦ **Wadi Aliane** is an attractive sandy beach with a small resort complex that is still in the process of being built.

Ksar es-Seghir

Ceuta

⑧

Malabata

S704

S601

S704

8312

8302

Tétouan

⑧ **At Ksar es-Seghir**, 33 km (20 miles) along a road with beautiful scenery, a splendid beach stretches out in front of woods and groves from which emerge the ruins of Almohad, Merinid and Portuguese buildings.

Key

▬ Motorway

▬ Major road

▭ Minor road

MEDITERRANEAN COAST & THE RIF

The great mountainous crescent of the Rif forms a natural barrier across northern Morocco. Its proud Berber-speaking inhabitants haughtily guard their traditions and independence, and historically the Rif has always resisted conquest. The Rif, today, is friendly and welcoming, with sandy Mediterranean coves and beaches, many of them with a backdrop of majestic cliffs.

Inaccessible and intricately partitioned, the Rif reaches a height of 2,452 m (8,047 ft) at Jbel Tidirhin, in the central part of the mountain range, then tails away eastwards towards the Moulouya estuary and the Algerian border. The northwestern Rif is a region of low mountains and hills dotted with villages, while the central part consists of lofty summits and enclosed valleys. To the east, what is regarded as the real Rif gently slopes away.

All Riffians fiercely defend their cultural identity. The Spanish, to whom the region fell when Morocco was divided under the French Protectorate, came face to face with this intransigence during the uprisings of 1921–6 and were soundly defeated at Anoual in 1921 *(see p60)*. The history of the Rif and its coastline is closely linked to that of Spain. For Morocco, the Mediterranean became a bridgehead for the conquest of Spain. From the 15th century, the Portuguese occupation, followed by that of the Spanish, cut Morocco off from the Mediterranean and accelerated its decline. Spain still maintains a foothold in Ceuta and Melilla, and on a few rocky islets. Morocco has worked for closer cooperation with Spain and Europe to tackle problems of illegal trafficking and emigration here. The increase of tourism in Tangier and Ceuta has resulted in dramatic changes to the area, including a modern port and airport.

The fishing harbour at Al-Hoceima

◀ A brightly painted wooden door in the town of Chefchaouen

Exploring the Mediterranean Coast & the Rif

Stretching from the land of the Jebala in the west to Morocco's eastern frontier, the Rif presents a great variety of landscapes. Here are high, steep valleys where almond trees blossom and oleanders flower, mountain roads that command wild and magnificent vistas, forests of cedar, fir and oak, and villages and isolated houses with pitched tin roofs. Between Ceuta and Cabo Negro, the coast is punctuated by sweeping beaches of golden sand and, from Wadi Laou to Al-Hoceima and Saïdia, by more secluded bays beneath rocky cliffs. The medinas of Tetouan and Chefchaouen are among the most picturesque in Morocco.

Carpets for sale in the medina in Oujda

Key

▬▬ Motorway

━━ Major road

═══ Minor road

--- Track

⎼⎼⎼ Railway

▬▬ International border

△ Summit

Sights at a Glance

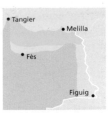

Area shown by map below

Getting Around

Air links to the region arrive in Tangier, Al-Hoceima, Melilla and Oujda. Once there, it is better to hire a car rather than use *grands taxis*. Having your own means of transport gives you the freedom to stop off at secluded beaches and seek out the high valleys. In this mountainous environment, the roads are sometimes in a bad state of repair, and there are often roadworks, particularly along the arterial routes.

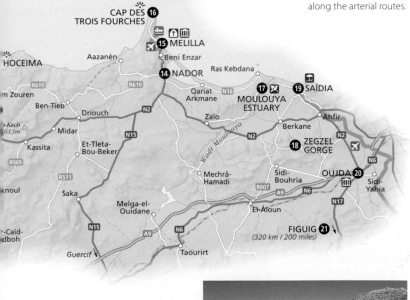

Snow-capped peaks in the Rif

For keys to symbols *see back flap*

❶ Cap Spartel

Road Map D1. 14 km (9 miles) west of Tangier.

From Tangier, the road leading to Cap Spartel runs through La Montagne, the city's western suburb, which is bathed in the perfume of eucalyptus and mimosa. Long walls surround the residences of Moroccan, Kuwaiti and Saudi kings and princes and the luxury villas dating from the golden age of Tangier's international period. Beyond stretch forests of holm-oak, cork oak, umbrella pine, mastic-tree, broom and heather, which all flourish here, watered by the highest rainfall in Morocco.

At the cape, the most northwesterly point of Africa, is the promontory known in antiquity as Cape Ampelusium or Cape of the Vines, and a lighthouse dating from 1865. From beneath the lighthouse, there is a breathtaking view of the ocean where the Mediterranean and Atlantic meet, and on clear days you can see the strait and coast of Spain from Cape Trafalgar to the Rock of Gibraltar.

The lighthouse at Cap Spartel, where sea and ocean meet

❷ Grottes d'Hercule

Road Map D1. 5 km (3 miles) southwest of Cap Spartel.

At the place known as Achakar, the sea has carved impressive caves out of the cliff. The people who, from prehistoric times, came to these caves knapped stones here and quarried millstones for use in oil presses. The opening to the caves, facing onto the sea, is a cleft shaped like a reversed map of Africa.

According to legend, Hercules slept here before performing one of his 12 labours – picking the golden apples in the Garden of the Hesperides. The location of the legendary garden belonging to these nymphs of darkness and guarded by the dragon with 100 heads is said to be further south, near Lixus.

The best time to visit the caves is in the late afternoon, after which the light of the setting sun can be enjoyed from the cafés nearby. Further south, beneath the level of the caves, are the **Ruins of Cotta** (1st century BC to 3rd century AD). With vats for salting fish, making *garum* and producing purple dye, this was one of the largest industrial centres of the Punic-Mauretanian period.

The Grottes d'Hercule, like a reversed map of Africa

The unfinished medieval "castle" at Cap Malabata

❸ Cap Malabata

Road Map D1. 12 km (7.5 miles) east of Tangier.

The route out of Tangier skirts an area of large tourist hotels and continues eastwards round the curve of the bay. Soon after a tiny estuary, at the edge of the road, are the remains of a 16th-century fortress, from which Moroccan soldiers could watch and attack the Portuguese, Spanish and English occupiers of Tangier. Nearby, white crenellated walls surround the lush and extensive grounds of the **Villa Harris**. It was once the residence of Walter Harris (1866–1953), a flamboyant journalist and diplomatic correspondent for *The Times*. He chronicled life in Tangier for many years from 1892.

The road ascending the hills passes through magnificent pine forests and by many small coves where there are cafés which, like Café Ryad, have an old-world charm. Just before the cape, a strange building appears. Conceived in the medieval style, it was the work of a whimsical Italian, who left it unfinished in the 1930s.

The view from Cap Malabata is stunning, especially in the morning, looking westwards over the city and suburbs of Tangier and across to the Straits of Gibraltar, and eastwards to Jbel Moussa, which rises over Ceuta.

❹ Ksar es-Seghir

Road Map D1. 33 km (20 miles) east of Tangier. 🚹 8,800. 🚌 Sat.

A town with a small fishing harbour and a fine beach, Ksar es-Seghir faces the Spanish town of Tarifa across the Straits of Gibraltar. The souk that takes place here on Saturdays is filled with women of the Rif, conspicuous in their white, red-striped *foutas*.

Since the 17th century, forts have stood on this well-sheltered spot on an estuary, and it was from here that Moroccan troops set sail for Spain. The Almohads made it an important centre of shipbuilding and skilled crafts. The remains of buildings in a small forest are those of a town built by the Merinids in the 14th century. The circular walls that surround it are unusual, but were obviously preferred to the customary square plan by the town's Muslim builders; the gateway facing the sea is the best-preserved. The Portuguese, who held the town from 1458 to 1549, strengthened it with new fortifications that reached to the sea.

Ksar es-Seghir, an attractive coastal town

❺ Ceuta

Road Map D1. 63 km (39 miles) east of Tangier. 🚹 75,000. 🅹 Calle Edrissis, Edif Baluarte de los Mallorquines; 00 34 856 20 05 60.

Standing on a narrow isthmus between Monte Hacho and the mainland, Ceuta occupies a favourable location opposite Gibraltar. The Rock of Gibraltar and Monte Hacho are the two legendary Pillars of Hercules.

Ceuta, like an amphitheatre on the isthmus linking it to the mainland

From the 12th century onwards, the town was visited by traders from Genoa, Pisa, Marseilles and Catalonia. In 1415, Ceuta became a Portuguese enclave, then passed to Spain in 1578. Today, it is an important garrison town. Its livelihood depends mainly on the tax-free trade that its status as a free port allows. Ceuta (like Melilla) is a self-governing town within the Spanish state. Morocco views the Spanish presence as anachronistic and claims sovereignty.

The 12-km (7.5-mile) circuit of Monte Hacho (part of it accessible by road) affords views over the town, the mountains and coast of the Rif and Gibraltar, especially from the lighthouse at Punto Almina. The Castillo del Desnarigado, a fortress that is now a military museum, encloses the Ermita de San Antonio. This chapel draws a large pilgrimage on 13 June each year.

The **Plaza de Africa** is, in architectural terms, the centre of the town, where the main public buildings are concentrated. The cathedral, whose present appearance dates from the 18th century, stands on the site of a Grand Mosque. Religious paintings and objects are displayed in its museum.

Nuestra Señora de Africa (the Church of Our Lady of Africa) was built in the early 18th century, also on the site of a mosque, in an arresting Baroque style. On the high altar stands a statue of the Virgin, patroness of Ceuta, who is believed to have saved the town from an epidemic of plague in the 16th century. The cathedral treasury contains some fine paintings, banners and 17th-century illuminated books.

The **Ayuntamiento** (town hall), built in 1929, is of interest to visitors for the paintings that it contains by Mariano Bertuchi, an artist active during the colonial period.

The **Museo Municipal El Revellin** (Archaeological Museum) is laid out above underground passages dug in the 16th and 17th centuries to supply the town with water. The displays include Neolithic, Carthaginian and Roman pottery, including amphorae, as well as coins and armour.

Through maps, photographs and visual displays, the **Museo de la Legión** documents the activities of the Spanish Foreign Legion and its efforts in 1921–6 to subdue the Rif uprising and the rebel leader Abdel Krim. The legion, formed in 1920, suffered serious losses during this war.

🏛 **Museo Municipal El Revellin**
On the corner of Paseo de Revellín and Calle Ingenieros. **Tel** 00 34 956 51 73 98. **Open** 11am–2pm, 5–9pm Tue–Sat & 11am–2pm public hols. 📷

🏛 **Museo de la Legión**
Paseo de Colón. **Open** 9am–5pm Tue–Sat & Mon. **Closed** Sun. 📷

❻ Tetouan

In the words of Arab poets, Tetouan is a white dove, "the sister of Fès", "the little Jerusalem" or "the daughter of Granada". The town, built partly on the slopes of Jbel Dersa, was inhabited by Jewish refugees from Granada in the 15th century, then by Moors from Andalusia in the 17th century. The town's Andalusian heritage can be seen in its medina, and also in its culinary traditions, as well as in its music and in the craft of embroidery. From the 15th to the 18th centuries, Tetouan was a lively centre of privateering, then of thriving trade with Europe, becoming a sort of city-state comparable to Florence or to Venice at the time of the doges. In the 18th century, the town was the diplomatic capital of Morocco. The Spanish, who held it from 1860 to 1862, made it their capital during the Protectorate, building a new town on the west side of the old Andalusian medina.

The church on Place Moulay el-Mehdi, built in 1926

Place Hassan II, a link between Ville Nouvelle and the medina

🏛 Ville Nouvelle

Place Moulay el-Mehdi and Boulevard Mohammed V.

It is on Place Moulay el-Mehdi – which is sometimes still referred to by the town's inhabitants as Place Primo (after the Spanish politician José Primo de Rivera) – that the Spanish colonial architecture of Ville Nouvelle (New Town) is at its most eloquent. With a main post office, bank and church (1926), the square looks like any other central town square in Spain. Elegant homes with doors, windows and balconies with Moorish-style ornamentation can be seen on Boulevard Mohammed V, the town's principal thoroughfare.

Place Hassan II links Ville Nouvelle and the medina. Modern tiling has replaced the old mosaic decoration of the royal palace that stands on the side of the square nearest the medina. Both the boulevard and the square come to life in the evenings with the *paseo* (promenade), a Spanish custom that is more deeply ingrained in Tetouan than elsewhere in Morocco.

🏛 Musée Archéologique

Boulevard El-Jazaïr, near Place El-Jala.
Open Mon–Fri pm only. 🖼

The rooms of the Archaeological Museum contain objects dating from the Roman period that were discovered at Volubilis, Lixus and Thamuda, a Roman site on the outskirts of present-day Tetouan (on the road to Chefchaouen). Mosaics, including a depiction of the Three Graces of classical mythology, as well as pottery, coins, bronzes and other pieces, are displayed. The most interesting exhibits – such as ancient inscriptions, mosaic floors and Muslim funerary stelae with the Star of David – are laid out in the garden.

🏛 Medina

Entry through Place Hassan II, then via Rue Ahmed Torres to the southeast.

Tetouan's medina, now a World Heritage Site, is the most strongly Andalusian of all Moroccan medinas. Emigrants from Spain who arrived in the 15th and 17th centuries implanted their architectural traditions here, including a taste for wrought-iron decoration and a liking for doors with elaborate metal fittings.

The aroma of spices, freshly sawn wood and *kesra* (bread) fills the medina's narrow streets, squares and souks, which bustle with carpenters, slipper-makers, drapers, tanners and sellers of second-hand goods. Rue El-Mokadem (between Place Souk el-Fouqui and Place Gharsa el-Kebira) is the street

Kesra (bread) on sale in the El-Fouqui Souk

The medina, on the slopes of Jbel Dersa

VISITORS' CHECKLIST

Practical Information
Road Map D1. 🏛 310,000.
ℹ️ 30 Bld Mohammed V; (0539)
96 19 15. 🔲 Wed, Fri, Sun by
Place Moulay-el-Medhi.

Transport
✈️ 5 km (3 miles). 🚌 Tnine-Sidi-
Lyamani. 🚌

most densely packed with shops, but also one of the most noteworthy for its impressive white buildings and its paving. Sellers of fabrics and pottery fill the small shady square where the El-Houts Souk takes place. It leads to the former mellah, Tetouan's Jewish quarter, where the balconied houses have large windows, wrought-iron gates and arcaded façades.

🏛 Musée d'Art Marocain
Avenue Hassan Ier and Rue Sqala, near Bab Oqla. **Tel** (0539) 97 27 21.
Open 9am–6pm Wed–Mon (times vary).

Occupying a bastion built in 1828, the museum is laid out in an Andalusian palace with a garden, a fountain clad in *zellij* tilework, and red-tiled awnings, typical of buildings in Tetouan. The furniture, the crafted pieces, the costumes and musical instruments illustrate the town's traditions. Tetouani rooms, with marriage scenes (such as putting together the trousseau and presenting the bride), have also been convincingly re-created.

The Craft School, near the museum, opposite Bab Oqla, occupies a residence built in 1928 in Moorish style. Specializing in local traditions, the school teaches leatherwork, pottery, mosaic-making, carpet-weaving and decorative plasterwork. The students' work is displayed in a domed exhibition hall.

Detail of a façade on Boulevard Mohammed V

Tetouan's Jews

A large Jewish community, expelled from Spain at the end of the Christian Reconquest, settled in Tetouan, thrived here and reached its height in the 16th century. Like the many Muslims who had also arrived from Spain, these Jews cherished the memory of Andalusia as a lost paradise. On feast days, they would listen to Andalusian music and don Andalusian costume and jewellery.

Exploiting their contacts in Gibraltar, Antwerp, Amsterdam and London, Tetouan's Jews played a central role in the economic life of the town and through them it became an important trade link with the West. At the beginning of the 19th century, subjected to violence and heavily taxed, the Jews repaired to a quarter of their own, the *judería*. Marginalized in professional and social life, many Jews left to settle in Melilla, Gibraltar or Iran, and also in Latin America. Despite an improvement in their situation under Spanish rule, the Jewish community – which still counted some 3,000 people in 1960 – continued to shrink progressively after independence, many leaving for Israel. By the early 1990s, there were no more than 200 Jews remaining in Tetouan.

Jewish Feast Day in Tetouan, painting by Alfred Dehodencq (1822–82)

❼ Chefchaouen

The white town of Chefchaouen nestles in the hollow of the two mountains – ech-Chaoua (The Horns) – from which it takes its name. Steep narrow streets with white and indigo limewashed buildings, small squares, ornate fountains and houses with elaborately decorated doorways and red tile roofs make this a delightful town. It was founded in 1471 by Idrissid *shorfa*, descendants of the Prophet Mohammed, as a stronghold in the fight against the Portuguese. Chefchaouen, esteemed as a holy town, has eight mosques and several *zaouias* and *marabouts*.

Courtyard of the kasbah, around which the museum is laid out

A café on Place Uta el-Hammam, in the heart of the town

🏛 Place Uta el-Hammam

The square is the heart of the old town and the focal point on which all the streets of the medina converge. It is lined with trees, and paved with stones and pebbles, and in the centre stands a four-sided fountain decorated with arches and crowned by a pavilion of green tiles. With shops and cafés, this is an ideal place for a relaxed stroll.

🄲 Grand Mosque

Place Uta el-Hammam. **Closed** to non-Muslims.

The Grand Mosque was founded probably in the 16th century and has been re-modelled several times since.

The *fondouk*, with rooms round the courtyard

The later minaret, which dates from the 17th century, is distinctive in being octagonal. It is decorated with three tiers of plain and lobed arches on a painted ochre background. The uppermost tier is decorated with *zellij* tilework.

🏛 Fondouk

Corner of Place Uta el-Hammam and Rue Al-Andalus.

The *fondouk* still serves the purpose for which it was originally built. About 50 rooms, arranged around the courtyard, still accommodate travellers and passing traders.

It is a building of strikingly simple design, with a gallery of semicircular arches lining the pebble-paved courtyard. The only contrast to this simplicity is provided by the main entrance; the doorway is surmounted by an awning and framed by a broken horseshoe arch surrounded by interlacing arches.

🏛 Kasbah and Museum

West corner of Place Uta el-Hammam. **Open** 9am–6pm Wed–Mon (till 1pm Fri). **Closed** Tue & Fri pm. 📷

The kasbah, with crenellated walls of red beaten earth and ten bastions, is the essential heart of the town. The fortress was begun in the 15th century by Moulay Ali ben Rachid, and was completed by Moulay Ismaïl in the 17th century, as was the residence within. The kasbah's plan and architectural style show Andalusian influence. A pleasant garden with fountains is laid out within, from where there is a good view of the walls and the rampart walk. The **Musée Ethnographique** (Ethnographic Museum) occupies the residence built in the garden. This is a traditional Moroccan house with a courtyard and gallery on the first floor. The museum contains displays of pottery, armour, embroidery, costume, musical instruments, palanquins and painted wooden chests.

🏛 Medina

A small street running between the kasbah and the Grand Mosque leads to the Souïka district. This is the oldest district of Chefchaouen, and the town's finest houses, with carved and decorated doors, are found here. The name *souïka*, meaning "little market", comes from the district's *kissaria*, where there are many small shops along its narrow streets.

The medina contains more than 100 weavers' workshops.

Narrow street with houses painted white and blue

🏠 Quartier Al-Andalus

This district is reached from the northwestern corner of Place Uta el-Hammam, leaving the *fondouk* on the left. The Quartier Al-Andalus received the second wave of immigrants – Muslims and Jews expelled from Spain – who arrived in 1492, after the fall of Granada.

Here, the houses, painted white, green or blue, have decorated doors and wrought-iron railings at some of their windows. They follow the steep gradient of the terrain, which makes for many exterior stairways and entrances at various levels.

🏚 Ras el-Ma and the Mills

The steep streets of Al-Andalus leading up towards the mountain pass through Bab Onsar, the town's northeast gateway, which has been restored and renovated.

VISITORS' CHECKLIST

Practical Information
Road Map D1.
🗺 45,000. ℹ (0539) 96 19 15/16. 🎪 Moussem of Sidi Allal el-Hadj (9 Aug). 🛒 Mon & Thu.

Transport
🚌

Beyond is the spring of Ras el-Ma, which is now enclosed by a building. The presence of this underground spring was the reason why the town was established here. It accounts for the town's lush gardens, and the water also powers the mills. Steps leading towards the metalled road run alongside the wash-houses, then the mills, whose origins go back to the arrival of the Andalusian refugees.

The route then leads to the bridge across Wadi Laou, which is built in the form of a semicircular arch with bevelled buttresses. With its cascades, wash-houses and cafés, this is one of the most pleasant quarters of Chefchaouen.

Indeed, Chefchaouen is famous for the woollen *jellabas* that are woven here, as well as for the red and white striped fabrics worn by the women of the Jebala, a tribe of the mountainous western Rif. One such weaver's workshop is located in Rue Ben Dibane, identifiable by an exterior stairway.

One of the most distinctive fountains in Chefchaouen is Aïn Souika, set in a recess in the district's main street. Covered by a porch, it has a semicircular basin and interlaced lobed arches.

Chefchaouen Town Centre

① Place Uta el-Hammam
② Grand Mosque
③ Fondouk
④ Kasbah and Museum
⑤ Medina
⑥ Quartier Al-Andalus

For keys to symbols *see back flap*

A mantle of olive trees covering the hills near Ouezzane

❽ Ouezzane

Road Map D2. 60 km (37 miles) south of Chefchaouen. 🏙 70,000. 🚌 🚍 Thu.

A large market town, Ouezzane spreads out over the slopes of Jbel Bou Hillal, in a landscape of extensive olive groves and plantations of fig trees fed by abundant springs. It is important for its textiles (*jellabas* and carpets) and olive oil.

In the 15th century, the town, which was populated by Andalusians, also counted many Jews among its inhabitants. It began to prosper in the 18th and 19th centuries under the influence of the Idrissid *shorfa*. In 1727, a descendant of Idriss II established the religious brother-hood of the Taïbia, whose influence spread throughout Morocco, Algeria and Tunisia. In the 19th century, the *shorfa* played a prominent religious and political role in Morocco. The sherif of Ouezzane's policy of openness also assisted trade relations with France. The Zaouia (or Green Mosque) and, with its *zellij*-covered minaret, the Mosque of Moulay Abdallah Cherif, founder of the Taïbia brotherhood, attract many pilgrims.

Jews also come to **Asjen**, 8 km (5 miles) west of the town, to venerate the tomb of Rabbi Abraham ben Diouanne, who died in about 1780. The pilgrimage that takes place 33 days after Easter is an occasion when Morocco's Jewish community acknowledges its allegiance to the king.

❾ The Rif

See pp158–9.

❿ Ketama

Road Map D-E1. 107 km (66 miles) east of Chefchaouen on the N2, the "Route des Crêtes" (Mountain Crests Road). 🚍 Wed.

Located in the heart of a forest, Ketama used to be a popular summer and winter resort but the presence and perseverance of illegal kif and hashish salesmen will make most visitors move on.

Leaving the town, the road leading eastward reveals the slopes of Jbel Tidirhin (or Tidiquin), at 2,448 m (8,034 ft) the highest peak in the Rif. In the valleys, the houses have pitched roofs, with a covering of planks and corrugated metal, the modern substitute for thatch. In some villages, such as Taghzoute, the craft of leather embroidery is very much alive.

View of the Peñon de Velez de la Gomera

⓫ El-Jebha

Road Map D1. 137 km (85 miles) east of Tetouan along the coast road N16; 73 km (45 miles) from Ketama on the N2 then the P4115. 🚍 Tue.

The small fishing town of El-Jebha nestles at the end of Fishermen's Point. Its one-storey, cube-like houses, covered in white roughcast, give it a typically Mediterranean air. On the right of the harbour, where *lamparo* boats are moored, is Crayfish Cove, which is ideal for underwater fishing. On the left, a soft sandy beach stretches away towards the west.

⓬ Torres de Alcalá

Road Map E1. 144 km (89 miles) from Chefchaouen and 72 km (45 miles) from Ketama on the N2 then the P5205.

Located on the estuary of Wadi Bou Frah, the fishing village of Torres de Alcalá lies at the foot of a peak crowned by the ruins of a Spanish fortress. About 5 km (3 miles) further east is **Peñon de Velez de la Gomera**, a tiny island attached to the mainland by a narrow spit of sand. Held by the Spanish from 1508 to 1522, it later became a hide-out for pirates and privateers. A convict station under the

Protectorate, it is still under Spanish sovereignty.

Some 4 km (2.5 miles) west of Velez is **Kalah Iris**, a cove that is an oasis of calm outside the summer season.

⑬ Al-Hoceima

Road Map E1. ⚐ 65,000. ✈ 17 km (10 miles). ➡ ℹ Zankat Al Bahia; (0539) 98 11 85. ⚑ Festival late Jul–early Aug. ⚑ Tue.

This ancient fishing and trading port, seat of the emirate of Nokour during the Middle Ages, was long the object of dispute between European traders. The modern town was founded by General Sanjurjo in 1926, at the place where the Spanish garrison landed, and was known initially as Villa Sanjurjo.

The town's location is one of the most beautiful along Morocco's Mediterranean coast. Whitewashed houses line the bay – an almost perfect semicircle between two hilly promontories. The coastline to the east, opposite the **Peñon de Alhucemas**, a small island held by Spain, commands

The Peñon de Alhucemas off the Moroccan Coast at Al-Hoceima

the most impressive view of the bay.

A few dozen trawlers are usually moored in the harbour; in the evenings their *lamparos* are lit up ready for a night's fishing. **Plage Quemado** stretches out in front of the town. This beach is better than others near Al-Hoceima, such as that at **Asfiha**, in the direction of Ajdir, opposite the small island known locally as Nokour's Rock.

The souk at **Im Zouren**, 17 km (10 miles) east on the

road to Nador, is unusual: for the first few hours in the day, only women may go there. Both **Im Zouren** and **Beni Bou Ayach**, large market towns on the road out of Al-Hoceima, have a slightly unreal appearance, created by largely empty residential blocks painted in ochres, blues, greens and pinks. The towns come to life for only a few weeks of the year, when emigrant workers based in Germany and Holland return.

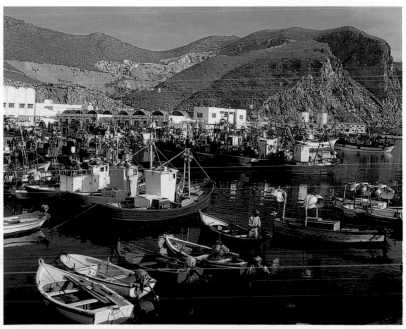

Trawlers and fishing boats moored in the harbour at Al-Hoceima, with warehouses in the background

❾ The Rif

This region is well known for its atmospheric and beautiful medinas but, covering an area of some 30,000 sq km (11,580 sq miles), it offers much else besides. Among its natural wonders are high mountains, capes, gorges and rock formations. The country souks held weekly in Riffian towns and villages provide the opportunity to come into contact with local people as they go about their daily business. In July, the *moussem* of Jbel Alam, one of Morocco's best-known pilgrimages, takes place: the object is the tomb of Moulay Abdesselam ben Mchich, a highly venerated Sufi mystic who died in 1228. In the environs of Chefchaouen, ramblers and those with four-wheel-drive vehicles can visit one of the rare collective granaries of the western Rif at Akrar d'El-Kelaa, and the nature reserve at Talassemtane, where the fir forests are protected.

Souk at Wadi Laou
The Saturday souk, where women in *foutas* sell their hand-made pottery goods, is the largest and most colourful in the Rif.

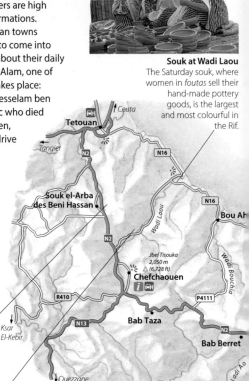

The Jebala District
In a landscape of hills and middle-altitude mountains, the villages of the Jebala tribe have taken root where springs cascade from the hillside, surrounded by olive groves and smaller cereal plantations.

Gorge of Wadi Laou
Running between sheer high cliffs and below precariously perched villages, the gorge offers stunningly beautiful sights.

Mountain Crests Road
This road commands breathtaking views of the mountains, villages and isolated houses of the Rif, as well as of the cultivated terraces, olive groves and forests of holm-oak that typify the region.

Riffian Coastline

East of the small village of Torres de Alcalá there are some attractive and unspoilt coves and bays, including Kalah Iris, a haven of calm and solitude.

Al-Hoceima

The coastal town of Al-Hoceima, which nestles around the bay, is a modest resort that is quiet outside the tourist season. The busy harbour has many restaurants.

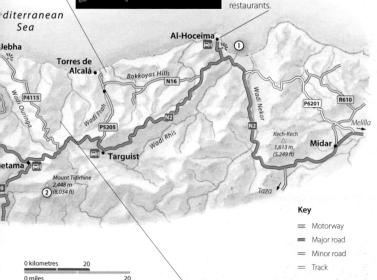

diterranean Sea

Jebha

Torres de Alcalá

Bokkoyas Hills
N16

Wadi Ouringa
P4115

Wadi Frah

P5205

Wadi Rhis

N2

Targuist

etama

Mount Tidirhine
2,448 m
② (8,034 ft)

Al-Hoceima
①

Wadi Nekor

N2

Kech-Kech
△
1,613 m
(5,249 ft)

P6201 R610

Melilla

Midar

Taza

Key

= Motorway
━ Major road
= Minor road
= Track

0 kilometres   20
0 miles   20

KEY

① **Al-Hoceima Bay**, into which flow the Wadi Nekor and Wadi Rhis, is lined by a pleasant, peaceful beach.

② **Mount Tidirhine**, the highest point in the Rif, has an imposing landscape of cedar and pine forests that can be explored on foot or by four-wheel-drive vehicle.

Almond Trees

When they blossom in the spring, almond trees bring a splash of brilliant colour to this landscape of hills and man-made terraces.

⓮ Nador

Road Map E1. 154 km (96 miles) east
of El-Hoceima and 13 km (8 miles)
south of Melilla. 🏛 200,000. 🚌 🚢
🍴 Sun & Mon.

With wide avenues, shops, a
multitude of cafés, restaurants
and hotels, banks and residential
blocks, Nador, somewhat
unexpectedly, has all the
trappings of a major town. It is,
indeed, enjoying great prosperity.

Nador's dramatic economic
growth has been fuelled both
by its traditional industries,
such as metallurgy (its metal-
processing complex is supplied
with iron ore from the Rif and
anthracite from Jerada) and by
modern ones, namely textiles,
chemicals and electrics. The
waves of emigration that have
affected the whole of the
eastern Rif have also contributed
significantly to Nador's development. While immigrants here
are key investors and consumers,
funds sent home by workers
from abroad have swelled the
town's economy.

Nador's location, 13 km
(8 miles) from the Spanish
enclave of Melilla, also accounts
for the town's prosperity,
through illegal trafficking.
Through well-oiled channels,
goods cross the border at many
points, including **Beni Enzar**,
the border post nearest Melilla.
Here, small consignments are
transported across the border
several times a day, packed in
small trucks or loaded onto
the backs of women and

The mountainous Mediterranean coastline near Melilla

children. The goods are then
disposed of in broad daylight
in two huge markets in Nador.

Beni Enzar, on the edge of
Nador, is the foremost fishing
port on the Mediterranean
coast, and it also has modern
naval dockyards.

⓯ Melilla

Sovereign Spanish town. **Road Map** E1.
167 km (104 miles) east of El-Hoceima
and 153 km (95 miles) northwest of
Oujda. 🏛 70,000. 🚌 ℹ️ Tourist and
information office near Plaza de Toros;
(952) 67 54 44. 🎭 Easter Week; Festival
of Spain (early Jul); Our Lady of Victory
(early Sep).

Although about 40 per cent of the
population of the Spanish town
of Melilla is Moroccan, the way
of life here is still very Andalusian.

It was once a Carthaginian, then
a Roman, trading post. Located
on the road from Fès and being
the destination of caravans from
Sijilmassa and the Sahara, Melilla
became a busy port during the
Middle Ages. The town has been
in Spanish hands since 1497.

Under the Protectorate, Melilla
underwent rapid development
thanks to its status as a free zone.
However, Moroccan independence and the closure of the
border with Algeria cut it off
from the hinterland. The town
is now experiencing a difficult
period. Consumer demand in
this Spanish town means that
tax-free goods find a ready
market. This has contributed
to a thriving illegal trade, which
in turn creates the appearance
of prosperity.

Set on a rocky peninsula
and enclosed within 16th- and
17th-century walls, the fortress-
like Medina Sidonia district
constitutes the upper town.
The Puerta de la Marina leads
through to a tracery of alleys,
vaulted passages, steps and
several small squares, some with
a chapel or church. The Puerta
de Santiago leads through to
Plaza de Armas, west of the
old town.

The church of **La Purísima
Concepción**, in the northwest
of the old town, contains some
fine Baroque altarpieces; on
the high altar stands an 18th-
century statue of Our Lady of
Victory, patron saint of Melilla.
Passing behind the church and
following the ramparts, you
will come to the **Museo
Municipal** (Town Museum).
Here, Melilla's Phoenician,
Carthaginian and Roman periods
are represented by ceramics,
coins and bracelets that were
discovered in the vicinity of
the town. Various stone
implements from the western
Sahara are also exhibited.

The circular Plaza de España
links the old town with the

Typical Mediterranean cactus seen
growing in the region

View of the popular Spanish town
of Melilla

◀ View of the Mediterranean coastal scenery and tower ruins at Torres de Alcalá

Kif plantation in the Rif

Kif

The cultivation of kif (cannabis) was once the preserve of a few tribes around Ketama. Kif plantations have multiplied and are now found in several provinces between Chefchaouen and Al-Hoceima. Once grown only in the high valleys of the central Rif, the plant is today also cultivated on the slopes of low-lying valleys. Growing *Cannabis sativa*, "the curative herb", as well as Indian hemp, is highly lucrative and underpins the entire economy of the Rif. Although growing and smoking it (which are traditional in the region) are tolerated on a localized basis, its commercial exploitation is illegal. This has given rise to a major smuggling trade, which the Moroccan authorities are fighting with financial assistance from the European Union. The proposed solution is to introduce alternative crops and to open up the Rif by building a coastal road from Tangier to Saïdia, passing through Ceuta and Al-Hoceima.

new, which was begun at the end of the 19th century. Avenida del Rey Juan Carlos is the new town's busiest street.

🏛 **Museo Municipal**

Plaza de D Pedro Estopinan.
Tel 952 97 62 16. **Open** Summer: 10am–1:30pm & 5–9:30pm Tue–Sat; Winter: 10am–1:30pm & 4–8:30pm Tue–Sat, 10am–2pm Sun.
Closed Sun. 🖾

⓰ Cap des Trois Fourches

Road Map E1. 30 km (18 miles) from Melilla by road then track.

The road from Beni Enzar to the Cap des Trois Fourches offers some stunning views of Melilla and the Mediterranean Sea. The part of the cape beyond the Charrana lighthouse is one of

the most beautiful promontories in Morocco.

The cape is lined with bays and beaches nestling against the rocky coast. However, the coast road is narrow and difficult to drive, so care should be taken.

⓱ Moulouya Estuary

Road Map E1. From Nador to Ras Kebdana, then on to Saïdia, road N16.

The whole area between the Bou Areg lagoon and the estuary of Wadi Moulouya is a rich and fascinating nature reserve. A great variety of birds – dunlin, plover, oystercatcher, little egret, redshank, black-tailed godwit and flamingoes, terns, and different species of gulls – come to spend the winter in this marshy area. The

A peasant woman working in the Moulouya valley

dunes are home to woodcock, plovers, herons and storks.

The vegetation in this area is equally diverse: spurge and sea holly grow on the dunes, while glasswort, reeds and rushes cover the marshes, which are the habitat of dragonflies, grasshoppers and sand spiders.

The Cap des Trois Fourches, offering some breathtaking views and stunning coastal landscapes

⑱ Zegzel Gorge

One of the most scenic routes in Morocco is road P6012 from Berkane to Taforalt. It follows the course of Wadi Zegzel as the river winds through deep gorges and along valleys and hillsides. Many of the caves that have been hollowed out of the cliffs by the action of water, such as the Grotte du Chameau and Grotte de Tghasrout, contain impressive stalactites and stalagmites. Continuing along this road offers breathtaking views of the mountains and the Angad plain, and of almond groves, villages and isolated *marabouts*. Road P6017 then road N2 lead back to Oujda, or Berkane via Ahfir, a town established by the French in 1910.

② Grotte du Chameau
Dug into the mountainside by an underground hot stream, Grotte du Chameau (Camel Cave) contains several great halls with stalactites and stalagmites.

① **Wadi Zegzel Gorge**
With the reddish cliffs of the mountainside towering above, the river valley traverses a lush green landscape, sometimes widening in places where it cuts through terraces planted with olive and fruit trees.

③ **Beni-Snassen Mountains**
In several places, the road offers spectacular views of the mountains, which bear the marks of erosion. Here also are hamlets with pisé houses and terraces with vines and olive trees.

⑲ Saïdia

Road Map F1. 50 km (31 miles) northwest of Oujda. 🏔 2,800. 🚌 🎭 Folk Arts Festival (Aug). 🛒 Sun.

At the northern extremity of the fertile Triffa plain, an agricultural and wine-growing area, is the little town of Saïdia, located on the Wadi Kiss estuary. For the last 20 km (12 miles) before it reaches the sea, this river constitutes the border between Morocco and Algeria.

Saïdia is a coastal resort with a fine beach edged with mimosa and eucalyptus, the reason behind the town's name "Blue Pearl". In summer the beach is crowded with Moroccan

tourists. A folk arts festival is held at the Palais du Festival on Boulevard Mohammed V in August.

Saïdia is also home to a modern resort that overlooks a marina and accommodates more than 1,000 guests.

⑳ Oujda

Road Map F2. 🏔 800,000. ✈ 15 km (9 miles). 🚌 🚆 ℹ Place du 16 Août 1953; (0536) 68 56 31, and railway station. 🎭 Moussem of Sidi Yahia (Sep). 🛒 Wed & Sun.

The history of Oujda has been shaped by its geographical location on a crossroads. In the Ville Nouvelle, the main

shops and the banks, and several large brasseries with spacious terraces, are concentrated on Avenue Mohammed V and around Place du 16 Août 1953.

The medina, still partly enclosed by ramparts, is easy to explore, being small enough to wander about in without becoming disoriented. Rue el-Mazouzi, a major axis, crosses the medina from west to east, ending at Bab Sidi Abdel Ouahab. Various souks are located on this main street. The *kissaria*, which is lined with arcades, has shops selling various types of textiles, kaftans and velvets as well as looms and skeins of wool. The small

④ **View of Jbel Fourhal**
The highest point of the Beni Snassen mountains, Jbel Fourhal (1,532 m/5,025 ft) is partly covered with forests of holm-oak and scarred by areas of limestone scree.

Key

▬ Suggested route

═ Other roads

0 km   3

0 miles   3

Saïdia ↖ P6000

P6002   ● **Ahfir**

N2

N2

Col de Guerbouss 539 m (1,769 ft)

ntains

Oujda ↘

Almou

P6017

④ ⑤ ⑥ ⑦

Tips for Drivers

Departure point: Berkane, 60 km (37 miles) from Oujda on the N2.
Length: 134 km (83 miles). Follow the P6012 for 20 km (12 miles) along the Zegzel Gorge. The Route de Corniche, skirts the Beni Snassen Mountains but is in a bad state of repair. Road P6017 leads back to the N2, for the return trip to Oujda.
Stopping-off points: Although it is possible to find a meal in Ahfir, it is best to take a picnic. Berkane (Hotel Laetizia) offers basic accommodation. For this trip it is more convenient to stay at Oujda (Hotel Ibis Moussafir, Blvd Abdellah). **Tel** (0536) 68 82 02.

⑤ **Oulad Jabeur Fouaga**
In this small village the houses that cluster around the mosque have roofs of earth and thatch, which is typical of the region. Some have a central courtyard.

⑥ **Almond Trees**
Grown on terraces, almond trees are widely cultivated in the region. Their blossom adds a splash of colour to this often harsh, high limestone environment.

⑦ **Beni-Snassen Mountain Road**
This mountain road winds up the hillsides and threads its way above dramatic precipices. On certain days there is a view of the Angad plain, where the town of Oujda was built.

squares where the El-Ma Souk (Water Market) and the Attarine Souk take place contain trees and fountains, and are the living centre of the medina.

The **Musée Ethnographique**, outside the ramparts, contains local costumes and items relating to daily life in the region.

🏛 **Musée Ethnographique**
Parc Lalla Meriem.
Tel (0536) 68 56 31.
Open daily, times vary. 📷

Environs
Sidi Yahia, 6 km (4 miles) east of Oujda, is an oasis with abundant springs. Nearby is the

tomb of Sidi Yahia ben Younes, patron saint of Oujda. Venerated by Muslims, Jews and Christians alike, he is equated with St John the Baptist.

㉑ Figuig

Road Map F3. 368 km (229 miles) south of Oujda. 👥 14,600. 🚌 from Oujda. ℹ Oujda; (0536) 68 56 31. 🎪 Tue & Sun.

Doorway in the medina at Oujda

An oasis located at an altitude of 900 m (2,955 ft), Figuig consists of seven villages, or *ksour*, spread out in a vast palm plantation that

covers almost 20 sq km (8 sq miles). The water provided by the artesian springs irrigates a large number of gardens, which lie behind clay walls. **Zenaga**, a typical *ksar*, is the largest of the villages, while El-Oudaghir is the administrative centre. The top of its minaret offers a view of the palm grove.

Figuig, at the crossroads of major caravan routes, was a busy caravanserai in the Middle Ages but lost its importance later. More recently, the closure of the border with Algeria deprived it of its role as a border post, which it once shared with Oujda.

FÈS

Located between the fertile lands of the Saïs and the forests of the Middle Atlas, Fès is the oldest of Morocco's imperial cities. It is the embodiment of the country's history and its spiritual and religious capital, and has been declared a World Heritage Site by UNESCO. Morocco's third-largest city, it consists of Fès el-Bali, the historic centre; Fès el-Jedid, the imperial city of the Merinids; and, located further south, the modern districts created under the Protectorate.

Idriss I founded Madinat Fas, on the right bank of the River Fès, in 789. In 808, his son, Idriss II, built another town on the left bank, which was known as El-Alya (High Town). In 818, these two cities, each within their own walls, received hundreds of Muslim families who had been expelled from Córdoba. Soon afterwards, some 300 refugee families from Kairouan, in Tunisia, found asylum in El-Alya, which then became known as Karaouiyine, after them. Within a few years, thanks to these two communities, the two towns became the centre of the Arabization and Islamization of Morocco.

In the mid-11th century, the Almoravids united the two towns, building a wall around them. The Almohads took the city in 1145, after a long siege. Fès then became the country's foremost cultural and economic metropolis, thanks in large part to the founding of its university. In 1250, the Merinids raised Fès to the status of imperial capital and endowed it with prestigious buildings. To the west of the old town they established a new royal city, Fès el-Jedid (New Fès). Conquered by the Alaouites in 1666, Fès was spurned by Moulay Ismaïl, who chose Meknès as his capital. The city's decline continued until the early 20th century.

When the Protectorate was established in 1912, a Ville Nouvelle (New Town) was built. After independence this was filled by the prosperous citizens of the old medina, while the country people, rootless and poor, crowded into the old town of Fès el-Bali. However, UNESCO's ongoing restoration programme has saved the old city. Today, Fès is home to over a million people.

The rooftops of the Karaouiyine Quarter, Fès el-Bali

◄ The entrance to the King's Palace Dar El Makhzen, Fès

Exploring Fès

Seen from the summit of the hill of the Merinid tombs, Fès appears as a compact and tightly woven urban fabric. Enclosed within its defensive walls, Fès el-Bali, the historic medina, is a sea of rooftops from which emerge minarets and domes. Wadi Fès separates the two historic entities: the Andalusian Quarter to the east, and the Karaouiyine Quarter to the west. Fès el-Jedid *(see pp184–7)* is built on a height south of the medina. Notable features here include the royal palace and the former Jewish quarter. The Ville Nouvelle (New Town), dating from the Protectorate, lies further south.

The crowded Rue Talaa Kebira in Fès el-Bali

Key

- Major sight
- Sight
- Medina
- Ramparts

Ville Nouvelle

0 metres 400
0 yards 400

Getting Around

Both Fès el-Bali and Fès el-Jedid can be explored only on foot since the labyrinthine layout of these quarters is unsuitable for motorized traffic. Parking is available near Bab Boujeloud or Bab el-Ftouh, or on Place des Alaouites. Buses (often very crowded) run between Ville Nouvelle and both Fès el-Bali and Fès el-Jedid. It is best to take a *petit taxi* (*see p362*). *Petits taxis* can be found near the post office, at Bab Boujeloud and in the vicinity of the large hotels.

Colourful carpets spread out on a terrace in the medina

Sights at a Glance

Historic Buildings

❶ Merinid Tombs
❻ Fondouk el-Nejjarine
❽ Zaouia of Moulay Idriss II

Streets, Squares and Historic Quarters

❹ Rue Talaa Kebira
❺ The Souks
⓬ Tanners' Quarter
⓭ Place el-Seffarine
⓯ Andalusian Quarter
⓲ *Fès el-Jedid pp184–7*

Mosques

⓮ Andalusian Mosque
⓱ *Karaouiyine Mosque pp180–81*

Medersas

❾ El-Attarine Medersa
❿ El-Cherratine Medersa
⓫ *Bou Inania Medersa pp176–7*

Museums

❷ Musée des Armes
❼ *Musée Dar el-Batha pp172–3*

Gates

❸ Bab Boujeloud
⓰ Bab el-Ftouh

For keys to symbols *see back flap*

The Merinid tombs, overlooking the medina of Fès

❶ Merinid Tombs

North of the medina, on the hill of the Merinid tombs.

Standing among olive trees, cacti and blue agaves, the 16th- century ruins that overlook Fès el-Bali are those of a Merinid palace and necropolis. Ancient chroniclers recorded that these tombs elicited wonderment because of their magnificent marble and the splendour of their coloured epitaphs. Today, the tombs are very dilapidated, and the area is popular with petty thieves, but it offers an impressive view of the city and is well worth the climb.

The stretch of wall immediately beneath the hill is the oldest part of the medina's defences. Parts of the curtain wall date from the Almohad period (12th century), notably Borj Kaoukeb, near which the lepers' quarter was once located.

The tombs overlook a tiered cemetery which stretches as far as Bab Guissa, an Almohad gateway dating from the 13th century.

❷ Musée des Armes

Borj Nord. **Tel** (0535) 64 75 66.
Open 9am–4:30pm Tue–Sun.

Borj Nord was built in 1582, on the orders of the Saadian sultan Ahmed el-Mansour (1578–1603). From its vantage point over the city, the fortress both defended and controlled Fès el-Bali. In 1963 the collection of weapons from the Musée Dar el-Batha (see pp172–3) was transferred here to create the Museum of Arms. Much of the collection, comprising more than 8,000 pieces, comes from

Silver dagger, Musée des Armes

The Musée des Armes, housed in a 16th-century fortress

the Makina, the arsenal built by Moulay Hassan I at the end of the 19th century, although it was enriched by donations from various Alaouite sultans.

Some 1,000 pieces of weaponry are exhibited in 16 rooms, in a chronological display running from prehistory to the first half of the 20th century. Moroccan weapons are well represented and demonstrate the technical knowledge of Moroccan craftsmen. There is also an interesting collection of weapons from all over the world.

❸ Bab Boujeloud

Place du Pacha el-Baghdadi.

Enclosed within high walls, the large Place Pacha el-Baghdadi links the medina and Fès el-Jedid. On one side of the square stands Bab Boujeloud. Built in 1913, this fine monumental gate is the principal entrance into Fès el-Bali.

With the development of heavy artillery, the fortified gates of Fès lost their effectiveness as defences and came to be seen as decorative buildings, contributing to the city's prestige and helping to justify the levy of city taxes.

Bab Boujeloud, built in the Moorish style, consists of three perfectly symmetrical horseshoe arches. A rich decorative scheme consisting of geometric patterns, calligraphy, interlaced floral motifs and glazed tilework of many colours, with blue predominating, graces the façade. From this entranceway the silhouette of the minaret of the Bou Inania Medersa can be glimpsed on the left.

❹ Rue Talaa Kebira

Reached via Bab Boujeloud.

This thoroughfare, whose name means "Great Climb" and which is partly covered by a cane canopy, is lined with small shops along almost its entire length. It is continued by the Ras Tiyalin and Aïn Allou souks and by spice

Rue Talaa Kebira, the main thoroughfare in the medina of Fès

markets. The street passes the *kissaria* and ends at the Karaouiyine Mosque *(see pp180–81)*. Running parallel to it at its southern end is another important street, Rue Talaa Seghira ("Short Climb"), which joins up with Rue Talaa Kebira at Aïn Allou. These streets are the two principal cultural and economic thoroughfares of Fès el-Bali. The city's most important buildings are located here.

Opposite the Bou Inania Medersa *(see pp176–7)* stands **Dar el-Magana** (House of the Clock), built by the ruler Abou Inan in 1357. It contains a water-clock built by Fassi craftsmen during the Merinid period.

Not far from here, level with a covered passage in the Blida Quarter, is the **Zaouia el-Tijaniya**, containing the tomb of Ahmed el-Tijani, master of *Tariqa el-Tijaniya* (The Way), a doctrine that spread widely throughout the Maghreb and sub-Saharan Africa. Further on are three musical instrument workshops. Makers of stringed instruments have almost completely disappeared from Fès; the only remaining practitioner is a craftsman in Rue Talaa Seghira, opposite Dar Mnebhi, who still makes *ouds* (lutes) by traditional methods. Beyond is the skin-dressers' *fondouk*, which contains leather workshops.

Across the Bou Rous bridge stands the **Ech Cherabliyine Mosque** (Mosque of the Slipper-Makers). Built by the Merinid sultan Abou el-Hassan, it is distinguished by its elegant minaret.

❺ The Souks

The souks of Fès el-Bali spread out beyond the Ech Cherabliyine Mosque.

The location of each souk reflects a hierarchy dictated by the value placed on the various goods on offer in each of them. Makers and sellers are grouped together according to the products that they offer. Every type of craft has its own street, or part of a street, around the Karaouiyine Mosque, which has resulted in a logical but relatively complex layout. While the **El-Attarine Souk** sells spices, there is also a **Slipper Souk** and a **Henna Souk**, which is laid out in an attractive shaded square planted with arbuses. A plaque records that the Sidi Frijthe *maristan*, which was the largest mental asylum in the Merinid empire, once stood on this square. Built by Abou Yacoub Youssef (1286–1307), it also functioned as a hospital for storks. It was still in

Skin-dressing workshops, unchanged since the Middle Ages

existence in 1944. In the 16th century, Leo Africanus, known today for his accounts of his travels, worked there as a clerk for two years.

The *kissaria*, near the Zaouia of Moulay Idriss, marks the exact centre of the souks. This is a gridwork of covered streets where shops selling luxury goods are especially conspicuous. Some of the fine silks and brocades, high-quality kaftans and jewellery on offer here supply the international market.

Fondouk el-Nejjarine, a UNESCO World Heritage Site

❻ Fondouk el-Nejjarine

Place el-Nejjarine. **Tel** (0535) 74 05 80. Musée du Bois: **Open** 9am–6pm daily.

Not far from the Henna Souk, the impressive Fondouk el-Nejjarine, with an elegant fountain, is one of the most renowned buildings in Fès. Built by the *amine* (provost) Adeyel in the 18th century, this former caravanserai provided food, rest and shelter to the traders in luxury goods arriving from the interior. Classed as a historic monument in 1916, it is now one of UNESCO's World Heritage Sites. Its restoration formed part of the preservation programme carried out on the whole medina. The *fondouk*'s three floors house the privately run **Musée du Bois** (Museum of Wooden Arts). The displays include carved doors from the magnificent Bou Inania Medersa *(see pp176–7)*.

❼ Musée Dar el-Batha

The palace of Dar el-Batha was begun between 1873 and 1875 by Moulay el-Hassan, and was completed by Moulay Abdel Aziz in 1897. The location of the palace was an area of neglected gardens, which had been irrigated by a river. The sultan, who wanted to make the palace a residence worthy of being used for official receptions, added an imposing courtyard covered with coloured tiles and featuring a large fountain. He also laid out a large and very fine Andalusian garden. Despite many later alterations, the traditional Moorish features of this building have survived.

Exploring the Collections of the Musée Dar El-Batha

In 1914, the Orientalist Alfred Bel made the first bequest to the future ethnographic musem which, by royal decree, became the museum of local crafts (Musée des Arts et des Traditions) in 1915.

Today, the permanent exhibition, which fills 12 rooms, consists of more than 500 objects selected from the 5,000 that the museum has acquired. They are shown in two large sections. The ethnographic section, featuring the arts and crafts of Fès and the rural crafts of neighbouring areas, fills the first eight rooms. The archaeological section is laid out in the four remaining rooms. Particularly notable is the display tracing the development of architecture in Fès, from the Idrissid period to that of the Alaouites.

A soup tureen with blue and white decoration

Books and Manuscripts

Room 1 contains some extremely fine leather-bound books dating from the 11th century. Their embossed and gold-painted decoration is a tradition peculiar to Fès that stayed alive until the 17th century. Also on display are manuscript copies of the Koran made on parchment in the 16th to 18th centuries; prayer books by the Sufi scholar El-Jazouli; and important manuscripts written in the Andalusian cursive style of calligraphy, which was widely used in Morocco in the 8th and 9th centuries. Examples of illuminated calligraphy with geometric decorative motifs, as well as other exhibits, highlight the role that Fès played in the development and diffusion of learning.

Ceramics

The original location of the potters' souk, next to the Karaouiyine Mosque, is proof of the respect and repute in which the makers of the famous Fès blue and white ware were held. As well as this pottery, Room 2 contains dishes and *jebbana* (traditional earthenware vessels) with polychrome decoration in blue, green, yellow and brown over a white tin glaze, or with *sboula* (herringbone) or *chebka* (scale) motifs. Some of the dishes with green motifs displayed in Case 11 are examples of *zarghmil*, the famous "centipede" style of decoration characteristic of Fès.

Leatherwork

The exhibits in Room 3 include a fragment of a 13th-century candelabra from the Karaouiyine Mosque, alms measures made in Fès in the 14th to 18th centuries, some fine astrolabes and a number of instruments for determining the times of day at which prayers are to be said, for indicating the direction of Mecca and for tracking the lunar calendar.

Alms measure (18th century)

There are also lamps, writing tables and a medicine bowl decorated with verses from the Koran and formulae; various equipment for use in the hammam and for brewing and drinking tea; and a fine 18th-century tray embellished with a complex geometric pattern. Each of these pieces demonstrates the consummate skill and exceptional creativity of the craftsmen of Fès, who in making them fulfilled the religious, scientific and symbolic needs of their time.

Wood, Embroidery and Weaving

The furniture in Room 4, including chests and sets of shelves, shows both the range of woods used (cedar, thuya, almond, walnut, ebony, citron and mahogany) and a range of cabinet-making skills. Shown here are carved

Lintel from the Andalusian Mosque, carved in 980

Detail of 19th-century embroidery from Fès

and painted or leather-covered furniture, and furniture with iron fittings, marquetry decoration and mother-of-pearl and ivory inlay. There is also a fine 14th-century Moorish chest, made to hold the most valuable pieces of a bride's trousseau as they were carried to her new home.

The exhibits in Room 5 consist of examples of the different types of Fassi embroidery. These include exquisite examples of *terz sqalli*, lamé embroidery in which gold thread and gold dust are used; *al-aleuj* embroidery, a technique very similar to Persian stitch; and *erz alghorza*, counted-thread embroidery, the most famous type of Fassi embroidery, usually in red, blue, purple

Double pitcher from the Rif (19th century)

and green silk. Women's costumes, headdresses and accessories in embroidered silk decorated with trimmings demonstrate the high degree of refinement in traditional Fassi dress.

Rural Crafts

Objects of everyday life from various regions of Morocco are exhibited in Room 6: pottery made by the women of the Rif, carpets from the Middle Atlas, and fine Berber jewellery, such as brooches, pectorals, necklaces, finger rings and bracelets. All these show the skills and inventiveness of Moroccan craftsmen and craftswomen.

Doors

A display of doors fills Room 7. Doors from ordinary houses and large palace doors carved and decorated with patterns of nails are shown with a selection of door locks from houses in Fès.

The Art of Zellij

Room 9 is devoted to *zellij* tilework made in Fès from the 14th to the 18th centuries and among the finest of its kind.

One of the exhibits, a remarkable panel from the Bou Inania Medersa, perfectly exemplifies this brilliant tradition of architectural decoration in Morocco. The rich aesthetic vocabulary of this art form brings to life plain surfaces with a lively play of patterns and colours.

Minbar dating from 1350, from the Bou Inania Medersa

Monumental Woodcarving

The displays in Rooms 10 and 11 trace the evolution of monumental woodcarving in Fès from the 9th century to the present day. Among the most interesting pieces are a lintel from the Karaouiyine Mosque (877) and the monumental door from the El-Attarine Medersa (1325). The splendid lintel from the Andalusian Mosque, made in 980, is a masterpiece of religious art of the early years of Islam in Morocco. The museum's collection also includes the minbar from the Andalusian Mosque, which is exhibited alternately with that from the Bou Inania Medersa (1350).

Funerary Architecture

Various pieces of Muslim funerary architecture and a selection of tombstones from Volubilis end the museum's displays.

Gallery Guide

The collections are divided into two large sections. The ethnographic section occupies eight rooms: Room 1 contains exhibits relating to the art of the book; Room 2 contains ceramics and paintings; Room 3 is devoted to leatherwork; Rooms 4 and 5 to marquetry, embroidery and weaving; Room 6 to carpets, Berber jewellery and objects from everyday life; Room 7 to wooden doors, and Room 8 to genealogy.

The archaeological section begins in Room 9 with *zellij* and ceramics, Rooms 10 and 11 contain displays of wood used in architecture; Room 12 is devoted to archaeology relating to Islam and funerary stelae. There is also a workshop which offers visitors the chance to watch the woodcarvers at work.

Arabic Calligraphy

Islam traditionally forbids all figurative representation, and since the 8th century this prohibition has encouraged the use of calligraphy in Arabic civilization. Decorative writing became an art form that was used not only for manuscripts but also to decorate buildings. Islamic calligraphy is closely connected to the revelation of the Koran: the word of God is to be transcribed in a beautiful script far finer than secular writing. Writing out not only the Koran, but also the 99 names of Allah is considered to be a very pious undertaking. The importance of this art form in Islamic civilization is shown by the carved, painted or tiled friezes that decorate the walls and domes of mosques and medersas, as well as by the thousands of scientific, literary and religious calligraphic manuscripts preserved in public and private libraries. Maghrebi script, used in the Maghreb, in Andalusia and in the Sudan, is derived from Kufic script, which is named after the town of Kufa, in Iraq, where this style of writing originated.

Manuscripts and Friezes

Quotations from the Koran are omnipresent in manuscripts and calligraphic friezes. Calligraphy appears in all dimensions and on a great variety of surfaces. Maghrebi script is characterized by rounded letters combined with slender descenders and ascenders.

This detail from an illuminated manuscript in Maghrebi script, produced in Rabat in the 8th century, features plant motifs.

Cursive script, like this example from the Bou Inania Medersa, may appear in the form of carved *zellij* work. Calligraphic friezes, often with a religious content, were made both for public buildings and private houses.

This illuminated manuscript of a *hadith*, recording the words and deeds of the Prophet Mohammed, is in Maghrebi script. With gold and bright colours, illumination enriches both religious and secular manuscripts. The finest illuminated manuscripts are preserved in the Royal Library in Rabat.

Decorative details, like this one from an anonymous manuscript of a musical score, shows that calligraphy was sometimes more ornamental than purely functional.

Calligraphy on marble, Hassan II Mosque.

Inkwells

Used for calligraphy and for illumination, inkwells were made in the shape of a koubba, the shrine of a Muslim saint.

The compartments in these *mejma* inkwells were designed to hold the inks of different colours that were used for illumination.

Fountain for ablutions at the Zaouia of Moulay Idriss II

❽ Zaouia of Moulay Idriss II

Closed to non-Muslims. Glimpses possible through the open doors.

The Zaouia of Moulay Idriss II, containing the tomb of the second Idrissid ruler (considered to be the founder of Fès) is the most venerated shrine in Morocco. Built in the centre of the city at the beginning of the 18th century, during the reign of Moulay Ismaïl, the building was restored in the mid-19th century. The pyramidal dome that covers the saint's tomb and its polychrome minaret give it a majestic silhouette. The courtyard of the mosque contains a fountain which consists of a white marble basin on a shaft, richly decorated with *zellij* tilework.

The *horm*, the perimeter wall around the *zaouia*, is also holy. The narrow streets leading to the shrine are barred at mid-height by a wooden beam that is supposed to prevent the passage of beasts of burden. The *horm* also made the shrine an inviolable place, so that in the past outlaws would find sanctuary here.

At the end of each summer, during a *moussem* lasting two to three days, this place of pilgrimage attracts not only the inhabitants of Fès but also people from the surrounding countryside and mountain-dwellers from distant tribes. They all come to receive a blessing and *baraka* ("beneficient force"). The motley crowd of the

faithful is made up of pilgrims and beggars, as well as nougat, candle and incense sellers whose goods are used as tomb offerings.

Decorative column and tilework in the El-Attarine Medersa

❾ El-Attarine Medersa

Opposite the Karaouiyine Mosque. **Tel** (0535) 62 34 60. **Open** 9am–6pm daily. **Closed** Fri.

The El-Attarine Medersa (Medersa of the Spice Sellers) stands in the neighbourhood of the Karaouiyine Mosque and the El-Attarine Souk. With the Bou Inania Medersa *(see pp176–7)*, it is considered to be one of the wonders of Moorish architecture. It was built between 1323 and 1325 by the Merinid sultan Abou Saïd Othman, and has all the elements specific to a medieval Muslim school.

The highly decorated entrance leads through to a

courtyard paved with *zellij* tilework in a two-colour pattern of brown and white, and enclosing an ablutions fountain. A cladding of polychrome tiles covers the base of the courtyard's four interior walls and its columns. A door with fine decoration and exquisite fittings leads from the courtyard to the prayer hall, which contains a mihrab. The prayer hall has a highly decorated ceiling, walls featuring luxuriant stuccowork and *zellij* work, and lintels with epigraphic decoration.

The students' rooms, looking onto the courtyard from the upper floor, have windows fronted by turned wooden railings. The terrace offers a view of the rooftops of Fès el-Bali and the courtyard of the Karaouiyine Mosque.

❿ El-Cherratine Medersa

Rue El-Cherratine.

Located southeast of the Karaouiyine Mosque, in Rue el-Cherratine (Street of the Ropemakers), this medersa was built by Moulay Rachid, the first Alaouite sultan, in 1670. Although it is structurally similar to the Merinid medersas, it is less elaborately decorated. Adding to the building's austerity are the high, narrow residential units known as *douiras*, which stand in three corners of the courtyard. The tiny cells inside were for the use of students.

Entry into the medersa is through beautiful double doors cased in engraved bronze. The doors open onto a passageway with a fine carved and painted wooden ceiling, which in turn leads to the Moorish courtyard.

The El-Cherratine Souk, where ropemakers sell their wares

⑪ Bou Inania Medersa

This is the largest and most sumptuously decorated medersa ever built by the Merinids. Constructed between 1350 and 1355 by the sultan Abou Inan, it is the only medersa in Morocco that has a minbar (pulpit) and a minaret. A mosque, cathedral, students' residence and school combined, its functions have determined its architectural complexity. The one-storey building, on a rectangular plan, is arranged around a square Moorish courtyard paved with marble and onyx, and surrounded on three sides by a cloister. It is one of the few Islamic religious buildings that is open to non-Muslims.

Stained-glass Windows
The windows of the prayer hall feature old stained-glass panels.

Capitals The carved motifs on the capitals in the medersa show Moorish influence.

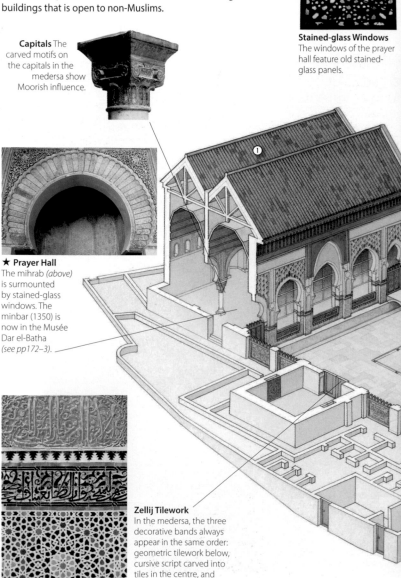

★ Prayer Hall
The mihrab (above) is surmounted by stained-glass windows. The minbar (1350) is now in the Musée Dar el-Batha (see pp172–3).

Zellij Tilework
In the medersa, the three decorative bands always appear in the same order: geometric tilework below, cursive script carved into tiles in the centre, and stuccowork above.

The Moroccan Medersa

Student at a medersa

The medersa was both a cultural and a religious establishment. It was primarily a residential college, designed for local students from the town or city and especially for those from the immediate or more distant rural areas, but also for anyone who came in search of learning. It was an extension of the great university-mosque, an institution once restricted to the study of religion, law, science and even the arts. It was finally a place of prayer and reflection. The medersas of Fès, home to the greatest scholars in the country, were the most highly esteemed in Morocco.

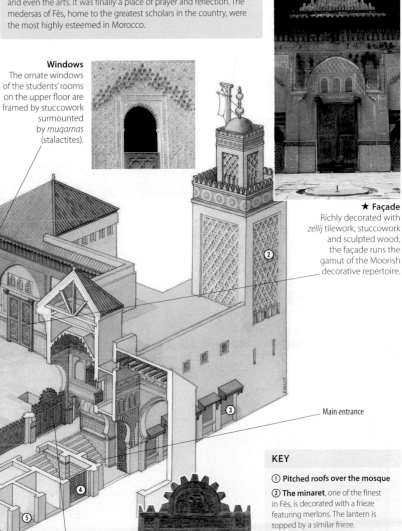

Windows
The ornate windows of the students' rooms on the upper floor are framed by stuccowork surmounted by *muqarnas* (stalactites).

★ **Façade**
Richly decorated with *zellij* tilework, stuccowork and sculpted wood, the façade runs the gamut of the Moorish decorative repertoire.

Main entrance

Wooden Screen
The magnificent carved wooden screen of the main entrance is framed by sturdy pillars. The adjoining door, of much plainer design, was known as Beggars' Gate.

KEY

① Pitched roofs over the mosque

② **The minaret**, one of the finest in Fès, is decorated with a frieze featuring merlons. The lantern is topped by a similar frieze.

③ Shops

④ Begger's Gate

⑤ Student's Cell

⑥ Courtyard paved with marble and onyx

The Tanneries of Fès

Often located near watercourses, and usually some distance from residential quarters because of the unpleasant odours that they produced, tanneries made a substantial contribution to a city's economy. Tanning is a craft with traditions that go back thousands of years. The process turns animal hides into soft, rot-proof leather. Once tanned, the hides are passed on to leatherworkers.

Vats, some of which have been in use for centuries, are used for soaking skins after the hair and flesh have been removed. The tanning solution that turns them into leather is obtained from the bark of pomegranate or mimosa.

The tanned hides are hung out to dry on the terraces of the medina, as here, or in other parts of Fès, such as the Bab el-Guissa cemetery. The roofs of houses and the hillsides around the city may also be used as drying areas.

Stages in the Tanning Process

In Fès, the tanneries (chouaras) are located near Wadi Fès. The hides of sheep, goats, cows and camels undergo several processes – including the removal of hair and flesh, followed by soaking in vats, then by drying and rinsing – before they are ready to be dyed and handed over to leatherworkers.

The dried hides are rinsed in generous quantities of water. They are then softened by being steeped in baths of fatty solutions.

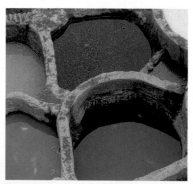

Natural pigments, obtained from certain plants and minerals, are still used by Moroccan craftsmen to colour the hides. However, chemical dyes are also used today.

Dyed leather is used to make many types of useful and decorative objects, such as embroidered bags, *babouches*, pouffes and clothing. These goods are offered for sale in the numerous souks in the medina of Fès.

⑫ Tanners' Quarter

North of Place el-Seffarine.

The Chouara, or Tanners' Quarter, has been located near Wadi Fès since the Middle Ages. Its dyeing vats, in the midst of houses in the Blida quarter, are best seen from neighbouring terraces. Although pervaded by an unpleasantly strong smell, this is the most lively and picturesque of all the souks in Fès.

⑬ Place el-Seffarine

Fès is the most important centre for the production of brass and silverware in Morocco. The workshops of brass-workers and coppersmiths lining Place el-Seffarine have been here for centuries. The pretty fountain with fleur-de-lis decoration is worth a look. It was probably built by French convicts in the 16th century.

North of the square is the 14th-century **Karaouiyine Library**, which was set up on the orders of the sultan Abou Inan. It was used by the greatest Moorish men of learning, including the philosopher and doctor Ibn Rushd, known as Averroës *(see p233)*, the philosopher Ibn Tufayl, the historian Ibn Khaldoun and the 6th-century traveller Leo Africanus. The manuscripts that once formed part of the library's collection have been transferred to the Royal Library in Rabat.

The **El-Seffarine Medersa**, opposite the Karaouiyine

Brass-worker making trays in Place el-Seffarine

Library, was built in 1280 and is the oldest medersa in Morocco that is still in use. The **El-Mesbahiya Medersa**, also north of the square, was built by the Merinid sultan Abou el Hassan in 1346. Further on, on the right, is the 16th-century **Tetouani Fondouk**, which accommodated traders and students from Tetouan.

Place el-Seffarine leads to **Rue des Teinturiers** (Dyers' Street), which runs parallel to the *wadi* and is where skeins are hung out to dry.

Karaouiyine Library
Place el-Seffarine. **Tel** (0535) 62 34 60. **Open** 9am–6pm Mon–Thu, 9am–1pm Fri (times may vary).

The north entrance of the Andalusian Mosque

⑭ Andalusian Mosque

Accessible via Rue el-Nekhaline or Bab el-Ftouh and Rue Sidi Bou Ghaleb. **Closed** to non-Muslims.

According to legend, this mosque was established by a religious woman, Mariam el-Fihri, sister of the founder of the Karaouiyine Mosque, and by the Andalusians who lived in the Karaouiyine Quarter. Its present appearance dates from the reign of the Almohad ruler Mohammed el-Nasser (13th century). The Merinids added a fountain in 1306 and funded the establishment of a library here in 1416. Non-Muslims can only admire the building from the exterior; notable are the great north entrance, with a carved cedar awning, and the domed Zenet minaret.

⑮ Andalusian Quarter

The Andalusian Quarter did not undergo the same development as the Karaouiyine Quarter, located on the opposite bank of Wadi Fès and better provided with water. Nevertheless, this part of the city, which is quieter and more residential, has monuments that are worth a visit.

The **El-Sahrij Medersa**, built in 1321 takes its name from the large water basin in one of the courtyards. This is considered to be the third-finest medersa in Fès after the Bou Inania and the El-Attarine medersas. The **Mausoleum of Sidi Bou Ghaleb**, in the street of that name, is that of a holy man from Andalusia who lived and taught in Fès in the 12th century.

El-Sahrij Medersa
Rue Sidi Bou Ghaled. **Tel** (0535) 62 34 60 (information). **Closed** for restoration.

⑯ Bab el-Ftouh

Southeast of the medina.

Literally meaning "Gate of the Aperture", the huge Bab el-Ftouh is also known as the Gate of Victory. It leads through to the Andalusian Quarter. The gate was built in the 10th century by a Zenet emir, and was altered in the 18th century, during the reign of the Alaouite ruler Sidi Mohammed ben Abdallah. Outside the ramparts, on a hill opposite the city, is the Bab el-Ftouh cemetery, where some of the most illustrious inhabitants of Fès are buried.

Bab el-Ftouh cemetery, resting place of some renowned teachers

⑰ Karaouiyine Mosque

Established in 859, the Karaouiyine Mosque is one of the oldest and most illustrious mosques in the western Muslim world. The first university to be established in Morocco, it was frequented by such learned men as Ibn Khaldoun *(see p185)*, Ibn el-Khatib, Averroës *(see p233)* and even Pope Sylvester II (909–1003). Named after the quarter in which it was built – that of refugees from Kairouan, in Tunisia – it was founded by Fatima bint Mohammed el-Fihri, a religious woman from Kairouan, who donated her worldly riches for its construction. It is still considered to be one of the main spiritual and intellectual centres of Islam and remains the seat of the Muslim university of Fès.

Pitched Roof
The roof of the mosque is covered in emerald-green tiles.

★ **The Prayer Hall**
The hall is divided into 16 aisles by 270 columns, parallel to the *qibla* wall (indicating the direction of Mecca). It is lit by a magnificent 12th-century Almohad candelabra.

★ **The Courtyard** The courtyard, or *sahn*, is paved with *zellij* tilework consisting of 50,000 pieces that were made especially for the floor of the mosque.

KEY

① **Women's Mosque**.

② **This door** is one of 14 entrances to the mosque.

③ **The prayer hall** can hold 20,000 people.

④ **The minaret**, in an early Almoravid style, is very similar in shape to a lookout tower.

Ablutions Basin
This basin, in the centre of the courtyard, is carved from a single block of marble. It rests on a marble fountain to which the faithful come to carry out their ablutions, an essential preparation for prayer.

VISITORS' CHECKLIST

Practical Information
Rue Bou Touil (which continues from Rue Talaa Kebira) runs parallel to the Karaouiyine Mosque. **Closed** to non-Muslims. Glimpses can sometimes be had through an open door, but be respectful.

The Role of the Mosque

Each quarter of Fès has one or more mosques and other places of worship. Friday prayers take place in both large and small mosques. *Msids*, small oratories without a minaret, are designed for prayer and for teaching the Koran. *Zaouias* are sanctuaries where religious brotherhoods gather. The mosque, which stands both as a civic and a social symbol, is simultaneously a place of worship, a university, a tribunal, an inviolable place of asylum and a friendly meeting place. The call to prayer is given by the muezzin five times a day.

Saadian pavilion

Mashrabiyya
The main doorway has a *mashrabiyya* screen to protect worshippers from prying eyes.

Dome Over the Entrance
The main entrance into the courtyard of the mosque faces Rue Bou Touil. The monumental doorway is surmounted by a small striated dome.

⓲ Fès el-Jedid

Fès el-Jedid, meaning New Fès or White Fès, was built in 1276 by Merinid princes as a stronghold against the permanent threat of the rebellious Fassis, and as a vantage point from which to survey their activities in the old town. Surrounded by ramparts, Fès el-Jedid was primarily a kasbah, and its political and military role predominated over the civic functions of a true Islamic town. It was the administrative centre of Morocco up to 1912.

Fès el-Jedid consists of several distinct units. In the west is the royal palace, and other buildings associated with it, and the Moulay Abdallah Quarter. In the south is the mellah, or Jewish quarter, a maze of dark, narrow streets. In the east are the Muslim quarters.

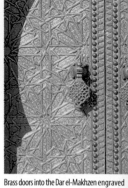

Brass doors into the Dar el-Makhzen engraved with a geometric pattern

Dar el-Makhzen, the royal palace in Fès

🏛 Dar el-Makhzen

Closed to the public.

This palatial complex in the centre of Fès el-Jedid is surrounded by high walls and covers more than 80 ha (195 acres). It was the main residence of the sultan, together with his guard and his retinue of servants. It was also where dignitaries of the *makhzen* (central government) came to carry out their duties. Part of the palace is still used by the king of Morocco when he comes to stay in Fès.

The main entrance to the complex, on the huge Place des Alaouites, is particularly imposing. Its magnificent Moorish gateway, which is permanently closed, is richly ornamented. The exquisitely engraved bronze doors are fitted with fine bronze knockers.

The walls enclose a disparate ensemble of buildings: palaces arranged around courtyards or large patios, as well as official buildings, notably the Dar el-Bahia, where Arab summit meetings are held; the Dar Ayad el-Kebira, built in the 18th century by Sidi Mohammed ben Abdallah; administrative and military buildings; and gardens, including the enclosed **Lalla Mina Gardens**.

The complex also includes a mosque and a medersa, which was built in 1320 by the Merinid prince Abou Saïd Othman. There is also a menagerie.

🏛 Moulay Abdallah Quarter

Accessible via Bab Boujat or Bab Dekaken.

Completely closed off on its western side by the palace walls and the ramparts of Fès el-Jedid, this quarter has two gateways linked by a central thoroughfare with a lattice-work of narrow streets leading off it. **Bab Dekaken**, the east gate, leads to the former *méchouar* (parade ground) and **Bab Boujat**, the west gate, pierces the city's walls. Nearby, in the main street, stands the **Grand Mosque**, a Merinid building dating from the 13th century that houses the necropolis of the sultan Abou Inan. Also on this street, in the direction of Bab Boujat, stands the **Mosque of Moulay Abdallah**, which was built in the mid-18th century.

🏛 Grande Rue de Fès el-Jedid and the Muslim Quarters

Accessible via Bab el-Semarine to the south and Bab Dekaken to the north.

The Muslim quarters – Lalla Btatha, Lalla Ghriba, Zebbala, Sidi Bounafaa, Boutouil and Blaghma – are the principal components of the urban agglomeration that Fassis know as Fès el-Jedid. The quarters are enclosed by the walls of Dar el-Makhzen to the west, and by a double line of walls to the east. Two gateways lead into the Muslim quarters; that on the northern side is Bab Dekaken, a simple opening in

A tower set in the walls of the *méchouar*

◀ View of the famous green rooftops of the Karaouiyine Mosque

Ibn Khaldoun

Abderrahman Ibn Khaldoun was born in Tunis in 1332 into a family of great scholars.

In about 1350 he came to Fès, which at the time was the leading intellectual centre in the Maghreb, and became diplomatic secretary to the sultan Abou Inan.

He taught in Cairo, where he died in 1406. His extensive writings include *Discourse on Universal History*. He is

considered to be the founder of sociology, and is without doubt one of the greatest historians of all time.

Modern-day portrait of Ibn Khaldoun

the fortifications that once led to the former *méchouar*. On the southern side is the monumental **Bab el-Semarine** (Gate of the Farriers). This is a monumental vaulted gateway, beneath which a souk for all sorts of food takes place; the stalls are laid out in the old Merinid grain stores.

The two gates are connected by **Grande Rue de Fès el-Jedid**, the main north–south artery through the city. The street, covered by a cane canopy at its northern extremity, is lined with an almost continuous succession of shops. This congested thoroughfare is the economic centre of the royal city. At intervals it is flanked by quiet residential quarters with a maze-like layout like that of all Muslim towns.

On the western side of the street, a small quarter huddles around the Lalla el-Azhar

Detail of Bab Segma, north of the old *méchouar*

Mosque (Mosque of the Lady Flower), which was built by the Merinid sultan Abou Inan in 1357. On the eastern side are the humble quarters inhabited by the families of old warrior tribes. There are two important mosques here: Jama el-Hamra (Red Mosque) with a 14th-century minaret, and Jama el-Beïda (White Mosque).

Fès El-Jedid City Centre

① Dar el-Makhzen
② Moulay Abdallah Quarter
③ Grande Rue de Fès el-Jedid and Muslim Quarters
④ Mellah
⑤ Grande Rue des Mérinides and Rue Boukhessissat
⑥ Danan Synagogue
⑦ Grand Méchouar
⑧ Vieux Méchouar
⑨ Petit Méchouar
⑩ Kasbah Cherarda

0 metres 200
0 yards 200

Richly ornamented door to a house in the mellah

🏛 Mellah
Accessible via Place des Alaouites or Bab el-Mellah.

Bab el-Semarine, then Bab el-Mellah leads into the mellah, the Jewish quarter of Fès. The name *mellah* probably comes from the Arabic word for "salt", the terrain on which the quarter grew.

This quarter, thought to be the first Jewish enclave to be established in Morocco, was originally located in the northern part of Fès el-Bali, in the El-Yahoudi Quarter next to the Karaouiyine district. In the early 13th century the Merinid rulers moved it near the palace, to the site of a former kasbah that was once occupied by the sultan's Syrian archers. The rulers of Fès had undertaken to protect the Jewish community, in return for an annual levy collected by the state treasury. The Jewish quarter's new location afforded the inhabitants greater security.

With its souks, workshops, schools, synagogues and a cemetery, the quarter flourished, providing the Jewish community with strong social cohesion and unrivalled opportunities for social advancement. Like the Muslims elsewhere, most of the Jews in the district were grouped according to their craft speciality. Thus Leo Africanus mentioned metal-working, recording that only the Jews worked with gold and silver. Today, the Jews of Fès have left to settle in Casablanca or have emigrated abroad, to Israel in particular.

Exploring the mellah reveals a striking contrast with the Muslim quarters. In architectural terms it is another world, the buildings being higher, narrower and more closely spaced. The present boundaries of the Jewish quarter were established only at the end of the 18th century, during the time of the Alaouite sultan Moulay Yazid, and the space available was small. As a result, the inhabitants were forced to build two-storey houses around tiny courtyards, and space to move around in was very restricted.

🏛 Rue des Mérinides and Rue Boukhessissat
Accessible via Bab el-Semarine or Place des Alaouites. Jewellery Souk: **Open** from 9am Sat–Thu.

A central rectilinear axis, lined with various workshops and a *kissaria*, divides the mellah into two. All the commercial activity in the quarter takes place in this street, which was once the economic and spiritual centre of the mellah. Rue des Mérinides cuts through the jewellery souk, where Jewish goldsmiths could once be seen at work.

Rue Boukhessissat separates the mellah from the Dar el-Makhzen. With some luxury residences, this was once the aristocratic area. The design of the houses here is the most unified and harmonious in the mellah. The rows of houses open onto the street, each house having a workshop on the ground floor. The upper storeys are fronted by generously proportioned, finely carved wooden balconies that are characteristic of the Jewish architecture of Fès.

The Danan Synagogue, nestling between houses in the mellah

✡ Danan Synagogue
Rue Der el-Feran Teati. **Open** 9am–5pm daily. No entrance fee but a small contribution is requested. Jewish Cemetery: **Closed** Sat.

The 17th-century synagogue, the property of a family of rabbis from Andalusia, looks as if it has been squeezed in between the houses in the mellah. The interior is divided into four aisles. A trap door in the aisle on the far right opens onto a stairway that leads down to a *mikve* – a bath for ritual purification where the faithful were cleansed of their sins. Above this fourth aisle is the *azara*, the women's gallery, which offers an overall view of

Tombs in the Jewish cemetery

The Vieux Méchouar, accessible via Bab el-Seba

the synagogue. It is worth going out onto the terrace for a sweeping view of the mellah, and of the white tombs of the Jewish cemetery below.

The Méchouars

Méchouars are wide, walled parade grounds used on ceremonial military occasions. Processions and ceremonies, such as acts of allegiance and the acknowledgment of the royal right to rule, are also performed here. There are three such esplanades in Fès. The **Grand Méchouar**, in the northwest, also known as the Méchouar de Bab Boujat, is an extensive parade ground. The **Méchouar de Bab Dekaken** (Gate of the Benches), or **Vieux Méchouar**, in the northeast, is a rectangular esplanade with the high ramparts of the Makina on one side. It links Bab Segma, the Merinid gate, and Bab el-Seba. It is here that the population gathered at sunset to watch dancers, musicians and storytellers. The **Petit Méchouar**, the smallest of the three, links the Méchouar de Bab Dekaken and Dar el-Makhzen. It can be reached through **Bab el-Seba** (Gate of the Lion), which once defended the entrance to the palace.

On Avenue des Français, just south of Bab el-Seba, a narrow street on the right, reachable through an opening in the wall, leads, after about 150 m (165 yards), to a large *noria* (water-wheel) built in 1287 by the Andalusians. The **Makina** was an arsenal, established by Moulay el-Hassan in 1855 with the help of Italian officers. It was built on the west side of the Méchouar de Bab Dekaken. Having fallen into disuse, the Makina was restored. It is now used as a concert hall and conference venue.

Kasbah Cherarda
North of the town, accessible via Bab Segma.

Once known as the Kasbah el-Khmis (Thursday Fort), after the El-Khmis Souk which took place along the northern and eastern walls, this kasbah was built by Moulay Rachid in the 17th century. Its present name is derived from a former kasbah built nearby by a Cherarda *caid* (chief) to defend his tribe's grain stores. With Bab Segma and Bab Dekaken, the kasbah formed a system of fortifications that controlled the road to Meknès and Tangier, and protected Fès el-Jedid and the intersection with Fès el-Bali.

Enclosed within crenellated walls set with sturdy square towers, the kasbah has two monumental gateways, one on the western and the other on the eastern side. The kasbah now contains a hospital and an annexe of the Karaouiyine university. Beneath the walls on the southern and western sides, in an area where Almoravid and Almohad grain stores once stood, are the tombs of the Bab el-Mahrouk cemetery. Among them the small Mausoleum of Sidi Boubker el-Arabi can be seen.

Walls of the Kasbah Cherarda, built by Moulay Rachid in the 17th century

MEKNÈS & VOLUBILIS

Located between the fertile plain of the Rarb and the Middle Atlas, Meknès and Volubilis lie at the heart of an agricultural area that has been Morocco's grain store since ancient times. The historical importance of the two cities can be clearly seen in the ruins of Volubilis, capital of Mauretania Tingitana and the most important archaeological site in Morocco, as well as in the grandeur of the Moorish buildings in Meknès.

From the time of its foundation in the tenth century to the arrival of the Alaouites in the 17th century, Meknès was no more than a small town overshadowed by Fès, its neighbour and rival. It was not until the reign of Moulay Ismaïl *(see pp58–9)*, which began in 1672, that Meknès first rose to the rank of imperial city. With tireless energy, the sultan set about building gates, ramparts, mosques and palaces. This ambitious building programme continued throughout his reign and involved robbing the ruins of Volubilis *(see pp206–209)* and the Palais el-Badi in Marrakech *(see p239)*. After 50 years, work was still not completed. Although the sultan's impatience was often a hindrance, he reinvigorated palace architecture.

Today, Meknès is one of the largest cities in Morocco, with a population approaching a million. It is a dynamic economic centre, renowned for its olives, wine and mint tea. The imperial city stands alongside the new town, on the banks of Wadi Boufekrane.

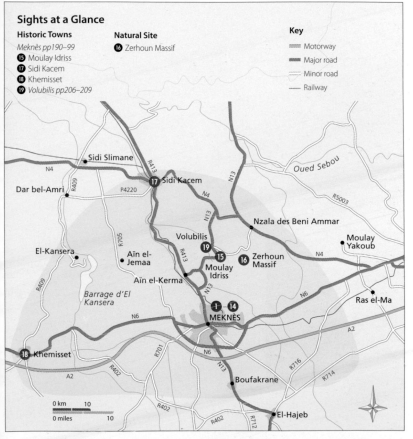

Sights at a Glance

Historic Towns
Meknès pp190–99
⓯ Moulay Idriss
⓱ Sidi Kacem
⓲ Khemisset
⓳ *Volubilis pp206–209*

Natural Site
⓰ Zerhoun Massif

Key
▨▨▨ Motorway
▬▬▬ Major road
▭▭▭ Minor road
——— Railway

◀ Ancient ruins in Volubilis

Exploring Meknès

Three well-defined quarters – the
medina, the imperial city and Ville
Nouvelle (the New Town) – make
up the city of Meknès. The medina
is a densely packed quarter. The
kasbah, or imperial city, contains
the finest of the lavish buildings
constructed by Moulay Ismaïl.
Ville Nouvelle is located on the
east bank of Wadi Boufekrane.

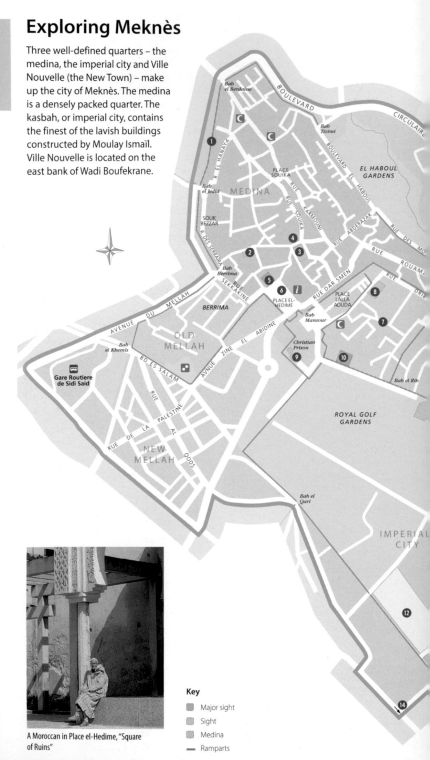

A Moroccan in Place el-Hedime, "Square
of Ruins"

Key

■ Major sight

■ Sight

■ Medina

— Ramparts

VISITORS' CHECKLIST

Practical Information
🗺 999,000. ℹ Place
Administrative (0535) 52 55 38.

Transport
🚌 🚍

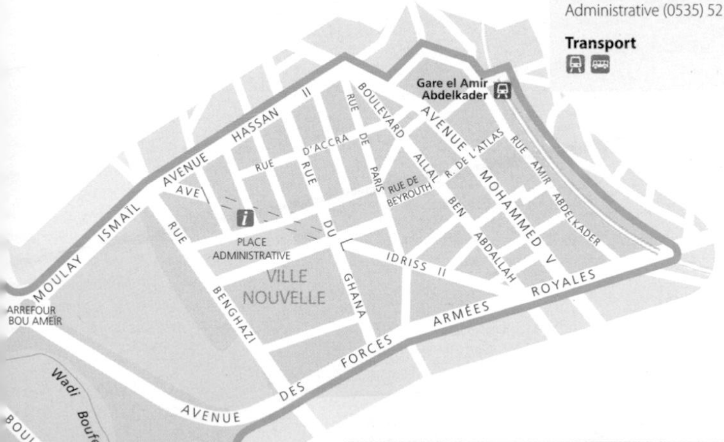

View over the rooftops of the medina in Meknès

Gare el Amir
Abdelkader

AVENUE HASSAN II

RUE D'ACCRA

BOULEVARD

RUE DE PARIS

AVE

AVENUE

RUE DU GHANA

RUE DE BEYROUTH

AVENUE ALLAL BEN ABDALLAH

R. DE L'ATLAS

RUE AMIR ABDELKADER

AVENUE MOHAMMED V

RUE

PLACE
ADMINISTRATIVE

VILLE
NOUVELLE

BENGHAZI

IDRISS II

ARMÉES

ROYALES

DES FORCES

AVENUE

MOULAY ISMAIL

ARREFOUR
BOU AMEIR

Wadi Boufekrane

BOULEVARD

ABDERRAHMANE

BEN

ZIDANE

MECHOUAR

Bab el Nouara

0 metres   400
0 yards   400

Sights at a Glance

Historic Sites and Quarters

❷ Souks and Kissaria
⓬ Bassin de l'Aguedal
⓮ Haras de Meknès

Buildings and Monuments

❶ Ramparts
❸ Grand Mosque
❹ Bou Inania Medersa
❻ Bab Mansour el-Aleuj and
   Place el-Hedime
❼ Dar el-Kebira Quarter
❽ Lalla Aouda Mosque
❾ Koubba el-Khayatine and
   Habs Qara
❿ *Mausoleum of Moulay Ismaïl*
   pp198–9
⓫ Dar el-Makhzen
⓭ Dar el-Ma and Heri es-Souani

Museum

❺ *Musée Dar Jamaï pp194–5*

For keys to symbols *see back flap*

Getting Around

Place el-Hedime is a good starting point
for exploring the medina and the imperial
city. Parking is available not far from this
square. From here, it is an easy walk to the
area around Bab Mansour and to the
Mausoleum of Moulay Ismaïl. To see the
rest of the imperial city, particularly Dar
el-Ma, a car is needed.

Bab el-Berdaïne, one of the gates into the medina of Meknès

❶ Ramparts

Encircling the medina, Meknès.

Protected by three stretches of wall that together amount to about 40 km (25 miles), the medina has the appearance of a sturdy fortress set with elegant gates. **Bab el-Berdaïne** (Gate of the Pack-Saddle-Makers), on the northern side, was built by Moulay Ismaïl. It is flanked by protruding square towers crowned by merlons, and stylized flowers in *zellij* tilework decorate its exterior façade. West of the gate, the walled cemetery contains one of the most highly venerated mausoleums in Morocco – that of Sidi Mohammed ben Aïssa, founder of the brotherhood of the Aïssaoua (see p202).

On the southern side of the cemetery stands **Bab el-Siba** (Gate of Anarchy) and **Bab el-Jedid** (New Gate, although in fact it is one of the oldest in Meknès). Further south is **Bab Berrima**, which leads into the medina's principal souks. To the west stands **Bab el-Khemis** (Thursday Gate), which once led into the mellah, now non-existent. The remarkable decoration of the gate's façade is on a par with that of Bab el-Berdaïne.

The layout of the medina, a medieval labyrinth, is identical to that of the other imperial cities. There are a few main thoroughfares.

Rue Karmouni, which runs through the quarter from north to south links Bab el-Berdaïne with the spiritual and economic heart of the medina. Rue des Souks runs from Bab Berrima, in the west, also to the heart of the medina. Several smaller streets radiate from this centre, which is marked by the Grand Mosque and the Bou Inania Medersa.

❷ Souks and Kissaria

Rue des Souks, Meknès. **Open** daily.

A network of small covered or open streets lined with shops and workshops, the souks are a fascinating encapsulation of the 17th- and 18th-century Moroccan urban environment. Rue des Souks, near Bab Berrima, is filled with hardware merchants *(akarir)*, corn chandlers *(bezzazine)*, and fabric sellers *(serrayriya)*, while metalsmiths *(haddadin)* are to be found in the old Rue des Armuriers.

Minaret of the En-Nejjarine Mosque, the Mosque of the Carpenters

Bab Berrima leads through to Souk En-Nejjarine, the Carpenters' Souk, which is next to that of the brass and coppersmiths, and to the Cobblers' Souk *(sebbat)*.

The **En-Nejjarine Mosque**, built by the Almohads in the 12th century, was restored by Mohammed ben Abdallah in about 1756, when it was given a new minaret. Set back from the En-Nejjarine Souk, in the **Ed-Dlala Kissaria**, is the location of a Berber souk. Every day from 3pm to 4pm, the mountain-dwellers of the Middle Atlas come to sell carpets and blankets here at auction.

Ablutions fountain in the Grand Mosque in Meknès

❸ Grand Mosque

Rue des Souk es Sebbat, Meknès. **Open** daily. **Closed** to non-Muslims.

The Grand Mosque, which stands near the souks and the Bou Inania Medersa, was established in the 12th century during the reign of the Almoravids. It was remodelled in the 14th century. The main façade is pierced by an imposing doorway with a carved awning. The green-glazed terracotta tiles of the roof and of the 18th-century minaret are particularly striking, the bright sunlight giving them an almost translucent appearance.

The **Palais el-Mansour**, a sumptuous 19th-century residence in Rue Karmouni, has been converted into a carpet and souvenir bazaar.

❹ Bou Inania Medersa

Rue des Souks es Sebbat, Meknès.
Open 8am–noon, 3–6pm daily.

This Koranic school opposite the Grand Mosque was established by the Merinid sultans in the 14th century. The building is divided into two unequal parts with a long corridor between them. On the eastern side is the medersa proper, while on the western side is an annexe for ablutions (now no longer in use). The main entrance is crowned by a flat-sided dome and faced with horseshoe arches with delicate stuccowork decoration.

A corridor leads to a beautiful courtyard in the centre of which is a pool. While three sides of the courtyard are lined with a gallery, the fourth opens onto the prayer hall. The green-tiled awnings, the sophisticated decoration of carved wood, stuccowork and colourful *zellij* tilework, as well as the mosaic-like tiled floor make the whole courtyard an entrancing sight.

The prayer hall, with carved stucco decoration and an elegant mihrab within a horseshoe arch, remains unaltered. Students' cells fill the rest of the ground floor and the upper floor. The terrace offers a fine view of the medina and the Grand Mosque next to the medersa.

Zellij tilework in the Bou Inania Medersa

❺ Musée Dar Jamaï

See pp194–5.

❻ Bab Mansour el-Aleuj and Place el-Hedime

South of the medina, Meknès.

Bab Mansour el-Aleuj (Gate of the Victorius Renegade) is named after the Christian who designed and built it. Standing like a triumphal arch before the imperial city, it pierces the walls of the kasbah and leads through

Place el-Hedime, once the grand entrance to the imperial city of Meknès

to Place Lalla Aouda and the Dar el-Kebira Quarter *(see p196)*.

Of monumental proportions and distinguished for its decoration, Bab Mansour el-Aleuj is held to be the finest gate in Meknès, or even in Morocco. It was begun by the sultan Moulay Ismaïl in about 1672, when the building of the kasbah, his first project, was under way. The gate was completed during the reign of his son, Moulay Abdallah, in 1732. The gate stands about 16 m (52 ft) high, while the arch has a span of 8 m (26 ft) wide and is surmounted by a pointed horseshoe arch. An intricate pattern of interlacing motifs is carved in relief on a background of predominantly green mosaics and tiles. The cornerpieces are filled with sgraffito floral decoration incised into dark-glazed terra-cotta. The gate is framed by protruding towers built in the style of loggias. Temporary exhibitions are sometimes held here.

Place el-Hedime (Square of Ruins) links the medina and the kasbah. It was laid out on the ruins of the Merinid kasbah that Moulay Ismaïl razed to make space for the palaces, water tanks, gardens, stables, arsenals and forts with which he planned to surround himself. The square has been restored and is now lined with modern residential buildings that are not in keeping with its historic character. Nearby, to the left of the square, is a covered food market.

Sacred Snakes

Expelled from Meknès by the sultan in the 16th century, Sidi Mohammed ben Aïssa, founder of the Aïssaoua brotherhood *(see p202)*, and his disciples fled to the desert. Famished, they ate whatever they could find – snakes, scorpions and cactus leaves. Ever since, the cobra has been the Aïssaoua's mascot, and no member ever kills one. Being immune to their venom, the Aïssaoua are often called upon to rid villages of the dangerous reptiles. Cobras also feature in the Aïssaoua's religious rituals, in which participants fall into a trance-like state.

An Aïssaoua in a trance

❺ Musée Dar Jamaï

This museum, in which Moroccan arts are displayed, is laid out in a delightful residence built in about 1882 by Mohammed Belarbi el-Jamaï, who was a grand vizier of Moulay el-Hassan in 1873–4. The sophisticated architecture of the palace includes painted wooden cornices. a green- tiled roof and a courtyard with two pools and *zellij* tilework. There is also an Andalusian garden planted with tall cypresses. Covering 2,845 sq m (30,600 sq ft), the palace also has several annexes and outbuildings.

The Museum of Moroccan Arts, occupying a large and elegant 19th-century palace

Painted wooden door from a house in Meknès

Exploring the Museum of Moroccan Arts

Before it was converted into a regional ethnographic museum, this palace incorporated a mosque, a garden, a *menzah* (pavilion), a courtyard, a small house, a kitchen and a hammam. Of the 2,000-plus objects in the museum's collection, some 670 are on display.

Woodwork

Room 1, on the ground floor, contains examples of architectural features in wood – pieces of carved and painted wood that were used in the building or decoration of the palaces and town houses of Meknès.

The exhibits also include a 17th-century minbar (pulpit) that originally stood in the Grand Mosque in Meknès.

Ceramics

Ceramics from Fès and Meknès are displayed in Room 2. Fassi potters attained unprecedented renown for their famous blue and white ware. Two kinds of blue pigment were used: a pale blueish-grey, which was in use up until the mid-19th century, and a clear blue with a violet tinge that was obtained by more modern industrial means.

The Fassi potting industry probably goes back to the 10th or 11th century. That of Meknès, by contrast, is much more recent, having been imported from Fès in about the 18th century. Three colours – brown, green and yellow – were used. Before the pottery was decorated, it was fired in a kiln and then covered in white glaze. The potter would decorate this surface with elegant motifs of Moorish inspiration.

Brass and painted wood coffer from Fès (19th century)

Perfume bottle from Tamegroute (late 18th century)

Carpets

The museum's richest section is that devoted to carpets, which fill Room 4. Most of the carpets and kilims on display come from the High and Middle Atlas. Among the latter, the most noteworthy pieces are those made by two Berber tribes, the Zemmour and the Beni M'Guild. Traditions of craftsmanship are still alive among these tribes – a relatively rare phenomenon in Morocco – and carpets similar to those on display here continue to be made.

Meknès carpets are characterized by a mixture of bright colours forming geometric patterns. This section of the museum also includes a fine collection of beautiful gold-thread embroidery, another craft speciality that has brought Meknès renown.

Gallery Guide

The eight exhibition rooms on the ground floor are arranged around the garden. Room 1 contains a display of carved and painted wood; Rooms 2 and 3 are devoted to ceramics; Room 4 to carpets and embroidery; Room 5 to kaftans and belts; Room 6 to jewellery; and Rooms 7 and 8 to the art of damascening *(see p195)*. On the upper floor, the reconstruction of a traditional Moroccan room can be seen. The museum has undergone renovation and its collections are now effectively displayed.

Costumes

The costumes of town- and city-dwellers, especially the kaftan (see pp40–41), is the theme of Room 5. The brightly coloured kaftan, a long robe worn by women on special occasions, is the quintessential garment of city-dwellers. Kaftans were often embroidered with silk, silver or gold thread, as was the belt (mdamma) worn with the kaftan. Wealthy women might even wear a belt made of silver or solid gold. The mdamma now forms part of a young townswoman's dowry.

Vase in damascened metal

Jewellery

Jewellery from several regions of Morocco is displayed in Room 6. Particular prominence is given to Berber jewellery.

Metalworking is a traditional craft that was once widespread throughout the country, and was particularly associated with Jewish craftsmen. Moroccan jewellery, which is typically made of gold or silver and sometimes set with precious or semi-precious stones, is made by age-old techniques. It forms an integral part of different types of dress (see pp40–41) and the way it is worn is highly significant. Jewellery also once indicated the wearer's geographical origin or tribal identity.

Modern copies of Berber jewellery can be seen today on offer in the souks.

Metalwork

While ceramics reached their apogee in Fès, the craftsmen of Meknès were distinguished masters of the art of damascening. The technique consists of covering a metallic surface with a patterned filigree of gold, silver or copper. There are some particularly fine damascened vases in Rooms 7 and 8. The craft is still very much alive in Meknès today, and some exquisite damascened pieces can be found in the souks of the old town.

This section of the museum also includes an interesting collection of keys decorated with the stylized names of their former owners.

The Moroccan Room

As in other ethnographic museums in the country, this museum features a reconstruction of a traditional Moroccan room. On the upper floor, it has walls covered with zellij tilework and a carved wooden domed ceiling. It is furnished with pieces from various houses and palaces in Meknès.

Reconstruction of a traditional Moroccan room, sumptuously decorated

Embroidery

Embroidery is a time-honoured craft practised by the townswomen of Morocco. Young girls start to learn embroidery as children, being taught either at home or in a workshop, and always under the supervision of a teacher (maalma). Fès, Meknès, Marrakech, Rabat, Salé, Tetouan, Chefchaouen and Azemmour are the main centres of embroidery. Each town has its own characteristic colours, stitches and repertoire of motifs. Fès embroidery is characterized by tree-like motifs, often depicted in a single colour. That of Salé alternates cross stitch and satin stitch. In Meknès embroidery (terz el-meknassi), motifs are peppered over the fabric, and bright colours are used to decorate tablecloths and scarves.

Cotton and silk embroidery from Rabat (19th century)

Chefchaouen gold-thread embroidery

Place Lalla Aouda and the minaret of the Lalla Aouda Mosque

❼ Dar el-Kebira Quarter

Behind Place Lalla Aouda (between Bab Moulay and the Lalla Aouda Mosque), Meknès.

This quarter forms part of what is known as the **Imperial City**, or the Kasbah of Moulay Ismaïl. Covering an area four times as large as that of the medina, the whole quarter is in keeping with the grand ambitions of this enterprising sultan. Protected by a double line of walls and monumental angled gates, the Imperial City has the appearance of an impregnable *ksar* (fortified village). It contains wide avenues and large squares, palaces with attractive pools and extensive gardens, as well as administrative buildings enclosed within their own ramparts.

The Imperial City comprises three palatial complexes: Dar el-Kebira, Dar el-Medrasa and Ksar el-Mhanncha. Dar el-Kebira, the Quarter of the Large House, is located southeast of the medina. It was the first palatial complex of the Imperial City that Moulay Ismaïl ordered to be built, in about 1672. It stands near Place Lalla Aouda, probably on the site of the former Almohad kasbah. The complex was cut off from the urban bustle by a double wall and by Place el-Hedime *(see p193)*.

Each palace in Dar el-Kebira contained a harem, reception rooms, hammams, kitchens, armouries, ovens and mosques. They were interlinked by a somewhat haphazard network of open or partially covered alleys. Today, the ancient heart of the Imperial City, which is partly in ruins, has become a poor district that has been filled with shanty dwellings.

The Mausoleum of Moulay Ismaïl, the Lalla Aouda Mosque and a monumental gate near Bab Bou Ameïr are the last surviving vestiges of the ostentatiously grand complex that the sultan had envisaged.

The second complex, which is now in complete ruins, was the Dar el-Medrasa. The palace comprised suites of residential rooms, some of which were used exclusively by the sultan and his harem.

❽ Lalla Aouda Mosque

Place Lalla Aouda, Meknès.
Open daily. **Closed** to non-Muslims.

The first major place of worship to be built by Moulay Ismaïl, in 1680, this mosque is one of the few of the sultan's projects to have survived intact. The building has three doorways. Two on the northwestern side open onto the former *méchouar* (parade ground) and a smaller one, on the side of the mosque where the mihrab is located, leads to a corridor running behind the mosque. It was probably the sultan's private entrance. The pitched roof is covered with green tiles.

❾ Koubba el-Khayatine and Habs Qara

Place Habs Qara. **Open** 9am–noon, 3–6pm daily. **Closed** public holidays. 🖼

This imperial pavilion, also known as the Pavilion of the Ambassadors, was used originally to receive diplomats who came to negotiate, among other things, the ransom of Christian prisoners. Later, the building was used by tailors *(khiyatine)*, who made military uniforms here. The building is crowned by a conical dome decorated with geometric and floral motifs.

Behind the pavilion are the former underground storage areas that were converted into the **Christian Prison**, or Habs Qara. The prisoners – probably Europeans captured by the corsairs of Rabat – were made to work on the sultan's herculean building projects. Chroniclers recorded that thousands of convicts were incarcerated in these underground galleries, which were later partly destroyed by an earthquake.

❿ Mausoleum of Moulay Ismaïl

See pp198–9.

⓫ Dar el-Makhzen

Place Bab el-Mechouar, Meknès.
Closed to the public.

This royal complex was formerly known as the Palace of the Labyrinth, after a white marble pool fashioned as a labyrinth. In contrast to Dar el-Kebira and Koubba el-Khiriyatine, the complex has a neat and compact layout.

It is divided into eight parts and is surrounded by walls set with bastions. In the centre stands a monumental gate,

Gate of the Kasbah Hedrach, Dar el-Makhzen

The Bassin de l'Aguedal, a water tank created by Moulay Ismaïl

the fulsomely decorated **Bab el-Makhzen** (Gate of the Warehouse), built by Moulay el-Hassan in 1888. A second gate, **Bab el-Jedid** (New Gate), was made on the northwestern side. Features of the complex include a *méchouar* and **Kasbah Hadrach**, the former barracks of the sultan's army of black slaves.

⓬ Bassin de l'Aguedal

Aguedal Quarter, Meknès.

This water tank *(sahrij)* was built within the kasbah by Moulay Ismaïl. It has a surface area of 40,000 sq m (430,000 sq ft) and its purpose was to supply water to the palace and the Imperial City, including its mosques, hammams, gardens and orchards. The women of the harem, so it is said, would sail on it in their pleasure boats. Only a few stretches of its crenellated walls survive.

The spot has suffered some unfortunate alterations carried out in an effort to create a place where the people of Meknès could come to walk.

⓭ Dar el-Ma and Heri es-Souani

L'Agdal Quarter, Meknès. **Open** 9am–noon, 3–6pm daily.

Dar el-Ma, the Water House, held the town's water reserves and was another of Moulay Ismaïl's grandiose projects. The huge barrel-vaulted building contains 15 rooms, each with

a *noria* (water wheel) once worked by horses to draw underground water by means of scoops. The terraces offer a fine view of the city.

Dar el-Ma gives access to **Heri es-Souani**, the so-called Grainstore Stables, which are

Horsemen in Heri es-Souani

considered to be one of the sultan's finest creations. This monumental building, with 29 aisles, was designed for storing grain. The thick walls, as well as a network of underground passages, maintained the temperature inside the grainstore at a low and constant level. The ceilings collapsed during the earthquake of 1755.

⓮ Haras de Meknès

Zitoune Quarter of Meknès, southwest of the town. From Dar el-Ma, 1 km (0.6 mile) towards Dar el-Beïda, turning right 400 m (440 yds) beyond Dar el-Beïda and continuing for 2 km (1 mile) to the south. **Open** 9am–noon, 2–6pm Mon–Fri. 🖼

Although it cannot rival the modern studs in Rabat and Marrakech, the Haras de Meknès is well known in Morocco. The stud was established in 1912 with the aim of improving blood lines and promoting various Moroccan breeds of horse for use in racing, competitive riding and fantasias *(see p39)*.

The stud can accommodate 231 horses, ranging from purebred Arabs and Barbs to English thoroughbreds and Anglo-Arabs. A visit here may include seeing horses being put through their paces.

The Royal Cities

The creation of royal cities in the Islamic world dates from the late 8th century. The Almohads, the Merinids and the Alaouites under Moulay Ismaïl continued this tradition, and it spread throughout the Maghreb, where it survived until recently. The royal city is an architectural complex built to protect the king and his courtiers. Several palaces and other buildings were needed to accommodate all the members of the royal household. Water tanks were built to irrigate the many gardens and to supply the baths and hammams of the harem. Designed both for royal receptions and for the king's private life, the royal city was architecturally the most sophisticated and most sumptuous component of a great urban centre.

Bab el-Makhzen, gateway of Dar el-Makhzen, Meknès

⓾ Mausoleum of Moulay Ismaïl

Featuring a suite of three rooms, 12 columns and a central sanctuary where the great sultan *(see pp58–9)* lies, the Mausoleum of Moulay Ismaïl is in some aspects reminiscent of the Saadian Tombs in Marrakech *(see pp242–3)*. The mausoleum was built in the 17th century and was remodelled in the 18th and 20th centuries. The wife of Moulay Ismaïl and his son, Moulay Ahmed al-Dahbi, as well as the sultan Moulay Abderrahman (1822–59), are laid to rest in the burial chamber, which is decorated with stuccowork and mosaics.

View of Meknès and the mausoleum

Mihrab
The mausoleum's mihrab is located in the open courtyard. This unusual position differs from the arrangement at the Saadian Tombs in Marrakech *(see pp242–3)*.

Finials
The roof of the mausoleum is topped with five brass spheres indentifying the building as a shrine or sacred place.

Prayer Hall
The floor of the prayer hall is covered with mats on which worshippers kneel to pray or to reflect before going into the burial chamber.

Decorated Door
This carved and painted wooden door between the ablutions room and the second room of the burial chamber is similar to those of the palaces and fine town houses of Meknès.

★ Burial Chamber
This consists of a suite of three rooms, including the ablutions room with central fountain *(above)* and the room containing the tomb of Moulay Ismaïl, and those of his wife and sons.

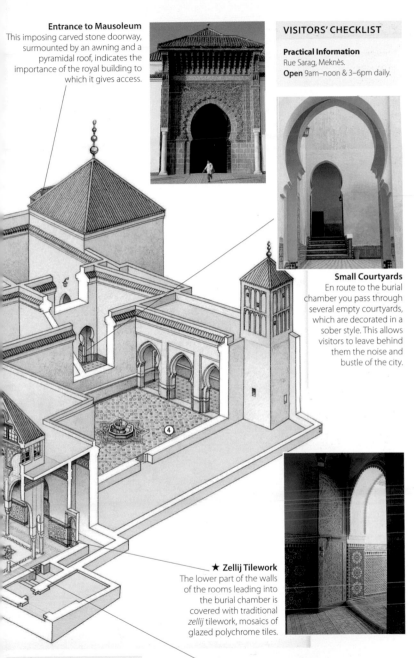

Entrance to Mausoleum
This imposing carved stone doorway, surmounted by an awning and a pyramidal roof, indicates the importance of the royal building to which it gives access.

Small Courtyards
En route to the burial chamber you pass through several empty courtyards, which are decorated in a sober style. This allows visitors to leave behind them the noise and bustle of the city.

★ Zellij Tilework
The lower part of the walls of the rooms leading into the burial chamber is covered with traditional *zellij* tilework, mosaics of glazed polychrome tiles.

★ Courtyard & Fountain
The ablutions room, paved with green glazed tiles, is a courtyard with a star-shaped fountain and bowl. Its 12 columns come from the el-Badi Palace in Marrakech.

KEY

① Tomb of Moulay Ismaïl
② Clock presented by Louis XIV, *(see pp58–9)*
③ Cemetery
④ Open courtyard

Spectacular interiors of the Mausoleum of Moulay Ismaïl ▶

Holy Men and Mystics

In Morocco, the Islamic faith of law-makers *(fkihs)* and learned men *(ulema)* coexists with popular forms of religion, in which the cult of saints and the role of brotherhoods (known as *tariqas*, meaning "ways") are prominent. Many followers of these religions are craftsmen and traders, who gather to perform spiritualist rites *(zikrs)*, involving singing, dancing and music, according to the teaching of their respective founder. These religions are connected to those of Eastern mystics, and they have spread well beyond the boundaries of Morocco. This spiritualist branch of Islam is widely known as Sufism, after the rough woollen garment *(suf)* worn by certain ascetics.

The pilgrimage to Sidi Ahmed Ou Mghanni takes place near Imilchil, in the territory of the Aït Haddidou. It is known as the Marriage Fair, as many betrothals are made on this occasion.

The Aïssaoua

This brotherhood came into being in the 16th century. Its beliefs are based on the teachings of Sidi Mohammed ben Aïssa, a mystic who was born in the 15th century. Through El-Jazouli, the holy man of Marrakech, it is connected to Chadhiliya, the great Sufi "way" that spread throughout the Muslim world. The Aïssaoua brotherhood exists in Meknès (see p193) and Fès, and also in Algeria.

The Mausoleum of Sidi Mohammed ben Aïssa, in Meknès, contains the tomb of the holy man who founded the Aïssaoua "way".

The spectacular ceremonies of the Aïssaoua, involving banners, drums and incense, have always made a deep impression on foreigners in Morocco. This scene, entitled *Les Aïssaouas*, was painted by Georges Clairin (1843–1919).

The Aïssaoua are always dressed in white. They have a fear of black.

Like the Hamadcha, the Aïssaoua are a popular brotherhood because of some of their practices. During their *moussem* (festival) they perform long drawn-out and impressive rituals, called *hadras*, which are accompanied by singing, dancing and drumming. These rituals may send them into a trance or lead followers to perform orgies of self-mutilation.

The *moussem* of **Moulay Abdallah**, near El-Jadida, can draw up to 150,000 visitors and a huge tent city springs up on the site.

The *moussem* in **Guelmim**, a town on the caravan route on the edge of the Sahara *(see p298)*, takes place each June in honour of the holy man Sidi el-Ghazi. Attended by the Reguibat, nomads known as the "blue men", this is also when a major camel fair takes place.

During the *moussem* of Moulay Idriss II in Fès, the various guilds of craftsmen, such as tanners, shoemakers, blacksmiths, brass-founders and coppersmiths *(above)* process through the medina, bringing gifts and sacrifices to the *zaouia* (shrine) of this highly venerated holy man.

Tombs of Holy Men

Marabout of Sidi Ahmad Ou Mghanni

Followers gather eagerly in order to make pilgrimages to the many tombs of holy men *(marabouts)* so as to seek a blessing *(baraka)*. These small mausoleums, which are often covered with a white dome known as a *koubba*, can be seen throughout the country. Some of the more important shrines – or *zaouias* – are the seat of a religious brotherhood and, besides the tomb of the holy man, consist of buildings in which pilgrims are accommodated and religious instruction given. Once a year, certain pilgrimages take the form of *moussems*, great gatherings that are simultaneously joyous occasions, festivals for the performance of traditional shows and commercial fairs.

Moussem in Guelmim

⑮ Moulay Idriss

Road Map D2. 27 km (38 miles) north of Meknès. 🚐 12,600. 🚌 from Meknès. 🛒 Sat. 🎪 last Thu in Aug.

The most spectacular view of Moulay Idriss is from the scenic route from Volubilis to Nzala des Beni Ammar, which runs above the more frequently used N13. In a superb setting, the bright white town clings to two rocky outcrops between which rises the **Tomb of Idriss I**, conspicuous with its green-tiled roof.

Fleeing the persecution of the Abbassid caliphs of Baghdad, Idriss found a haven in Oualili (Volubilis). A descendant of Ali, son-in-law of the Prophet Mohammed, he founded the first Arab-Muslim dynasty in Morocco. He died in 791 and was buried in the town that now bears his name. It was not until the 16th century that the town began to prosper, and it was still in the process of developing in the 17th century, during the reign of Moulay Ismaïl (see pp58–9). The latter

The grand entrance to the Tomb of Idriss I in Moulay Idriss

endowed it with defensive walls and a monumental gate, as well as Koranic schools, fountains and a new dome for the mausoleum.

The Tomb of Idriss I is closed to non-Muslims, and a wooden beam across the entrance marks this as sacred ground, or *horm*. However, from the terrace, near the Mosque of Sidi Abdallah el-Hajjam, which perches above the town, there is a splendid

view of the town and the mausoleum. The minaret (1939), whose cylindrical shape is unusual in the Maghreb, is covered with green tiles with verses from the Koran.

⑯ Zerhoun Massif

Road Map D2. About 50 km (31 miles) northwest of Meknès.

Culminating in Jbel Zerhoun, which rises to a height of 1,118 m (3,670 ft), the massif forms part of an extensive range of hills bordering the southern side of the Rif and running from the region of Meknès to the environs of Taza in the east.

This pre-Riffian terrain, consisting mostly of clay and marl, is very susceptible to fluvial erosion. As a result, a few outcrops of harder limestone and sandstone have emerged, one of which is Jbel Zerhoun, whose gorges, peaks and cliffs have all been created by erosion.

Water is abundant here, and the Romans tapped the springs to supply Volubilis. Large villages grew up on the hillsides, along the line of springs and at the foot of the massif. While fig trees, orange trees and olive trees grow on the higher slopes, corn and barley thrive in the valleys and on the lower hillsides. Enclosures (*zriba*) made of loose stones or thorny branches, for small herds of cattle, sheep and goats, can be seen near the villages.

Moulay Idriss, clinging to an outcrop of rock

For hotels and restaurants see pp306–313 and pp320–31

The verdant Zerhoun Massif, where water is plentiful

For Moroccans, Zerhoun is a holy mountain, the home of many religious men, and the setting of numerous stories and legends.

⑰ Sidi Kacem

Road Map D2. 46 km (29 miles) northwest of Meknès. ⛟ 70,000. 🚉 from Meknès. 🚌 Thu.

Sidi Kacem grew out of a military outpost that was set up in 1915 near a *zaouia* and the souk of the local Cherarda tribe. It is now an important agricultural and industrial centre on the plain of the eastern Rharb.

The three building complexes that dominate the town bear witness to the history and economic activity of Sidi Kacem. One is the railway station, at the intersection of lines running between Rabat and Fès and between Tangier and Fès. The second is the oil refinery (initially for local, then for imported fuel). Thirdly, there are the grain silos, at the heart of a well-watered and productive region.

Sidi Kacem is a major centre of agricultural food production and of brickmaking. These industries have made the town an important banking and commercial hub.

⑱ Khemisset

Road Map D2. ⛟ 90,000. 🚌 from Meknès. 🚌 Tue.

This town was founded in 1924, on the site of a military outpost on the road from Rabat to Fès. Now a provincial capital,

Carpet made by the Zemmour, with graphic geometric motifs

Khemisset is also the "capital" of the confederation of the Berber-speaking Zemmour tribes.

This is a good place to stop, since there are many cafés and restaurants. The town also has a crafts cooperative where you can buy regional specialities, such as carpets and mats woven in palm fibre or wool. Every Tuesday, Khemisset is the venue for one of the most important country souks in Morocco, with almost 1,900 stalls.

Country Souks

At daybreak, hundreds of country people travelling on foot, on donkeys or in heavily laden trucks make their way to a site where tents and stalls are being set up. Around 850 country souks – named after the day on which they take place – are held every week in Morocco, drawing people from up to 10 km (6 miles) around. On an area of open ground, alleys between the stalls form according to a well-defined plan. The pattern on which the goods are laid out is similar to that of the economic layout of a medina. In the centre are such prized goods as fabric and clothing, followed by basketwork, carpets and blankets; on the periphery are second-hand items, scrap metal, humble traders such as cobblers and hairdressers, and also food stalls. Beyond, various livestock markets are laid out in separate areas.

Returning from the souk

Souks allow townspeople to buy agricultural produce and craft items brought in by country people, who in turn stock up with groceries, sugar, tea and fruit. They provide services, entertainment and food, but also attract charlatans and storytellers. The civic authorities also use souks to set up temporary registry offices, post offices and health centres. Permanent shops that may appear on the site of a weekly souk sometimes lead to the establishment of a new town.

A country souk, with tents set up for a day

⑲ Volubilis

The ancient town of Volubilis backs on to a triangular spur jutting out from the Zerhoun Massif. The site was settled and began to prosper under the Mauretanian kings, from the 3rd century BC to AD 40. Temples from this period, as well as a strange tumulus, have been uncovered. When Mauretania was annexed by the Roman emperor Claudius in AD 45, Volubilis was raised to the status of *municipia* (free town), becoming one of the most important cities in Tingitana. The public buildings in the northeastern quarter date from the 1st century, and those around the forum from the 2nd century. After Rome withdrew from Mauretania in the 3rd century, the city declined. It was inhabited by Christians but had been Islamicized when Idriss I arrived in 788.

Mosaic from the House of Dionysus and the Four Seasons

House of the Columns
This house is arranged around a huge peristyle courtyard with a circular pool. Columns with twisted fluting and composite capitals front the grand reception room.

KEY

① *Macellum* (market)

② House of the Athlete

③ House of the Dog

④ Knight's House

⑤ **The House of the Labours of Hercules** is named after a mosaic found here depicting the Greek hero's 12 labours.

⑥ *Decumanus maximus*.

⑦ House of Dionysus and the Four Seasons

⑧ House of the Bathing Nymphs

⑨ Gordian Palace

⑩ Tangier Gate

⑪ House of the Golden Coins

⑫ Aqueduct

⑬ Artisans' quarters

⑭ House of Orpheus

★ Triumphal Arch
Bestriding the *decumanus maximus*, the triumphal arch overlooks plantations of cereals and olive trees. The fertile plain to the west of Volubilis has provided the area with grain and oil since antiquity.

The Site of Volubilis Today

The forum, basilica and capitol were built in the 2nd century, under the Severi dynasty. Richly appointed residences paved with mosaics also graced the city. These buildings are still easily identifiable today. Excavations have shown that the site was still inhabited during the Almoravid period (see pp48–9).

VISITORS' CHECKLIST

Practical Information
Road Map D2.
31 km (19 miles) northwest of Meknès; 5 km (3 miles) from Moulay Idriss. **Open** 8am–one hour before sunset daily. 🎫 🚻 🛍

Transport
🚌 from Meknès to Moulay Idriss, then by *grand taxi* to the site.

★ Diana and the Bathing Nymphs
In this mosaic in the House of the Cortège of Venus, the nymphs admire Diana as she receives water from Pegasus, the winged horse. A similar scene is depicted in a mosaic in the House of the Bathing Nymphs.

★ Basilica
Apart from the triumphal arch, this was the only building whose ruins were still impressive when excavations began. The interior is divided into three aisles and two apses.

Visitors' entrance

The Capitol
Of the original building (dating from the early 3rd century) only the foundations remain. The sacrificial altar, identifiable by its moulded base, stood in front of the steps.

Exploring Volubilis

The ancient site of Volubilis was known from the 18th century, but it was not until the late 19th century that it was first investigated. Excavations resumed in 1915, and have continued almost uninterrupted since, although extensive areas still remain to be explored. Although Volubilis is not as large as some other Roman towns, it shows how thoroughly romanized Mauretania Tingitana had become. This is seen in the public buildings and sophisticated town houses within the 2nd-century walls, which enclose an area of more than 400,000 sq m (4,300,000 sq ft). The site, a pre-existing settlement on which the Romans imposed their way of life, features baths, oil presses, bakeries, aqueducts, drains and shops that evoke the inhabitants' daily lives. Volubilis is well-signposted and easy to explore.

Reconstruction of an oil press, showing the baskets used for pressing the olives

geometric patterns and bath suites with hypocausts (underfloor heating).

The House of Orpheus
Located in the southern quarter of the city, the House of Orpheus is remarkable not only for its size but for the rooms that it contains. Opposite the entrance is a large peristyle courtyard, with a slightly sunken square pool that is decorated with a mosaic of tritons, cuttlefish, dolphins and other sea creatures. The *tablinum*, looking onto the courtyard, is the main reception room; the centre is paved with the Orpheus Mosaic, the largest of the circular mosaics that have been discovered in Volubilis. A richly dressed Orpheus is depicted charming a lion, an elephant and other animals with his lyre. The house also has an oil press with purification tanks, as well as private areas. These have further rooms paved with mosaics in

Oil Press
The reconstruction of an oil press near the House of Orpheus shows how this device worked in Roman times. The olives were crushed in a cylindrical vat by the action of a millstone fixed to a vertical axis. The resulting pulp was emptied into rush or esparto baskets laid beneath planks of wood on which pressure was exerted by means of a beam that acted as a lever. The oil ran out along channels and into purification tanks set up outside. Water poured into the tanks forced

Reconstruction of Volubilis

Most of the major public and private buildings date from the 2nd and 3rd centuries AD, when the city was at its peak. Only the centre of the city has been excavated.

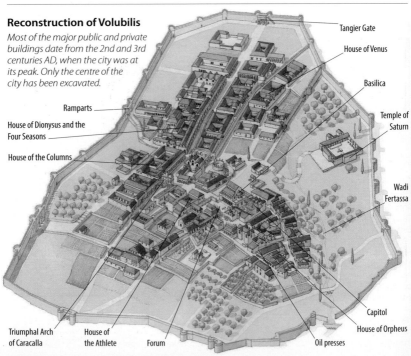

Tangier Gate

House of Venus

Basilica

Temple of Saturn

Ramparts

House of Dionysus and the Four Seasons

House of the Columns

Wadi Fertassa

Capitol

House of Orpheus

Triumphal Arch of Caracalla

House of the Athlete

Forum

Oil presses

the better-quality oil to float to the surface. It was then poured off into large earthenware jars for local use or for export.

The Forum, Basilica and Capitol

Like the other major public buildings in the heart of the city, the unusually small forum dates from the early 3rd century. It was the focal point of public life and administration, as well as a meeting place where business was done. It is continued on its western side by the *macellum*, a market that was originally covered.

On the left of the entrance, from the direction of the oil press, stands the stele of Marcus Valerius Servus, which lists the territory that the citizens of Volubilis possessed in the hinterland.

On the eastern side of the forum, a short flight of steps and three semicircular arches leads into the basilica. This was the meeting place of the curia (senate), as well as the commercial exchange and tribunal, and somewhere to take a stroll. On the capitol, south of the basilica, public rites in honour of Jupiter, Juno and Minerva were performed.

The *decumanus*, linking Tangier Gate and the triumphal arch

House of the Athlete

The athlete that gives this house its name is the *desultor*, or chariot jumper, who took part in the Olympic Games. He would leap from his horse or his chariot in the middle of a race and remount or get back in immediately.

The Chariot Jumper, parodied in this mosaic

The mosaic here depicts the *desultor* as a parody. The naked athlete is shown bestriding a donkey backwards, and holding a *cantharus*, a drinking vessel given as a prize. The scarf, another emblem of victory, flutters in the background, behind the horseman.

House of the Dog and House of the Ephebe

The House of the Dog, behind the triumphal arch on the western side, is laid out to a typical Roman plan. A double doorway opens onto a lobby leading through to the atrium. This room, which is lined on three sides by a colonnade, contains a pool and leads in turn to a large dining room, or *triclinium*. In 1916, a bronze statue of a dog (*see p83*) was discovered in one of the rooms off the *triclinium*.

Opposite the House of the Dog stands the House of the Ephebe, where a beautiful statue of an ivy-wreathed ephebe (youth in military training) was found in 1932. It is now in the Musée Archéologique in Rabat (*see pp82–3*).

Triumphal Arch and Decumanus Maximus

According to the inscription that it bears, the triumphal arch was erected in AD 217 by the governor Marcus Aurelius Sebastenus in honour of Caracalla and his mother Julia Domna. The statues that originally filled the niches in the arch were surmounted by busts of Caracalla and his mother within medallions. Above the inscription, at the top of the monument, ran a

frieze and a band, and the whole was crowned by a chariot drawn by six horses.

The arch, which stands over 8 m (26 ft) high, was reconstructed in 1933. It faces west onto the plain and east onto the *decumanus maximus*. This main axis through the city, 400 m (1,312 ft) long and 12 m (39 ft) wide, leads from the triumphal arch in the southwest to the gateway known as Tangier Gate in the northeast.

Parallel with the *decumanus maximus,* and a few metres away on its southern side, ran an aqueduct, substantial parts of which survive. This brought water from the Aïn Ferhana, a spring 1 km (0.6 mile) east-southeast of Volubilis, on Jbel Zerhoun. The largest of these fountains can be seen between the basilica and the triumphal arch.

Aristocratic Quarter

Fine houses, such as the elegant House of the Columns, House of the Knight and House of the Labours of Hercules, constituted the aristocratic quarter. The House of Dionysus and the Four Seasons, and the House of the Bathing Nymphs, have high-quality mosaics. The Gordian Palace, named after Emperor Gordian III (238–44) and probably the residence of the Roman governor, is notable for the 12 columns that front it and the horseshoe-shaped pool with almost perfectly semicircular outlines.

Autumn, from the Four Seasons

Cortège of Venus

Busts of Cato the Younger (*see p83*) and Juba II were found south of the *decumanus.* The mosaic depicting the Cortège of Venus, which paved the *triclinium*, is displayed in the Musée Archéologique in Tangier (*see pp136–7*). Some of the mosaics have motifs very similiar to those seen in Berber carpets today.

MIDDLE ATLAS

A wild region of rare beauty, the Middle Atlas is surprisingly little visited. The great cedar forests that cover the mountain sides between deep valleys stretch as far as the eye can see. Bordered by the fertile plain of the Saïs and the cities of Fès and Meknès, the mountainous heights of the Middle Atlas are the territory of Berber tribes, whose population is thinly scattered over the area.

The mountains of the Middle Atlas are traversed by one of the main routes through to southern Morocco, running from Fès to the Tafilalt. It is worth taking some time here to appreciate the beauty and serenity of the region's landscapes.

This mountain chain northeast of the Atlas is 350 km (217 miles) long, and is delimited on its eastern side by Tazzeka National Park, whose terrain is scarred with caves and gorges. South of Sefrou, forests of cedar, holm-oak and cork oak form a patchwork with the bare volcanic plateaux and small lakes brimming with fish.

The Oum er-Rbia rises in the heart of the mountains. The longest river in Morocco, it runs for 600 km (375 miles) before reaching the Atlantic. To the west,

the Middle Atlas abuts the foothills of the High Atlas. Here, the Cascades d' Ouzoud crash down 100 m (328 ft) to the bottom of a natural chasm wreathed in luxuriant vegetation.

Nicknamed the Switzerland of Morocco, the Middle Atlas also features some exquisitely scenic small towns at mid-altitude. Ifrane, which has stone-built chalets with red-tiled roofs, Azrou, a resort on the slopes of a cedar plantation, and Imouzzer du Kandar are among the most attractive; they also serve as bases for hikes and tours in the mountains.

A tour of the lakes takes in the wild and arid mountain landscape, which is populated only by Berbers. Forest roads darkened by towering stands of cedar are patrolled by peaceable macaques.

Berber shepherd with his flock of sheep in the lakes region of the Middle Atlas

◀ One of the most popular sights in Morocco, the Cascades d'Ouzoud

Exploring the Middle Atlas

A varied landscape characterizes the Middle Atlas. The eastern part receives scant rainfall and is thus only sparsely covered with vegetation, but above the deep valleys rise Jbel Bou Naceur and Jbel Bou Iblane: reaching a height of 3,340 m (10,962 ft) and 3,190 m (10,470 ft) respectively, these are the highest peaks of the Middle Atlas. In the thinly populated central high plateaux between Azrou and Timhadit, lakes (known as *dayet* or *aguelmame*) fill the craters of extinct volcanoes and are surrounded by forests. The western part receives the highest rainfall and arable areas have attracted denser populations. Here, plateaux and valleys are covered in forests of cedar, cork oak and maritime pine. From December, peaks over 2,000 m (6,564 ft) are covered with snow. The Middle Atlas is the territory of the semi-nomadic Beni M'Gild and Zaïana peoples.

■ **Area shown by map below**

Sidi Ka

ME

← Rab

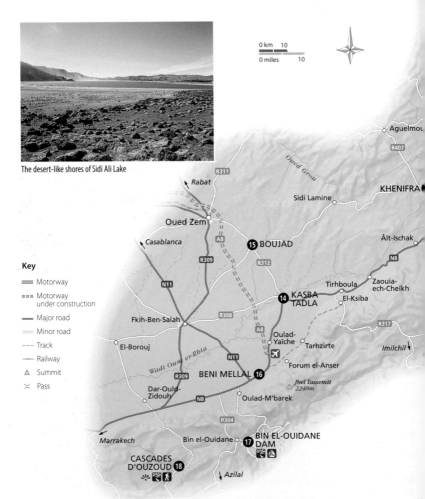

The desert-like shores of Sidi Ali Lake

0 km 10
0 miles 10

Key

═══ Motorway
=== Motorway under construction
━━ Major road
══ Minor road
--- Track
━━ Railway
△ Summit
✕ Pass

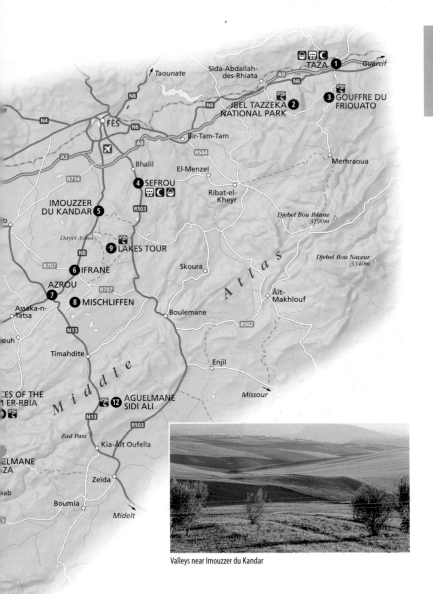

Valleys near Imouzzer du Kandar

Sights at a Glance

1. Taza
2. Jbel Tazzeka National Park
3. Gouffre du Friouato
4. Sefrou
5. Imouzzer du Kandar
6. Ifrane
7. Azrou
8. Mischliffen
10. Sources of the Oum er-Rbia
11. Aguelmane Azigza
12. Aguelmane Sidi Ali

13. Khenifra
14. Kasba Tadla
15. Boujad
16. Beni Mellal
17. Bin el-Ouidane Dam
18. Cascades d'Ouzoud

Tour
9. Lakes Tour

Getting Around

The major roads between Fès and Khenifra and between Fès and Midelt are in a reasonably good state of repair. By contrast, the minor roads are narrow and the distances that they cover are long because the terrain is hilly; they can be impassable in winter. These minor roads are, however, the only means of exploring the Middle Atlas. In the eastern part of the mountains, many tracks lead to small isolated lakes.

For keys to symbols *see back flap*

Taza, between the Rif and the Middle Atlas, on the route towards eastern Morocco

❶ Taza

Road Map E2. 120,000. from Oujda, Fès and Meknès. from Nador, El-Hoceima, Fès and Oujda. 56 Avenue Mohammed V. Moussem of Sidi Zerrouk (Sep).

Located on the route between Fès and Oujda, in the lower foothills of the Rif and the Middle Atlas, the town of Taza is a stopping-place that seldom figures on the tourist route. It is, however, one of the oldest towns in Morocco.

Taza was founded in the 8th century by the Meknassa, a Berber tribe, and was regularly seized by sultans who wished to establish their authority before going on to take Fès. The old town, built on a rocky hill, overlooks the new town, 3 km (2 miles) below, which the French began to build in 1920. The 3-km (2-mile) walls surrounding the medina date mostly from the 12th century, the Almohad period, and were restored on several occasions, notably by the Merinids in the 14th century. Moulay Ismaïl, of the Alaouite dynasty, embellished the town and heightened its role as a military stronghold on the eastern frontier.

The Andalusian Mosque, with a 12th-century minaret, stands at the entrance to the medina, from where the main street runs through to the **Grand Mosque**. Founded by the Almohad sultan Abd el-Moumen in 1135, this is one of the oldest mosques in Morocco. It is closed to non-Muslims, who are therefore unable to see the interior of the magnificent pierced dome or the fine bronze candelabrum.

There is a lively souk in the medina, as well as an unusual minaret whose summit is wider than the base of Djemma Es Souk, the Market Mosque. Bab er-Rih, in the north of the town, offers a splendid view of the orchards and olive trees below, the hills of the Rif and the slopes of Jbel Tazzeka.

❷ Jbel Tazzeka National Park

Road Map E2. 76-km (47-mile) tour starting from Taza. Sun, at Es-Sebt.

Established in 1950 to protect the cedar forests of Jbel Tazzeka, this national park offers a spectacular tour southwest of Taza.

In the middle of a valley of almond, cherry and fig trees are the **Cascades de Ras el-Oued** (falls which only flow between November and April). The winding road crosses the fertile plateau of the **Chiker**, a punch-bowl which at certain times of year becomes a small lake (*dayet*) fed by underground water.

Beyond Bab Taka, a mountain pass at an altitude of 1,540 m (5,054 ft), a narrow track leads over 9 km (5.5 miles) to the summit of Jbel Tazzeka. The peak, at an altitude of 1,980 m (6,498 ft), supports a television mast. There is a fine view north over the mountains of the Rif, west over the plain of Fès and south to the higher foothills of the Middle Atlas and the snow peaks of the Jbel Boulblanc. The road then winds through the Wadi Zireg gorge. Caves in the cliffs here are used by local shepherds.

A single-storey house in the foothills of Jbel Tazzeka

❸ Gouffre du Friouato

Road Map E2. 22 km (13.5 miles) southwe st of Taza.

This natural chasm, which was first explored in 1934, is open to visitors, although sturdy walking boots are necessary. A flight of 500 slippery steps leads down to the cave. It is 180 m (590 ft) deep and contains galleries and halls filled with fascinating stalactites, stalagmites and other formations. The adjacent **Chiker Caves** are open only to speleologists.

The impressive canyons of the Sebou gorge

❹ Sefrou

Road Map D2. 230,000. from Fès and Midelt. Thu. Cherry Festival (Jun); Moussem of Sidi Lahcen Lyoussi (Aug).

This ancient town has always stood in the shadow of Fès, the imperial capital. It takes its name from the Ahel Sefrou, a Berber tribe that was converted to Judaism 2,000 years ago, and that was then Islamicized by Idriss I in the 8th century. In the 12th century, trade with the Sahara brought Sefrou prosperity. A century later, it became home to a large colony of Jews who had fled from the Tafilalt and southern Algeria. In 1950, a third of Sefrou's population was Jewish. The majority of Jews emigrated to Israel in 1967, and the town's population is now mostly Muslim.

Sefrou is surrounded by crenellated ramparts pierced by nine gates. These ochre pisé walls have been restored on several occasions.

The town is bisected by Wadi Aggaï, which irrigates the surrounding fertile plain. Four bridges link the two parts of the town. South of the *wadi* is the mellah, the former Jewish quarter, a district of narrow winding streets. North of the *wadi* is the old medina, with its souks centred around the Grand Mosque and the *zaouia* of Sidi Lahcen Lyoussi, who became patron saint of Sefrou in the 18th century. On the north side of the town, outside the ramparts, is a crafts centre where leather goods, pottery and wrought-iron items are made.

The Cherry Festival, marking the end of the cherry harvest in June, is a major event in the town, which is surrounded by cherry orchards. The festival goes on for several days, and the major event is a grand procession marked by the coronation of the Cherry Queen. Folk dancers and musicians from the Middle Atlas, Fès and the Rif perform and there are sometimes fantasias.

The road following the river upstream for 1 km (0.6 mile) west of Sefrou leads to the **Kef el-Moumen Caves**, natural caves in the cliff face containing tombs that are venerated by Muslims and Jews. One of them is said to be that of the prophet Daniel. The **Wadi Aggaï Falls** here bring a welcome freshness to the surrounding hills.

The green-roofed **Koubba of Sidi bou Ali Serghine**, 2 km (1 mile) west of Sefrou, offers a scenic view over Sefrou and the Kandar hills. Nearby is the miraculous spring of **Lalla Rekia**, which is reputed to cure madness.

The village of **Bhalil**, 7 km (4 miles) north of Sefrou, has troglodytic dwellings. Its population, Christian during the Roman period, was converted to Islam by Idriss II.

A minor road east of Sefrou leads to the small town of El-Menzel. The kasbah here overlooks the **Sebou Gorge**, which has impressively sheer cliffs.

Fortified gateway into the mellah in Sefrou

❺ Imouzzer du Kandar

Road Map D2. 12,000. Mon. Apple Festival (Jul).

Built by the French, the small hillside town of Imouzzer du Kandar overlooks the Saïss plain, which abuts the plateaux of the Middle Atlas. At an altitude of 1,345 m (4,414 ft), the town is pleasantly cool in summer, providing a welcome respite from the heat of Fès and Meknès. Many Moroccans come here for the weekend.

The dilapidated kasbah of the Aït Serchouchène, where the souk takes place, contains troglodytic dwellings, of which there are many in the region. The caves were dug into the hillside and, in times gone by, protected Berbers from attacks by their enemies. Some are still inhabited. Steps or just a slope lead up to the entrance. The openings – no more than a small door and a few ventilation holes – are small so as to keep out the cold, and the spartan interiors have neither water nor electricity.

Troglodytic dwelling in the kasbah of Imouzzer du Kandar

The King's summer residence at Ifrane, set in a dense cedar forest

❻ Ifrane

63 km (39 miles) south of Fès on road N8. 🏔 10,000. 🚌 from Fès and Azrou. 🛈 Avenue Mohammed V; (0535) 56 68 21.

Established in 1929 during the Protectorate, Ifrane is a small, noticeably clean town with a European rather than a Moroccan character. Located at an altitude of 1,650 m (5,415 ft), it is cool in summer and may be snow-bound from December to March. On the descent into the valley, a green-roofed palace, the King's summer residence, comes into view. Al-Akhawaya University, inaugurated by Hassan II in 1995, has contributed considerably to the town's development.

Ifrane serves as the departure point for many tours, including a trip to the waterfalls known as the **Cascades des Vierges**, 3 km (2 miles) west (follow the signs to Source Vittel), and north to the **zaouia** of Ifrane, which is surrounded by caves and *koubbas*.

Holm-oak in the forests surrounding the town of Azrou

Environs
Road R707 out of Ifrane, going up to the Tizi-n-Tretten Pass, leads to the **Forêt de Cèdres**. After running along the Mischliffen and Jbel Hebri, it reaches a legendary 900-year-old cedar, the Cèdre Gouraud.

❼ Azrou

48 km (30 miles) south of Ifrane on road N8. 🏔 45,000. 🚌 from Meknès, Fès, Marrakech and Er-Rachidia; Grands taxis. 🛈 Ifrane; (0535) 566821. 🛒 Tue.

A large outcrop of volcanic rock at the entrance to the town gave Azrou (meaning "rock" in Berber) its name. At an altitude of 1,250 m (4102 ft), it is located at the crossroads of routes linking Meknès and Erfoud, and Fès and Marrakech.

Wooden chalet in Ifrane

The town nestles in the centre of a geological basin, with Jbel Hebri to the southeast. It is circled by a dense belt of cedar and holm-oak, where the Beni M'Gild, the most prominent Berber tribe in the region, once came to spend their summers. These nomadic pastoralists from the Sahara gradually adopted a sedentary lifestyle and founded the town.

Azrou is still a regional market town, with a large weekly souk. At the **crafts centre** (opposite the police station) items made of cedar, thuya, walnut and juniper are on sale, as are wrought-iron objects and the renowned carpets, with geometric motifs on a red background, made by the Beni M'Gild.

During the Protectorate the town became a health resort, and highly reputed treatment centres are still found here. It is also the departure point for tours of the cedar forests and plateaux. The lakes in the vicinity offer fishing for trout, pike and roach (a permit is compulsory).

Environs
North of Azrou, the road to El-Hajeb runs along the edge of the **Balcon d'Ito** plateau, offering good views of the "lunar" landscape. The Berber hill village of **Aïn Leuh**, 32 km (20 miles) south of Azrou, hosts the Middle Atlas Arts Festival in July. There is a souk here on Mondays and Thursdays.

The ski resort on the Mischliffen, located in a volcanic crater

❽ Mischliffen

Road Map D2.

A shallow bowl surrounded by cedar forests, the Mischliffen is the crater of an extinct volcano. The villages here are outnumbered by the tents of the shepherds who bring their flocks for summer grazing. A small winter sports resort (also called Mischliffen) has been set up, at an altitude of 2,000 m (6,564 ft), among the trees. The resort's facilites, which consist of just two ski-lifts, are, however, relatively basic.

❾ Lakes Tour

Three attractive lakes – Dayet Aoua, Dayet Ifrah and Dayet Hachlaf – lie 9 km (6.5 miles) south of Imouzzer du Kandar. A turning off road N8 leads to Dayet Aoua, which formed in a natural depression. The narrow road running along it leads to Dayet Ifrah, surrounded by a cirque of mountains, and on to Dayet Hachlaf. Beyond a forestry hut, a track on the right leads to the Vallée des Roches (Valley of the Rocks). Ducks, grey herons, cranes, egrets, birds of prey and dragonflies populate these arid expanses.

② Bird sanctuary
When the lakes are full, the area becomes a nature reserve for many species of birds. It attracts waders – such as avocets, cattle egrets, grey herons and crested coots – wildfowl, birds of prey – such as red kites and kestrels – and swallows.

① Dayet Aoua
This lake sits in a natural depression surrounded by hills. It sometimes remains dry for several years in a row and this is due to persistent drought and the fact that the water table has been tapped to irrigate orchards in the area.

③ Dayet Ifrah
Surrounded by a natural amphitheatre of hills, this is one of the largest lakes in the area. Shepherds set up their tents on the lakeshore, and two hamlets face each other across the water, their white minarets rising up into the sky.

⑤ Rock formations
Continuing along track P7231 in the direction of the Ifrane-Mischliffen road, a rough track branching off to the right leads to this circle of rocks which, shaped by natural forces, have the appearance of ruins.

④ Vallée des Roches
A track on the right, beyond the forestry hut, leads to these outcrops of limestone, strangely shaped by erosion, and to caves inhabited by bats.

0 kilometres   5

0 miles   5

Tips for Drivers

Tour length: about 60 km (37 miles).
Departure point: 16 km (10 miles) north of Ifrane on the N8, forking left to Dayet Aoua.
Duration: one day.
Stopping place: Chalet du Lac, on the shores of Dayet Aoua.

Key

■■ Tour route (track)

══ Road

═ ═ Track

The sources of the Oum er-Rbia, the "Mother of Spring"

❿ Sources of the Oum er-Rbia

160 km (99 miles) from Fès and from Beni Mellal. Please note: there are no hotels or petrol stations on road N8 between Azrou and Khenifra.

A winding road runs above the valley of the Oum er-Rbia, then leads down to the *wadi*. The river's sources – more than 40 springs – form cascades that crash down the limestone cliffs, joining to form the Oum er-Rbia, the longest river in Morocco. The springs can be explored via a footpath.

Aguelmane Azigza, a lake in a verdant setting

⓫ Aguelmane Azigza

12 km (7.5 miles) south of the sources of the Oum er-Rbia.

The rivers whose sources lie in the heart of the Middle Atlas have formed lakes in the craters of extinct volcanoes. One such is Aguelmane Azigza. It is enclosed by cliffs and forests of cedar and holm-oak and contains plenty of fish.

◄ View of the Tigrigra Valley, Azrou

⓬ Aguelmane Sidi Ali

Junction with road N13.

A right turn off road N13 from Azrou to Midelt leads to Aguelmane Sidi Ali, a deep, fish-filled lake that is 3 km (2 miles) long and lies at an altitude of 2,000 m (6,564 ft). With Jbel Hayane rising above, it is surrounded by rugged hills and desolate pasture where the Beni M'Gild's flocks are brought for summer grazing.

Continuing towards Midelt, this very scenic road climbs up to the Zad Pass, which at 2,178 m (7,148 ft), is the highest in the Middle Atlas.

⓭ Khenifra

160 km (99 miles) from Fès; 130 km (81 miles) from Beni Mellal. 🚊 15,000. 🚌 from Fès and Marrakech. 🛒 Sun & Wed.

In the folds of the arid hills and on the banks of the Oum er-Rbia stand houses painted in the carmine red that is typical of Khenifra. Until the 17th century, the town was the rallying point of the Zaïane tribe, which resisted attempts by the French to pacify the region. In the 18th century Moulay Ismaïl asserted his authority by building imposing kasbahs in which armies were garrisoned. The livestock market here is one of the few interesting aspects of the town.

A typical intricately designed gate in Khenifra

The Lions of the Atlas

Before World War I, the roaring of lions in the Moroccan Atlas could be heard at dusk and during the night. The last Atlas lion was killed in 1922. During the Roman period, lions were plentiful in North Africa. They flourished in Tunisia until the 17th century, although by 1891 not one remained. In Algeria, the last lion was killed in 1893, about 100 km (60 miles) south of Constantine. The lions of the Atlas were large, with a thick mane, which was very dark or almost black. Because the genetic make-up of the Atlas lion is known, it should be possible to bring this extinct sub-species back to life. With this end in view, a breeding programme is under way, using lions bred in circuses and in zoos, most particularly the zoo in Rabat.

Lion of the Atlas (1829), portrayed by Eugène Delacroix (Musée Bonnat, Bayonne)

Olives and Olive Oil

Olive groves are a common sight around Meknès and Beni Mellal and in the Rif. The gnarled and knotty olive tree survives in poor soil, taking root in rough and uneven ground. Olive oil is extracted by time-honoured methods. In the autumn, the green, black and violet-tinged olives are harvested, the mixture of all three determining the flavour and aroma of the oil. A heavy grindstone turned by donkeys grinds the olives, crushing both the flesh and the kernel. The resulting dark-hued pulp is emptied into large, shallow, circular porous containers placed beneath the oil press. The oil seeps out and runs into vats, where, mixed with water, it floats to the surface, free of debris. A whole 5 kg (11 lb)

Piles of olives set out for sale in the souk

Grindstones, carved from a single block

of olives makes just 1 litre (1.76 pints) of oil. On the colourful stalls in the souks, the different kinds of olives are piled up into pyramids; there are green olives with herbs, violet-hued olives with a sharp taste, piquant olives spiced with red peppers, olives with bitter orange, crushed black olives that have been sun-dried and steeped in oil, and olives for making *tajine*.

Environs

he village of **El-Kebab** lings to a hillside southeast of henifra. Here craftsmen make ottery and carpets. Above the illage is the hermitage where ather Albert Peyriguère, a octor and companion to he French ascetic Charles de oucauld, lived from 1928 o 1959. A souk is held n Mondays.

Kasba Tadla

2 km (51 miles) southwest of henifra on road N8. ⟨⟩ 36,000. ⟨⟩ from Beni Mellal and Khenifra. ⟨⟩ Beni Mellal. ⟨⟩ Mon.

he focal point of this former arrison town is, predictably, e kasbah, which was built y Moulay Ismaïl in the 1600s. o as to subdue rebellious ibes, Moulay Ismaïl made is son governor of the rovince. The latter built a econd kasbah, contiguous ith the one that his father ad built. A double line of alls thus surrounds the town, nclosing two dilapidated osques, the former governor's alace and grain stores. Below e town, a ten-span bridge osses Wadi Oum er-Rbia.

Environs

Plantations of olive trees cover the Tadla plain between Kasba Tadla and Khenifra, and many traditional olive mills line the road at **Tirhboula**, about 10 km (6 miles) from Khenifra. In the autumn, visitors can see the various stages in the oil-producing process and buy

olive oil here. **El-Ksiba** is an attractive village on the edge of the forest 22 km (13.5 miles) east of Kasba Tadla. It has a souk, which is very busy on Sundays. Beyond El-Ksiba, the road becomes a track that crosses the High Atlas via Imilchil, descending to Tinerhir, in the southern foothills.

The ten-span bridge over the Oum er-Rbia at Kasba Tadla

The Mountains of Morocco

From the high peaks down to altitudes above 600 m (1,970 ft), the climate is permanently moist. Annual precipitation ranges from 650 mm (25 in) in the eastern Grand Atlas to over 2 m (80 in) in the Rif, and snowfall is often heavy. The vegetation in this band is particularly luxuriant, and many forests thrive in this well-watered environment. The forests consist mostly of cedar, cork oak, deciduous oak, evergreen holm-oak and, in the Rif, Moroccan pine.

Holm-oak grows at altitudes of 600 to 2,700 m (1,970 to 8,860 ft) and makes up a quarter of all Morocco's forested areas.

Aleppo pine, which grows naturally in the mountains, is planted almost everywhere since its timber is used for a wide range of purposes.

Forests of Atlas cedar are impressive for their sheer size, and the trees for their beauty, their majestic appearance and their height, which can exceed 50 m (164 ft).

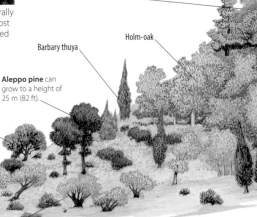

Atlas cedar

Holm-oak

Barbary thuya

The carob produces sugar-rich pods that are a nutritious food for both humans and animals.

Aleppo pine can grow to a height of 25 m (82 ft).

Argan

Kermes oak

Wild olive can be used as grafting stock. Its timber is suitable for carpentry and is also used as firewood.

The argan (see p131) is a small tree that grows exclusively in southwest Morocco. Argan nuts are a favourite food of goats which climb up into the branches to reach them. Oil extracted from the kernels is used in foods, cosmetics and as a tonic

High-Altitude Vegetation

At altitudes above 2,700 m (8,860 ft), the mountains consist of cold and arid steppe, which is often covered in snow. No trees grow here but there are abundant streams. The low-growing vegetation, including some endemic species, is varied and forms a covering of spiny, cushion-like clumps.

Juniper

The Tizi-n-Test Pass commands a view of the snowy heights of the Atlas and the Souss valley, 2,000 m (6,564 ft) below.

Mountain Fauna

The Barbary sheep, Africa's only wild sheep, inhabits the High and Middle Atlas. It can also be seen in Jbel Toubkal National Park *(see p253)*, which was created especially to ensure its survival. Three-quarters of the country's population of macaques live in the cedar forests of the Middle Atlas. Wild boar is found in all mountainous areas and the Barbary stag was reintroduced in 1990. Birds are plentiful at altitudes between 2,200 and 3,600 m (7,220 and 11,815 ft). They include the golden eagle, Bonelli's eagle, booted eagle, the huge lammergeier, Egyptian vulture, partridge, Moussier's redstart and the rare crimson-winged finch, which nests only at altitudes above 2,800 m (9,190 ft).

Barbary sheep

Adult booted eagle, feeding chicks in the nest

Female macaque carrying her newborn on her back

M'Goun, which rises to a height of more than 4,000 m (13,128 ft), is the second-highest peak in the High Atlas.

The Aïn-Asserdoun springs, "Springs of the Mule"

⓯ Boujad

24 km (15 miles) north of Kasba Tadla on road R312. 🔼 15,000. 🚌 Thu.

The holy town of Boujad, which is filled with *koubbas* (tombs) and shrines, is set in the Tadla plain, on the caravan route that once ran between Marrakech and Fès. It was established in the 16th century by Sidi Mohammed ech-Cherki, patron saint of Tadla, who built an important *zaouia* here. The saint and his descendants, bearers of *baraka* (blessing, luck or good fortune) from one generation to the next, have always been highly venerated by the Beni Meskin and Seguibat, local Berber tribespeople. In 1785, sultan Sidi Mohammed ben Abdallah, who was resentful of this power, razed the town, including the *zaouia*. The latter was rebuilt in the 19th century and is still inhabited by the saint's descendants.

The tombs of the saintly dynasty can be seen around the market square in the north of the town. The largest, the **Koubba of Sidi Othman**, is open to visitors. There are many other mausoleums here, most notably that of the sheik Mohammed ech-Cherki, which is closed to non-Muslims. On a promontory outside Boujad, in the direction of Oued Zem on the northern side of the town, stand five white *koubbas*, to which crowds of pilgrims come for annual gatherings.

⓰ Beni Mellal

30 km (18.5 miles) southwest of Kasba Tadla on road N8. 🔼 140,000. 🚌 from Khenifra, Marrakech and Demnate. ℹ Avenue Hassan II; (0523) 48 78 29. 🛒 Tue; Sun in Sebt-Oulad-Nemaa 35 km (22 miles) to the west.

The modern town of Beni Mellal lies at the foot of the Middle Atlas, on the edge of the great Tadla plain, where cereals are extensively cultivated. Although it is devoid of any obvious appeal, it is still a convenient stopping-place.

Inhabited by Berbers and Jews well before the arrival of Islam, the town was known successively as Day, Kasba Belkouche and Beni Mellal. In the 13th century, it stood on the border between the kingdoms of Fès and Marrakech, which were the object of bitter dispute between the Merinid and Almohad dynasties. In 1680 Moulay Ismaïl built a kasbah here, which was restored on several occasions.

The town is surrounded by orange groves (oranges from Beni Mellal are renowned), and olive groves stretch to the horizon. Beetroot and sugarcane have replaced bananas as cultivated crops. All are unusually well watered thanks to the Bin el-Ouidane dam.

South of the town, in the lower foothills of the Middle Atlas, a road marked "Circuit

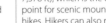

Cedar-dwelling macaque

touristique" leads to the **Aïn Asserdoun springs**, which run between trees and small gardens. It is worth making the short detour to **Ras el-Aïn**, a little further up. This stone and pisé *borj* (tower) offers a picturesque view of Beni Mellal and its orchards.

Environs
The area around Beni Mellal has many waterfalls, springs, caves and wooded gorges populated by monkeys. About 10 km (6 miles) east, a road leads to **Foum el-Anser**, where a waterfall crashes into a gorge. The rockface here is marked by artificial caves, access to which is difficult. South of Beni Mellal, a hillside track leads up to **Jbel Tassemit** (2,248 m/ 7,378 ft), which is the departure point for scenic mountain hikes. Hikers can also reach the **Tarhzirte Gorge** and the Wadi Derna valley, 20 km (12 miles) northeast of Beni Mellal.

⓱ Bin el-Ouidane Dam

43 km (27 miles) southwest of Beni Mellal on road N8, branching left on road R304. ℹ Beni Mellal.

From Beni Mellal the road climbs through wooded hills to reach the grandiose site of an

The *borj* of Ras el-Aïn, offering a spectacular view over the Tadla plain

The Bin el-Ouidane reservoir, at the foot of the High Atlas

artificial lake, the Bin el-Ouidane reservoir. The dam here is 285 m (935 ft) long and 133 m (436 ft) high and the reservoir, with a surface area of 380,000 sq m (94 acres), is the largest lake in Morocco. Fed by Wadi el-Abid and Wadi Ahansalt, it irrigates the intensively culvitated Tadla plain, while the hydroelectric generator provides a quarter of Morocco's electricity. The turquoise waters of the lake, which are broken by spits of land and small islands, are surrounded by red hills, and the lakeshore is dotted with a few isolated houses.

Watersports and fishing are permitted on the lake and Wadi el-Abid is suitable for kayaking and rafting in spring, when the water level is sufficiently high. A track leading from the lake ends at a rock formation known as La Cathédrale. This rock, with a covering of red soil and a setting among Aleppo pines, is well known to abseilers.

From the dam, Azilal and the Aït Bouguemez valley *(see pp258–61)* can be reached on road R304.

⑱ Cascades d'Ouzoud

65 km (40 miles) southwest of Bin el-Ouidane on road R304, or 156 km (97 miles) from Marrakech via Demnate. 🚌 for Beni Mellal-Azilal then grand taxi.

One of the most spectacular sights in Morocco, the Cascades d'Ouzoud attract large numbers of visitors. The waterfall is particularly impressive in spring, when the waters pour down from the top of reddish cliffs, crashing off a succession of rocky ledges to fall into the canyon of Wadi el-Abid 100 m (328 ft) below.

The road to the site leads to a spot above the waterfall, which can be reached along a footpath with steps cut into the earth. From platforms set at intervals on the path, visitors can marvel at the majestic succession of cascades and admire the permanent rainbow created by the mist thrown up by the water. Mills, whose only vestiges are small rectangular recesses, once worked a grindstone on which corn and barley were ground to make flour. The fig trees and carobs that grow beside the path are often full of monkeys – the beige-coated macaques whose eyes are outlined in black. Bathing is permitted in the natural pools.

Starting from the bottom of the waterfall, energetic visitors wearing strong walking boots can hike to the Wadi el-Abid gorge.

Environs

Six kilometres (4 miles) southwest of Demnate, on road R304, is **Imi-n-Ifri**, a natural bridge that has been partly carved out by the *wadi*. A track leads down to the bottom of the chasm.

The Cascades d'Ouzoud in spring, at their most spectacular

MARRAKECH

Such is the importance of Marrakech that it gave its name to Morocco. For more than two centuries, this Berber city at the point of interchange between the Sahara, the Atlas and the Anti-Atlas was the hub of a great empire, and the achievements of illustrious builders can be seen within the city's walls. It is the capital of the great South and, although it is now only Morocco's fourth city after Casablanca, Fès and Rabat, with a population approaching a million, its fabulous palaces and luxuriant palm grove continue to hold a powerful fascination for visitors.

Marrakech was founded in 1062 by Almoravids from the Sahara. These warrior monks soon carved out an empire that stretched from Algiers to Spain. In 1106, Ali ben Youssef hired craftsmen from Andalusia to build a palace and a mosque in the capital. He also raised ramparts around the city and installed *khettaras* (underground canals), an ingenious irrigation system that brought water to its great palm grove.

The Almohads took the city in 1147. Abd el-Moumen built the Koutoubia, a masterpiece of Moorish architecture, and his successor was responsible for building the kasbah. But the Almohad dynasty collapsed, to the benefit of the Merinids of Fès, and for over 200 years Marrakech stagnated. It was not until the 16th century that the city was reinvigorated by the arrival of the Saadians, most notably by the wealthy Ahmed el-Mansour. The Saadian Tombs, the Ben Youssef Medersa and the remains of the Palais el-Badi mark this golden age. In 1668, Marrakech fell to the Alaouites, who made Fès, then Meknès, their capital.

In the 20th century, Marrakech embraced the modern age with the creation of the Quartier Guéliz, built during the Protectorate. Visitors continue to flock to this magical city, and tourism is central to its economy today.

A woman leaving the *zaouia* of Sidi bel Abbès

◄ The Koutoubia Mosque, the largest mosque in Marrakech

Exploring Marrakech

The rich history of Marrakech is reflected in its various quarters. The medina, above which rises the minaret of the Koutoubia Mosque, the emblem of the city, corresponds to the old town. Place Jemaa el-Fna, the hub of all activity, is its heart. Within the ramparts are the souks (north of Place Jemaa el-Fna), the kasbah and the mellah (the Jewish quarter). Guéliz, in the northwest, is the new town laid out by Marshal Lyautey under the Protectorate. It is filled with Western-style offices, businesses and a residential area. Avenue Mohammed V is the district's main thoroughfare. Extending Guéliz in the southwest is Hivernage, a verdant quarter with many hotels that also dates from the Protectorate. The district is bordered on its western side by the Menara Gardens, and on its eastern side by the walls of the medina.

Key

- Major sight
- Sight
- Medina
- — Ramparts

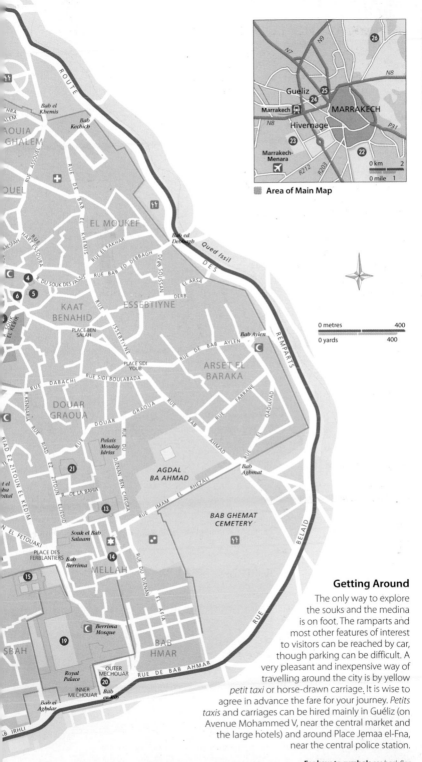

Area of Main Map

0 metres 400
0 yards 400

Getting Around

The only way to explore the souks and the medina is on foot. The ramparts and most other features of interest to visitors can be reached by car, though parking can be difficult. A very pleasant and inexpensive way of travelling around the city is by yellow *petit taxi* or horse-drawn carriage. It is wise to agree in advance the fare for your journey. *Petits taxis* and carriages can be hired mainly in Guéliz (on Avenue Mohammed V, near the central market and the large hotels) and around Place Jemaa el-Fna, near the central police station.

For keys to symbols *see back flap*

The monumental entrance to the Zaouia of Sidi bel Abbès

❶ Zaouia of Sidi bel Abbès

Sidi bel Abbès quarter (north of the medina). **Closed** to non-Muslims. Pilgrimage on Thu.

From Bab el-Khemis, Rue Sidi Rhalem leads to the Zaouia of Sidi bel Abbès. The sanctuary is a focal point for the pilgrimage of the Regraga (the Seven Saints), which was instituted by Moulay Ismaïl so as to obtain forgiveness for his depredations in Marrakech.

Sidi bel Abbès (1130–1205) is the city's most highly venerated patron saint. A disciple of the famous Cadi Ayad, he devoted his life to preaching and to caring for and defending the weak and the blind. Because of him, it was said throughout Morocco that Marrakech was the only city where a blind man could eat his fill. To this day, the gifts of pilgrims are distributed to the poor and the blind.

In 1605, the Saadian sultan Abou Faris raised a mausoleum for the saint in the hope of curing his epilepsy. Moulay Ismaïl added a dome in the 18th century and the mausoleum was given its present appearance by Sidi Mohammed ben Abdallah a few years later.

The *zaouia* also includes a mosque, a hammam, a home for the blind, a small market, an abattoir and a cemetery.

South of the *zaouia* is the **El-Mjadlia Souk**, the Passementerie Souk, built in a covered alley during the reign of Sidi Mohammed ben Abderrahman, at the end of the 19th century. Going from here towards the centre of the medina, you will pass **Bab Taghzout**, an Almoravid gate that has been integrated into the surrounding architecture.

❷ Zaouia of Sidi ben Slimane el-Jazouli

North of the medina (near Rue Dar el-Glaoui). **Closed** to non-Muslims. Pilgrimage on Fri.

After Bab Taghzout, if you follow Rue de Bab Taghzout, then take the first right, and then go right again, you will reach this *zaouia*, which also features in the Regraga pilgrimage *(see p42)*. The mausoleum dates from the Saadian period and was remodelled in the late 18th century during the reign of Sidi Mohammed ben Abdallah.

Sidi Mohammed ben Slimane el-Jazouli, another venerated mystic, founded Moroccan Sufism in the 15th century. Under the Wattasids, this religion spread to every level of the population. A champion of the holy war against the Portuguese and a politically influential figure, this holy man attracted thousands of followers; his reputedly occult powers even worried the sultan.

Interior of the Zaouia of Sidi ben Slimane

❸ Chrob ou Chouf Fountain

Rue Amesfah, near the Mosque of Ben Youssef.

As its name – meaning "Drink and Admire" – suggests, this Saadian fountain is one of the most beautiful in the medina. It was built during the reign of Ahmed el-Mansour (1578–1603), and it is shaded by a carved cedar awning with coloured *zellij* tilework and inscriptions in cursive and Kufic script engraved into the wood.

In a town like Marrakech, located at the head of pre-Saharan valleys, water was a very precious commodity. An underground network of channels supplied the mosques and the houses and fed the fountains. Obeying the precepts of the Koran, according to which water must be given to the thirsty, many of the leading citizens of Marrakech financed the building of fountains.

Detail of the cedar awning over the Chrob ou Chouf Fountain

The Ramparts of Marrakech

Skirting the Guéliz and Hivernage quarters on their eastern side, the ramparts completely encircle the medina. From the time of its foundation, Marrakech was defended by sturdy walls set with forts. Although their outline has hardly altered from the time of the Almoravids, they were extended to the south by the Almohads and to the north by the Saadians in the 16th century. These pisé walls are 19 km (12 miles) long, up to 2 m (6 ft) thick and up to 9 m (30 ft) high. Some of the monumental gates that pierce them are very fine examples of Moorish architecture. The best time to walk around the ramparts is in the early morning or just before sunset. Their warm ochre colour changes according to the time of day and the intensity of the light. In the evening, they take on an almost rust-coloured hue.

Bab el-Khemis was remodelled after the Almoravid period (1147–1269). An open-air market is held outside the gate on Thursdays. The tomb of the Seven Saints is a small dome-topped building dedicated to a *marabout*.

The Gates

Bab Aghmat and Bab Aylen, on the eastern side of the ramparts, date from the 12th century, and are relatively plain. Bab ed-Debbagh, dating from the same period, opens onto the tanners' quarter. On the northern side stands Bab el-Khemis and on the southern, Bab el-Robb (1308). The latter takes its name from a grape liqueur in which the city once did a brisk trade. Bab el-Jedid, on the western side, leads to La Mamounia hotel (see p238).

These lower pisé walls, which are just high enough to close a harem off from a house or a garden, or to shield a sanctuary from prying eyes, were not built for defensive purposes.

Bab Agnaou *(see p243)*, whose name is derived from the Berber for "hornless black ram", is one of the finest gates in Marrakech. It is carved in an ochre stone with tinges of pink. It once led into the Almohad palace.

The ramparts of Marrakech, which date from the 12th century, are the most impressive city walls in Morocco. The well-preserved defences encircle the old town, with its palaces and gardens.

Zellij tilework in the Ben Youssef Medersa

❹ Ben Youssef Medersa

Place ben Youssef (in the medina). **Tel** (0524) 44 18 93. **Open** 9am–6pm daily.

This Koranic school is not only one of the finest but also one of the largest in the Maghreb, with a capacity for up to 900 students.

It was founded by the Merinid sultan Abou el-Hassan in the mid-14th century, and was rebuilt by the Saadian sultan Moulay Abdallah in the 16th century. This fact is recorded by the inscriptions carved into the lintel above the entrance, together with the date, 1564.

The medersa takes its name from the Almoravid mosque of Ali ben Youssef to which it was once attached. For four centuries this mosque was the focal point of worship in the medina, and with the medersa it constituted an important centre of religion.

Architecturally, and with its sumptuous decoration, it is on a par with the Merinid medersas, particularly the Bou Inania Medersa of Fès *(see pp176–7)*. By building it, Moulay Abdallah was expressing his desire to restore to Marrakech the prestige of an imperial capital and simultaneously to affirm his devotion to Allah.

Bronze door of the Ben Youssef Medersa

Covering an area of some 1,720 sq m (18,514 sq ft), this harmoniously proportioned medersa appears as it was originally designed, with no later alteration. The dome, decorated with exquisite stalactites within, can be seen from the street. The main entrance, a bronze door topped by a carved cedar lintel, opens onto a mosaic-paved corridor, which in turn leads to the courtyard. This masterpiece of Moorish design is paved with white marble and has an ablutions pool in the centre. The walls are decorated with *zellij* tilework below and carved plaster above. A double tier of galleries supported on thick columns lines both sides of the courtyard. The students' cells on the ground and upper floors opened onto the courtyard. Those that are arranged around seven smaller interior courtyards are shielded from daylight.

A magnificently ornate doorway leads through to the large prayer hall. The room is crowned by a pyramidal cedar dome and divided into three by marble columns with capitals with calligraphy praising Moulay Abdallah. The mihrab is decorated with verses from the Koran in calligraphic script and is lit by 24 windows decorated with a tracery of plasterwork.

❺ Musée de Marrakech

Place ben Youssef. **Tel** (0524) 44 18 93. **Open** 9am–6:30pm daily.

This museum is laid out in the Dar Menebhi, a palace built at the end of the 19th century by the grand vizier of Sultan Moulay Mehdi Hassan. The building is in the style of a traditional Moorish house.

The decorated door – which, as in many Moorish houses, is the only opening in the otherwise featureless external walls – leads through to an open courtyard with *zellij* tilework and three marble basins in the centre. The courtyard gives access to the rooms on the ground and upper floors.

The museum's collection is displayed in two wings. One contains contemporary art, Orientalist paintings and a series of original engravings of Moroccan subjects.

The second wing contains a rather haphazard display of objects: coins from the Idrissid period of the 9th century to that of the Alaouites in the present day; illuminated copies of the Koran, including a 12th-century Chinese example and a 19th-century book of Sufi prayers; southern Moroccan jewellery; Tibetan dress, 17th- and 18th-century ceramics; and some fine decorated Berber doors.

Zellij tilework in the courtyard of the Musée de Marrakech

The Koubba Ba'Adiyn, the only vestige of the Almoravid mosque

❻ Koubba Ba'Adiyn

Place ben Youssef. **Tel** (0524) 44 18 93. **Open** 9am–6pm daily.

This brick-built dome is the only example of Almoravid architecture in Marrakech. Built by Ali ben Youssef in 1106, originally it formed part of a richly decorated mosque that was demolished by the Almohads. Miraculously spared, the rectangular pavilion was rediscovered in 1948. It contained an ablutions pool fed by three reservoirs. While the exterior is decorated with chevrons and pointed arches in relief, the interior is graced by scalloped and horseshoe arches and floral ornamentation. These elements anticipate the full-blown artistic creativity of Islamic architecture.

❼ Bab Doukkala Mosque

Rue de Bab Doukkala. **Closed** to non-Muslims. Dar el-Glaoui: **Closed** to visitors.

This place of worship was built in the mid-16th century by the mother of the Saadian ruler Ahmed el-Mansour. Its slender minaret, crowned by four golden orbs, and its refined decoration are reminiscent of the Kasbah Mosque (see p242). Next to the building stands an ornate fountain with a bowl surmounted by three domes.

From here, Rue de Bab Doukkala, going towards the centre of the medina, leads to **Dar el-Glaoui**, the palace built by El-Glaoui, the famous pasha

Averroës

Born in Córdoba in 1126, Averroës (Ibn Rushd) was one of the most renowned Muslim scholars of his day. Like other men of learning at the time, his knowledge encompassed medicine, law, philosophy, astronomy and theology. Born into an important Cordoban family, he was the grandson of an imam at the Great Mosque in Granada. Under the patronage of Abou Yacoub Youssef, Averroës divided his time between Seville, Córdoba and Marrakech. He took the place of his friend and teacher, the famous physician Abubacer (Ibn Tufayl). Basing his approach on his own reading of Aristotle, he promoted a rationalist, rather than an esoteric, interpretation of the Koran. This brought him condemnation from Córdoba. However, he was soon rehabilitated by the Almohad ruler Yacoub el-Mansour, who gave him asylum in Marrakech until his death in December 1198.

Averroës, the great 12th-century philosopher

of Marrakech (see p61), at the beginning of the 20th century. While one part of the building contains a library, another is used to receive heads of state during official visits.

The palace has several beautifully decorated court-yards lined with *zellij* tilework, stuccowork, painted wood and *muqarnas* (stalactites). It also features a fine Andalusian garden planted with fruit trees. The palace is reputed to have been the venue for some wild and extravagant parties.

❽ The Souks

See pp234–5.

❾ Mouassine Mosque

Mouassine Quarter. **Closed** to non-Muslims.

The Saadian sultan Moulay Abdallah established this place of worship, which was built between 1562 and 1573 on what is thought to be a former Jewish quarter. Its design as well as its decoration bear certain similarities

to the Koutoubia Mosque (see pp240–41) and the Kasbah Mosque (see p242).

The minaret, which is crowned by a gallery with merlons, is of strikingly simple design. The adjacent Mouassine Fountain consists of three large drinking troughs for animals and a fourth for people. The fountain is enclosed within a portico with decorative stuccowork and carved wooden lintels.

Dar el-Glaoui, palace of the popular pasha, El-Glaoui

ⓑ The Souks

The souks of Marrakech are among the most fascinating in the Maghreb. Arranged according to the type of goods on offer, they are laid out in the narrow streets north and east of Place Jemaa el-Fna. On the map shown here, the area marked in orange denotes the historic heart of the souks, which stretches from the Ben Youssef Mosque in the north to the Souk Smarine in the south. Many of the souks are known by the name of whatever is sold here. Today a very wide range of goods, from fabric to jewellery and slippers, is on offer. Leatherwork is particularly prominent. Around this commercial hub are the crafts traditionally associated with country people, such as blacksmithing, saddle-making and basketry. Because of rank odours, the tanneries are banished to the edge of the city.

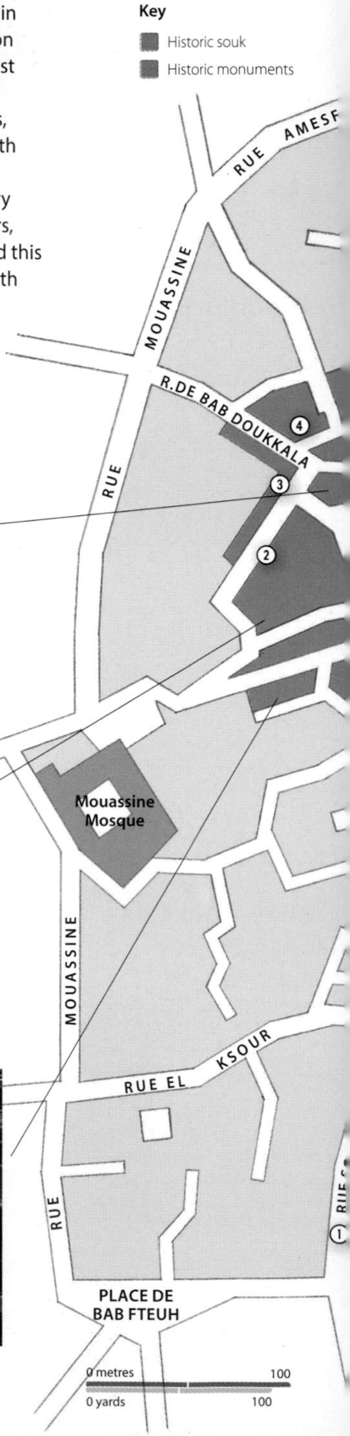

Key
- Historic souk
- Historic monuments

Souk Addadine (metalwork)
Amid a deafening clatter, brass and copper workers tirelessly hammer hot metal, shaping it into a range of everyday items such as trays, ashtrays, lanterns, wrought-iron grilles, locks and keys.

Souk Chouari (basketry and woodturning)
The *chouari* is the double pannier that is put on the backs of donkeys. These baskets are woven from palm fibre.

Dyers' Souk
Skeins of wool or silk, freshly dyed and still wet, are hung out to dry in the sun and warm air.

For hotels and restaurants see pp306–313 and pp320–31

Souk Smata (slippers and belts)
The craftsmen of Marrakech are master-leatherworkers. The craft of leatherworking is said to have originated in the city.

VISITORS' CHECKLIST

Practical Information
Place Jemaa el-Fna (via Rue du Souk Smarine or Bab Doukkala). A *petit taxi* or horse-drawn carriage can be taken as far as the entrance to the souks, which must be explored on foot.
Open 9am–7pm daily.
Closed noon–4pm Fri.

Ben Youssef Mosque

Ben Youssef Medersa

Musée de Marrakech

Koubba Ba'Adiyn

Kissarias
Clothing, fabric, leather goods and passementerie are on sale in these lit and covered galleries. This was once where the most highly prized goods, some of them imported, were sold.

RUE SOUK EL KEBIR

⑤
⑥
⑦
⑨ ⑧
RAHBA KEDIMA
⑩

Souk el-Btana (skins)
Thousands of skins for use in leatherwork are sold in the skinners' souk.

KEY

① Souk Smarine (clothing)

② Souk Atarin (brass and copper)

③ Souk El-Bradiia (pitchers)

④ Souk Kimakhin (stringed instruments)

⑤ Souk Siyyaghin (jewellery)

⑥ Souk Fakharin

⑦ Souk El-Kebir (leatherwork)

⑧ Souk Zarbia (the Criée Berbère, the main carpet market)

⑨ Souk El-Maazi (goatskins)

⑩ Rahba Kedima, "Old Square" is where magicians and healers buy their supplies, and country people sell fruit, vegetables and live chickens.

⑪ Former slave market

Small open-air restaurants on Place Jemaa el-Fna

⑩ Place Jemaa el-Fna

East of Gueliz (off the southern extremity of Avenue Mohammed V).

For centuries, this unique and extraordinary square has been the nerve centre of Marrakech and the symbol of the city. Although it is in fact no more than an irregular space devoid of a harmonious ensemble of buildings, it is of interest to visitors mainly because it is a showcase of traditional Morocco. UNESCO has declared it a World Heritage Site.

It has a gruesome past: until the 19th century, criminals on whom the death sentence had been passed were beheaded here. Sometimes up to 45 people were executed on a single day, their heads pickled and suspended from the city gates.

No traces are left of this today. A large market is held in the mornings, and medicinal plants, freshly squeezed orange juice as well as all kinds of nuts and confectionery are sold.

From sunset, the life and bustle on the square reaches its peak. It becomes the arena of a gigantic, multifaceted open-air show. As the air fills with smoke from grilling meat and the aroma of spices, the square fills with musicians, dancers, storytellers, showmen, tooth-pullers, fortune-tellers and snake-charmers, who each draw a crowd of astonished onlookers.

⑪ Koutoubia Mosque

See pp240–41.

⑫ La Mamounia Hotel

Avenue Bab el-Jedid. **Tel** (0524) 38 86 00. See also *p311*.

Opened in 1923, the legendary hotel La Mamounia stands on the site of a residence that, in the 18th century, belonged to the son of the Alaouite sultan Sidi Mohammed. All that remains of that residence is the magnificent 130,000-sq-m (32-acre) garden, planted with olive and orange trees and containing a pavilion that was probably built by a Saadian ruler in the 16th century.

The original hotel was designed by Henri Prost and Antoine Marchisio, who achieved a pleasing mix of Art Deco and Moorish styles. Many famous people, including Winston Churchill and Richard Nixon, have stayed here. The Mamounia reopened in 2009 following renovations.

⑬ Palais Bahia

Riad Zitoun Jedid (medina).
Tel (0524) 38 91 79.
Open 9am–4:30pm daily.

This palace, whose name means "Palace of the Favourite", was built by two powerful grand viziers – Si Moussa, vizier of Sultan Sidi Mohammed ben Abderrahman, and his son Ba Ahmed, vizier of Moulay Abdelaziz – at the end of the 19th century.

The palace complex consists of two parts, each built at different times. The older part, built by Si Moussa, contains apartments arranged around a marble-paved courtyard. It also has an open courtyard with cypresses, orange trees and jasmine, with two star-shaped pools.

The newer part, built by Ba Ahmed, is a huge palace without a unified plan. It consists of luxurious apartments looking onto courtyards planted with trees. So as to make it easier for the obese master of the house to move around, almost all the apartments were located on the ground floor. The main courtyard is paved with marble and *zellij* tilework. It is surrounded by a gallery of

The entrance to the hotel La Mamounia (*see p311*)

◄ Tourists at the Medersa Ben Youssef, the old Islamic school

Beautiful arch leading to Palais Bahia

finely fluted columns, while three fountains with bowls stand in the centre. This courtyard, once used by the viziers' concubines, faces the main reception room. It has a cedar ceiling painted with arabesques. The decoration of the palace apartments and of the council chamber is equally splendid.

Ba Ahmed hired the best craftsmen in the kingdom to build and decorate this palace. It is decked out with highly prized materials, such as marble from Meknès, cedar from the Middle Atlas and tiles from Tetouan. Not surprisingly, Marshal Lyautey chose to live here during the Protectorate.

Maison Tiskiwin, at No. 8 Rue de la Bahia, houses the **Bert Flint Museum**. This charming residence with a courtyard is an example of a traditional 19th-century Marrakech house. Here, Bert Flint, a Dutch anthropologist who fell in love with Morocco and settled here in the 1950s, amassed a collection of folk art and artifacts from the Souss valley and the Saharan region (see pp287–99). Exhibits include jewellery and daggers from the Anti-Atlas, pottery from the Rif and carpets from

the Middle Atlas. The museum is close to another museum, the Dar Si Saïd (see pp244–5).

🏛 **Bert Flint Museum**
8 Rue de la Bahia, Riad Zitoun Jedid. **Tel** (0524) 38 91 92. **Open** 9am–12:30pm & 2:30–6pm daily.

⑭ Mellah

East of Palais el-Badi and south of Palais Bahia.

Once accommodating some 16,000 inhabitants, the former Jewish quarter of Marrakech was the largest mellah in Morocco until the country's independence. Previously located on what became the site of the Mouassine Mosque, the mellah was established in the mid-16th century by the Saadian sultan Moulay Abdallah, and it was almost identical to the mellah in Fès (see p186). Until 1936, it was surrounded by a wall pierced by two gates, one opening east onto the cemetery and the other leading into the city. The jewellers' souk is held opposite the Palais Bahia.

⑮ Palais el-Badi

Hay Salam, Rue Berrima. **Open** 9am–4:45pm daily.

Five months after acceding to the throne, Ahmed el-Mansour decided to consolidate his rule and banish the memory of earlier dynasties. Having emerged victorious over the

Door opening onto a narrow street in the mellah of Marrakech

Portuguese at the Battle of the Three Kings on 4 August 1578 (see p56), Ahmed el-Mansour, "the Golden", ordered a luxurious palace to be built near his private apartments. It was to be used for receptions and audiences with foreign embassies. Its construction was financed by the Portuguese whom he had defeated in battle, and work continued until his death in 1603.

El-Badi, "the Incomparable", is one of the 99 names of Allah. For a time, the palace was indeed considered to be one of the wonders of the Muslim world. Italian marble, Irish granite, Indian onyx and coverings of gold leaf decorated the walls and the ceilings of the 360 rooms.

In 1683, Moulay Ismaïl demolished the Palais el-Badi and salvaged the materials to embellish his own imperial city of Meknès (see p196). Today, all that remains of the palace are empty rooms.

The remains of the Palais el-Badi, built in the 16th century

⑪ Koutoubia Mosque

In about 1147, to mark his victory over the Almoravids, the
Almohad sultan Abd el-Moumen set about building one of
the largest mosques in the Western Muslim world. The minaret,
a masterpiece of Islamic architecture, was completed during the
reign of Yacoub el-Mansour, grandson of Abd el-Moumen. It later
served as the model for the Giralda in Seville, as well as for the
Hassan Tower in Rabat *(see pp78–9)*. The "Booksellers' Mosque" takes
its name from the manuscripts souk that once took place around
it. The interior of the minaret contains a ramp used to carry building
materials up to the summit. The mosque has been restored to
reveal the original pink colour of the brickwork.

★ Minaret
This splendid tower in
pink Gueliz stone stands
like a sentinel above the
city. It is 70 m (230 ft) high
and its proportions obey
the canons of Almohad
architecture: its height
equals five times its width.

Entrance to the Koutoubia Courtyard
This restrained and simple entrance
follows the design of most gateways
to important Moroccan buildings:
a horseshoe arch with
moulded arcature.

**Detail of the East Side
of the Minaret**
Each side of the minaret has
a different decorative scheme.
Common to all, with variations,
are floral motifs, inscriptions,
bands of moulded terracotta
and, as here, windows with
festooned arches.

West View of the Minaret
The minaret is the highest building in the city and it stands as a landmark for many miles around. Only Muslims may enjoy the unforgettable view from the top of the building.

VISITORS' CHECKLIST

Practical Information
Place de la Koutoubia.
i (0524) 43 61 31/79.
Closed to non-Muslims.

Eastern Entrance to the Prayer Hall
This is the main entrance for the faithful. The design of the doorway is relatively plain, with minimal ornamentation.

KEY

① **The interior of the minaret** contains six superimposed rooms.

② **Denticulate merlons**

③ **Four gilt-bronze spheres** surmount the lantern.

④ **Roof of green tiles**

⑤ **Courtyard and pool**

⑥ **The interior of the mosque** consists of 16 parallel aisles of equal width bisected by a wider nave.

⑦ **The original mosque** was superseded by another, built on the orders of the Almohad ruler Abd el-Moumen. This was because the *qibla* wall of the earlier mosque was not accurately oriented towards Mecca. Its foundations can still be seen today.

★ **Prayer Hall** This can accommodate some 20,000 faithful. The white columns supporting horseshoe arches and the braided pattern of the floor create a striking perspective.

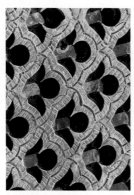

Detail of the minaret of the
Kasbah Mosque

⑯ Kasbah Mosque

Rue de la Kasbah, near Bab Agnaou.
Closed to non-Muslims.

Built by Yacoub el-Mansour
(1184–99), the Kasbah Mosque
is the only other Almohad
building besides Bab Agnaou
to survive in Marrakech. Its
distinctive minaret, a beautiful
stone and brick construction
in shades of ochre, was used
as a model by later builders.
Successive remodelling in the
16th and 17th centuries has
robbed the mosque of its
original appearance. Even so,
it is not without interest.

Built to a rectangular plan,
77m (253 ft) long by 71 m
(233 ft) wide, the mosque
consists of a prayer hall and
five interior courtyards
separated by arcades. The
80-m (263-ft) long façade is
topped by crenellations and
denticulate merlons. According
to Almohad custom, the minaret
is devoid of ornamentation
up to the height of the walls.
Above this, it has restrained
decoration and is crowned by
an attractive terracotta frieze.
Turquoise tiles moulded with
a magnificent pattern of
interlaced lozenges almost
completely cover the four
faces of the minaret.

Two-fifths of the tower are
taken up by the lantern, which
is crowned by three spheres.
These are made of brass, but
legend has it that they are made
of gold, hence their popular
name, the Golden Apples.

⑰ Saadian Tombs

Rue de la Kasbah. 📞 (0524) 43 61 31.
Open 9am–noon & 2:30–
6pm daily. 🎟

Although they were neglected
for more than two centuries, the
tombs of the Saadian dynasty
constitute some of the finest
examples of Islamic architecture
in Morocco. Their style is
in complete contrast to the
simplicity of Almohad architecture, as the Saadian princes
lavished on funerary architecture the same ostentation
and magnificence that they
gave to other buildings.

A necropolis existed here
during the Almohad period
(1145–1248), continuing in
use during the reign of the
Merinid sultan Abou el-Hassan
(1331–51). The Saadian Tombs
themselves date from the late
16th to the 18th centuries. Out
of respect for the dead, and
even though he had been at
pains to erase all traces of his
predecessors, the Alaouite
sultan Moulay Ismaïl raised a
wall round the main entrance.

It was not until 1917 that the
tombs were made accessible to
the public. They consist of two

Mausoleum of Ahmed el-Mansour, with
marble-columned mihrab

mausoleums which are set in
a garden planted with flowers
symbolizing Allah's paradise.

The central mausoleum is
that of Ahmed el-Mansour
(1578–1603). It consists of
three funerary rooms laid out
to a plan reminiscent of that
of the Rawda in Granada.
The first room is a prayer hall
divided into three aisles by
white marble columns. The
mihrab is decorated with
stalactites and framed by
a pointed horseshoe arch
supported by grey marble
pilasters. The prayer hall is

Ornate capitals on the columns in the Saadian Tombs

it by the three windows of the lantern, which rests on a cedar base decorated with inscriptions.

The central room, a great masterpiece of Moorish architecture, is crowned by a remarkable dome with stalactites. Of carved cedar with gold-leaf decoration, it is supported by 12 columns of Carrara marble. The walls are completely covered – the lower part by a graceful interlacing pattern of glazed tiles, and the upper part by a profusion of stuccowork.

In the centre of the room lie Ahmed el-Mansour and his successors. The ivory-coloured marble tombstones are covered with arabesques and inscriptions arranged on two levels: above are verses from the Koran, and below a framed epitaph in verse. The third room, known as the Hall of the Three Niches, has an equally sumptuous decorative scheme. It contains the tombs of young princes.

The second mausoleum, a green-roofed building, has more modest proportions. It consists of a room with two loggias and a prayer hall. A cedar lintel carved with inscriptions links the columns of the loggias. In the prayer hall, the dome hung with stalactites is a splendid sight.

In the burial chamber the tomb of Lalla Messaouda, mother of Ahmed "the Golden", who died in 1591, fills a honeycombed niche.

⑱ Bab Agnaou

Rue de la Kasba, opposite the Kasbah Mosque.

Like its twin, Bab Oudaïa in Rabat *(see pp72–3)*, this monumental gate was built by Yacoub el-Mansour. Its name means "hornless black ram" in Berber.

Protected by Bab el-Robb *(see p231)*, the outer defensive gate, Bab Agnaou marked the main entrance to the Almohad palace, and its function was thus primarily decorative.

Although the gate no longer has its two towers, the façade still makes for an impressive sight. In the carved sandstone

Bab Agnaou, the royal entrance to the old Almohad palace

tinges of red meld with tones of greyish-blue.

The sculpted façade consists of alternating layers of stone and brick surrounding a horseshoe arch. The floral motifs in the cornerpieces and the frieze with Kufic script framing the arch are unusually delicate.

This is another example of the sober, monochrome style of decoration that is typical of Almohad architecture and that gives the gate a dignified and majestic appearance.

⑲ Dar el-Makhzen

Southeast of the Saadian Tombs. **Closed** to the public.

When Sidi Mohammed ben Abdallah arrived in Marrakech in the 18th century, he found the Almohad and Saadian palaces in a state of ruin. On an extensive area within the kasbah that he enclosed within bastioned walls, he ordered a royal palace, Dar el-Makhzen, to be built, next to the ruins of the Palais el-Badi.

Sidi Mohammed's building project is notable because, unlike the design of other palaces in Marrakech, it took into account the perspective and dimensions of the terrain.

Restored countless times, Dar el-Makhzen consists of several groups of buildings: the Green Palace (el-Qasr el-Akhdar), the Nile Garden (Gharsat el-Nil) and the main house (el-Dar el-Kubra), as

well as outbuildings and several pavilions *(menzah)* set in the park. The palace is still a royal residence today.

⑳ Méchouars

Near Dar el-Makhzen.

Dar el-Makhzen has three large parade grounds, known as *méchouars*. where royal ceremonies are held.

The inner *méchouar*, located south of the palace, is connected to it by Bab el-Akhdar and is linked to the Aguedal Gardens. The outer *méchouar*, east of the palace, is connected to the Berrima quarter by Bab el-Harri. The large *méchouar* south of the inner *méchouar* is outlined by a wall set with merlons.

Procession gathering on one of the *méchouars* at Dar el-Makhzen

㉑ Dar Si Saïd Museum

A stone's throw from the Palais Bahia *(see pp238–9)* is the contemporary Dar Si Saïd. This delightful palace, now a museum, was built in the late 19th century by Si Saïd ben Moussa, brother of Ba Ahmed and a vizier of Moulay Abdel Aziz. Consisting of *zellij* tilework, intricate plasterwork and carved or painted wooden domes, the decoration alone is worth the visit.

The Palace

Following Islamic tradition, the palace is enclosed within solid walls and consists of a two-storey central building arranged around courtyards with graceful arcades. It also has an Andalusian garden, with a pavilion and fountain in the centre.

The sumptuous **Reception Room** on the upper floor is a jewel of Moorish design. The cedar dome and the walls, with *zellij* tilework and a stuccowork frieze, are a mesmerizing sight.

The room contains a wooden candelabrum, a cedar sofa and benches covered with colourful fabric. From the topmost floor there is a view over the medina and towards the High Atlas.

The Collections

Converted into a museum in 1932, Dar Si Saïd houses a fine collection of carpets, doors, chests, weapons, ceramics, costumes and jewellery illustrating the skill of the craftsmen and women of southern Morocco, particularly of the High Atlas, the Tafilalt, the Anti-Atlas, the Souss and the Tensift.

Also on display are a few archaeological pieces and architectural fragments from Fès. The museum's collections are laid out thematically on three levels.

Detail of the door of the reception room

Doors and Carriages

Entry to the museum is through an imposing door studded with nails and fitted with locks. A map at the entrance shows the geographical location of the main centres of craft production in southern Morocco.

Marble basin for ritual ablutions

Arranged along the walls are a cedar chest and some interesting old doors from the region's kasbahs and *ksour* (fortified villages). These unusual and finely worked doors consist of a single panel of oak, almond wood, poplar or walnut. Some of them are decorated with applied relief patterns of wood cut to geometrical shapes. Others are decorated with engraved or painted motifs. As these doors were made by craftsmen working in isolation in a rural environment, they are unique pieces, each one different from the next.

At the end of the corridor a splendid basin for ritual ablutions is on display. The basin was carved from a single block of marble in Andalusia in the late 10th or early 11th century. The decoration features three tiers of ornament: floral motifs, four-legged creatures and heraldic eagles.

The next room contains a display of antique children's carriages and swings.

Jewellery

Located to the left of the entrance, the room in which jewellery is displayed holds a collection of headdresses typical of southern Morocco as well as earrings, diadems, finger rings, necklaces, fibulas (pin-like brooches), bracelets

The pavilion and fountain of the *riad* (Andalusian garden)

For hotels and restaurants see pp306–313 and pp320–31

and anklets. These pieces are engraved, inlaid with niello (a black compound) or enamelled, and are set with polished gems, shells, coral, amber or coins. Geometric shapes such as rectangles, triangles, lozenges, circles, crosses and zigzags are the principal Berber motifs. Some have a symbolic meaning: for example, motifs arranged in sets of five refer to the fingers of one hand, symbolizing life, creativity and representing a lucky charm. Arabesques and floral motifs, by contrast, belong to the Moorish canon of decorative motifs.

Mastered by Jewish metalworkers, these various styles led to the creation of jewellery inspired both by city and rural traditions.

Cedar dome on the ceiling of the reception room

Pottery

The room on the right of the entrance contains a display of everyday objects consisting mostly of pottery from Amizmiz, stone oil lamps from Taroudannt, amphorae, pitchers, storage jars, churns, cooking pots and

various dishes. These pieces, most of which are made of terracotta, have incised, relief or painted decoration.

Two major regional types of pottery can be seen in this room. One is from Safi *(see p122)*, a continuation of the Fassi tradition and characterized by restrained polychrome decoration, often on a white ground. The other is from Tamegroute *(see p273)*, south of Zagora, typified by glazed monochrome ware in which green predominates.

Silver pendant from the Tafilalt

Carpets

The upper floor is devoted to village carpets, most notably those from the Tensift and Boujad. The display includes antique carpets and thick woollen blankets *(hanbel)* in which madder-red predominates. The latter are loosely woven so as to retain more warmth.

The display continues in the second courtyard with carpets from the High Atlas. These include Glaoui and Ouaouzguite carpets, which are both embroidered, woven and knotted and which feature bright colours. Carpets from Chichaoua, with a red or rosewood background, display a variety of motifs: geometric patterns including zigzags, chevrons and squares; animal motifs depictings snakes, scorpions and camels; and motifs derived from everyday objects

VISITORS' CHECKLIST

Practical Information
Riad Zitoune Jedid. **Tel** (0524) 38 95 64. **Open** 9am–4:30pm daily.

such as teapots and combs. Certain motifs are based on tribal tattoos.

The more unusual figure of a horseman was brought from the Sudan by slaves who worked in local plantations.

Woodwork

The interesting collection of woodwork displayed in the second courtyard includes house doors, house frontages and delicate *mashrabiyya* (screenwork), some of it painted in bright colours. These architectural elements, most of them carved in cedar, originate from old houses and shops in Marrakech. The beautiful pieces in wood and marble dating from the Saadian period (16th century) are not to be missed.

A room in the richly decorated former palace

Costume

The corridor leading to the exit contains a display of boots and burnouses worn by the shepherds of the Siroua mountains. Made of black wool, they are decorated with motifs worked in cotton or in silk. Such garments are still worn today, although the workmanship is less refined.

Gallery Guide

The building has three storeys. The exhibition rooms on the ground floor open onto the riad. Beyond the entrance, large-scale pieces such as wooden doors and chests are displayed. To the left of the entrance is the jewellery room, and on the right of it are displays of everyday objects. Next comes the pottery room. The room at the far end of the garden contains objects made of brass and copper, and in the second courtyard is a display of woodwork. The reception room is on the first floor while village carpets can be seen on the second floor. The corridor leading to the exit displays the traditional costume of the Ouzguita tribe.

The pool and pavilion in the Menara imperial garden

㉒ Aguedal Gardens

Rue Bab Ahmar. Reached via the outer méchouar near Bab Ighli. **Open** daily.

This vast enclosed space, 3 km (2 miles) long and 1.5 km (1 mile) wide, contains an orchard planted with lemon, orange, apricot and olive trees.

The historic gardens were laid out in the second half of the 12th century by the Almoravids, who also installed two large irrigation pools connected by *khettaras*, or underground channels *(see pp280–81)*. Enlarged and embellished by the Almohads, and later by the Saadians, the gardens were then completely neglected until the 19th century. At that time the

Alaouite sultans Moulay Abderrahman and Sidi Mohammed ben Abdallah restored the gardens and the pavilions. So as to provide irrigation, they also diverted the course of Wadi Ourika. Gates were also built into the surrounding wall.

While the public have free access to the gardens, the pavilions, on the northern side, are for the exclusive use of the king's guests. Dar el-Hana, the largest pool, located south of the garden, dates from the Almohad period. The terrace of the small Saadian pavilion

Pavilion window in Aguedal Gardens

that stands next to it commands stunning views in two opposite directions: northwards across olive groves and the city rising in tiers to the hill of Jbilet, and southwards to the serene and distant snowcapped peaks of the High Atlas.

One of the many orange trees in the Aguedal Gardens

㉓ Menara

Avenue de la Ménara (west of Hivernage). **Open** 8am–6pm daily.

A welcome haven of coolness and shade, this imperial garden, covering almost 90 ha (220 acres) and enclosed within pisé walls, is filled mostly with olive and fruit trees. In the 12th century, an enormous pool was dug in the centre of the garden to serve as a reservoir for the Almohad sultans. In the 19th century, Moulay Abderrahman refurbished the garden and built the pavilion with a green-tiled pyramidal roof. This attractive building was used by the sultans for their romantic meetings. It is said that every morning one of them would toss into the water the concubine that he had chosen the night before. The ground floor is fronted by three arches opening onto the pool. The upper floor has a large balustered balcony on its north side. Although the interior decoration is plain, the building's overall conception and location are remarkable, and the view from any point within, with the peaks of the Atlas as a backdrop, is quite unforgettable.

㉔ Guéliz

Northwest of the medina.

Established during the Protectorate, Guéliz is the Ville Nouvelle (New Town). Taking its name from the hill that rises above it, this commercial district was designed by Henri Prost. It has a spacious layout in line with the principles of modern town planning.

The wide avenues, municipal gardens, large hotels and cafés with shady terraces make Guéliz a pleasant quarter to visit. Avenue Mohammed V, which runs between Guéliz and the medina, is lined with offices, banks, restaurants, bars, pavement cafés and chic shops.

Despite the number of modern buildings, a few vestiges of the European architecture introduced by the French remain. A notable example of this style, known as "Mauresque", is the **Renaissance Café**, on Place Abdel Moumen ben Ali. It is decorated in typical 1950s style and has a dining area on the top floor with panoramic views.

A large municipal market takes place daily in Place du 16 Novembre. It is worth a visit to take in the atmosphere as local shoppers purchase their fresh fruit, vegetables, herbs and spices.

An apartment block in Guéliz, Marrakech's Ville Nouvelle

❷❺ Majorelle Garden

Avenue Yacoub el-Mansour (near the bus station). **Open** Summer: 8am–5pm; Winter: 8am–5:30pm.

This wonderful garden is like a small paradise in the heart of Ville Nouvelle (the new town). In 1923, Jacques Majorelle *(see above)* fell in love with Morocco and built himself a splendid Moorish villa, which he called Bou Safsaf, in Marrakech. He designed the patterns of the *zellij* tilework, painted the front door, and decorated the interior in tones of deep blue, green and dark red. Around the house he laid out a luxuriant garden. In 1931,

Villa Majorelle, the painter's residence in Marrakech

Jacques Majorelle

The painter Jacques Majorelle was born in Nancy, in northeastern France, in 1886. The son of the renowned cabinet-maker Louis Majorelle, one of the leading figures of the École de Nancy, he was raised in the artistic milieu of Art Nouveau. He seemed destined to follow in his father's footsteps. However, after studying at the École des Beaux-Arts in Paris, Majorelle decided to devote himself to painting. He travelled to Spain, Italy and Egypt. Recovering from health problems, he went to Morocco in 1919 and fell in love with its intense light. Aided by Marshal Lyautey, he settled in Marrakech, in his now-famous villa. Finding fascination in the souks, kasbahs and villages of the High Atlas, he stayed in Morocco until his death in 1962.

at Majorelle's request, the architect Sinoir built an Art Deco studio with pergolas and bright blue walls. The garden, which is separate from the house, opened to the public in 1947.

The house was later bought by Yves Saint-Laurent, the famous couturier, and Pierre Bergé. Skilfully restored, the garden is divided by four walkways that cross each other to create parterres of brightly coloured tropical flowers. Besides yucca, bougainvillea, bamboo, laurel, geraniums, hibiscus and cypresses, the garden has over 400 varieties of palm tree and 1,800 species of cactus. Water lilies grow in a pool bordered by papyrus.

The studio has been converted into a small museum that contains a selection of Moroccan crafts such as antique carpets, Fassi ceramics and Berber doors, and some 40 engravings of the villages and kasbahs of the Atlas executed by Jacques Majorelle.

❷❻ La Palmeraie

On the road to Casablanca, 22 km (14 miles) north of Marrakech. This interesting tour, 22.5 km (14 miles) long, can be made by car or horse-drawn carriage.

Legend has it that, after eating dates brought back from the Sahara, the soldiers of the 11th-century Almoravid sultan Youssef ben Tachfine spat out the stones around their encampment. The stones are supposed to have germinated and led to the creation of La Palmeraie (Palm Grove) in Marrakech.

Covering an area of some 120 sq km (46 sq miles), the grove consists of fields, gardens and orchards irrigated by ditches and wells supplied by *khettaras*. Although it contains 150,000 trees, the agricultural function of the grove is being pared away by the advance of buildings and the greed of developers who are making inroads into it by building desirable residences here.

La Palmeraie (Palm Grove) in Marrakech, with 150,000 trees

HIGH ATLAS

Little-known because of its relative inaccessibility, the High Atlas makes up the largest massif in the Atlas chain. It is also the highest mountain range in North Africa. In this geographical isolation Berber culture and identity prospered. Over the centuries, the tribes established their own economic and social framework, and a unique collective way of life, based on blood ties and solidarity.

Extending from the plains of the Atlantic seaboard to Morocco's border with Algeria, the High Atlas forms an impregnable barrier some 800 km (500 miles) long and, in certain places, 100 km (60 miles) wide. Consisting of great massifs rising to heights of 3,000–4,000 m (10,000–13,000 ft), and steep valleys, desolate rocky plains and deep narrow canyons, the High Atlas has played a decisive role in the history of Morocco.

From earliest times these mountains have been a place of refuge for populations fleeing from invaders. For centuries, nomads forced northwards by the desertification of the Sahara have come into conflict with the sedentary mountain-dwelling tribes, disputing possession of prized pasture.

This tumultuous feudal past led to the development of a strikingly beautiful form of fortified architecture. Today, although the Berbers no longer need to guard their safety, they still live in *tighremts*, old patriarchal houses with thick walls. Hamlets built of pisé still cling to mountainsides, while every last plot of land is used to grow barley, corn, maize, turnips, lucerne and potatoes – crops that can be cultivated at high altitudes. The Berbers channel river water to irrigate small squares of land and graze their flocks of sheep and goats, which they raise for milk, butter and wool.

Sometimes isolated by snowfall in winter, the Berbers of the High Atlas live and work by the seasons, the constant round of labour punctuated by a variety of festivals.

The kasbah in Telouet, abandoned in 1956

◄ Skiing at Oukaïmeden, the Atlas Mountains

Exploring the High Atlas

Crowned with high peaks, the chain of the High Atlas culminates in the west in Jbel Toubkal. At 4,167 m (13,676 ft), this is the highest peak in North Africa, with pisé villages nestling on its lower slopes. In the centre, Jbel M'Goun, at 4,068 m (13,351 ft), rises over the Tessaout, Aït Bouguemez and Aït Bou Oulli valleys. The only channels of communication between these valleys are mule trails and high passes. On the banks of the *wadi* that snakes along the valley bottoms, villages cluster around fortified houses, punctuating expanses of cultivated land. The eastern end of the High Atlas is marked by the imposing outline of Jbel Ayachi, 3,737 m (12,265 ft) high. Here high desert plateaux stretch to the horizon. From late spring to early autumn they are filled with flocks of grazing sheep.

Marrakech

■ **Area shown by map below**

Key

═══ Motorway
━━ Major road
⋯⋯ Minor road
--- Track
〜〜 Railway
△ Summit
✕ Pass

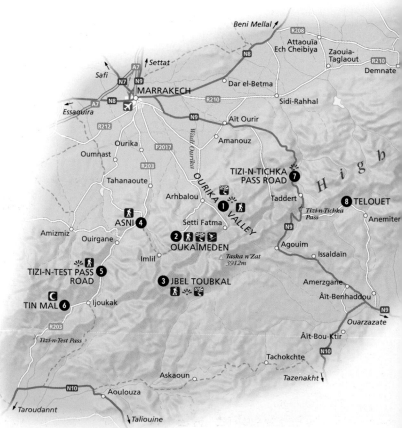

Sights at a Glance

① Ourika Valley
④ Oukaïmeden
④ Asni
⑤ Tizi-n-Test Pass Road
⑥ Tin Mal
⑦ Tizi-n-Tichka Pass Road
⑧ Telouet
⑨ *Aït Bouguemez Valley pp258–61*
⑩ Imilchil

Tour

③ The Jbel Toubkal Massif

Harvesting barley in the Aït Bouguemez valley

The village of Dar Caïd Ouriki, at the entrance to the Ourika valley

Getting Around

With the High Atlas forming an imposing east-to-west barrier, the most westerly north-to-south route in this region is the R203. Running from Marrakech, it crosses the Tizi-n-Test Pass and leads to Taroudannt and Agadir. South-east of Marrakech, another road, the N9, via the Tizi-n-Tichka Pass, leads to Ouarzazate. In the central stretch of the mountain chain, there is no road over the High Atlas for 200 km (124 miles). Only a track, which is often impassable in winter, crosses the lake-filled plateau to reach the Dadès valley. On the eastern side, a road from Fès runs along the Middle and High Atlas, leading via Midelt to the Tafilalt valley.

For keys to symbols *see back flap*

Wadi Ourika, irrigating a valley of fruit tree plantations

❶ Ourika Valley

Road Map C4. 68 km (42 miles) from Marrakech on road P2017. 🚌 from Marrakech; alternatively, by taxi. 🛈 Marrakech; (0524) 43 61 31. 🎭 Moussem of Setti Fatma (mid-Aug).

The trip to the Ourika valley, 68 km (42 miles) southeast of Marrakech, offers a pleasant tour of the lower foothills of the Atlas. Beyond the village of **Tnine-de-l'Ourika**, the valley, through which flows the Ourika, becomes verdant. The largest souk in the valley takes place in the village on Mondays.

All along the road that follows the course of the *wadi*, small houses, cafés, grocery shops and small hotels cling to the hillside. Gardens and plots of cultivated land shaded by many fruit trees are laid out along the valley bottom. The Ourika river is occasionally subject to sudden and devastating flooding, such

as in August 1995, when many houses were swept away.

Beyond Arhbalou, at an altitude of 1,500 m (4,923 ft), the valley narrows and gently rises. The road comes to an end at **Setti Fatma**, a good starting point for hikes. Seven waterfalls flow down the rocky scree above the village. The first of these is easy to reach by walking up the course of the *wadi*. The walk up to the others is over more uneven ground, and some climbing is involved, so that you will need strong walking boots. From that vantage point there is a superb view over Setti Fatma.

The village may also be used as the starting point for longer hikes to Jbel Toubkal and Yagour Plateau, whose peak is well known for the hundreds of rock engravings that can be seen here.

The tomb of Setti Fatma is the focus of a *moussem* that takes place in the village in mid-August. This religious pilgrimage is also an occasion when Berbers from a wide area can gather together.

❷ Oukaïmeden

Road Map C4. 74 km (46 miles) from Marrakech on road P2017. 🚌 from Marrakech, then taxi. 🛈 Marrakech; (0524) 43 61 31.

A ski resort in winter and base for mountain hikes in summer, Oukaïmeden is a haven of fresh air, just over one hour from Marrakech. The resort is easily

reached on a road that forks off to the right at the village of Arhbalou, with the Ourika valley on the left. Shaded by olive, oak and walnut trees, the road then winds upwards in a series of hairpin bends through a stony landscape.

The chalets and winter sports facilities are in the village itself, encircled by mountain peaks: Jbel Oukaïmeden, rising to a height of 3,273 m (10,742 ft), Jbel Ouhattar, at 3,258 m (10,693 ft), and Jbel Angour, at 3,614 m (11,861 ft). The great Oukaïmeden plateau is carpeted in pasture, the grazing of which is controlled by tradition.

From November to April, if the snow is sufficiently deep, a chair lift – the highest in North Africa – runs up to the summit of Jbel Oukaïmeden, while several ski lifts allow beginners to practise on the lower slopes. The resort also offers long-distance and cross-country skiing.

Rock engravings can be seen in the village and on the plateau. Dating from the Bronze Age, they depict mainly daggers, halbards, shields and humans.

About 2 km (1 mile) from the resort, the site of a transmission mast at an altitude of 2,740 m (8,993 ft) commands a magnificent view of the Atlas and the plain where Marrakech is located. In summer, Oukaïmeden is also the starting point for mountain hikes, particularly up to the Tizi-n-Ouaddi Pass, the beautiful village of Tacheddirt, and to Imlil and the Tizi-n-Test Pass.

The ski resort at Oukaïmeden, built in 1950

❸ Tour of the Jbel Toubkal Massif

As well as the opportunity to climb to the top of Jbel Toubkal, at 4,167 m (13,676 ft) the highest peak in the Atlas, the Jbel Toubkal massif offers great scope for hikes lasting several days. Climbing Toubkal is not particularly difficult, but the fact that it is a high-altitude hike over rough terrain should be taken into account. From the Toubkal Refuge, the summit of Jbel Toubkal can be reached in about four hours. For the finest view over the High Atlas, it is best to reach the summit in the late morning.

⑦ **Tacheddirt** This pretty village, at 2314 m (7,595 ft) and set amid mountains, is reached via the Tizi-n-Tamatert Pass, east of Imlil.

⑧ **Lepiney Hut** Located at the start of the hike up the Azzaden valley and across the Tazarhart plateau, at 3,000 m (9,846 ft), the hut is used by seasoned hikers and rock climbers.

① **Imlil** Surrounded by walnut and fruit trees, this mountain village is the starting point for the climb up Jbel Toubkal and also for many other mountain hikes.

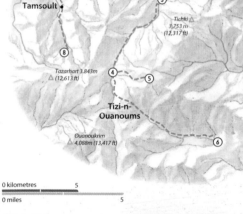

② **Aremd** The village, in the Mizane valley, lies at 1,900 m (6,236 ft). Its stone houses cling to the rocky mountainside, surrounded by cultivated terraces.

③ **Sidi Chamharouch** At the end of a deep gorge, the *koubba* of Sidi Chamharouch, king of the *djnouu* (genies), attracts pilgrims all year-round.

④ **Toubkal Refuge** This is the last stopping place before the summit of Jbel Toubkal. The refuge, at 3,200 m (10,502 ft), is open all year-round.

Tips for Hikers

Reasonably fit hikers can climb to the summit of Jbel Toubkal without a guide.
Starting point: Imlil, 17 km (10.5 miles) from Asni on road P2015, or 1 hour and 30 minutes from Marrakech.
When to go: April to October offers the best conditions.
Huts: Toubkal (5 hours from Imlil), Lépiney (two days' walk from the Tazarhart plateau) and Tacheddirt (2 hours and 30 minutes from Imlil).
Information: Detailed maps of the area can be obtained from the guides' office at Imlil. Mules can also be hired for walks lasting several days.

⑥ **Lake Ifni**
The lake, five hours' walk from Toubkal Refuge, lies in a mineral-rich environment. Shepherds' huts stand on the lakeshore.

⑤ **Jbel Toubkal**
You can climb to the top at the end of winter: it offers breathtaking views over the whole of the High Atlas.

Key

-- Tour route (footpath)

== Track

The village of Asni, encircled by the Tamaroute mountains

❹ Asni

Road Map C4. 42 km (26 miles) from Marrakech on road R203. 🚌 from Marrakech, then by taxi. 🛒 Sat.

With an interesting red-walled kasbah, Asni is the first large village on the road from Marrakech to the Tizi-n-Test Pass. Attractive orchards surround the village and there are many mule tracks leading up to the plateaux in its vicinity.

From this small settlement, a metalled road leads to the village of Imlil, which is the starting point for hikes to Jbel Toubkal (see p253).

Environs

The very popular *moussem* at **Moulay Brahim**, 5 km (3 miles) from Asni, takes place one to two weeks after the festival of Mouloud (see p45). Moroccans ascribe to the saint Moulay Brahim the power to cure barren women. Pilgrims come to lay their gifts before his tomb and to hang small pieces of fabric from the shrubs here. When one of these fragments falls from the shrub, the woman who hung it may expect a child.

❺ Tizi-n-Test Pass Road

Road Map B-C4. Accessible from Marrakech on road R203. 🚌 from Marrakech or Taroudannt. 🛒 Thu in Ouirgane; Wed in Ijoukak.

Beyond Asni, the road crosses the High Atlas, then runs down into the Souss plain. This road, in a good state of repair although narrow and meandering in places, was built by the French in the 1930s.

Just before Ouirgane, a small road to the right leads to **Amizmiz**, a pretty village with a ruined kasbah, set in the midst of olive trees. The souk here is renowned for Berber pottery made in the village itself. **Ouirgane** is a resort whose coolness in summer makes it popular with the inhabitants of Marrakech. A few salt mines are still worked here.

As the road climbs further up to the Tizi-n-Test Pass, snaking through red, almost purple terrain, the landscape becomes more wild. Starting from **Ijoukak**, keen hikers can reach the Agoundis valley, walking in the direction of Taghbart and El-Maghzen, or make for the Jbel Toubkal massif. Beyond Ijoukak, the massive Tin Mal mosque is visible on the right.

Below the Tizi-n-Test Pass, imposing deserted kasbahs perch on arid outcrops. They all date from the end of the 19th century and belonged to the Goundafa, a powerful Berber tribe that controlled access to the pass. From November to April, the pass, at an altitude of 2,093 m (6,869 ft) is sometimes blocked by snow. The descent offers a beautiful view of the Souss plain and of hills covered with argan trees, 2,000 m (6,564 ft) below.

Tizi-n-Test pottery

❻ Tin Mal

Road Map B4. About 25 km (15.5 miles) south of Asni on road R203. Mosque: **Open** daily, except Friday for non-Muslims. To visit the mosque, ask the caretaker in the village of Tin Mal.

In an isolated setting at the foot of the Atlas, 10 km (6 miles) beyond Ijoukak on the Tizi-n-Test Pass road, the **Mosque of Tin Mal** situated uphill from the village, is the last remaining sign of the Almohad conquest in the 12th century. Tin Mal, once a fortified holy town, was founded by the theologian Ibn Toumart in 1125. From here, he fomented a holy war against the Almoravids and was recognized as a religious leader by the Berber tribes of the High Atlas.

In 1276, the town was sacked and pillaged by the Merinids. Only the sumptuous mosque was left standing. It was built in 1153 by Abd el-Moumen, Ibn Toumart's successor and the first Almohad ruler. The mosque has been restored and as a UNESCO

The tortuous road winding up to the Tizi-n-Test Pass

◀ Road leading to Tizi-n-Test Pass in the High Atlas Mountains

The mosque at Tin Mal, with pink brickwork and plaster stalactites

World Heritage Site, it is one of the few religious buildings in Morocco that is open to non-Muslims. Its high walls and sturdy towers give it a fortress-like look.

❼ Tizi-n-Tichka Pass Road

Road Map C4. From Marrakech or Ouarzazate on road N9. 🚌 Marrakech or Ouarzazate. 🏪 Tue in Aït Ourir.

Built by the French in the 1920s, this winding road runs through a landscape that is, by turn, arid, mineral-rich environments and fertile valleys. Pisé villages, in tones of red or grey, huddle at the foot of hillsides.

The first pass, **Tizi-n-Aït Imger**, at an altitude of 1,470 m (4,825 ft), offers a panoramic view of the Atlas chain. Here, the road is lined with stalls selling pottery, mineral rocks and stones whose colours are a little too bright to be natural.

From here up to the **Tizi-n-Tichka Pass** – which, at an altitude of 2,260 m (7,417 ft), is the highest road pass in Morocco – crops gradually give way to a landscape of bare red soil. The mountains become more rounded and the houses are built higher, with more decoration, anticipating those of the Moroccan south. The impressive fortified grainstore on the way out of **Igherm-n-Ougdal** is open to visitors. Beyond Agouim, on the other side of the *wadi*, stands the restored kasbah at **El-Mdint**, its towers decorated with relief patterns. Palm trees come into view, and a wide stony desert plain with tones of pink and beige leads to Ouarzazate.

Interior of the fortified grainstore at Igherm-n-Ougdal

❽ Telouet

Road Map C4. Accessible from road N9. **Open** daily; caretaker on the premises.

About 5 km (3 miles) along the road running down from the Tizi-n-Tichka Pass, towards Ouarzazate, a narrow metalled minor road leads off to the left. It drops down into a steep valley, and 20 km (12 miles) further on reaches the kasbah of Telouet.

This was one of the principal residences of Al-Thami el-Glaoui, pasha of Marrakech, whose fiefdom covered a large part of the High Atlas. El-Glaoui served the sultan, then switched to the French in 1912. His opposition to Sultan Mohammed V cost him dear, for on his death his family was exiled and his possessions dispersed.

Thus it was that Telouet, a town with an illustrious past, has been the victim of neglect since 1956. The glazed tiles are disintegrating, the lookout towers crumbling, the walls cracking and the windows shattered. Most of the rooms are inaccessible since the roof has fallen in.

However, low-ceilinged, bare-walled corridors lead to two reception rooms that have miraculously survived the passage of time. They are vestiges of the opulence treasured by El-Glaoui. The Andalusian-style rooms have engraved stuccowork, painted cedar ceilings and doors, and colourful *zellij* tilework. Daylight entering through a glass-covered dome and a small window framed with decorative wrought iron lights the rooms from dawn to sunset.

Environs

From Telouet, a narrow, winding metalled road offers a picturesque route to the village of **Aït Benhaddou** *(see p269)*. In this fertile valley, planted with palm, fig and olive trees, and irrigated by Wadi Ounila, kasbahs signal the past importance of El-Glaoui's fiefdom. The attractive village of **Anemiter**, standing at the head of the Ounila valley some 11 km (9 miles) from Telouet, is unusually well preserved.

Painted wooden ceiling in the kasbah of Telouet

❾ Aït Bouguemez Valley

The wide, flat Aït Bouguemez valley is flanked by a landscape of high, arid hilltops. This is the domain of the Aït Bouguemez tribe, who are settled farmers. The tribe is thought to be the oldest established in the region. The valley is covered in meticulously tilled plots of land surrounded by ditches, and walnut trees grow in undulating fields of barley and corn. On the dry slopes, pisé hamlets cluster around *tighremts*, old fortified houses. The valley is the starting point for hikes through spectacular scenery up to the massif of Jbel M'Goun. There are 28 villages scattered along the valley between Agouti and Zaouïa Oulemsi.

Threshing the Corn
Mules attached to a post in the centre of the threshing ground circle slowly, trampling the corn. This separates the grain from the husks and straw.

★ **Painted Ceilings** In the *tamsriyt*, a room set aside for overnight guests, the ceilings – particularly in Agouti – are decorated with geometric motifs and thin coloured lines skilfully drawn freehand or with a compass.

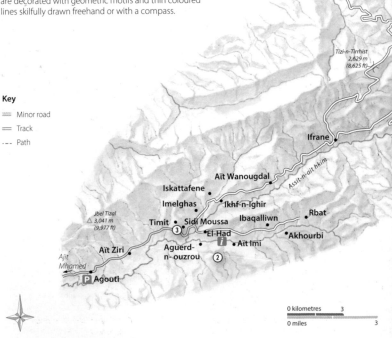

Key

- ⚌ Minor road
- ═ Track
- --- Path

Tizi-n-Tirrhist 2,629 m (8,625 ft)

Ifrane

Assit-n-aït hkim

Aït Wanougdal

Iskattafene

Imelghas · Ikhf-n-Ighir

Jbel Tizal 3,041 m (9,977 ft)

Timit · Sidi Moussa · Ibaqalliwn · Rbat

El-Had 🛈 · Aït Imi · Akhourbi

Aït Ziri · Aguerd-n-ouzrou

Ajit Mhamed

🅿 Agouti

0 kilometres 3

0 miles 3

Maize Drying on the Rooftops
In the autumn, maize is laid out carefully on the tiered rooftops. When it has dried, the grain is separated from the cob on a concrete floor by hand.

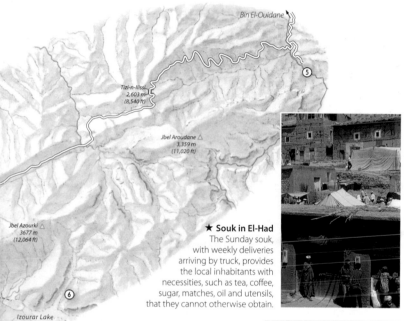

★ **Souk in El-Had**
The Sunday souk, with weekly deliveries arriving by truck, provides the local inhabitants with necessities, such as tea, coffee, sugar, matches, oil and utensils, that they cannot otherwise obtain.

Valley Landscape Drawn to the pastures in the region, the industrious Berbers have irrigated the land so as to extract the most from it, and built fortified villages to ensure their safety.

KEY

① **Zaouïa Oulemsi** is the departure point for hikes to Lake Izourar.

② **Tabant** is the valley's administrative centre. The souk at El-Had takes place on Sundays.

③ **The restored circular granary** in Sidi Moussa is famous in the region.

④ **The direct route to Aït Mohammed** is best avoided. Instead take the easier road from Agouti.

⑤ **Zaouïa Ahansal** contains *tighremts*, old fortified houses.

⑥ **Many nomadic herdsmen** camp on the shores of Lake Izourar.

Exploring the Aït Bouguemez Valley

Clinging to the mountainside, the hamlets of the Aït Bouguemez valley blend into their setting, being almost the same colour as the landscape. The houses are stacked together like building blocks, the flat roof of the house serving as a terrace for the inhabitants of the house above. Looking down onto the river and the village's communal land, these cube-like houses catch the warmth of the rising sun and are adapted to the rigours of the climate. Houses in the valley bottom are built of pisé, raw earth dug at the spot where the house is to be built, mixed with water and sometimes straw. In villages at altitudes above 2,200 m (7,220 ft), dry stone is used, since pisé is unsuited to cold and wet conditions.

Detail of a painted ceiling, typical of the houses of the Aït Bouguemez

Setting off for the souk in a village below Jbel Ghat

Agouti

At the western extremity of the Aït Bouguemez valley.

The first of the villages that line the valley, Agouti is located at 1,800 m (5,908 ft). As an outpost of the Aït Bouguemez tribe, it once defended access to the high valley against rival tribes.

A ruined *igherm* (fortified communal granary), set on a sheer rocky promontory, towers above the village. The villagers once kept their possessions and their crops here. In the valley, many houses have electricity, as well as some form of running water.

In Agouti, as in some of the other villages in the valley, visitors can see some beautiful wood

Mules in the Aït Bou Oulli valley

ceilings in the houses of wealthier families. The painted decoration is executed by craftsmen of renown and features an infinite variety of geometric patterns.

Aït Bou Oulli Valley

West of Agouti.

From Agouti, a day trip can be made to the Aït Bou Oulli valley on mule-back or by four-wheel-drive vehicle. A sheer-sided track leads down into the valley, whose name means "the people who raise ewes". The narrow wooded valley, thickly covered with walnut trees, winds the length of the *wadi*, which irrigates small fields.

Jbel Ghat, rising above the valley, is a peak with mythical associations to which

the Berbers come on a pilgrimage in years of drought. **Abachkou**, an interesting, high-set village at the far end of the valley, is renowned for the beautiful white capes produced by the villagers and found nowhere else in Morocco.

Sidi Moussa

East of Agouti.

Perched on the summit of a pointed hill, in the centre of the Aït Bouguemez valley, Sidi Moussa **granary** has benefited from a complete restoration and is on UNESCO's World Heritage list. It is reached by a steep path from the village of Timit.

This collective granary, one of three in the region, is a sturdy circular building with incorporated watch towers.

In the interior, which is lit by sparse loop-hole windows, a spiral staircase leads to the two upper floors. In the half-light, compartments arranged along the walls can be made out. This was where the inhabitants kept their possessions.

Sidi Moussa, the holy man renowned for his good deeds and his powers as a healer, is buried here. Sterile women of the Aït Bouguemez valley and from more distant valleys visit the shrine, where they spend the night and sacrifice a chicken as an offering to him.

From the granary, it is possible to look over the rest of the valley, with the outlines of nearby villages dotting the surrounding hillsides.

Aït Ziri, Timit, Imelghas and Iskattafène

East of Agouti. 🚍 at El-Had on Sun.

Walking around these villages, visitors will observe such details as decorated doors (either carved or painted in bright colours) and windows with interlacing wrought iron or *mashrabiyya* screens. Some very fine *tighremts* (fortified houses) dating from the early 20th century are still inhabited by village chiefs and their large families.

Close to Tabant, the administrative centre of the valley, **El-Had** is well known for its Sunday souk. This is the only place in the valley where supplies can be purchased. The village is also the starting point for mountain hikes to the M'Goun.

Zaouïa Oulemsi

On the way from Agouti, on a narrow track.

Zaouïa Oulemsi is the last village in the Aït Bouguemez valley, which it overlooks from an altitude of 2,150 m (7,056 ft). It consists of low, red-hued dry-stone houses. Here, the snowfall comes early and tends to be heavy.

The village is the starting point for hikes to **Lake Izourar**, which lies in the heart of the mountains at an altitude of 2,500 m (8,205 ft). Many nomadic shepherds camp beside the lake, which is often dry in summer, when it turns into pasture, the use of which is

Cultivated fields in the Aït Bouguemez valley

carefully controlled to prevent over-grazing.

The shepherds include the Aït Bouguemez, who come for the summer, living in the stone-built sheepfolds, and the Aït Atta, with their sheep, goats and camels, who in summer come up to the High Atlas from Jbel Sarhro. Seeking good pasture, they settle on the slopes of M'Goun, around Lake Izourar or on the Imilchil plateau, moving south again at the first frosts.

Fortified granary, Aït Bouguemez valley

Zaouïa Ahansal

On the track towards Bin el-Ouidane. 🚍 Mon.

A track running along the continuation of the Aït Bouguemez valley goes up to the Tizi-n-Tirrhist Pass, at 2,629 m (8,628 ft). The mountains are very bare here. The track passes a "fossilized forest" of juniper, with gnarled, dying trunks; the species faces extinction.

Zaouïa Ahansal, consisting of some old *tighremts* and the tomb of its founder, Saïd Ahansal, dates from the 14th century, when the *marabout* movement loomed large in the history of this mountain region. *Zaouias* (sanctuaries set up around the tombs of *marabouts*, holy figures and the leaders of brotherhoods) were then protected holy places, where pilgrims and the needy found refuge. In exchange for the protection given by the *marabout*, the Berbers maintained the land around the *zaouia*, were taught Arabic and received Koranic instruction.

Heedless of the power of the sultans, the leaders of some *zaouias* controlled the lives of the mountain people, settling disputes over land ownership and imposing their will. Zaouïa Ahansal was a major influence on the local Berber populations, but the descendants of Saïd Ahansal came into conflict with the fiefs of the *caïds* (chief of a defined territory) of the High Atlas. They held out against the French until 1934.

The track continues for 40 km (25 miles) before reaching **La Cathédrale**, an impressive rock formation, then Lake Bin el-Ouidane.

Animals grazing around Lake Izourar, in summer

Lake Tiselit, on the Plateau des Lacs, near Imilchil

⓿ Imilchil

Road Map D3. Accessible via Kasba Tadla (on road N8) and El-Ksiba (on road R317). 🚗 🚌 Sat.

On its eastern end, the chain of the High Atlas descends as if it had been crushed, forming a desert plateau surrounded by rolling mountains. Imilchil is at the heart of this sparsely populated region – the territory of the Aït Haddidou.

This group of semi-nomadic shepherds came originally from Boumalne du Dadès, located in the high Dadès valley, where some of them still live. They arrived in Morocco during the centuries immediately after the introduction of Islam, and there is evidence of their presence in the Boumalne du Dadès region durng the 11th century. For several years they were in conflict with the powerful Aït Atta tribe in disputes over pasture, then settled in the Assif Melloul valley in the 17th century.

The village of Imilchil is dominated by a sumptuously decorated kasbah. Its towers have a curious feature: the angles of the crenellation are set with finials resembling inverted cooking pots. This decorative device is also related to superstitious belief, as it gives protection against lightning and the "evil eye" and is a symbol of prosperity.

Chimney with "cooking pot" finial, Imilchil

Although Imilchil is remote, its claim to fame is the annual **Marriage Fair**, a *moussem* at which women may choose a fiancé and many pilgrims and traders from the mountains gather. It takes place at the end of September at a spot known as Aït Haddou Ameur, some 20 km (13 miles) from Imilchil. Arriving on foot, by truck or by mule, all the tribes of the area flock to this great yearly commercial, social and religious gathering. The pilgrims throng around the pisé walls of the shrine of Sidi Ahmed ou Mghanni, a venerated holy man, to present their offerings.

The origin of the Marriage Fair goes back to the story of two lovers, Hadda and Moha, members of rival tribes who were kept apart by their parents. Their tears created two lakes, Iseli, "the fiancé", and Tiselit, "the fiancée", on the Plateau des Lacs (see *below*). Ever since, young girls who come to the *moussem* with their family may converse freely with men from other tribes, although they must be accompanied by a sister or a female friend. Young couples who wish to can visit the tent of the *adouls* (lawyers) and sign a betrothal agreement. These unions are often engineered by the respective families ahead of the *moussem*.

The event, which for some years has attracted crowds of tourists, has lost some of its authenticity. The presentation and parade of the couples and the evenings of folk dance and song are but a superficial aspect of what is a great commercial and religious gathering.

The colourful tents of the great souk spread out across the wide plateau. Traders sell basketry, cooking utensils, blankets and handwoven carpets, metalware, clothing, basic foodstuffs, and other items. On the hillside, herds of cows and camels and flocks of sheep await buyers.

The Plateau des Lacs can be reached either by following a long track that runs from El-Ksiba, crossing narrow gorges and undulating passes, or on a surfaced road via Rich, further east. This mineral-rich environment, at an altitude of 2,000– 3,500 m (6,500–11,500 ft), is dotted with isolated *tighremts*, and a splash of colour is provided by the emerald waters of lakes Tiselit and Iseli. In summer, sheep are brought to the lush pasture here.

A couple at the Imilchil Marriage Fair

Berbers of the High Atlas

The Berbers of the High Atlas are non-nomadic peasants. Many of them have a completely self-sufficient lifestyle, and in certain valleys mule tracks are the only channel of communication with the outside world. The inhabitants of these remote valleys live by the pattern of the seasons and the round of work in the fields. In the autumn, the men till the soil with a wooden plough and buy and sell goods and produce at the weekly souk. In winter, the women collect water from the river, gather wood and weave thick woollen blankets. In spring, the men dig and maintain vital irrigation channels. In summer, the women harvest and thresh the grain, while the men winnow barley on threshing floors.

At the Marriage Fair in Imilchil, the *raïs*, the dance leader of this folk troupe, beats out the rhythm on his *bendir*, a kind of tambourine, with his right hand.

Family Festivals

The daily life of the Berber women of the High Atlas is enlivened by family festivals. The women, dressed in dazzling clothes, dance the ahwach or the ahidous, according to the region, while the men intone chants as they beat out a regular rhythm on their bendir.

A woman carries barley on her back to the threshing ground. There the unripe barley will be deposited.

Berber women from the Aït Haddidou tribe wear differently striped cloaks to signal that they belong to a certain clan.

This weaver from Abachkou, in the Aït Bou Oulli valley, washes, cards and spins sheep's wool. She weaves the yarn into cloth to make white capes, which are then decorated with pieces of metal.

Men come to the souk at Imilchil to buy and sell livestock and to stock up with vital supplies for the winter.

OUARZAZATE & THE SOUTHERN OASES

This fascinating region begins at the southern edge of the High Atlas, where desert and mountains meet. The stony desert is broken by green oases where shade-giving date palms grow in profusion. Cut by steep canyons and studded with arid hills, it is criss-crossed by wadis right up to the edge of the Sahara. Here, the light is intensely bright and the colours sumptuously rich.

The history of Morocco is closely linked to this region bordering the Sahara desert, the birthplace of the great Moroccan dynasties. In the 11th century, Almoravid warriors, who came from the Sahara, set out from the south to extend their empire from Senegal to Spain. In the 16th century, the Saadians, who came from Arabia, left the Draa valley to conquer Morocco. Lastly, the Alaouites, the dynasty that holds power in Morocco today, settled in the Tafilalt region in the 13th century.

Trade in gold, salt and slaves between black Africa and Morocco melded the local populations, so that Arabs, Berbers and Haratines, descendants of ancient black populations, lived side by side. Life here centres on three great *wadis*, the Draa, the Dadès and the Ziz. These rivers have created stunning landscapes, carving gorges and canyons out of the sides of the High Atlas and Anti-Atlas. The date palm that brings welcome shade to small plots of corn and barley accounts for the region's wealth. The palm groves are punctuated by hundreds of kasbahs and *ksour*. These fortified villages and houses protected the sedentary populations against attack from nomadic tribes. Many of them are still inhabited today, although they are slowly crumbling. The desert begins south of the oases. Every year, aided by drought, it encroaches further onto arable land.

The central patio of the kasbah at Oulad Driss, in the southern Draa valley

◄ The Dadès Gorge with a dramatic backdrop in the Atlas Mountains

Exploring Ouarzazate and the Southern Oases

The Draa Valley, south of Ouarzazate, and the Tafilalt valley, south of Er-Rachidia, are the two great routes to the Sahara. The valleys are interconnected by the Dadès valley, which covers 120 km (75 miles) between Ouarzazate and Boumalne du Dadès. It cuts through a desert plateau at an average altitude of 1,000 to 1,500 m (3,282 to 4,923 ft), set between the High Atlas on its northern side and the foothills of Jbel Sarhro on its southern side. Other valleys, irrigated by *wadis* flowing down from the Atlas, impinge on the Dadès valley. Negotiable on foot or by four-wheel-drive vehicle, they give access to the interior of the High Atlas. Exploring this region, experiencing the scenic oases and visiting the most interesting *ksour*, takes at least a week.

Getting Around

Roads in a good state of repair run between Ouarzazate and Zagora, Er-Rachidia and Erfoud. However, distances are great, and the mountainous terrain and passes to be negotiated must be taken into account. Although certain tracks can be followed only in a four-wheel-drive vehicle, an ordinary car is sufficient to drive on the major roads. Buses and *grands taxis* from Ouarzazate cover the whole region.

Msemrir, a village at the foot of the High Atlas *(see p277)*

For hotels and restaurants see pp306–313 and pp320–31

Area shown by map below

Elaborately designed door of the *zaouia* in Tamegroute

Key

— Major road

==== Minor road

--- Track

△ Summit

✕ Pass

An austere kasbah in the Dadès Gorge

Sights at a Glance

1 Ouarzazate
2 Taourirt Kasbah
3 Aït Benhaddou
4 Jbel Sarhro
5 Draa Valley
6 Zagora
7 Tamegroute
8 Mhamid
9 Skoura
10 El-Kelaa M'Gouna
11 Boumalne du Dadès
12 Dadès Gorge
13 Tinerhir
14 Todra Gorge
15 Tamtattouchte
16 Goulmima
17 Midelt
18 Ziz Gorge
19 Er-Rachidia
20 Source Bleue de Meski
21 Erfoud
22 Tafilalt Palm Grove
23 Rissani
24 Merzouga

For keys to symbols *see back flap*

A shop in the crafts centre opposite the Taourirt Kasbah

❶ Ouarzazate

Road Map C4. 🔼 70,000. 🚌 Avenue Mohammed V (to Marrakech, Tinerhir, Taroudannt and Zagora) and grands taxis (Tue, Fri, Sat, Sun). 🛈 Avenue Mohammed V; (0524) 88 24 85. Grands taxis, Land Rovers and 4x4 vehicles for hire. 🎭 Crafts Festival (May); Moussem of Sidi Daoud (Aug).

A former garrison town of the French Foreign Legion, Ouarzazate was founded in 1928, having been chosen by the French as a strategic base from which to pacify the South. Located at an altitude of 1,160 m (3,807 ft) at the intersection of the Draa and Dadès valleys, with the Agadir region to the west, it is on the main route between the mountains and the desert. It is also a good base from which to visit Aït Benhaddou and the Skoura palm grove.

Ouarzazate is a peaceful provincial town with wide streets, many hotels and municipal gardens. Avenue Mohammed V, the only main street, crosses the town and leads to the Dadès valley.

About 6 km (4 miles) outside Ouarzazate, off the road to Marrakech, are the **Atlas Film Studios**, surrounded by high pisé walls that look as if they are defended by giant Hollywood-style, pseudo-Egyptian figures. The studios, which cover 30,000 sq m (322,920 sq ft) of desert, provide the livelihood of a considerable portion of the population of Ouarzazate. For a century, hundreds of films have been shot in this region, including Bertolucci's *The Sheltering Sky* (1990) and Scorsese's *Kundun* (1997). On the other side of the town, opposite the Taourirt Kasbah, are the Andromeda Italian film studios.

Atlas Film Studios

On road N9, 6 km (4 miles) northwest of Ouarzazate. **Tel** (0524) 88 22 23. **Open** Studios: 8am–6:30pm daily; 🎥 8:15am–5:15pm (until 6:45pm in summer) daily, except when filming is going on.

Environs

About 10 km (6 miles) to the south is the **Finnt Oasis**, with fine pisé *ksour*. A little further on is the **El-Mansour Eddahbi Dam**, fed by the Dadès and Ouarzazate rivers, which join to form the Draa. The dam provides water for the golf course, the Draa's palm groves and electricity for the valley.

About 7 km (4 miles) northwest of Ouarzazate is the majestic **Tiffoultoute Kasbah**, offering fine views from its terrace. It was converted into a hotel in the 1960s to provide rooms during the shooting of David Lean's *Lawrence of Arabia*. It is now a restaurant.

❷ Taourirt Kasbah

Road Map C4. Opposite the crafts centre on the road out of Ouarzazate leading to the Dadès valley. 🖼

Ouarzazate's only historic building, the Taourirt Kasbah stands as a monument to Glaoui expansionism. At the beginning of the 20th century, the Glaoui family were the lords of the South and controlled access to the High Atlas. They were the first to collaborate with the French in the expansion of the latter's rule in the South.

Begun in the 18th century and renovated in the 19th, the kasbah has been undergoing restoration from time to time since 1994. It once housed the large Glaoui family, together with their servants.

The façade, consisting of high smooth earth walls, is pitted and decorated with geometric patterns in negative relief.

Inside, a maze of staircases at every level of the building leads to rooms of various sizes lit by low windows. The larger rooms have plasterwork decoration featuring floral and geometric motifs, and colourfully painted wooden ceilings. There are also some tiny rooms with low rush-matted ceilings, doorless arches, red-tiled floors and white walls. Next to the kasbah is a former

Detail of a window in the Taourirt Kasbah

Aït Benhaddou, which has often been chosen as a film location

Berber village, which probably predates the kasbah. It is inhabited by a busy population. In the narrow winding streets of the *ksar* (fortified village), you will find an Internet café, a former synagogue that now serves as a carpet shop, and a herbalist. The crafts centre opposite the Taourirt kasbah offers carpets, stone carving, jewellery and pottery, all at relatively high prices.

❸ Aït Benhaddou

Road Map C4. 30 km (19 miles) northwest of Ouarzazate, off road N9. 🛈 Ouarzazate; (0524) 88 24 85.

Backing onto a pinkish sandstone hill, the *ksar* of Aït Benhaddou stands on the left bank of Wadi Mellah. It is reached on foot from the village on the opposite bank. The *wadi* is usually dry, except in winter and spring.

The picturesque village of Aït Benhaddou, which has often been used as a film location, can be explored without a guide. It was once fortified and has a now-ruined *igherm* (communal granary). Built near water and arable land, in a place safe from foreign attack, it contains an impressive group of ochre pisé kasbahs.

Since the village was made a UNESCO World Heritage Site, some of its kasbahs have undergone restoration to their upper sections. The kasbahs' crenellated towers are decorated with blind arches and geometric designs in negative relief, creating a

play of light and shadow. Behind the kasbahs stand plain earth houses. Today, the *ksar* is inhabited by fewer than ten families.

Beyond Aït Benhaddou, a minor road leads to the ruined fortress of **Tamdaght**, once a kasbah inhabited by the Glaoui. Its towers are now inhabited by nesting storks. The road continues to Telouet, 32 km (20 miles) away.

❹ Jbel Sarhro

Road Map: D4. 98 km (61 miles) south of Ouarzazate. From Tansikht to Nekob on road R108, or from Boumalne du Dadès. 🛒 Sun in Nekob; Mon in Ikniounn.

Stretching for over 100 km (60 miles), Jbel Sarhro is a wild and inhospitable region that is still off the tourist track. It is separated from the main Anti-Atlas chain by the Draa valley to the west and from the High Atlas by Wadi Dadès to the north.

Jbel Sarhro is the territory of the Aït Atta, who, from the 17th and 19th centuries, were the

most important tribe in southern Morocco. This semi-nomadic people never bowed to the power of the sultans, and they were the last to resist the French at the Battle of Bou Gafer in 1933. They live in *ksour*, but take to tents for part of the year, when they drive livestock to seasonal pastures.

Jbel Sarhro is a region of sheer rockfaces, plateaux and blackish rocky escarpments. The rugged territory is crossed from north to south by tracks, which are best driven in a four-wheel-drive vehicle (routes are seldom signposted).

At the **Baha Kasbah** in Nekob guides can be hired for hikes and tours in four-wheel-drive vehicles. The route from Nekob to the Tizi n'Tazazert Pass, at 2,200 m (7,220 ft), is difficult, but the spot known as Bab n'Ali is worth the visit for some striking needle-like volcanic rock formations. The track to Boumalne du Dadès crosses the **Vallée des Oiseaux** (Valley of Birds), which is home to over 150 species of birds.

The Baha Kasbah in Nekob, at the foot of Jbel Sarhro

Camels grazing in the rocky landscape of Jbel Sarhro

The Kasbah

Kasbahs (*tighremt* in Berber) have long fulfilled the role of fortified castles, being places of refuge from attack for people and animals, and affording protection from the cold and other threats to safety. A lordly residence or family dwelling, the kasbah is an imposing edifice built to a square plan. While kasbahs in the mountain valleys are thick-set, those in the southern oases have a taller, more slender outline. At the four corners are towers crowned with merlons rising above the height of the walls.

Fortified Citadels
High walls set at a slightly oblique angle give the kasbah a perfectly proportioned outline.

Stepped merlons

Bricks are made from earth mixed with water, sometimes with chopped straw added. They are pressed into wooden moulds and dried in the sun.

A Typical Kasbah

Their dimensions being dictated by the size of the horizontally placed beams, the rooms are often longer than they are wide. The largest room is the reception hall, which often has a painted ceiling and which is reserved for men. The stable and sheepfold are located on the ground floor.

Water Jar
Ancient pieces of pottery like this one can be seen in restored kasbahs.

Windows
Mashrabiyya screens and wrought-iron grilles, made with no soldering, allow the inhabitants to look out without being seen.

Defensive Walls
The upper parts of the walls are decorated with geometric patterns, incised motifs and blind arches cut into the pisé.

Fortified Granary
The interior of the *igherm* or *agadir* is divided into compartments where maize, barley, sugar and cooking vessels are stored.

The Kitchen
Circular loaves of bread, made by the women, are baked in a small igloo-like earth oven. The kitchen is often dark and badly ventilated, and cooking is done on the earth floor.

Maize drying on the roof

Painted Ceilings
Ceilings are painted with volutes, rosettes and interlacing patterns, executed freehand or with a compass. They are a feature of reception rooms of kasbahs and wealthy houses.

Wooden Doors
They can be opened only from within.

Detail of the interior of the *ksar* at Tamnougalt, in the Draa valley

❺ Draa Valley

Road Map C-D4. 200 km (124 miles) between Ouarzazate and Zagora on road N9. 🚍 Thu in Agdz.

Rock engravings discovered near Tinzouline show that the Draa valley was inhabited by warriors from prehistoric times. The valley, where buildings are in a good state of preservation, contains a wealth of *ksour* and kasbahs.

The road between Ouarzazate and **Agdz** crosses the desert plateaux of Jbel Tifernine. Beyond Aït Saoun, hills of black rock give way to steep canyons as the road climbs towards the Tizi-n-Tinififft Pass, at 1,660 m (5,448 ft). To the north appear the foothills of the High Atlas and to the east, Jbel Sarhro.

Agdz, an unassuming town on the edge of a palm grove, is convenient for a short stop. Between Agdz and Zagora, the road follows a string of oases. Villages have grown up around the old kasbahs, on the edge of the road and in the palm grove.

About 6 km (4 miles) from Agdz, a track branching off to the left leads to the majestic *ksar* of **Tamnougalt**, which once controlled access to the trade routes of the Draa valley. The interior reveals some striking frescoes, which were painted in pale colours for the shooting of a film.

Continuing along the left bank of the Draa, the track leads to the pisé village of Tamnougalt, with narrow, partly covered streets. Visitors wishing to see the old kasbah may like to bring a torch, which is useful for viewing its superb painted ceilings. Tamnougalt, which is currently undergoing restoration, also has a former mellah (Jewish quarter) with a synagogue.

Back on the Draa valley road, the elegant **Timiderte Kasbah** comes into view on the left bank of the *wadi*, backing onto Jbel Sarhro. Villages and *ksour* here are rarely signposted. In Tansikht, a narrow road turns off to the left towards Nekob, Jbel Sarhro and Rissani, 233 km (145 miles) away. The bridge over the *wadi* joins a sandy track that passes through villages in the palm grove. To rejoin the road, the river can be forded in several places.

Still leading in the direction of Zagora, the road passes the **Igdaoun Kasbah**, with towers in the shape of truncated pyramids. At Tinzouline, a track to the right leads to a site with rock engravings, 7 km (4 miles) away.

The valley narrows in the approaches to the Azlag gorge, to the right of which is a high, smooth cliff. Soon after, a signpost indicating "Circuit Touristique de Binzouli" leads to the palm grove, which reaches Zagora on the other side of the river. Ochre pisé *koubbas* line the valley, while cemeteries are filled with the vertical flat stones that are typical of Muslim graveyards. Between Tissergate and Zagora, the palm grove stretches away to the distant foothills of Jbel Rhart.

❻ Zagora

Road Map D4. 🔼 30,000. 🚌 Ouarzazate or grands taxis. 🛈 (0524) 88 24 85. 🚍 Wed & Sun. 🎪 Moussem of Moulay Abdelkader Jilali at Mouloud.

Established by the French authorities during the Protectorate, Zagora is the most convenient base for exploring the region. The sign saying "Timbuctu, 52 Days by Camel" evokes the great age of the trans-Saharan caravans, although the illusion is spoiled by the presence of the large concrete *Préfecture* behind it.

The village of **Amazraou**, set amid lemon, almond and olive trees and gardens on the southern side of the town, is a haven of peace on the edge of

A camel trek through the peaceful palm grove in Zagora

Green-glazed pottery vessels characteristic of Tamegroute

the desert. In the former mellah, the mosque stands next to the abandoned synagogue. Amazraou is inhabited by Arabs, Haratines and Berbers, who continue the Jewish tradition of making silver jewellery. By following a footpath from the La Fibule hotel, the summit of Jbel Zagora can be reached in one hour. It is crowned by a military post and commands a breathtaking view of the valley. The remains of walls indicate the presence of the Almoravids in the 11th century.

Several hotels offer tours in four-wheel-drive vehicles or on camels. Lasting from a day to two weeks, the tours take in the Chigaga dunes south of Mhamid, and Foum-Zguid, west of Zagora.

Mule in the Draa valley

❼ Tamegroute

Road Map D4. 🚌 Sat. 🎪 Moussem of Sidi Ahmed ben Nasser (Nov).

Surrounded by ramparts, the *ksar* at Tamegroute contains a *zaouia* and a library. This great centre of Islamic learning was founded in the 17th century by Mohammed Bou Nasri, and its influence extended throughout southern Morocco.

Beneath the arcades of the courtyard, near the entrance to the tomb of Mohammed Bou Nasri, invalids and disabled people gather, hoping to be cured.

The holy man's works laid the foundations of the **Koranic Library**. A collection of priceless manuscripts is displayed in one of the rooms. It includes an 11th-century gazelle-skin Koran, books of calligraphy with gold dust and saffron illuminations, and treatises on algebra, astronomy and Arabic literature. Exposed to heat and light, these works are, unfortunately, not in the best condition.

In the potters' workshop outside, members of seven families produce traditional functional pots with a green glaze typical of Tamegroute ceramics.

Environs
About 5 km (2 miles) south of Tamegroute, and off to the left, are the **Tinfou Dunes**, an isolated ridge of sand rising up abruptly in the middle of the stony desert. From Tagounite, a difficult track leads to the foot of Jbel Tadrart and the beautiful **Nesrate Dunes**.

❽ Mhamid

Road Map D4. 🏘 2,000. 🚌 Mon.

This border post and small administrative centre is the last oasis before the great expanse of the Sahara. To the south stretches a stony desert, the Hammada du Draa. From Mhamid, Wadi Draa sinks beneath the sand to reappear on the Atlantic coast 540 km (338 miles) to the west.

The ruins of a *ksar* indicate the former existence of a great caravan centre, from which Ahmed el-Mansour's army set out in the 16th century to take Timbuctu.

Environs
Coming from Zagora, the Tizi-Beni-Selmane Pass, at an altitude of 747 m (2,451 ft), offers a stunning view of Jbel Bani and the desert, which looks black since it is covered with volcanic stone. A little further on, a track to the left leads to **Foum-Rjam**, one of the largest prehistoric necropolises in the Maghreb. Tumuli mark thousands of graves. About 45 km (28 miles) south of Mhamid, the **Chigaga dunes**, which can be reached only by four-wheel-drive vehicle, stretch to the horizon.

Camel and rider on the Tinfou Dunes, south of Tamegroute

The palm grove at Skoura

❾ Skoura

Road Map C4. 🚌 from Ouarzazate and Tinerhir. 🏪 Mon.

The small sleepy town of Skoura is surrounded by an impressive palm grove, which was laid out in the 12th century by the Almohad sultan Yacoub el-Mansour. The most beautiful kasbahs in southern Morocco are to be found here. Some of these are still partially inhabited, and some are attached to private houses. Many of Skoura's inhabitants, however, have moved into the breeze-block villages that line the road.

The **Ben Morro Kasbah** stands on the left of the road above Skoura. It was built in the 17th century and, now completely restored, has been converted into a guesthouse. The entrance to the palm grove is on the other side of Wadi Amerhidil. The grove can be explored only on foot, by bicycle or on mule-back. The grove is irrigated by *khettaras*

(underground channels) and wells dug at regular intervals. Ruined kasbahs stand among palm trees, fig trees, birch and tamarisk – whose tannin-rich flowers are used in the processing of skins. The most imposing is **Amerhidil Kasbah**, which was once owned by the Glaoui family and which dominates the *wadi*. The restored interior is now open to visitors. The kasbahs of Aït Sidi el-Mati, Aït Souss, El-Kebbaba and Dar Aïchil are also worth a visit.

Further east, **Aït Abou**, built in 1863 and the oldest kasbah in the palm grove, has six storeys and walls 25 m (82 ft) high. Its outbuildings have been turned into a small short-stay gîte. An orchard with pomegranate, apple, pear, fig, quince and olive trees provides the necessary shade for growing crops.

Twenty-five kilometres (15 miles) northeast of Skoura is the village of **Toundout**, where there are some highly decorated kasbahs. The **Marabout of Sidi M'Barek** served as a stronghold where the semi-nomadic people stored their crops, under the protection of the saint.

A little way beyond Skoura, towards El-Kelaa M'Gouna, unexpected plantations of grasses imported from Australia in the 1990s help to preserve a little moisture in the arid ground.

Spectacular landscape at the approach to the M'Goun valley

❿ El-Kelaa M'Gouna

Road Map D4. 🛈 guides office; (0524) 88 24 85 (Ouarzazate). 🏪 Wed. 🎪 Rose Festival (May).

This town, whose name means "fortress", is located at an altitude of 1,450 m (4,759 ft), in the heart of rose country. In the 10th century, pilgrims returning from Mecca brought *Rosa damascena* back with them to Morocco. These peppery-scented flowers have developed a resistance to the cold and dry conditions in which they are now grown.

Each spring, rose-picking produces 3,000 to 4,000 tonnes of petals. The harvest is taken to two local distillation factories. One of them, in El-Kelaa M'Gouna, is laid out in a kasbah, and it is open to visitors in April and May. While a proportion of the roses is used to make rosewater for local distribution, the rest is processed and exported for use in the perfume industry.

The Rose Festival takes place after the harvest and is attended by all the inhabitants of the valleys of the Dadès. Accompanied by a *bendir* (a tambourine), young girls from El-Kelaa M'Gouna perform a sinuous dance, their long hair braided with coloured wool.

On the road out of the town is a craft cooperative with about 30 workshops. Daggers are made here, the craftsmen continuing a Jewish tradition of making sheaths and dagger handles out of cedar or camel bone. The steel blades are made in the mountain village of Azlague, not far from El-Kelaa M'Gouna.

The Amerhidil Kasbah, in the palm grove at Skoura

◀ The Aït Benhaddou *ksar*, at sunrise

The Rose Festival in El-Kelaa M'Gouna

Environs

Between Skoura and El-Kelaa M'Gouna, kasbahs are set among greenery throughout the Dadès valley. The modern concrete houses that line the roads here are an artless imitation of these fine traditional buildings. Ruined kasbahs are now part of the local landscape. From offices on the way out of El-Kelaa M'Gouna, many hikes and tours by four-wheel-drive vehicle are organized, particularly to the **Vallée des Roses** and to the *ksar* at **Bou Thrarar**, a breathtaking mountain tour.

Further into the interior of the High Atlas some impressive gorges lead to the remote M'Goun valley. It is best to hire a guide because the tracks are not signposted.

⓫ Boumalne du Dadès

Road Map D4. 🚶 13,000.
ℹ️ Tizzarouine kasbah; (0524) 88 24 85 (Ouarzazate). 🚌 Wed.

This pleasant stopping place at the beginning of the Dadès gorge is a regional administrative centre. From the edge of the plateau above the town,

the view stretches over the fertile Dadès Oasis. At Tizzarouine Kasbah, from where there are fine views, guides offer tours and camping trips in the High Atlas and Jbel Sarhro.

The Aït Mouted Kasbah, in the Dadès gorge

⓬ Dadès Gorge

Road Map D3. Grand taxi from Boumalne du Dadès.
🚌 Sat in Msemrir.

Bordered by greenery, the course of Wadi Dadès stands out against the rocky landscape. Cultivated land on the banks of the *wadi* is surrounded by fig, almond and walnut trees and poplars.

About 2 km (1 mile) from Boumalne, in a bend in the road, stands the **Aït Mouted Kasbah**, which once belonged to the Glaoui. Here and there, large constructions in brown breeze-block, built by emigrants who have returned to Morocco, stand out as unfortunate blots on the landscape.

As it rises, the road passes some dramatic geological limestone folds which have been shaped by erosion. At the foot of these natural formations stand the ruins of the **Aït Arbi Kasbah**. Further on are the stone and pisé **Tamnalt Kasbahs**, whose slender towers rise up against a backdrop of rocks that seem to be pressed together sideways like the fingers of a human hand.

Beyond Aït Oudinar, the road crosses Wadi Dadès, following the bottom of the gorge between sheer cliffs. It then runs along the edge of deep canyons, home to royal eagles and vultures. On the plateau, the valley widens again, and attractive stone and pisé villages overlook the opposite riverbank.

The road running up the gorge from Boumalne du Dadès is metalled as far Msemrir, 60 km (37 miles) to the north. The final stretch before Msemrir passes through much wilder country than in the lower part of the gorge. Beyond Msemrir, a track that is passable only by four-wheel-drive vehicle leads east to the Todra gorge and north to the High Atlas and Imilchil.

Tamnalt Kasbah in the Dadès gorge with a dramatic rocky backdrop

For hotels and restaurants see pp306–313 and pp320–31

The Tinerhir oasis, stretching out along the banks of Wadi Todra

⑬ Tinerhir

Road Map D3-4. ⚐ 40,000. 🚌 from Er-Rachidia and Ouarzazate, and grands taxis. 🛈 Hôtel Tombouctou; (0524) 88 24 85 (Ouarzazate). 🗓 Mon.

This lively town, the region's administrative centre, lies midway between the Draa valley and the Tafilalt. Built on a rocky outcrop, it has an elongated layout. On its northern and southern sides it is bordered by a lush palm grove laid out at the foot of arid hills and containing dozens of *ksour* and kasbahs.

With several silver mines in the vicinity, Tinerhir is a wealthy town known for its silver jewellery. To the west stands a kasbah once owned by the Glaoui and now in a state of disrepair. To the southeast is Aït el-Haj Ali, the former mellah (Jewish quarter), whose houses make an interesting architectural ensemble. North of the town stretches a palm grove irrigated by Wadi Todra.

About 2 km (1 mile) from the bridge across the *wadi*, on the road to the **Todra Gorge**, a viewing platform commands a stunning view. Here, guides with camels offer their services. However, visitors need no assistance to walk down into the palm grove and follow the network of shady paths that

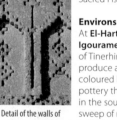

Detail of the walls of Tinerhir Kasbah

lead through orchards and run along irrigation ditches. This is a wonderful walk, as the Todra palm grove stretches for 12 km (7.5 miles).

On the other side of the *wadi* are many semi-ruined *ksour*, where 50 to 100 families once lived. The most interesting and most easily reached are the **Aït Boujane Ksar** and **Asfalou Ksar**.

Further north, about 5 km (3 miles) before the start of the gorge, there is an alternative route to the palm grove; this is via the Imarighen spring, the "Spring of the Sacred Fish".

Environs
At **El-Hart-n-Igouramene**, south of Tinerhir, craftsmen produce a bronze-coloured local pottery that is sold in the souk. The sweep of road taking in El-Hart, Tadafalt and Agoudim offers the opportunity to see many *ksour*, some of which are still inhabited.

⑭ Todra Gorge

Road Map D3.

Sheer cliffs 300 m (985 ft) high rise up dramatically each side of the narrow corridor that forms the Todra gorge. These are the most impressive cliffs in southern Morocco, and they are well known to experienced mountaineers.

Wadi Todra flows through this great geological fault and on into the Tinerhir palm grove (*see above*).

Two hotels make possible an overnight stop in the Todra gorge. The best time of day to view the gorge is in the morning, when the rays of the sun break through between the high cliffs on either side.

The cliffs soon widen and a stony track leads to the village of Tamtattouchte, 22 km (14 miles) further on.

The Todra gorge, sandwiched between sheer cliffs

⑮ Tamtattouchte

Road Map D3. 36 km (22 miles) north of Tinerhir.

The picturesque village of Tamtattouchte is located at the other extremity of the Todra gorge, its earth houses blending into the red-ochre tones of the mountains. Here, small plots of land that stand out from their arid, rocky surroundings are irrigated by Wadi Todra.

Tamtattouchte is the starting point of tracks to the Dadès gorge to the west and Imilchil to the north, leading over passes, through gorges, across plateaux and over mountains. Ask a local for information about the state of tracks negotiable by four-wheel-drive vehicles, particularly after periods of

The village of Tamtattouchte, at the northern end of the Todra gorge, with several fine *ksour*

rainfall. Visitors should also be aware that no destinations are signposted.

🔟 Goulmima

Road Map D3. 🚐 from Er-Rachidia and Tinejdad. 🗓 Mon & Thu.

Although it is set in the heart of the Rheris oasis, where about 20 *ksour* stand on the banks of Wadi Rheris, the modern village of Goulmima is of no great interest to visitors. The inhabitants of neighbouring *ksour* come to the village to buy supplies.

The sturdiness of their fortifications make the *ksour* here unusual. Their towers are remarkably high and, when tribal feuds were rife, they protected the inhabitants against the incursions of the Aït Atta, who came to pillage their harvests.

The *ksar* at Goulmima, a labyrinth of narrow streets and alleys

The old fortified village of Goulmima, 2 km (1 mile) east on the road to Erfoud, is worth the detour. Still inhabited, the **Goulmima *ksar***, which exemplifies southern Moroccan defensive architecture, is surrounded by walls set with two massive towers. Cows and sheep are enclosed within small corrals outside. A gate set at an angle opens onto a second gate. On a small square within the walls stand a mosque and the well that provides the *ksar* with water. The upper floors of some of the houses span the narrow streets, providing a strange contrast of light and shadow.

Morocco's Architectural Heritage

The vestiges of past ages and of a unique way of life, kasbahs, *ksour* and granaries – all of them built of earth – are the victims of neglect. The kasbahs are crumbling, the once-luxurious residences are abandoned and clay walls are slowly disappearing into the ground. The Moroccan government seems indifferent to the unique value and interest of these

Detail of the Taourirt kasbah in Ouarzazate

buildings. Aside from sparse and sporadic activity, action to protect Morocco's architectural heritage goes little further than listing its monuments and drawing up conservation programmes that produce no concrete results. The only active conservation in Morocco is that resulting from European initiatives. Besides the uncompleted restoration of the *ksar* at Aït Benhaddou, funded by UNESCO, that of the granary at Igherm-n-Ougdal, on the road to the Tizi-n-Tichka Pass, and of the Taourirt Kasbah in Ouarzazate, the small number of kasbahs in the Dadès valley that have been restored were saved by private funding. Private initiatives are also responsible for the skilful restoration of the Ben Morro kasbah and Aït Abou kasbah in Skoura and the Hôtel Tombouctou in Tinerhir. Unfortunately, most of the Glaoui fortresses in the valleys of the Atlas are being left to their fate.

The Southern and Eastern Oases

Southern and eastern Morocco have many oases. Their existence depends on the presence of water, which is either supplied by rivers flowing down from the mountains or provided by an underground water table. Underground water rises naturally at the foot of dunes or is pumped by artesian wells or along underground channels known as *khettaras*, some of them covering considerable distances. This accounts for the fact that the oases are strung out in a line along the Dadès, Draa and Ziz valleys.

Seguias are man-made channels that criss-cross the oasis, bringing water to the crops and trees. Clay plugs are sometimes used to divert the water along particular routes.

Irrigation in the Oases

Set in particularly hostile surroundings, oases are a very fragile ecological environment that survives thanks only to ceaseless human intervention. Many dams are built to control the flow of water in the wadis, *which, when they are in flood, can devastate the plantations in the oases in a few hours. Khettaras and seguias must be regularly cleared.*

Clay plugs are used to direct the flow of water to other parts of the oasis.

Date palms, of which there are many varieties, produce abundant fruit. A single tree can provide 30 to 100 kg (66 to 220 lb) of dates a year. They are harvested in autumn.

Animal-s container

Barley

Crops such as tomatoes, carrots and lettuce, as well as fruit trees such as fig and apricot, thrive in the shade provided by the palm trees.

Irrigation is produced by *khettaras*, underground channels that bring water to the oasis. Here, the water is either drawn from a well or is simply forced to the surface by gravity. The exact amount of water needed for each crop is provided by *seguias*.

Work in the fields is done by women, who carry out all stages in the cultivation of cereals and various kinds of vegetables.

The tops of the shafts that are sunk to dig and then maintain the *khettara* are visible on the surface.

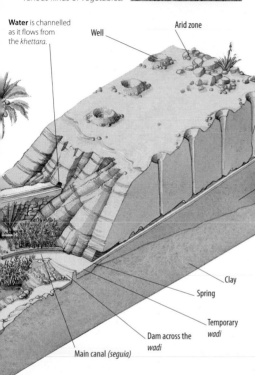

Water is channelled as it flows from the *khettara*.

Well

Arid zone

Underground water gently flows into the oasis.

Impervious layer

Clay

Spring

Temporary *wadi*

Dam across the *wadi*

Main canal *(seguia)*

Temporary wadis, across which dams are built, feed water to the various *seguias* in the oasis.

At Tinerhir, many *seguias* channel water from Wadi Todra, bringing it to the beautiful palm grove nearby.

Animals of the Oasis

The common bulbul, rufous bush robin, house bunting and doves are some of the more familiar birds seen in the oases. Toads frequent the banks of the watercourses, geckos and lizards cling to stone walls and the trunks of trees, and scorpions hide under stones. During the night, jackals occasionally approach places of human habitation. The fennec, horned viper and herbivorous lizard rarely venture beyond the dunes and rocks where they were born.

Herbivorous lizard

Horned viper

Fennec

Majestic Jbel Ayachi, rising over extensive and sparsely populated desert plateaux

⑰ Midelt

Road Map D3. ⚐ 20,000. 🚌 from Meknès, Rabat, Erfoud, Er-Rachidia and Azrou. ℹ Timnaï Cultural Centre, 20 km (12 miles) north of Midelt; (0535) 36 01 88. 🛒 Wed & Sun. 🎉 Apple Festival (Oct).

On the border between the High and Middle Atlas, Midelt is considered to be part of southern Morocco. The small villages on each side of the road leading out of the town consist of traditional buildings that are very similar to those typical of southern Morocco. While, at the beginning of the 20th century, Midelt was no more than a modest *ksar*, under the Protectorate it became a French garrison town.

Located at the foot of **Jbel Ayachi**, which rises to a height of 3,737 m (12,264 ft), Midelt is the starting point for tours. At an altitude of 1,500 m (4,923 ft), the town enjoys a continental climate – very cold in winter and very hot in summer. Beautiful Middle Atlas carpets,

as well as fossils and mineral stones, are on sale in Souk Jedid. There is also a workshop in Kasbah Myriem, on the road to Tattiouine, where carpets, blankets and high-quality embroidery are produced. It used to be run by Franciscan nuns who taught the local Berber women these handicrafts, thus ensuring an income for many families.

Environs
The **Cirque de Jaffar**, a limestone gorge on the way out of Midelt, makes for the most interesting tour here. However, the tracks that go there and back, covering 79 km (49 miles), are tough going, being passable only from May to October and only by four-wheel-drive vehicle.

The track along the hillside is overshadowed by the imposing outline of Jbel Ayachi, which can be climbed without much difficulty. The Cirque de Jaffar is set in a wild landscape of cedar, oak and juniper growing in stony ground. The winding track

passes through remote Berber hamlets. A turning off to the left, at the Mit Kane forestry hut, leads back to Midelt. The track that continues west leads eventually to Imilchil.

Disused lead and silver mines in the impressive **Aouli Gorge**, 25 km (15 miles) northeast of Midelt, are sunk into the mountainside. They were abandoned in the 1980s, but the machinery is still in place.

⑱ Ziz Gorge

Road Map D-E3. 88 km (55 miles) south of Midelt on road N13.

Wadi Ziz, which springs near Agoudal, in the heart of the High Atlas, runs in an easterly direction, then obliquely south, level with the village of Rich. It then carves a gorge in the mountains, irrigates the Tafilalt then disappears into the Saharan sands.

South of Midelt, beyond the Tizi-n-Talrhemt Pass, at an altitude of 1,907 m (6,259 ft), forests give way to arid plains. The fortified villages of the Aït Idzerg tribe, as well as a few old forts of the French Foreign Legion, line the road.

The **Tunnel de Foum-Zabel**, or Tunnel du Légionnaire, was driven through the limestone rock here by the French Foreign Legion in 1927, thus opening a route to the south. The tunnel opens on

Berber women used to learn embroidery with the Franciscan sisters of Midelt

Dates drying after the autumn harvest in the Ziz gorge

Ksour in the Oases

The Ziz valley is *ksar* country. The *ksar* (plural *ksour*) was developed originally as a communal stronghold for sedentary populations, to protect them against the incursions of bandits and nomadic tribes that raided the oases when the harvests had been brought in. The defensive design of these fortified villages is connected to this warlike past. The *ksar* usually overlooks the oasis. Originally, the *ksar* consisted of no more than a central alley with family houses on each side. Over time, it expanded to become a village, with a mosque, a medersa and granaries. Built of pisé and earth bricks in its upper part, every *ksar* bears the individual stamp of its builders, who devised elaborate incised geometric patterns.

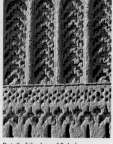

Detail of the *ksar* of Oulad Abdelhalim in Rissani

to the Ziz gorge, whose impressive red cliffs jut into the Atlas. Two fine *ksour*, Ifri and Amzrouf, both surrounded by palm trees, stand here.

The Hassan-Addakhil dam, contained by a thick dyke of red earth, demarcates the lower foothills of the Atlas. Built in 1970, it irrigates the Tafilalt and Ziz valleys and provides electricity for Er-Rachidia.

⓳ Er-Rachidia

Road Map D3. 🚹 62,000. ✈
🚌 from Erfoud, Midelt, Ouarzazate and Figuig. ℹ Tourist office; (0535) 57 09 44. 🛒 Tue, Thu & Sun.

As a result of its strategic location between northern and southern Morocco, and between the Atlantic seaboard and Figuig and the Algerian border, Er-Rachidia became the main town in the

province. Here the palm groves of the Ziz and Tafilalt begin, and the town also stands at the start of the road to the south. Er-Rachidia, also an administrative and military centre, was built by the French in the early 20th century, when it was known as Ksar es-Souk. Its present name was bestowed in 1979 in memory of Moulay Rachid, the first of the Alaouites to overthrow Saadian rule in 1666. Many *ksour* here were abandoned after 1960, when the Ziz broke its banks, causing serious floods and washing away land.

Although they are busy, the town's perfectly straight, gridlike streets hold scant appeal. A craft centre offers locally made pottery, carved wooden objects and rush baskets.

⓴ Source Bleue de Meski

Road Map E3. 23 km (14 miles) south of Er-Rachidia on road N13.

The spring, located 1 km (0.6 mile) off the main road, is a reappearance of Wadi Ziz, which runs underground for part of its course. The blue spring waters flow from a cave at the foot of a cliff into a pool built by the Foreign Legion. The water provides a natural swimming pool for the campsite in the palm grove.

The clifftop offers a view of the oasis and the ruined *ksar* of Meski. The road to Erfoud *(see p284)* also offers fine views of the Ziz valley and the oases of Oulad Chaker and Aourfous.

Er-Rachidia, a town at the junction of roads leading south

Shop in Erfoud, selling fossils – a local speciality – and a range of craft items

㉑ Erfoud

Road Map E4. 🏠 10,000. 🚌 from Fès, Er-Rachidia, Midelt, Rissani and Tinejdad, and grands taxis. 🛒 daily. 🎉 Date Festival (Oct).

Before the development of the town began in 1930, the French had set up a military post here to watch over the Tafilalt valley. The Berber tribes put up a long drawn-out resistance to the establishment of French rule, and the valley was one of the last parts of southern Morocco to surrender.

Erfoud's checkerboard layout is a vestige of this military past. This peaceful town, with an extensive palm grove, is the base for tours of the dunes of the Erg Chebbi. From the top of the eastern *borj*, a small bastion 3 km (2 miles) southeast of Erfoud, the view takes in a wide swathe of desert and palm groves.

In October, the souk at Erfoud overflows with dates of every variety. This is also when the three-day Date Festival, at the end of the date harvest, takes place. Both a religious and a secular event, the festival attracts local tribes. It begins with prayers at the mausoleum of Moulay Ali Cherif in Rissani, 17 km (11 miles) to the south, and continues with processions of people dressed in traditional costume and with folk dances.

Polished marble containing fossils is Erfoud's other main source of income. The cutting workshops, the **Usine de Marmar**, is open to visitors.

The road is also bordered with many small craters – the tops of shafts down to *khettaras*.

Usine de Marmar
On road R702 to Tinejdad.
Open 8am–noon & 2–4pm Mon–Sat.

㉒ Tafilalt Palm Grove

Road Map E4. South of Erfoud on road N13.

Stretching out along the bends of Wadi Rheris and Wadi Ziz, which run from Erfoud, the Tafilalt oasis nestles in a stretch of greenery, extending beyond Rissani. The oasis was once a welcome stopping-place for caravans, as they arrived exhausted after weeks in the desert.

Today, the inhabitants of the Tafilalt rely on it for their livelihood: the 800,000 date palms that grow here are renowned for their fruit.

Date harvest in the Tafilalt Palm Grove

Unfortunately, and despite care, for a century the trees have suffered from Bayoud palm sickness – caused by a microscopic fungus – and the effects of excessive drought, both of which can kill them.

The October date harvest in the palm grove is a spectacular sight. Each owner climbs to the top of his tree and, as the grove resonates to the sound of machetes, bunches of dates crash to the ground, falling in large orange heaps (they turn brown as they ripen).

Symbols of happiness and prosperity, dates figure in many rituals, and in birth, wedding and burial ceremonies.

㉓ Rissani

Road Map E4. 🏠 15,000. 🚌 from Meknès, Erfoud and Er-Rachidia, and grands taxis. 🛒 Tue, Thu & Sun.

This small town on the edge of the Sahara marks the end of the metalled road and the start of tracks into the desert. To the east is the Hammada du Guir, a stony desert notorious for its violent sandstorms.

Rissani, built close to the ruins of Sijilmassa, was once the capital of the Tafilalt. Sijilmassa is said to have been founded in 757–8 as an independent kingdom, becoming a major stopping place on the trans-Saharan caravan routes. Over the centuries, it became prosperous from trade in gold, slaves, salt, weapons, ivory and spices, reaching its peak in the 13th and 14th centuries.

However, religious dissent and the instability of the rival tribes that regularly launched raids on the city led to its destruction. The first town had a pisé wall on stone foundations pierced by eight gates, and contained a palace, fine houses, public baths and many gardens. A few vestiges of these emerge from the sand just west of Rissani.

The **Rissani Souk** is one of the most famous in the area. Donkeys, mules, sheep and goats are enclosed in corrals. Stalls are piled with shining pyramids of dates, as well as with vegetables and spices. Beneath roofs made of palm-matting and narrow pisé alleyways, jewellery, daggers, carpets, woven palm fibre baskets, pottery and fine local leather items, made from goat skins tanned with tamarisk bark, are laid out for sale.

South of Rissani, a 20-km (13-mile) route marked by many *ksour* crosses the palm grove. After 2.5 km (1.5 miles) stands the **Mausoleum of Moulay Ali Cherif**, where the father of Moulay er-Rachid, founder of the Alaouite dynasty, is laid to rest. The mausoleum was rebuilt in 1955, after it was damaged by a serious flooding of Wadi Ziz. A courtyard leads to the burial chamber, to which non-Muslims are not admitted. Behind the mausoleum are the ruins of the 19th-century **Abbar Ksar**. This former residence once housed exiled Alaouite princes, the widows

Well in the Oulad-Abdelhalim *ksar*

of sultans and, protected by a double earth wall, part of the royal treasury.

About 2 km (1 mile) from the mausoleum stands the **Oulad Abdelhalim Ksar**. It was built in 1900 for the elder brother of Sultan Moulay Hassan, who was made governor of the Tafilalt. The monumental entrance, with elaborate decoration in its upper part, opens onto a labyrinth of dilapidated rooms. Two rooms still have their painted ceilings.

The route takes in many other *ksour*, including those of Assererhine, Zaouïa el-Maati, Irara, Gaouz, Tabassamt and Ouirhlane. The *ksar* of Tinrheras, set on a promontory, also comes into view.

The road leading to the Draa valley via Tazzarine and Tansikht starts from Rissani.

Erg Chebbi and the small rain-filled lake Dayet Srji

㉔ Merzouga

Road Map E4. 53 km (33 miles) southeast of Erfoud. 🚌 Sat.

The small Saharan oasis of Merzouga, much damaged by floods in 2006, is famous for its location at the foot of the **Erg Chebbi Dunes**. These photogenic dunes, which rise up out of the stony, sandy desert, extend for 30 km (19 miles), and reach a maximum height of 250 m (820 ft). At sunrise or dusk, the half-light gives the sand a fascinating range of colours.

Although they are nearer to Rissani, Merzouga and the Erg Chebbi dunes are easier to reach from Erfoud. The services of a guide are not necessary, except when high winds whip up the sand. From Erfoud, going in the direction of Taouz, the metalled road degenerates into a track after 16 km (10 miles). Beyond the Auberge Derkaoua, visitors should follow the line of telegraph poles.

The dunes come into view on the left. At Merzouga, camel drivers offer one-hour to two-day tours of the dunes.

Dayet Srji, a small lake west of the village, sometimes fills with water during the winter, after sudden rainfall. It attracts hundreds of pink flamingoes, storks and other migratory birds.

Procession at the foot of the Erg Chebbi dunes, during the Date Festival

SOUTHERN MOROCCO & WESTERN SAHARA

The vast southwestern region of Morocco embraces a variety of spectacular landscapes. The fertile Souss plain, an area dotted with oases and extensive stony deserts, is bordered by the rugged mountains of the Anti-Atlas. On the southern Atlantic coast, sheer cliffs give way to large areas of dunes linking Morocco to the Sahara and the republic of Mauritania.

Six thousand years ago, hunters forced northwards by the desertification of the Sahara moved into southwestern Morocco, as shown by the thousands of rock engravings that have been discovered in the Anti-Atlas. The Arab conquest in the 7th century inaugurated the age of the independent kingdoms. An important point for trans-Saharan trade between Morocco and Timbuctu, the Atlantic coast was coveted from the 15th century by the Portuguese and the Spaniards, who eventually colonized it in the late 19th century, re-naming it Río de Oro (Golden River).

When Spain withdrew from western Sahara in 1975, King Hassan II initiated the Green March during which 350,000 civilians reasserted Morocco's claim to the region (see p62).

The great Souss plain, east of Agadir, lies at the heart of this isolated region. The commercially grown fruit and vegetables here are irrigated by the underground waters of Wadi Souss, and the surrounding argan trees provide food for herds of black goats. To the south, the Anti-Atlas is the final mountainous barrier before the Sahara. Its almost surreal geological folds, shaped by erosion, alternate with verdant oases. Stone-built villages, often with an *agadir* (fortified granary), cluster along *wadis* or at the foot of mountains. Further south, the wide deserted beaches are sometimes cut off by lagoons that attract thousands of migratory birds.

Camel in the Sahara desert, southern Morocco

◄ Houses with pink plaster in Agadir with the Anti-Atlas as a backdrop

Exploring Southern Morocco and Western Sahara

All roads heading into the deep South begin at Agadir, Morocco's foremost coastal resort. To the east lies the great Souss plain, which stretches north as far as the High Atlas and south as far as the Anti-Atlas. This mountain chain of rocky peaks and stony plateaux culminates on its eastern side in Jbel Siroua, a remarkable volcanic massif that reaches a height of 3,304 m (10,844 ft), and whose western side, pitted with isolated valleys, slopes down towards the Atlantic. The resort of Agadir is linked to Tafraoute to the southeast, and to the numerous oases on the Saharan slopes of the Anti-Atlas. The road south links Agadir with the Saharan provinces, which start at the coastal town of Tarfaya. The focal points of human life in the Sahara are a few large towns surrounded by banks of dunes seemingly stretching to infinity.

Area shown by map below

Sights at a Glance

1 Agadir pp290–91
2 Taroudannt
3 Igherm to Tata
4 Akka
5 Souss Massa National Park
6 Tiznit
7 Sidi Ifni
8 Tafraoute
9 Guelmim
10 Tan Tan and Tan Tan Plage
11 Tarfaya
12 Laayoune

Sand dunes along the coast between Tan Tan Plage and Tarfaya

Key

— Motorway
— Major road
⋯ Minor road
--- Track
▬ International border
▬ ▬ Disputed territory border
△ Summit
╳ Pass

Essaouira
Marrakech
N1
A7
N8
TAROUDANNT ②
AGADIR ①
Ouarzazate
Wadi Souss
N10
Tioute
R109
Biougra
Inchaden
Aït-Baha
Igherm
SOUSS MASSA NATIONAL PARK ⑤
R105
Tizi-Touzlimt Pass
Had-Belfa
Tioulit
R106
Atlas
IGHERM TO TATA ③
Jbel Lekst 2359m
Souk-Khemis-d'Issafen
Tata
Sidi Moussa Aglou
TIZNIT ⑥ Ⓒ
Assaka
TAFRAOUTE ⑧
Foum Zguid
R109
Mirleft
Anti
R104
Jbel Tillit 1739m
N12
Ida Oussemlal
Bou-Zarif
SIDI IFNI ⑦
Souk-Tlata-des-Akhasass
AKKA ④
Oua-Belli
Bou-Izakarn
N12
Aït-Herbil
Wadi Draa
GUELMIM ⑨
Foum-el-Hassan
iar
N1
Aït Bekkou
Targoumait
R103
Assa
Djebel Taskalouine
Aoulnet-Torkoz
Ouarkziz
Wadi Draa
Djebel
El-Mahbas

Tata, with many kasbahs and a palm grove

Getting Around

Although the network of roads has improved considerably, the roads that cross the Anti-Atlas between Igherm and Tata, and between Tiznit and Tafraoute, are long and tiring to drive because they are narrow and follow the contours of the mountainside. By contrast, the 650 km (404 miles) between Agadir and Laayoune are relatively easy to cover, except when there are sandstorms. When travelling through the Saharan provinces it is extremely unwise to leave the road because landmines laid during the war between Morocco and the Polisario Front in the 1970s are still in place. The border with Mauritania can be crossed easily, as long as the required formalities are observed.

For keys to symbols *see back flap*

● Agadir

Agadir, the regional capital of the South beyond the Atlas, draws thousands of visitors a year. Its gentle climate – temperatures range from 7 °C to 20 °C (45 °F to 68 °F) in January, the coolest month – together with its sheltered beach and hotels make it Morocco's second tourist city after Marrakech. Having been completely rebuilt in the 1960s after the terrible earthquake that destroyed the city, Agadir has none of the charm of traditional Moroccan towns, although its wide-open spaces and its modernity appeal to many holiday-makers. The industrial quarter consists of oil storage tanks and cement works, as well as factories where fish is canned (Agadir is Morocco's foremost fishing port) and where fruit from the fertile Souss plain is processed.

Camel and horses seen on the beach at Agadir

Nouveau Talborj

Agadir's modern centre, the Nouveau Talborj, was built south of the old city, which was completely razed as the result of the earthquake of 1960.

The main streets of the city centre run parallel to the beach. Pedestrian areas, lined with restaurants, shops and crafts outlets are concentrated around Boulevard Hassan II and Avenue du Prince Moulay Abdallah.

There are some fine modern buildings, including the post office, the town hall and the stately law courts. The city's bright white buildings are interspersed by many gardens.

Traditional doorway

🏛 Musée Municipal du Patrimoine Amazighe

Avenue Hassan II, passage Aït Souss. **Tel** (0528) 82 16 32. **Open** 9:30am–5:30pm Mon–Sat. 🅿

This museum was opened on 29 February 2000, on the day of the commemoration of the reconstruction of Agadir, forty years after the violent earthquake that destroyed the city. The museum exhibits everyday objects derived from the peoples of the Souss plains and the pre-Saharan regions. Among the exhibits is a rich collection of magnificent Berber jewellery, superbly displayed alongside information on how the jewellery was made.

🎭 Open-Air Theatre

Boulevard 20 Août.
Concerts, shows and music festivals take place here throughout the year.

🐦 Vallée des Oiseaux

Avenue Hassan II. **Open** 9am–noon & 3–6pm Tue, pm–Sun.
This open space in the heart of the city, laid out on a narrow strip of greenery, contains aviaries with a multitude of exotic birds. A small zoo features mouflons (wild mountain sheep) and macaques. There is also a play area for children.

Polizzi Medina

Ben-Sergaou. 10 km (6 miles) south of Agadir, towards Inezgane. **Tel** (0528) 28 02 53. **Open** 9am–6pm daily. **Closed** Tue. 🅿

This medina was created by Coco Polizzi, an Italian architect, who used traditional Moroccan building methods. Houses, restaurants and craft workshops have been built in the medina.

🏖 Beach

South of the city, the sheltered beach, in a bay with 9 km (6 miles) of fine sand, is Agadir's main attraction, offering some of the safest swimming off Morocco's Atlantic coast. However, although the city enjoys 300 day of sunshine a year, it is often shrouded in mist in the morning. Sailboards, jet-skis and water scooters can be hired on the beach, and rides, on horses or camels, are also on offer. Many cafés, hotels and restaurants line the beach.

🏰 Old Kasbah

At an altitude of 236 m (775 ft), the hilltop ruins of the kasbah, within restored ramparts, offer a stunning view of Agadir and the bay. The kasbah was built in 1540 by Mohammed ech-Cheikh, to keep the Portuguese fortress under surveillance. It was restored in 1752 by Moulay Abdallah and accommodated a garrison of renegade Christians and Turkish mercenaries.

White houses in Agadir, a city completely rebuilt in the 1960s

For hotels and restaurants see pp306–313 and pp320–31

The German cruiser *Berlin* off Agadir in 1911

Agadir's History

The origins of Agadir are not fully known. In 1505, a Portuguese merchant built a fortress north of the present city. This was acquired by King Manuel I of Portugal and converted into a garrison. By then, Agadir had become a port of call on the sea routes to the Sudan and Guinea. A century of prosperity began in 1541, when the Portuguese were expelled by the Saadians. The Souss fell under the control of a Berber kingdom in the 17th century, but Moulay Ismaïl later reconquered the region. In 1760, Sidi Mohammed ben Abdallah sealed the city's fate when he closed its harbour and opened one in Essaouira. In 1911 Agadir was the object of a dispute between the French and the Germans relating to its strategic location. On 29 February 1960 an earthquake destroyed the city.

VISITORS' CHECKLIST

Practical Information
609,000. ℹ Immeuble Ignouan, Boulevard Mohammed V; (0528) 84 63 77. Tue–Sun.

Transport
✈ Agadir El- Massira, 22 km (13.5 miles) on the road to Taroudannt. from Casablanca, Essaouira, Marrakech & Tiznit.

The busy, bustling port at the popular city of Agadir

Port

Located on the edge of the city, the port consists of a large complex with about 20 canning and freezing factories where the produce of the sea is processed. An auction takes place in the fish market here every afternoon. Agadir also exports citrus fruit, fresh vegetables, canned food and ore.

Agadir City Centre

① Nouveau Talborj
② Musée Municipal du Patrimoine Amazighe
③ Open-Air Theatre
④ Vallée des Oiseaux
⑤ Beach

0 metres 400
0 yards 400

For keys to symbols *see back flap*

The imposing ramparts of Taroudannt

❷ Taroudannt

80 km (50 miles) east of Agadir.
🏙 36,000. 🚌 from Casablanca,
Agadir, Marrakech & Ouarzazate, or
grands taxis; Thu & Sun. 🏛 Berber
souk daily. 🎭 Moussem (Aug).

Enclosed within red-ochre
ramparts and encircled by
orchards, orange groves and
olive trees, Taroudannt has all
the appeal of an old Moroccan
fortified town. It was occupied
by the Almoravids in 1056 and
in the 16th century became
the capital of the Saadians, who
used it as a base from which
to attack the Portuguese in
Agadir. Although the Saadians
eventually chose Marrakech
as their capital, they made
Taroudannt wealthy through
the riches of the Souss plain,
which included sugarcane,
cotton, rice and indigo.

Under the Alaouites, the town
resisted royal control, forming

an alliance with Ahmed Ibn
Mahrez, the dissident nephew
of Moulay Ismaïl. The latter
regained control of the region
by massacring the inhabitants.

Taroudannt is a generally
peaceful town, except during
the annual olive harvest when it
is enlivened by itinerant pickers.
On its two main squares, Place
Assarag and Place Talmoklate,
horse-drawn carriages can be
hired for a tour of the **ramparts**,
which are 7 km (4 miles)
long. Set with bastions and
pierced by five gates, they are
in a remarkably good state of
preservation, a part of them
dating from the 18th century.

The **souks**, between the two
squares, are the town's main
attraction. The daily Berber
market sells spices, vegetables,
clothing, household goods,
pottery and other items. In the
Arab souk the emphasis is on
handicrafts: terracotta, wrought
iron, brass and copper, pottery,
leather goods, carpets and
Berber jewellery of a type once
made by Jews can be seen.
Carvings in chalky white stone
are a speciality of Taroudannt.

Outside the ramparts is a
small tannery, which is open
to visitors. Its shop sells goatskin
and camel-hide sandals, lambskin
rugs, soft leather bags, belts
and slippers.

Environs
The peaks of the western High
Atlas – particularly Jbel Aoulime,
at a height of 3,555 m (11,667 ft)
– can be reached via road 7020,
north of the town. About 37 km
(23 miles) southeast of Taroudannt,
the imposing **Tioute Kasbah**

dominates the palm grove.
This was the location for the
film *Ali Baba and the Forty
Thieves*, made by Jacques
Becker in 1954.

A restaurant adjacent to the
kasbah rather spoils the site.
On the banks of Wadi Souss,
which attracts migratory birds,
stands the older Freija kasbah,
now uninhabited.

Between Taroudannt and
Ouarzazate, the road (N10)
passes through a landscape of
wild beauty. Plains covered with
argan trees give way to the
volcanic massif of Jbel Siroua,
which bristles with peaks and
where soft geological folds
alternate with rocky plateaux.

Taliouine, a town between
two mountain chains at an
altitude of 1,180 m (3,873 ft),
has a stately kasbah once owned
by the Glaoui *(see p61)*. Though
dilapidated, it is still inhabited.
The town is the centre of the
world's biggest saffron-growing
area. In **Tazenakht**, 85 km
(53 miles) east of Taliouine,
beneath Jbel Siroua, carpets
with an orange weft are woven
by the Ouaouzguite tribe.

Hot and arid desert landscape in the
Anti-Atlas

❸ Igherm to Tata

Road N10 east from Taroudannt, then
road R109 to Tata. 🚌 Taroudannt,
Tiznit, Agadir & Bouizarkane. 🏛 Souk
Wed in Igherm, Thu in Tata.

A relatively new road (built in
1988), the N10 crosses the
Anti-Atlas, passing through
some remarkable landscapes.
Between Taroudannt and
Igherm, argan fields alternate
with dry-stone villages overlooking terraced plantations.

The daily Berber market in the town
of Taroudannt

Saffron flowers, harvested for their stigmas

Saffron from Taliouine

Saffron (*Crocus sativus*) is a bulbed herbaceous plant that belongs to the iris family. It grows at altitudes of 1,200 to 2,000 m (4,000 to 6,600 ft), in slightly chalky soil. Almost 6 sq km (2.3 sq miles) of saffron fields around Taliouine are cultivated by families, each of which tends its own plot of land. The bulbs are planted in September at a density of 7,500 per 1,000 sq m (10,760 sq ft), and the mauve flowers appear at the end of October. Harvesting takes place before sunrise and goes on for 15 to 20 days. It is a delicate process, involving the separation of the red stigmas that contain the colorant from the plant. After drying, 100,000 flowers produce 1 kg (2.2 lb) of saffron, and just 1 gram (a tiny pinch) is enough to colour 7 litres (12 pints) of liquid. The precious powder is then poured into airtight boxes and stored away from daylight to preserve its flavour. Good-quality saffron is sold in the form of whole filaments. Saffron is used in food, as a dye for carpets and pottery, and for dyeing the hair and hands of brides. It is also a medicinal plant that is thought to aid digestion and calm toothache.

Igherm, 94 km (58 miles) southeast of Taroudannt, is a large mountain village at an altitude of 1,800 m (5,908 ft). It is the base of the Ida Oukensous tribe, renowned for the daggers and guns that they make. The houses here are built of pink stone, their windows outlined in blue. Women dressed in black and wearing coloured headbands fetch water in tall copper jars (*situle*) which they carry on their heads.

Between Igherm and Tata the road crosses a rugged desert plain, with mountains of folded strata in hues of ochre, yellow and violet. The Tizi-Touzlimt Pass, at 1,692 m (5,553 ft), is followed by a succession of oases. In the Souk-Khemis-d'Issafen palm grove women dressed in indigo can be seen walking around the well-watered gardens, except when the Thursday souk is on. Some 30 *ksour* stand in the great **Tata Palm Grove**, where Berber and Arabic are spoken.

Crossing Wadi Tata, which irrigates the grove, the road leads to Agadir-Lehne, where a stone *koubba* stands below a spring. Some 4 km (2.5 miles) further on are the Messalite caves, which are inhabited sporadically by shepherds.

❹ Akka

62 km (39 miles) southwest of Tata on road N12. 🗠 6,500. 🚆 Souk Thu & Sun.

The Akka palm grove lies north of the village. A dozen *ksour* are interspersed among the date palms and the pomegranate, fig, peach, apricot and nut trees. On a hill is Tagadirt, a mellah, now in ruins, where the rabbi Mardoch was born in 1883. He discovered ancient rock engravings in the area and accompanied the French ascetic Charles de Foucauld, disguised as a Jew, on his peregrinations *(see p221).*

The Aït-Rahhal springs in the palm grove supply the oasis. A strange brick-built minaret dating from the Almohad period can also be seen here.

The troglodytic granary at Aït-Herbil, still in use

Environs

Many rock engravings can be seen at **Foum-el-Hassan**, 90 km (56 miles) southwest of Akka on the road to Bouizarkane (road N12), and at **Aït-Herbil**. To visit them, you need to hire a guide (details from Café-Hôtel Tamdoult in Akka). There are also many *igherm* (granaries) here, some dug into the cliff face.

The *koubba* at Agadir-Lehne, in the Tata Palm Grove

Greater flamingoes flying in the Souss Massa National Park

❺ Souss Massa National Park

65 km (40 miles) south of Agadir on road N1; 50 km (31 miles) north of Tiznit on road N1.

Created in 1991, the Souss Massa National Park extends along the banks of Wadi Massa, which, en route to the Atlantic, irrigates a large palm grove. This nature reserve, where river and sea water meet, where tides ebb and flow, and where winter temperatures are mild, attracts hundreds of migratory birds.

The reed beds on the banks of the *wadi* are inhabited by greater flamingoes from the Camargue, in southern France, and from Spain, as well as godwit, turnstone, snipe, dunlin, coots, grey heron and many other species. The primary purpose of creating the park was to preserve the bald ibis, a species threatened with extinction. Morocco is home to half the world's population of this curious bird, which has a pink featherless head.

Only certain areas of the park are open to the public. Visitors should approach the *wadi* from Sidi Rbat. The best time to see the birds is early in the morning, from March to April and October to November.

❻ Tiznit

91 km (57 miles) south of Agadir on road N1. 🚹 45,000. 🚌 from Agadir, Safi, Guelmim and Tafraoute, or grands taxis. ℹ️ ONMT Agadir. 🛒 Souk Wed & Thu. 🎪 Moussem of Sidi Ahmed ou Moussa (Aug), 35 km (22 miles) east of Tiznit.

Located slightly inland from the coast, Tiznit is a small town where the proximity of both the Atlantic and the desert can be felt. In 1881, Sultan Moulay Hassan settled here in order to exert greater control over the dissident Berber tribes of the Souss.

The town came to fame in 1912, when El-Hiba, a populist rebel leader, was proclaimed sultan of Tiznit in the mosque. Opposed to the establishment

of the French Protectorate in Morocco, El-Hiba conquered the Souss by rallying the tribes of the Anti-Atlas and the Tuareg to his cause. He launched an attack on Marrakech, where he was repulsed by French troops.

It is possible to walk round the 5-km (3-mile) pink pisé ramparts that encircle the town. The *méchouar*, a rectangular parade ground that functioned as the pasha's reception courtyard, is lined with arcades beneath which are cafés and shops. The renowned craftsmen of Tiznit still work with silver here, as the Jews once did, producing chunky Berber jewellery, daggers and sabres with inlaid handles.

The vertical poles on the clay walls of the minaret of the Grand Mosque are put there to help the souls of the departed enter paradise.

Environs
Sidi Moussa Aglou, 15 km (9 miles) northwest of Tiznit, is a fine beach used by surfers. Caves in the cliffs are used by local fishermen.

❼ Sidi Ifni

75 km (47 miles) south of Tiznit. 🚹 20,000. ℹ️ ONMT Agadir. 🚌 Tiznit or grands taxis. 🛒 Souk Sun. 🎪 Moussem (end of Jun).

From Tiznit, a scenic minor road leads to the coast, which it follows until Sidi Ifni. Formerly a Spanish coastal enclave, the town, on the crest of a rocky plateau overlooking the ocean, is buffeted by wind and is often shrouded in sea mist. The

Women spreading washing out to dry on the banks of Wadi Massa

◀ Beach with the backdrop of the red cliffs of Legzira, around Sidi Ifni colonial style of some of the buildings – such as the former Spanish Consulate and the Hispano-Berber Art Deco church that is now the law courts – gives the town an unusual aspect.

❽ Tafraoute

143 km (89 miles) southeast of Agadir. Road N1 from Agadir then road R105; road R104 from Tiznit. 🚗 1,700. 🚌 Tiznit and Agadir, or grands taxis. ℹ️ ONMT Agadir. 🛒 Souk Tue & Wed. Mountain bikes can be hired in the town centre.

At an altitude of 1,200 m (3,938 ft), Tafraoute stands in the heart of a stunning valley of the Anti-Atlas. It is surrounded by a cirque of granite whose colours at the end of the day change from ochre to pink. The palm groves here are lush and, for the brief period of their flowering – two weeks in February – the almond trees are covered with clouds of pink and white blossom.

The square dry-stone houses consist of a central courtyard and a tower. They are rendered with pastel pink plaster and their windows are outlined with white limewash.

Tafraoute is the territory of the Ameln, the best known of the six tribes of the Anti-Atlas. They are renowned for their acumen as traders. As spice merchants, they have spread throughout Morocco and also abroad.

Monk Seals

The largest colony of monk seals (Monachus monachus) in the Mediterranean area is found along the Atlantic coast, in the very south of Morocco. In 1995, 200 seals still existed here but half the colony was destroyed by disease in 1998, and it faces a very uncertain future. This brown seal can grow to a length of 3 m (10 ft) and weigh up to 300 kg (660 lb). During the 20th century it has disappeared from the Canary Islands archipelago, Madeira and most of the islands of the Mediterranean. Today, it is still to be found in the Black Sea and on the Bulgarian and Turkish coasts, and it may still survive in Sicily and Sardinia.

The monk seal, facing an uncertain future in Morocco

The fortified village of Tioulit perched on a hilltop

Limited local resources have forced them to leave their homeland, so that their villages are today inhabited only by children, elderly people and women shrouded in black. However, as soon as they can, the émigrés return to build comfortable houses.

Tafraoute is also a centre for the manufacture of round-toed slippers, in natural, red, yellow or embroidered leather.

Environs

Jean Vérame's **painted rocks** can be seen 3 km (2 miles) north of Tafraoute. The smooth, rounded rocks, painted by the Belgian artist in 1984, rise chaotically from a lunar landscape. Although their colours – red, purple and blue – have faded, the effect is still surreal.

About 4 km (2.5 miles) further north is the fertile **Ameln Valley**, carpeted with orchards and with olive and almond trees. It is dotted with 26 Berber villages perching on the mountain side, above which runs a precipitous mountain chain culminating in Jbel Lekst, at 2,359 m (7,743 ft). **Taghdichte**, the highest village, is the starting point for the ascent of Jbel Lekst.

North of Tafraoute, on the road to Agadir, is the *igherm* (communal granary) of Ida ou Gnidif, on the top of a hill. A little further on is the fortified village of **Tioulit**, perched on another outcrop and looking down into the valley.

About 3 km (2 miles) south of Tafraoute a cluster of huge, strangely shaped rocks known as Napoleon's Hat overlooks the village of Agard Oudad. A one-day detour from Tafraoute leads to the **Afella Ighir Oasis**. Laid out along the *wadi*, it is filled with tiny gardens, palm trees and almond trees clinging to the cliffs. Beyond the point where the road becomes a rough track, a four-wheel-drive vehicle is needed.

Houses in Tafraoute, covered in pink plaster

Angling from the cliff-top near Tan Tan Plage

⑨ Guelmim

56 km (35 miles) south of Sidi Ifni.
38,000. ℹ (0528) 87 29 11.
from Agadir, Marrakech, Laayoune
and Tan Tan, or grands taxis. Camel
souk (Sat). Moussem of Asrir (Jul).

Also known as Goulimine,
this small settlement of red
houses with blue shutters was an
important centre on the caravan
route from the 11th to the 19th
centuries. Today, it is known chiefly
for its camel souk. The *moussem*
of Asrir, 6 km (4 miles) southeast, is
attended by the Sahraouis, known
as the "blue men" because of their
indigo clothing.

Environs

Fourteen kilometres (9 miles) to
the north are the **Abeino** thermal
springs with bathing pools for
men and women. The vast **Plage
Blanche** (White Beach), 60 km
(37 miles) west of Guelmim, can
be reached along tracks. The

A trader at the famous camel souk
in Guelmim

beautiful **Aït Bekkou Oasis**,
17 km (11 miles) to the southeast,
is the largest in the area.

⑩ Tan Tan and Tan Tan Plage

125 km (78 miles) southwest of
Guelmim on road N1. 50,000.
Agadir, Tarfaya and Laayoune, or
grands taxis. Moussem of Sheikh
Ma el-Ainin (May/Jun).

The province of Tan Tan is
sparsely populated by pastoral
nomads and fishermen. The road
from Guelmim is good but police
checks are frequent since the
region remains a military zone.

Tan Tan has a certain raffish
charm, with everything from
shops and mosques to the *petits
taxis* painted in blue or mustard.
In the medina, Saharan-style
bric-a-brac is for sale and there
is a colourful Sunday souk. A
moussem held in May or June,
honouring local resistance
hero Sheikh Ma el-Ainin, is
the occasion of a huge camel
market. At night women dance
the *guedra* in tribal tents.

On the coast, 25 km (15 miles)
away, is Tan Tan Plage where
low-key tourism development
has begun.

Environs

Road R101 leads across the
desert to **Smara**, about 245 km
(152 miles) south of Tan Tan.
Today no more than a garrison
base, this legendary town put
up fierce resistance to the
expansion of French rule.

⑪ Tarfaya

235 km (146 miles) south of Tan Tan.
from Tan Tan or grands taxis.

The spectacularly scenic route
between Tan Tan and Tarfaya
follows the coastline, where
cliffs give way to dunes of
white sand.

Tarfaya, today an expanding
fishing port, was a stop on the
Service Aéropostale, the French
airmail service, in the 1920s and
1930s. There is a statue of writer
and airman Saint-Exupéry who
has left vivid descriptions of
flying over this desolate region
in terrible sandstorms. It was
also the rallying point for the
Green March of 1975 *(see p62)*.

Boundless expanses of desert near
Laayoune

⑫ Laayoune

117 km (73 miles) south of Tarfaya.
100,000. from Agadir,
Dakhla and Tan Tan. from Agadir,
Dakhla and Tan Tan. ℹ Avenue de
l'Islam; (0528) 89 16 94.

A large oasis on Wadi Sagia
el-Hamra, Laayoune is today
the economic capital of the
Saharan provinces. Since Spain
relinquished the territory in
1975 *(see p62)*, Morocco has
invested in making Laayoune
a modern town.

Dakhla, 540 km (335 km)
further south, stands on the tip
of an attractive peninsula. The
bay is one of the most beautiful
places in the country and an
internationally renowned spot
for kite surfing. Dakhla is the last
town before the border with
Mauritania, 350 km (217 miles)
away. The border can be
crossed easily.

The Nomad's Tent

The *khaïma*, or nomad's tent, seen on the desert plateaux of the High Atlas, outside the towns of Zagora and Guelmim, is the moveable home of shepherds who travel to provide their flocks with seasonal grazing. The sturdy tent is easy to set up and gives protection against the heat. The brown fabric is woven from goat or camel hair. It consists of *flijs*, strips 40 to 60 cm (16 to 24 in) wide, sewn together edge to edge. It rests on a ridgepole supported on two vertical wooden poles. The interior of the tent is divided into two. One side, with basic cooking equipment and a loom, is for the women. The other side, separated by a screen, is reserved for the men and for visitors.

Nomads are rarely seen because they mostly frequent mountain or desert environments that are remote from civilization. However, for a few weeks of the year, some of them settle in an oasis. Their tents are very simply furnished, with little more than thick, heavy carpets and wooden chests where the women keep their most prized possessions. The hospitality of the nomads is legendary.

The nomad's tent is set up on level ground. In summer, the covering is laid over the poles in such a way as to allow air to circulate freely. In winter, the sides are drawn together and are insulated with long woollen blankets and carpets.

Nomadic Berber women card wool before spinning it into yarn. Using a loom unchanged since ancient times, they weave blankets and lengths of cloth.

These nomads, portrayed in a century-old photograph, lived in a way that hasn't changed much to this day. Nomads still travel from one source of water to another.

Driving animals to seasonal pastures occurs in Morocco's more arid regions. In summer, the nomads take their herds and flocks up to the high pastures of the Atlas, returning to the south in winter.

TRAVELLERS' NEEDS

WHERE TO STAY

Choosing a hotel in Morocco depends primarily on its location and the types of services travellers seek during their stay in the country. In recent years, a rise in eco-tourism and exploration, rather than simple holiday-making, has resulted in greater accommodation choices. There are still the ultra-flamboyant and opulent alternatives – most often found in Marrakech – and beach resorts in places such as Agadir, but there are also the guesthouses of Essaouira, the *riads* of ancient Fès, the kasbahs of the mountains, and an increasing number of desert-style encampments in and around the Sahara. The range of decor, price, amenities and standards is huge, and visitors should have no trouble finding accommodation to suit their budget and needs. For those with smaller budgets, youth hostels and guest rooms are attractive alternatives so long as visitors are happy to observe the ground rules.

Be Live Grand Saidia *(see p309)*, perfect for large groups and families

Choosing a Hotel

The location of a hotel, especially in large towns and cities, is an important criterion. It is usually best to stay somewhere near the old town, where the main tourist sites are often found. The disadvantage of such a location, however, is that the hotel will probably be noisy and unlikely to offer parking. For those desirous of more space, especially a garden – and many gardens also have swimming pools – it is best to choose a hotel on the edge of the old town or in a modern quarter.

Smaller towns rarely offer high-class accommodation, especially in the south. Here, your choice of hotel should be governed by your itinerary. In the south, most places of interest to tourists are not in the towns themselves but along the roads between them, so that rather than planning an itinerary route according to the desirability of a hotel, it is best to choose where to stay in relation to the distance you intend to cover each day.

Information about hotels is available from the **Fédération Nationale de l'Industrie Hôtelière** in Casablanca.

Classification of Hotels and Services

The Moroccan Ministry of Tourism has devised an official system of classification for hotels. Accordingly, hotels are graded on a scale of one to five stars, with two sub-categories, A and B. In principle, each grade corresponds to certain standards of comfort, as well as other criteria such as the size of the establishment.

Once bearing little relation to reality, the system by which stars are awarded has been overhauled. Although some hotels may still be over-ambitiously graded, many have been downgraded to reflect more accurately the standard of accommodation that they offer. Note, however, that these stars may not quite match European standards.

As a general rule, four- and five-star hotels are well equipped, with satellite televisions, telephones, en-suite bathrooms and room service, as well as many other features such as a restaurant, swimming pool, sports centre and hammam. Two- and three-star hotels are comfortable and clean, with private baths or showers. The small one-star hotels, or hotels without classification, are often quite basic and may not be very clean. It is advisable to ask to see the room before deciding.

Jardins De Roses in the Husa Casablanca Plaza *(see p306)*, Rabat

◀ Colourful ceramics on display at a souk in Essaouira

Prices

By law, prices must be shown in the reception area of a hotel as well as in the rooms, and this requirement is widely fulfilled. Be aware, however, that advertised prices rarely include tax (ranging from 1 to 25 dirhams, according to the town and the hotel) and that they do not include the cost of breakfast.

The average price of a single room in a small one-star or unlisted hotel is 150 dirhams. A two- or three-star establishment will charge 250 to 400 dirhams, and a three-star category-A hotel or a four-star hotel can charge anywhere from 400 to 1,000 dirhams. The numerous five-star hotels charge 1,200 dirhams, and some over 2,000 dirhams. There is no official upper limit.

Prices vary according to the season, and it is not unusual to see prices double around the holiday periods at the end of the year as well as in spring, and during the summer in the coastal resorts. Prices also vary according to the number of people renting the room. For example, for a child or a third adult sharing a room, a supplement will be charged, though usually with a reduction of 5 to 50 per cent.

Negotiating a lower price for a hotel room is common practice, and it bears results. At slack times, it is possible to obtain reductions of up to 30 per cent. However, it is a waste of time trying to negotiate at the peak of the high season, or in the very smart hotels, such as Marrakech's La Mamounia *(see p311)*.

Reservations

During the high seasons, the crowds of holiday-makers can be unexpectedly large. At such times, in small towns that have a limited number of hotels (particularly in the south), it can be quite impossible to find a room. This may also be true in towns with a much larger choice of hotels, such as Marrakech or Fès.

At these busy times, it is essential to make a reservation in advance. This can be done at a travel agency, through a tour operator that covers all of Morocco, on the Internet, or by contacting hotels directly.

One consequence of the European-style hotel management that has taken root in Morocco is the practice of over-booking. Put simply, the hotel accepts more reservations than it has rooms, so as to compensate for any cancellations. Unfortunately, if you happen to be a victim of this practice, there is little that can be done to salvage the situation. The best way to try to avoid this happening is to pay for your stay in full at the time of booking and check in at the hotel earlier rather than later in the day.

Chain and Luxury Hotels

The Accor Group manages multiple international hotel brands such as **Sofitel** and **Mercure**, which can be found in most major towns and cities throughout the country. Leading international hotel chains such as Hyatt and Le Méridien also have several establishments in Morocco. The **Ibis** group manages several hotels belonging to the **Moussafir** chain.

Of the large number of luxury hotels in Morocco, many boast slick, modern facilities, but the country also offers some legendary establishments, such as the charming La Mamounia in Marrakech. The Sofitel Palais Jamaï in the imperial city of Fès *(see p310)*, converted from a former palace, is not only an architectural marvel but has a unique location above the medina. The luxurious and elegant Hôtel El-Minzah in Tangier *(see p309)* looks like something from a film set and, although it is showing its age, it is still one of Morocco's great hotels.

Campsites

Campsites can be found in every large town, and there are many dotted on the Atlantic and Mediterranean coasts. As a general rule, standards of cleanliness in campsites leave much to be desired, and it is not safe to leave property unattended in tents. Staying in a campsite in Morocco is also something that best suits those who are not too fussy about hygiene and facilities.

Finding your own place to set up camp outside designated sites is not officially unlawful, but it is definitely not recommended for reasons of personal safety and also because the authorities do not like tourists camping anywhere they please.

Rooftop of the Sefrou's Dar Attamani *(see p311)* offering fine views of the town

Warm and inviting interiors of The Repose *(see p307)* in Salé

Guesthouses and Guest Rooms

Guesthouses can be a useful option for those spending a few days away from the large tourist coastal resorts.

In small seaside villages, where it is sometimes very difficult to find accommodation, many Moroccans offer rooms in their own houses. Comforts are often basic and, before accepting the room, it is wise to check the cleanliness of the bedclothes and that toilets and washing facilities are in working order.

Often, when travelling in the Atlas, rather than left to camp in the open, visitors may be offered space in a living room, or on the roof of a pisé house, which can be a magical experience. The owner of the house (often the village chief) will steadfastly refuse money, and may even invite guests to share a meal. You can always offer a gift, or deal with the women of the house, who will often accept remuneration or a present for their children. Never give children gifts directly as this might offend.

Youth Hostels

There are several youth hostels in Morocco, and these make it possible to stay in the country for a minimal cost. However, most youth hostels are not centrally located and are quite basic, although they are usually clean. Travellers without an international Youth Hostel Association

membership card may be asked to pay a little extra. The easiest way to obtain a card is to join your country's Youth Hostel Association, for example the **YHA** in Britain or the **Hostelling International USA** in the United States.

Information in Morocco is available from the **Fédération Royale Marocaine des Auberges de Jeunes** in Casablanca.

Unmarried Couples

In Morocco, strict rules apply to the accommodation of couples. A Muslim cannot sleep with a woman if the couple is unmarried. Some hoteliers scrupulously respect this ruling, although allowances are normally made for Western couples.

However, it is possible that you will be asked to present your marriage certificate. Similarly, same sex couples may encounter difficulties when dealing with highly devout hoteliers.

Disabled Visitors

Apart from some modern hotels, few establishments in Morocco are equipped for disabled visitors. Nevertheless, Moroccans are very well disposed to anyone needing help, so that people with disabilities will be pleasantly surprised at the thoughtfulness and helpfulness that they encounter across the country.

Riads

The literal translation of the Arabic word *riad* is "garden". Thus a *riad* should consist, theoretically, of a garden planted with trees. By extension, the word *riad* is applied to all old houses that have at least a patio or courtyard. These old-style houses can be found in the medinas, and many have become available to visitors, especially in Marrakech, Fès and Essaouira.

These traditional residences each have their own particular architectural design and have usually been restored very well. Converted into guesthouse accommodation, they are very pleasant places to stay in, particularly because they are quiet, naturally cool and because of their often excellent location. By contrast to a large international hotel, staying in a *riad* is usually a more culturally enriching experience.

Either individual rooms or the whole *riad* can be rented, and many also offer breakfast and an evening meal. No official grading applies to

The atmospheric interiors of Riad d'Or *(see p310)* in Meknès

this type of accommodation, and standards, service and prices vary widely according to the individual *riad*.

It is worth noting that a riad, by its very nature, is traditional and is therefore unlikely to offer the spacious lounges and glittering bars that a top-priced modern hotel would supply.

While some riads are run by people who have only a vague idea of the hotel business, others are exceptional and better options than standard hotels, such as the Villa des Orangers *(see p312)* in Marrakech, which will delight those who love old buildings and who expect a high standard of service.

Organizations such as **Marrakech-Medina** and **Fès Medina Morocco** (US based) can help book *riads*.

Recommended Hotels

Morocco is a country of great contrasts, of lush valleys and high mountains, stretches of open fertile fields, crashing waves of the Atlantic coast, calmer waters of the Mediterranean and sweeping sandy dunes, peppered with the occasional oasis. With so many different

Stylish and sohisticated decor at the La Sultana *(see p308)* in Oualidia

regions and so many exceptional cultural contrasts to shape its architecture, cities and views, it can be difficult for visitors to choose a place to stay. This guide takes into account the needs of many different styles of travel, loosely categorizing accommodation on offer in each area: Value, Modern, Historic, Boutique and Luxury. These choices are intended to help find something for everyone. In some cases – such as in Marrakech – the choice is too diverse to list all

the establishments of note, while in the Middle Atlas and Sahara, the entries are limited by the scarcity of options available.

The entries marked "DK Choice" in this guide are a range of accommodation options. All offer something unique and memorable: from the grandest of ancient palaces in Fès to a white-washed *pension* in the Atlas mountains, where one can sit on the roof terrace and gaze at the stars.

DIRECTORY

Choosing a Hotel

Fédération Nationale de l'Industrie Hôtelière
320 Boulevard Zerktouni, 2040 Casablanca.
Tel (0522) 26 73 13/14.
Fax (0522) 26 72 73.
W **fnih.ma**

Hotel Chains

Hôtels Ibis Moussafir
(Accor group)
Tel (001) 80 02 21 45 42 (central reservations).
W **accorhotels.com**

Hôtel Mercure (Rabat)
Tel (0530) 20 03 94.
Fax (0537) 72 45 27.
W **mercure.com**

Hôtel Novotel (Casablanca)
Tel (0520) 48 00 01.
Fax (0522) 46 65 01.
W **mercure.com**

Hôtel Sofitel (Marrakech)
Tel (0524) 42 56 00.
W **sofitel.com**

Youth Hostel Associations

England & Wales Youth Hostel Association (YHA)
Trevelyan House, Matlock, Derbyshire DE4 3YH.
Tel 01629 592 700.
W **yha.org.uk**

Hostelling International USA
8401 Colesville Road, Suite 600, Silver Springs, MD 20910, USA.
Tel 240 650 2100.
W **hiayh.org**

Fédération Royale Marocaine des Auberges de Jeunes
Parc de la Ligue Arabe, Casablanca.
Tel & Fax (0522) 22 76 77.
W **frmaj.ma**

Riads

Fès Medina Morocco
516 San Miguel Canyon Rd, Royal Oaks, California 95076.
Tel (831) 724 5835.
Fax (904) 212 8814.
W **fesmedina.com**

Marrakech-Medina
Rue Dar el Bacha, Marrakech.
Tel (0524) 29 07 07.
W **marrakech-medina.com**

Where to Stay

Rabat

AGDAL: Ibis
Modern Map C2
Pl de la Gare, Agdal
Tel *(0530) 20 03 93*
W ibishotels.com
Convenient location and predictably good standards of cleanliness, decor and service.

CITY CENTRE: Art Riad
Value Map C2
16 Rue Essam
W artriad.com
Sister property of nearby Riad Kalaa, this is a very stylish, yet reasonably priced, place to stay.

CITY CENTRE: Dar Mayssanne
Value Map C2
13 Rue Faran Khechen
Tel *(0661) 06 66 66*
W rabat-riad.com
Cosy, stylish rooms, tastefully decorated with great attention to detail. Welcoming staff.

CITY CENTRE: A L'Alcazar
Historic Map C2
4 Impasse Benabdellah Bab Laalou
Tel *(0537) 73 69 06*
W lalcazar.com
Stunning century-old building with impressive traditional interiors. Close to the main sights.

CITY CENTRE: Golden Tulip Farah
Modern Map C2
Place Sidi Makhlouf
Tel *(0537) 23 74 00*
W goldentulipfarahrabat.com
Well-reputed and known for its reliable standards of amenities and service. Offers relaxed poolside dining and barbecue facilities.

The luxurious Sofitel Rabat Jardins de Roses in Souissi

CITY CENTRE: Hotel Balima
Historic Map C2
Av Mohammed V
Tel *(0537) 70 77 55*
W hotel-balima.net
Worn and faded Art Deco dame that nevertheless continues to be an important city landmark.

CITY CENTRE: Hotel Mercure Sheherazade
Modern Map C2
21 Rue de Tunis
Tel *(0530) 20 03 94*
W mercure.com
Small for a hotel bearing such a name, this is a welcoming place with jewel-like decor.

CITY CENTRE: Riad Dar El Kebira
Modern Map C2
Rue des Consuls No.1, Impasse Belghazi, Ferrane Znaki
Tel *(0537) 72 49 06*
W darelkebira.com
Unlike other modernized high-end hotels, the Riad Dar El Kebira is a gem of Moorish architecture.

CITY CENTRE: Riad El Maati
Modern Map C2
15 Sidi el Maati
Tel *(0537) 72 57 16*
W riadelmaati.com
Little-known, expertly run and beautiful *riad*, owned by a French/Moroccan couple.

DK Choice

CITY CENTRE: Riad Kalaa
Historic Map C2
3–5 Rue Zebdi
Tel *(0537) 20 20 28*
W riadkalaa.com
Has all the nooks, crannies, tiled stairways and alcoves befitting a 200-year-old medina mansion. Classy interiors and impeccable attention to detail throughout. Learn to cook in the *riad's* kitchens, have a steam or treatment in the traditional hammam or simply cool off in the rooftop pool.

CITY CENTRE: La Tour Hassan
Luxury Map C2
26 Rue Chellah BP 14
Tel *(0537) 23 90 00*
W palaces-traditions.ma
Typical Moorish architecture that oozes Moroccan style, and yet has a distinctive European flavour. The tastefully presented rooms are well-equipped.

Price Guide
Prices are based on one night's stay in high season for a standard double room, Inclusive of service charges and taxes.

Dh	up to 1,000 dirhams
Dh Dh	1000 to 2,000 dirhams
Dh Dh Dh	over 2,000 dirhams

SKHIRAT PLAGE: Hotel L'Amphitrite Palace
Modern Map C2
Skhirat Plage
Tel *(0537) 62 10 00*
W lamphitrite-palace.com
Comfortable out-of-town option for families with kids and larger groups.

SOUISSI: Villa Mandarine
Luxury Map C2
19 Rue Ouled Bousbaa
Tel *(0537) 75 20 77*
W villamandarine.com
Luxurious mansion-like place with airy, light-filled rooms and peacocks in magnificent gardens. Great option for families.

SOUISSI: Sofitel Rabat Jardins de Roses
Luxury Map C2
Aviation Souissi
Tel *(0537) 67 56 56*
W sofitel.com
Glistening after a breathtaking revamp, this urban oasis has impressive gardens and a bar.

Northern Atlantic Coast

ASILAH: Berbari
Boutique Map D1
Medchar Ghanem
Tel *(0660) 29 54 54*
W berbari.com
Quirky, much-loved bohemian retreat that is a great place for families to let off steam.

ASILAH: Dar Manara
Value Map D1
23 Rue M'Jimaa
Tel *(0539) 41 69 64*
W asilah-darmanara.com
Good option for those on a budget who do not wish to sacrifice comfort. Book ahead.

KENITRA: Hotel Europe
Value Map C2
63 Av Mohammed Diouri
Tel *(0537) 37 14 50*
Simple, basic establishment with decent, clean rooms, an adequate little restaurant and friendly service.

LARACHE: La Maison Haute (Dh)
Value   Map D1
6 Derb Ibn Thami
Tel *(0539) 34 48 88*
W lamaisonhaute.free.fr
More a guesthouse than a hotel,
affording a glimpse into real
Morocco. As the name suggests,
there are plenty of stairs.

MOULAY BOUSSELHAM:
Driftwood (Dh)
Value   Map D1
Fronte de Mar
Tel *(0537) 43 21 95*
Tiny, tranquil place to watch
birds flock over the lagoon
and experience the simple life.
Also offers self-catering.

MOULAY BOUSSELHAM:
Hotel Le Lagon (Dh)
Value   Map D1
Centre de Moulay Bousselham
Tel *(0537) 43 26 50*
Offers both lagoon and Atlantic
views, expansive if somewhat
plain communal areas, neat
rooms and a good bar.

SALÉ: Riad Marlinea (Dh)(Dh)
Value   Map C2
17 Derb Hrarta, Bab Lamrissa,
Medina
Tel *(0537) 88 37 34*
Traditionally decorated rooms
and ample communal seating
areas. Can be difficult to find,
so phone ahead for directions.

DK Choice

SALÉ: The Repose (Dh)(Dh)
Boutique   Map C2
17 Zankat Talaa, Salé Medina
Tel *(0537) 88 29 58*
W therepose.com
Unique guesthouse with lots
of character and elegant decor.
Strikes a good balance between
traditional and serene and is
very reasonably priced for
what it offers, including a
complimentary three-course
breakfast. The *riad*'s few rooms –
all suites – are in high demand,
so book ahead.

Casablanca

BOUZNIKA: Riad des
Plages (Dh)(Dh)
Historic   Map C2
Plage Essanaoubar Nord
Tel *(0659) 21 73 09*
W riaddesplages.com
Small and delightful *riad*
that has direct access to the
beach. Can be booked per
room or as a whole.

Simple and classy bedroom interiors at The Repose in Salé

CITY CENTRE:
Hotel Guynemer (Dh)
Value   Map C2
2 Rue Mohammed Belloul, Casa-Anfa
Tel *(0522) 27 57 64*
Family-run budget option
that stands out because of the
personal quality of service offered.

CITY CENTRE: Best Western
Toubkal (Dh)(Dh)
Modern   Map C2
9 Rue Sidi Belyout
Tel *(0522) 31 14 14)*
W hoteltoubkal.com
A good choice for tourists and
business travellers due to its
amenities and reliable reputation.

CITY CENTRE: Golden Tulip (Dh)(Dh)
Modern   Map C2
160 Av des FAR
Tel *(0522) 31 12 12*
W goldentulipfarahcasablanca.com
Excellent location, and all the
usual extensive amenities for
a hotel of this standing.

CITY CENTRE: Novotel
Casablanca (Dh)(Dh)
Modern   Map C2
Corner Rue Zaid Ouhmad &
Rue Sidi Belyout
Tel *(0522) 46 65 00*
W accorhotels.com
Reliable mid-range option with
views over the port and Hassan II
mosque. Practical for families.

CITY CENTRE:
Palace D'Anfa (Dh)(Dh)
Modern   Map C2
171 Blvd d'Anfa
Tel *(0522) 95 42 00*
W lepalacedanfa.ma
Not very swanky, but it has good
amenities, including a pool. Great
ocean views.

CITY CENTRE:
Hyatt Regency (Dh)(Dh)(Dh)
Luxury   Map C2
Place des Nations Unies
Tel *(0522) 43 12 34*
W hyatt.com
All the expected comforts. A
full list of amenities and facilities,

and well-trained, efficient staff.
Has several restaurants and
bars on site.

CITY CENTRE:
Kenzi Tower Hotel (Dh)(Dh)(Dh)
Luxury   Map C2
Blvd Mohammed Zerktouni
Tel *(0522) 97 80 00*
W kenzi-hotels.com
On the 28th floor of one of the
Twin Center skyscrapers. Incredible
views and excellent service.

CITY CENTRE: Le Doge Hotel
and Spa (Dh)(Dh)(Dh)
Luxury   Map C2
9 Rue du Docteur Veyre
Tel *(0522) 46 78 00*
W hotelledoge.com
Arty interiors and sumptuous
fabrics have infused new life into
this wonderful 1930s structure.

CITY CENTRE: Le Royal
Mansour Meridien (Dh)(Dh)(Dh)
Luxury   Map C2
27 Av de L'Armee Royale
Tel *(0522) 45 88 88*
W leroyalmansourmeridien.com
Extremely sophisticated, with
full amenities and an enviable
location. Choice of restaurants, a
piano bar and a health complex.

DK Choice

CITY CENTRE: Sofitel
Tour Blanche (Dh)(Dh)(Dh)
Luxury   Map C2
Rue Sidi Belyout
Tel *(0522) 45 62 00*
W sofitel.com
Elegant and extremely
impressive, with attractive
interiors and a popular and
very stylish lounge and bar.
Offers sweeping views of the
Atlantic and local landmarks.
There are two superb fine-
dining restaurants, as one
would expect in a luxury
hotel of this calibre, as well
as the usual package of
treatments, services and
conference facilities.

For more information on types of hotels *see page 305*

Southern Atlantic Coast

DAR BOUAZZA:
Hotel des Arts 🏠🏠
Modern   Map C2
1120 Jack Beach
Tel *(0522) 96 54 50*
Stylish hotel occupying a prime location in this pleasant beach resort and surfers' paradise.

EL-JADIDA: L'Igelsia 🏠🏠
Historic   Map B2
Eglise Espagnole de Saint-Antoine de Padoue
Tel *(0523) 37 34 00*
🅆 liglesia.com
A 19th century building that was once a Spanish convent, is now beautifully decorated in 1930s style.

DK Choice

EL-JADIDA: Mazagan
Beach Resort 🏠🏠🏠
Modern   Map B2
Mazagan Beach Resort
Tel *(0523) 38 80 00*
🅆 mazaganbeachresort.com
One of the most extensive resorts on the entire Moroccan coast. Has so many facilities on site that guests rarely venture out of the complex to visit nearby El-Jadida or Casablanca. Offers extensive spa and golf facilities, as well as several activities for families with kids. All in all, an unforgettable luxury experience.

ESSAOUIRA: Dar L'Oussia 🏠
Value   Map B4
4 Rue Mohammed Ben Messaoud, Bab Sbaa, Medina
Tel *(0524) 78 37 56*
🅆 darloussia.com
A *riad*-style building that is both bright and airy. Great roof terrace and extensive spa.

ESSAOUIRA: Riad
Mogador 🏠🏠
Modern   Map B4
Route de Marrakech
Tel *(0524) 78 35 55*
🅆 ryadmogador.com
The interplay of neutral colours and contemporary decor here gives the impression of a chic apartment rather than a hotel.

ESSAOUIRA: Villa De L'O 🏠🏠
Historic   Map B4
3 Rue Mohammed Ben Messaoud
Tel *(0524) 47 63 75*
🅆 villadelo.com
Colonial and traditional styling at this 18th-century *riad*. The monochrome interiors give it a fashionable boutique feel.

Sophisticated decor at the Mazagan Beach Resort, El-Jadida

ESSAOUIRA: Villa Maroc 🏠🏠
Boutique   Map B4
Rue Abdellah Ben Yassine
Tel *(0524) 47 31 47*
🅆 villa-maroc.com
Smartly interconnected *riads* provide an impressive 21 rooms. Carefully crafted boho-chic decor.

ESSAOUIRA: Heure Bleue
Palais 🏠🏠🏠
Luxury   Map B4
2 Rue Ibn Batouta, Bab Marrakech
Tel *(0524) 78 34 34*
🅆 heure-bleue.com
Elegant French-colonial in style, this high-end establishment has a rooftop pool, banana palms and splendid rooms.

ESSAOUIRA: Sofitel Medina
and Spa 🏠🏠🏠
Luxury   Map B4
Domaine Mogador
Tel *(0524) 47 94 00*
🅆 accorhotels.com
White Moorish architecture and lush gardens combine to impart a distinct character.

OUALIDIA: La Sultana 🏠🏠
Modern   Map B3
3 Parc a Huitres
Tel *(0524) 38 80 08*
🅆 lasultanahotels.com
With luxurious linens and marble floors, this small but high-end place is among the best in town.

Tangier

CITY CENTRE: Dar Jameel 🏠
Value   Map D1
6 Rue Mohammed Bergach, Medina
Tel *(0539) 33 46 80*
🅆 magicmaroc.com
Small hotel with five floors set around a central courtyard. Lives up to its name, "The House of Beauty", perfectly.

CITY CENTRE: Ibis 🏠
Value   Map D1
Lotissement Tanger Offshore Plazza
Tel *(0539) 32 85 50*
🅆 ibishotel.com
The reliable Ibis provides good service as well as modern, comfortable rooms.

CITY CENTRE: Dar Chams
Tanja 🏠🏠
Boutique   Map D1
2 Rue Jnan Kabtan
Tel *(0539) 33 23 23*
🅆 darchamstanja.com
Artistic accommodation; a great favourite with regular visitors to the city. Book ahead.

CITY CENTRE:
Hotel Continental 🏠🏠
Historic   Map D1
36 Rue Dar Baroud
Tel *(0539) 93 10 24*
🅆 continental-tanger.com
In 1888, this eccentric hotel welcomed Queen Victoria's son, Alfred, among its first guests. Today it is something of a Tangerine institution.

CITY CENTRE:
La Tangerina 🏠🏠
Historic   Map D1
19 Riad Sultan Kasbah
Tel *(0539) 94 77 31*
🅆 latangerina.com
Charming colonial-style building, with wonderful views over the medina and Strait of Gibraltar from the roof terrace. No credit cards.

CITY CENTRE: Maison
Arabesque 🏠🏠
Historic   Map D1
73 Rue Naciria, Medina, Place Sakaya
Tel *(0679) 46 68 76*
🅆 maison-arabesque.com
Built in 1898 in the Spanish-Moorish style, this guesthouse manages to effortlessly blend the old and new. No credit cards.

CITY CENTRE:
El-Minzah Hotel
Luxury   **Map** D1
85 Rue de la Liberté
Tel *(0539) 93 58 85*
Historical landmark with lots of
glamour. Outstanding service
and facilities. Wireless Internet
is available in all rooms.

DK Choice

FURTHER AFIELD:
Villa Josephine
Luxury   **Map** D1
231 Rue de la Vieille Montagne
Tel *(0539) 33 45 35*
Ⓦ villajosephine-tanger.com
Stunning property that
has more of a French Riviera
or country house feel than a
riad or *dar*. Timeless, romantic
decor, stunning gardens, great
service and delicious food.
Steeped in legend and history,
it makes for a remarkable stay.

Mediterranean Coast & the Rif

AL-HOCEIMA: Suites Hotel
Mohammed V
Value   **Map** E1
Pl Mohammed VI
Tel *(0539) 98 22 33*
Ⓦ hrm.ma
Small, refurbished establishment
that is a good base from which
to explore the region.

CAP SPARTEL:
Le Mirage
Luxury   **Map** D1
Les Grottes d'Hercule
Tel *(0539) 33 33 32*
Ⓦ lemirage.com
Luxurious bungalows on clifftops,
overlooking the Atlantic and the
Mediterranean; a memorable
place to unwind.

The plush and comfortable Be Live
Grand Saidia

CHEFCHAOUEN: Casa Perleta
Value   **Map** D1
Bab el Souk
Tel *(0539) 98 89 79*
Ⓦ casaperleta.com
Quaint blue-and-white option
with tiled floors and antique
painted doors. Ask for an AC room.

CHEFCHAOUEN: Dar Gabriel
Boutique   **Map** D1
Bab Souk
Tel *(0539) 98 92 44*
Ⓦ dargabriel.com
Pretty and snug getaway
with views of Rif mountain and
welcoming wood-burning stoves
during winter. No credit cards.

OUJDA: Atlas Terminus
and Spa
Value   **Map** F2
Blvd Zerktouni, Place De La Gare
Tel *(0536) 71 10 10*
Ⓦ hotel-atlas-terminus-oujda.com
A touch on the dated side, but
with comfortable rooms and an
impressive set of amenities.

OUJDA: Ibis
Value   **Map** F2
Blvd Abdellah
Tel *(0532) 11 02 80*
Ⓦ ibishotel.com
Attractive whitewashed place
with well-equipped rooms and
lots of charm.

SAÏDIA: Be Live
Grand Saidia
Luxury   **Map** F1
Parcela H7, Station Balnéaire
Tel *(0536) 63 33 66*
Ⓦ belivehotels.com
Huge resort suited to groups and
families, offering many amenities
plus access to golf and beaches.

TETOUAN: Blanco Riad
Historic   **Map** D1
25 Rue Zawiya Kadiria
Tel *(0539) 704 202*
Ⓦ blancoriad.com
Historic building that once housed
the Spanish Consulate, refurbished
as a lovely boutique hotel.

DK Choice

TETOUAN: Riad El Reducto
Value   **Map** D1
No. 38, Zawya Zanqat
Tel *(0539) 96 81 20*
Ⓦ riadtetouan.com
Intricately tiled rooms and
heavily adorned communal
areas are the highlights of
this great-value, well-run,
family lodging. The rooms are
impressive and the location is
excellent, just a stone's throw
from the royal palace.

TETOUAN: Barcelo Marina
Smir
Luxury   **Map** D1
Rue de Sebta
Tel *(0539) 97 12 34*
Ⓦ barcelo.com
Sprawling whitewashed building
in beautifully kept gardens. One
of the finest options in the area.

Fès

CITY CENTRE:
Dar Bensouda
Historic   **Map** D2
14 Zkak el Bghel, Elquettanine
Tel *(0524) 42 64 63*
Ⓦ riaddarbensouda.com
Restored palace with surprisingly
affordable rooms that offer
gorgeous mountain views.

CITY CENTRE: Riad
Laaroussa
Historic   **Map** D2
3 Derb Bechara, Talaa Sghira
Tel *(0674) 18 76 39*
Ⓦ riad-laaroussa.com
Deluxe guesthouse in a 17th-
century palace. Cool courtyard in
summer, blazing fires in winter.

CITY CENTRE: Riad
Numero 9
Modern   **Map** D2
Derb Lamside
Tel *(0535) 63 40 45*
Ⓦ riad9.com
Antique-filled interiors make for
delightful rooms and lounges. No
credit cards. Closed in August.

DK Choice

CITY CENTRE: Palais Amani
Sofitel
Luxury   **Map** D2
12 Derb El Miter
Tel *(0535) 63 32 09*
Ⓦ palaisamani.com
Remarkable building that was
once a palace. The beautiful
interiors display muted but
traditional design and offer all
modern comforts. It also has
ornate formal gardens. Regarded
as the top place to stay in the old
town, with some rooms offering
excellent medina views.

CITY CENTRE:
Riad Ibn Battouta
Luxury   **Map** D2
Av Allal El Fassi
Tel *(0535) 63 71 91*
Ⓦ riadibnbattouta.com
Renovated mansion located
on the edge of the medina.
Has high-spec suites and a
series of terraces.

For more information on types of hotels *see page 305*

CITY CENTRE: Zalagh Parc Palace
Luxury Map D2
Lotissement Oued
Tel *(0535) 94 99 49*
W zalagh-palace.ma
One of the city's largest hotels, with suites, full amenities and excellent views. No credit cards.

MEDINA: Dar Seffarine
Historic Map D2
14 Derb Sbaa Louyate
Tel *(0671) 11 35 28*
W darseffarine.com
Restored by skilled local craftsmen, this medina palace shines as it did in the Middle Ages.

MEDINA: Dar El-Ghalia
Historic Map D2
15 Ross Rhi Medina
Tel *(0535) 63 41 67*
W riadelghalia.com
Little gem of a palace, with authentic Moroccan decor, comfortable suites and fine food.

MEDINA: Ryad Mabrouka
Historic Map D2
Talaa K'bira Derb el Miter
Tel *(0535) 63 63 45*
W ryadmabrouka.com
Historic property with columns, sculpted plasterwork, mosaic tiles and an inner courtyard.

MEDINA: Sofitel Palais Jamaï
Luxury Map D2
Bab El Guissa
Tel *(0535) 63 43 31*
W sofitel.com
Former 19th-century palace built in an authentic, extravagant Moorish style. Five-star amenities.

VILLE NOUVELLE: Dar Roumana
Value Map D2
30 Derb El Amer, Zkak Roumana
Tel *(0535) 74 16 37*
W darroumana.com
This spectacular Fasian *dar* offers mountain views. Attentive staff.

VILLE NOUVELLE: Hotel Jnan Palace
Luxury Map D2
Av Ahmed Chaouki
Tel *(0535) 65 22 30*
W sogatour.ma/jnanpalace.htm
Set in extensive parkland, with luxurious rooms and amenities.

VILLE NOUVELLE: Palais Sheherazade and Spa
Historic Map D2
23 Arsat Bennis Douh
Tel *(0535) 74 16 42*
W sheheraz.com
Intensely romantic and sumptuous palace with carved

cedar ceilings, ornate columns with mosaic detail and rooms still worthy of royalty.

Meknès and Volubilis

DK Choice

MEKNÈS: Riad Anne de Meknes
Value Map D2
4 Derb Sidi M'Barek Biab Bardaine
Tel *(0679) 15 63 38)*
W riadannedemeknes.com
With excellent service and a lovely decor for a hotel in the budget bracket, this charming little place is a lesson on how to run a good establishment in an area that does not present the traveller with a wide-range of choices. No credit cards.

MEKNÈS: Riad La Maison D'a Cote
Value Map D2
25 Derb Lakhouaja
Tel *(0535) 53 51 01*
W riadmaisondacote.com
Intimate guesthouse with serene rooms and a central courtyard shaded by mature orange trees and a banana palm. Cash only.

MEKNÈS: Riad D'Or
Historic Map D2
17 Rue Ain El Anboub and Lalla Aicha Adouia
Tel *(0641) 07 86 25*
W riaddor.com
Large townhouse with traditionally styled rooms, winding staircases, intricate carvings and great city views.

Extravagant interiors at the Sofitel Palais Jamaï in Medina

MEKNÈS: Riad Meknes
Historic Map D2
79 Ksar Chaacha-Dar Lakbira
Tel *(0535) 53 05 42*
W riadmeknes.com
Part of the palace of the 17th-century ruler Moulay Ismail. Rooms vary in size. Cash only.

MEKNÈS: Palais Didi
Luxury Map D2
7 Dar Lakbira
Tel *(0535) 55 85 90*
W palaisdidi.com
Rich, colourful decor, and terraces with fine views of the old imperial city. Get an air-conditioned room.

MOULAY IDRISS: Dar Ines
Value Map D2
57 Derb Amajout, Hay Tazga
Tel *(0667) 15 67 95*
W dar-ines.com
In a town with few good hotels, this small guesthouse is a bright and spotlessly clean option.

MOULAY IDRISS: Dar Zerhoune
Value Map D2
42 Derb Zouak, Tazga
Tel *(0535) 54 43 71*
W darzerhoune.com
Great guesthouse with views of the ruins. Provides electric blankets and duvets in winter.

VOLUBILIS: Volubilis Inn
Modern Map D2
Ruins of Volubilis
Tel *(0535) 54 44 05*
Old-fashioned hotel in a good location. Neat, tidy rooms with all the basic comforts.

Middle Atlas

BENI MELLAL: Hotel Chems Le Tazarkout
Value Map D3
Afourer-Beni Mellal
Tel *(0523) 44 01 01*
An ideal base from which to explore the area. Pleasant rooms.

BENI MELLAL: Hotel Ouzoud
Value Map D3
Rue de Marrakech km 3
Tel *(0523) 48 37 52*
A little nondescript from the outside, but has a traditional Moroccan interior. No credit cards.

IFRANE: Hotel des Perce Neige
Value Map D2
Hay Riad, Blvd Mohammed VI
Tel *(0535) 56 63 50/51*
W hotelperceneige.com
A no-frills, central hotel which is popular with locals and visitors.

Good budget option in an otherwise pricey town. Has an international restaurant on site.

DK Choice

IFRANE: Michlifen
Luxury   Map D2
Av Hassan II
Tel *(0535) 86 40 00*
w michlifenifrane.com
Unashamedly deluxe, this five-star hotel is fashioned on an ultra-glamorous ski-lodge of enormous proportions. The fairy-tale "chalet" offers only the best in terms of accommodation, service, fine dining and style. It also has its own heliport.

KHOURIBGA: Golden Tulip Farah Khouribga
Modern   Map C3
13 Blvd Moulay Youssef
Tel *(0523) 56 23 50*
w goldentulipfarahkhouribga.com
Modern, resort-style hotel with comfortable rooms and good amenities.

SEFROU: Dar Attamani
Value   Map D2
414 Bastna
Tel *(0645) 29 89 30*
w darattamani.com
Simple but prettily painted guesthouse with a charm of its own. No credit cards.

SEFROU: Dar Kamel Chaoui
Value   Map D2
60 Kaf Rhouni, Bhalil
Tel *(0678) 83 83 10*
w kamalchaoui.com
Chic, yet good-value guesthouse with clean, bright rooms and amazing views. Cash only.

Marrakech

GUÉLIZ: Bab Hotel
Modern   Map C3
Corner of Blvd Mansour Eddahbi & Rue Mohammed El Beqqal
Tel *(0524) 43 52 50*
w babhotelmarrakech.com
Ultramodern option. The sleek decor is predominantly white with intense splashes of colour.

HIVERNAGE: Four Seasons Resort
Luxury   Map C3
1 Blvd de la Menara
Tel *0524 359 200*
w fourseasons.com
Extravagant resort with sumptuous suites, private *riads*, extensive conference facilities and excellent children's activities.

Warm and inviting room at Michlifen in Ifrane

HIVERNAGE: Sofitel Marrakech
Luxury   Map C3
Av Harroun Errachid Tel
Tel *(0524) 42 56 00*
w accor-hotels.com
Antique furniture, fine crystal, lavish drapes and an almost decadent luxury that meets every need.

LA PALMERAIE: Amanjena
Luxury   Map C3
Rue de Ouarzazate km 12
Tel *(0524) 39 90 00*
w amanjena.com
Brad Pitt and Angelina Jolie have stayed here, perhaps lured by the opulence. It was also used as a set for part of the *Sex and the City* movie.

LA PALMERAIE: Dar Ayniwen
Luxury   Map C3
Tafrata, La Palmeraie
Tel *(0524) 32 96 84*
w dar-ayniwen.com
Richly decorated high-end guesthouse. Quiet, relaxing and a lovely place to unwind.

LA PALMERAIE: Dar JL
Luxury   Map C3
Arset Sdiguia Talaint
Tel *(0661) 22 34 62*
w darjl.com
Sumptuous estate in impressive grounds. Guests are given mobile phones with numbers for the front desk, butler, driver and maid.

LA PALMERAIE: Palais Namaskar
Luxury   Map C3
88–69 Rue de Bab Atlas
Tel *(0524) 29 98 00*
w palaisnamaskar.com
Much-fêted five-star offering lavish suites, huge ornamental gardens, hot-air ballooning and access to the hotel's private jet.

MEDINA: Hotel Tresor
Value   Map C3
77 Sidi Boulokat Riad Zitoun Kdim
Tel *(0524) 37 51 13*
w hotel-du-tresor.com
Tiny but memorable rooms decorated with items from the local collector's bazaar. Cash only.

MEDINA: Riad 72
Historic   Map C3
72 Arset Awsel, Bab Doukkala
Tel *(0524) 38 76 29*
w riad72.com
Stylish Italian-owned *riad* with a black-and-white colour scheme and sleek furniture.

MEDINA: La Maison Arabe
Luxury   Map C3
1 Derb Assehbe
Tel *(0524) 38 70 10*
w lamaisonarabe.com
Characterful and luxurious rooms and suites in an establishment that began as a restaurant in the 1940s.

DK Choice

MEDINA: La Mamounia
Luxury   Map C3
Avenue Bab Jdid
Tei *(0524) 38 86 00*
w mamounia.com
Surrounded by ancient gardens and the city's ramparts, this world-famous hotel from the 1920s lies within walking distance of the major tourist attractions. Features splended Art Deco and Moorish decor and four top-class restaurants.

MEDINA: Le Meridian N'Fis
Luxury   Map C3
Av Mohammed VI
Tel *(0524) 33 94 00*
w lemeridiennfis.com
Spectacularly situated amid palm trees and sprawling Andalusian-style gardens.

For more information on types of hotels *see page 305*

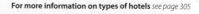

Understated elegance at the La Sultana in Medina

MEDINA: La Sultana (Dh)(Dh)(Dh)
Luxury   Map C3
403 Rue de la Kasbah
Tel *(0524) 38 80 08*
W lasultanamarrakech.com
Close to the Royal Palaces. Hard-to-beat elegance, with a lavish spa and opulent fittings.

MEDINA: Riad Kaiss (Dh)(Dh)(Dh)
Luxury   Map C3
65 Derb Jdid Zitoune Kedim
Tel *(0524) 44 01 41*
W sanssoucicollection.com
Period *riad* that is tastefully decorated with antiques. Very knowledgable and helpful owner.

**MEDINA: The Royal
Mansour** (Dh)(Dh)(Dh)
Luxury   Map C3
Rue Abou Abbas El Sebti
Tel *(0529) 80 80 80*
W royalmansour.com
Breathtaking *riads*, complete with private rooftop swimming pools and individual butlers.

**MEDINA: Villa des
Orangers** (Dh)(Dh)(Dh)
Luxury   Map C3
6 Rue Sidi Mimoun
Tel *(0524) 38 46 38*
W villadesorangers.com
Beautifully styled hotel with a rooftop pool, Koutoubia views, lounges and gorgeous spa.

High Atlas

ASNI: Kasbah Tamadot (Dh)(Dh)(Dh)
Luxury   Map C4
Post Office Box 67
Tel *0208 600 0430 (UK)*
W kasbahtamadot.virgin.com
Richard Branson's destination hotel offers fine rooms and deluxe Berber tents. Children allowed only during UK school holidays.

IMLIL: Kasbah Toubkal (Dh)(Dh)
Modern   Map C4
Imlil.
Tel *(0524) 48 56 11*
W kasbahdutoubkal.com
Simple place that champions local trekking trade and supports the surrounding community. Superlative views.

**OUIRGANE: Auberge de
Sanglier Qui Fume** (Dh)
Value   Map C4
Km 61, 5 Route Taroudant-Ouirgane par
Tel *(0524) 48 57 07*
W ausanglierquifume.com
This rustic but charming mountain lodge once housed the Foreign Legionnaires. Cash only.

**OUIRGANE: Domaine
Malika** (Dh)
Modern   Map C4
Douar Marigha Commune de Ouirgane, Route d'Amizmiz, par Asni
Tel *(0661) 49 35 41*
W domaine-malika.com
Hugely successful establishment with French owners who have paid meticulous attention to the quirky, modern interiors.

**OUKAÏMEDEN: Club Alpin
Francais** (Dh)
Historic   Map C4
Club Alpin Francais
Tel *(0524) 31 90 36*
W ffcam.fr
Historic place, highly valued by regulars and newcomers to the surrounding ski and trekking slopes. No credit cards.

DK Choice

**OURIKA VALLEY:
Bab Ouirka** (Dh)(Dh)(Dh)
Luxury   Map C4
Tniine Ourika
Tel *(0661) 63 42 34*
W kasbahbabourika.com
Clinging to a crag above a national park, this lofty *kasbah* was built using traditional Berber building techniques. All rooms have stunning views of the Atlas Mountains. The extensive organic vegetable gardens provide fresh produce for the restaurant's seasonally changing menu. The hotel also actively promotes eco-tourism.

**OUZOUD FALLS: Riad Cascades
D'Ouzoud** (Dh)
Value   Map C3
Chemin des Moulin, Azilal
Tel *(0523) 42 91 73*
W ouzoud.com
Characterful place in a stunning setting, by far the best in town. Run by a lovely French owner.

TISSELDAY: Irocha (Dh)(Dh)
Modern   Map C4
Village de Tisselday, Ouarzazate
Tel *(0667) 73 70 02*
W irocha.com
Pleasing rooms with lots of charm. The roof terrace is perfect for stargazing.

Ouarzazate & the Southern Oases

**AÏT BENHADDOU: Hotel
Auberge Etoile Filante D'Or** (Dh)
Value   Map C4
Centre of Aït Benhaddou
Tel *(0524) 89 03 22*
W etoilefilantedor.com
Compact structure overlooking the *ksar*, creatively designed to blend with its surroundings.

**ERFOUD: Kasbah Hotel
Chergui** (Dh)
Value   Map E4
Erfoud to Errachidia Rd km 5
Tel *(0535) 57 85 04*
W hotelchergui.com
Out in the desert, with impressive views and lots of facilities. Large enough to cater for groups.

DK Choice

**ERFOUD: Xaluca
Bivouac** (Dh)(Dh)
Luxury   Map E4
Rd Arfoud to Errachidia km 5
Tel *(0535) 57 84 50*
W xaluca.com
Tented desert hotel offering an unforgettable experience, with nomad's tents, traditional feasts, camel treks and endless dunes. Xaluca Bivouac is the perfect choice for a safe, ecologically sound and exciting way to experience a night in the desert. Also offers 4WD and dromedary excursions.

ERFOUD: Hotel Xaluca (Dh)(Dh)(Dh)
Luxury   Map E4
205 Rue d'Errachidia km 5
Tel *(0535) 57 84 50*
W xaluca.com
Experience the desert in style, with all amenities and entertainment facilities. Excellent option for large groups.

OUARZAZATE: Dar Rita (Dh)
Value   Map C4
Rue de la Mosquée 39, Tassoumaat
Tel *(0654) 16 47 26*
W darrita.com
Simple but highly attractive *riad*-style guesthouse with an impressive eco-friendly stance. Great value for money.

OUARZAZATE: Le Berbere Palace
Luxury   Map C4
Quartier Mansour Eddahbi
Tel *(0524) 88 31 05*
W leberberepalace.com
One of the top choices in the region, with deluxe individual bungalows set in gardens.

OUARZAZATE: Le Temple Des Arts
Luxury   Map C4
173 and 174, Hay Al Wahda
Tel *(0524) 88 88 31*
W templedesarts-ouarzazate.com
Shimmering with gold and movie props, this excellent hotel appeals to guests of all ages.

ZAGORA: Dar Nekhla
Value   Map D4
Palmeraie d'Amezrou
Tel *(0524) 84 64 72*
W riadzagora.fr
Large, clean rooms and a lovely oasis garden in which to listen to the birds. Cash only.

ZAGORA: Villa Zagora
Value   Map D4
Piste du Djebel de Zagora
Tel *(0524) 84 60 93*
W mavillaausahara.com
Traditional house and hospitality; choose a private room or a bed in the Berber tent. Friendly service.

ZAGORA: Sahara Safari Camp
Luxury   Map D4
N9 Tagounite, SE of Zagora
Tel *0044 (020 7193 2461 (UK)*
W specialistmorocco.com
Pop-up-style camp with luxurious trappings. Stargazing, camel treks and 4WD excursions. Run by an experienced UK-based firm.

Southern Morocco & Western Sahara

AGADIR: Atlantic Hotel
Modern   Map B4
Av Hassan II
Tel *(0528) 84 36 61*
W atlantichotelagadir.com
A modern and lavishly decorated four-star with comfortable rooms and a great terrace to sit out on.

AGADIR: Iti Agadir Beach Club
Value   Map B4
Rue de Oued Souss
Tel *(0528) 84 43 43*
W Iti.de
One of best and most popular spots in Agadir's tourist area.Family-friendly rooms, with balconies that offer ocean views.

AGADIR: Hotel Beach Albatross
Modern   Map B4
Blvd Mohammed V
Tel *(0528) 84 32 32*
W pickalbatros.com
One of the better budget options in Agadir. Bright and modern with good standards of service.

DK Choice

AGADIR: Riad Villa Blanche
Luxury   Map B4
Baie des Palmiers, N°50 Cité Founty, Sonaba
Tel *(0528) 21 13 13*
W riadvillablanche.com
Magnificent yet understated elegance, far removed from the hustle and bustle of Agadir. Has a wide range of tastefully decorated rooms that offer panoramic ocean views. The many facilities include indoor and outdoor pools, a hammam, a spa and a library.

AGADIR: Sofitel Royal Bay Resort
Luxury   Map B4
Cité Founty Baie des Palmiers
Tel *(0528) 84 92 00*
W sofitel.com
Sizable and luxurious five-star that combines the traditional Moroccan *kasbah* style with contemporary amenities.

GUELMIM: Fort Bou-Jerif
Historic   Map A5
Fort Bou-Jerif, Pierre Gerbens
Tel *(0672) 13 00 17*
W fortboujerif.com
A quirky 1930s desert fort with a restaurant and bar. Organises excellent excursions. Cash only.

SIDI IFNI: Hotel Bellevue
Value   Map A5
Pl Hassan II
Tel *(0528) 87 52 42*
Spectacular clifftop location with outstanding ocean views.

Comfortably fitted rooms and an attractive common terrace. No credit cards.

TAROUNDANNT: Hotel Zitoune
Modern   Map B4
Boutarial El Berrania, 83000
Tel *(0528) 55 11 41*
W darzitoune.com
The Swiss owners of "The House of Olives" built it as an eco-hotel, restaurant and retreat.

TAROUNDANNT: Hotel La Gazelle D'Or
Luxury   Map B4
Centre of Taroudannt
Tel *(0528) 85 20 39*
W gazelledor.com
Legendary establishment that is one of the region's most luxurious hotels and has an impressive list of former guests.

TATA: Dar Infiane
Historic   Map C5
Maison d'Hôtes Dar Infiane, Douar Indfiane
Tel *(0524) 43 72 92*
W darinfiane.com
Stay in this marvellous 16th-century guesthouse, featuring a foot-and-a-half-thick walls, rich carpets, painted woodwork and mesmerizing views.

TIZNIT: Bab El Maader
Value   Map B5
132, Rue El Haj Ali
Tel *(0673) 90 73 14*
W bab-el-maader.com
Modest guesthouse, reflecting this simple area. Colourful, clean and comfortable rooms, some with shared bathrooms.

TIZNIT: Riad Janoub
Value   Map B5
93 Rue de la Grande Mosquée
Tel *(0528) 60 27 26*
W riadjanoub.com
Simple, spacious and serene *riad* nestled in the medina. The management can help organize tours of the surrounding area.

The Sofitel Royal Bay Resort in Agadir

For more information on types of hotels *see page 305*

WHERE TO EAT AND DRINK

Standing as it does on the crossroads of geography and culture, Morocco offers much in terms of international and regional cuisine. Seasonal foods and a myriad of spices make its food among the best in the world. That said, Moroccans prefer to eat traditional dishes at home with the family, opting for international dishes when they dine out. Luckily for travellers, the growth of food tourism, ecological concerns relating to importation and a greater interest in the diversification of culture, mean that even more mid- to high-class establishments are offering Moroccan dishes on their menus.

Spectacular view from the rooftop restaurant at Nord-Pinus *(see p324)*, Tangier

Cultural Aspects

Given the pleasantly warm climate in Morocco, many restaurants prefer to serve their customers outdoors, setting out tables in a quiet and pleasantly shaded courtyard, in the corner of a garden or even on the pavement outside the restaurant.

As a general rule, do sample what is traditional to each region (fish by the coast, for example, or Spanish-influenced dishes towards Tangier). By seeking out where some of the locals are eating (even if it is a street stall), visitors are guaranteed a delicious meal.

A word of warning to the hungry: if possible, check your facts before dining. Life in Morocco is lived by the day, which means that any information you might have in advance may not pan out as expected. Opening hours, exact menus, and even addresses, may suddenly change – often for no apparent reason. Wherever possible, telephone a restaurant before heading there, or if language is an issue, get your hotel to do this for you. Discuss their opening hours and address, planned entertainment (if any) and access. If it is in a medina, they may need to send someone to collect you or explain their location.

Moroccan Specialities

A traditional Moroccan meal begins with a large number of starters, consisting of soup, salad, or vegetables flavoured with different kinds of spices. Then follows the main course, often couscous or *tajine*.

A kind of stew made with fish, chicken, beef or lamb, and including prunes or almonds, *tajine* can be found in many varieties, which differ according to the region. All, however, are prepared and served in a terracotta dish with a conical lid; this cooking vessel is called a *tajine*, hence the dish's name.

Moroccan desserts, especially milk *pastilla*, are mouth-watering. Meals are usually accompanied by mint tea, although more and more restaurants now offer wine.

Opening Hours and Reservations

Heavily influenced by the French, Moroccan restaurants generally open for a certain period at lunch, close in the afternoon, and re-open in the evening. Lunch is generally served between noon and 3pm, and supper generally between 7pm and 10pm. Consequently, it might be difficult to dine out outside these times.

During the fasting month of Ramadan *(see p45)*, or other religious festivals, opening times and menus vary. Small eateries, for example, will not open for lunch during Ramadan, and few restaurants, whatever their size, will serve alcohol during major religious periods.

In very fashionable restaurants, particularly those in the centre of the largest towns and cities, it is advisable

Beautiful dining interiors of Le Mirage *(see p324)* in Cap Spartel

The exquisite Mazagan Beach Resort *(see p308)* in El-Jadida

for large parties to reserve ahead, especially on Thursdays, Fridays and Saturday evenings.

Reservation is absolutely essential for the tables d'hôte in Marrakech and Fès. In these places, it is often necessary to reserve several days in advance, since space can be limited, as can the number of sittings each evening.

Prices and Tipping

Prices vary widely according to a restaurant's quality. They may range from 50 dirhams for a basic meal to about 300 dirhams for a meal with wine in a classic establishment, and between 400 and 600 dirhams in a high-class restaurant. Prices are higher in large towns and cities and in places that attract lots of foreign visitors, such as Casablanca, Marrakech and Agadir. Prices given on menus usually include service and tax.

Tipping is a widely accepted custom in Morocco. It is usual to give 5 to 10 per cent of the bill. The tip should be in cash, and should be left on the table when leaving the restaurant. Do not add it to the total when making a payment by cheque or bankers' card because the waiters will not receive it.

Alcoholic Drinks

Morocco is a Muslim country where stringent laws apply to the sale of alcohol. However, most restaurants from a certain level upwards have a license to serve alcohol, as do Moroccan restaurants with a largely Western clientele.

Unlicensed restaurants may sometimes serve wine discreetly. Visitors should not, however, insist on being served alcohol in an unlicensed restaurant since it may be against the rules of the management.

Dress

Moroccans usually dress quite smartly when they go out to eat. Restaurants rarely insist on a particular type of dress. It is best, however, to avoid too relaxed a style of dress, and revealing clothes, such as shorts, plunging neck-lines and beachwear, are likely to be considered offensive.

Children

Children are universally adored by Moroccans, who tend to take them everywhere. Even the fanciest restaurants will gladly serve children. However, mid-range to high-end hotels can usually arrange a babysitter for those trying to plan a quiet night out.

Street Stalls

Stalls selling cheap food are seen everywhere in Morocco. Typical dishes are soup, skewered meat or fish and sandwiches. Eat where the locals are eating to sample some of the freshest, most delicious food Morocco has to offer.

At dusk, Place Jemaa el-Fna in Marrakech *(see p238)* turns into a huge open-air restaurant. In coastal towns and villages, usually on the quays of harbours where fishing boats come in, trestle tables serving freshly cooked seafood are often set up.

Recommended Restaurants

The restaurants featured in this guide have been selected across a wide price range for their value, good food, location and atmosphere. From authentic, no-frills eateries to pricier, more sophisticated options, these restaurants run the gamut across all price levels and cuisine types.

For the best of the best, look out for the restaurants in each region or major town highlighted as the 'DK Choice'. In the mountains, the choice will likely be a restaurant with stunning views by the sea, it could be one that consistently supplies the freshest fish, or in a town, it might be the fanciest place to dine. Wherever possible, we have tried to keep these choices varied in terms of price and cuisine.

Traditional dining room in a restaurant in Agadir

The Flavours of Morocco

From the indigenous, rural Berber people come the basics of Moroccan cuisine, such as couscous, but Moroccan food owes much to influences from neighbouring lands. In the 1600s the Arabs introduced bread, pulses and spices, notably chickpeas (garbanzos), cinnamon, ginger, saffron and turmeric, from their empire in the East. In the 11th century Bedouin tribes brought dates and milk from their wandering flocks. The Arabs returned from Andalusia with produce such as olives and lemons, and, later, tomatoes and peppers from the Americas.

Dried couscous

Meat and other products on sale at a market food stall in Morocco

Meat

Lamb is the cornerstone of Moroccan cookery, and is found in the form of grills, *merguez* (thin, spicy red sausages) and brochettes (skewers); in *tagines* or a couscous; and roasted whole on a spit with aromatics such as the traditional *m'choui*. You

will also find beef on the menu, usually served as kebabs, as well as rabbit, served as a couscous or *tagine*. Chicken and turkey are also readily available. Pigeon is more rarely on the menu these days, but is still a feature of *b'stilla*. This extravagant pie, a speciality of Fès, is made with tissue-thin *warkha* pastry. Offal, such as brains, heart, liver and tripe, are also popular.

Fish & Seafood

Morocco has long coasts on the Atlantic and the Mediterranean, which provide a wide variety of seafood. Fish such as bream and bass are typically marinated in a garlicky, spicy mixture called *chermoula*, and are usually cooked whole. They may also be served stuffed, with an almond crust, as steaks or brochettes, or as fishcakes, known as *boulettes*, with a

Ginger   Saffron   Ras el hanout   Coriander seeds   Cloves   Cinnamon   Dried rose pet   Cumin

Some of the many spices used in traditional Moroccan dishes

Moroccan Dishes and Specialities

A restaurant meal in Morocco will typically start with a full-flavoured soup, such as *harira*, a comforting soup of diced lamb, lentils and chickpeas with tomato, onion, coriander and parsley, or a selection of vibrant salads. A *tagine* is a common main course, served with flat bread (*matlouh*). The meat and vegetables are flavoured with saffron, garlic, coriander and cumin. Garnishes include olives, eggs, mint and preserved lemons. Another main course is couscous. Made with vegetables, chicken, lamb, *merguez*, rabbit, or even fish, it is usually served with a hot sauce made from *harissa* and tomato purée.

Preserved lemons and mint

Harira, a meal-like soup, is a dish traditionally served at sunset during Ramadan, in order to break the fast.

Food stall at dusk in the Place Jemaa el-Fna in Marrakech

spicy tomato sauce. Prawns, squid, oysters and mussels are also available and good quality.

Vegetables

Morocco has many inventive and refreshing salad dishes. Often served as a starter, they include *mezgaldi*, which combines onions with saffron, ginger, cinnamon, sugar and celery. Aubergines (eggplants) are ubiquitous, served as a salad, fried or stuffed. Combinations of tomatoes, green peppers, hot red or sweet red peppers and red onions, all add colour and flavour to the table. Olives and their oil are abundant, and nutty argan oil is widely used. (Goats adore the outer pulp of the nut, and can be seen "grazing" in the branches of argan trees.)

Fruit

Most Moroccan meals end with a dish of fruit, often a simple sliced-orange salad, sprinkled with cinnamon and orange-flower water, and sometimes chopped dates and almonds. Other common fruits include

Array of cakes and pastries in a patisserie in Fès

peaches, figs, melons, bananas, plums, pomegranates and all types of citrus fruits. Lemons, preserved in brine, add piquancy to many dishes.

Spices & Flavourings

Key Moroccan spices include aniseed, black pepper, cayenne, cardamom, cinnamon, coriander, cumin, ginger, paprika, parsley, saffron and turmeric. Three spice blends are important: *chermoula*, for marinades; *harissa*, a hot red pepper condiment; and *ras el hanout* ("top of the shop"), a blend of over 20 spices, used in *tagines*.

MOROCCAN PASTRIES

Briouats Triangular *warkha* pastries filled with almond and cinnamon paste.

Ghoriba Macaroons made with sugar, almonds, lemon zest, vanilla and cinnamon.

Kaab el ghzal Pastry crescents filled with sweet almond paste, dipped in orange-flower water and icing sugar.

M'hanncha "Coiled serpent" cake of pastry stuffed with almonds and decorated with icing sugar and cinnamon.

Sfenj Deep-fried doughnuts.

Shebbakia Deep-fried pastry ribbons, dipped in hot honey and coated in sesame seeds.

B'stilla is a rich pie of pigeon, eggs, almonds and raisins, flavoured with lemon, sugar, saffron and cinnamon.

Tagine, a slow-cooked stew, is named for the earthenware dish with a conical lid in which it is cooked.

Couscous is the Moroccan national dish – a semolina-based grain served with an accompanying stew.

What to Drink in Morocco

Green mint tea is the national drink in Morocco. It is served several times a day at home, in the office, in shops and on café terraces. Moroccans are also very fond of coffee, which is usually served with milk but may sometimes be flavoured with cinnamon, orange-flower water or a few grains of pepper. Freshly squeezed orange juice is delicious, as are all fruit juices – cherry, grape and pomegranate being the most widely available choices. Although the Koran forbids the consumption of alcohol, fairly good-quality wines are produced in Morocco, and these can be bought in certain shops.

The tea ceremony, performed in front of guests

Tea

Known for 3,000 years in China, green tea, with long fine leaves, reached Morocco in 1854. It was introduced by the British; and immediately became popular in every Moroccan home. All over Morocco, from the sophisticated town house to the simple nomad's tent, green mint tea has become the national drink. This thirst-quenching drink, which is made with varying amounts of sugar and mint, is a symbol of hospitality, and it is considered very ill-mannered to refuse it.

Glass of mint tea

The tea ceremony is almost always performed in front of guests and according to immutable rules. Mint tea is always served in small, slender glasses decorated with a gold or coloured filigree pattern. The tea leaves are rinsed in the scalded teapot so as to remove their excessive bitterness. Whole mint leaves, complete with stems, are then added, together with large lumps of sugar, which prevent the leaves from rising to the surface. After being left for a few minutes to infuse, a little tea is poured into a glass and returned to the pot. This is repeated several times. The host finally tastes the tea, which will not be served to guests until it is deemed to be perfect.

Traditionally served mint tea

Coffee

Although it is less widely drunk than tea, Moroccans are also fond of coffee, which they like to drink very strong. It is accceptable to ask for a little boiling water with which to dilute it. Unless you request otherwise, your coffee will automatically be served with milk. A black coffee is a *qahwa kahla*; a *noss noss* is half coffee and half milk; and *café cassé* consists of more coffee than milk.

Coffee with milk (*noss noss*)

Black coffee (*qahwa kahla*)

Cold Drinks

Although lemonade and cola are sold on every street corner, freshly squeezed orange juice is the real Moroccan speciality. It is absolutely delicious, so long as it is served undiluted. The sweet, juicy and famously flavoursome Moroccan oranges can be seen laid out for sale everywhere, piled up in glossy pyramids on barrows and on market stalls. On Place Jemaa el-Fna in Marrakech (see p238), they are almost a sideshow in themselves. Almond milk, banana milk, apple juice and pomegranate juice are also popular drinks.

Orange juice

Almond milk

Beer and Spirits

All kinds of imported alcoholic drinks can be purchased in supermarkets. Flag Spéciale is a light ale brewed in Tangier and Casablanca. Stork is brewed in Casablanca. *Mahia* is a Moroccan fig distillation, 40 per cent proof. The sale of wine and other alcohol is forbidden to Muslims during Ramadan and after 7:30pm.

Casablanca beer

Flag Spéciale, from Tangier

Mineral Water

Although the tap water in towns is safe to drink, it tastes strongly of chlorine. Mineral water – such as Sidi Ali and Sidi Harazem, which are still, and Oulmès and San Pellegrino, which are sparkling – is much more palatable.

Sidi Ali mineral water

Sidi Harazem mineral water

Oulmès mineral water

Moroccan Wines

Wine has been produced in Morocco since Roman times, and local wine production was encouraged during the Protectorate. The country has three major wine-producing areas: around Oujda, in the northeast, in the Fès and Meknès area, and in the west, between Rabat and Casablanca.

The most popular wines include red and white Médaillon, red, white and rosé Siroua, and the higher-quality wines produced by the winemakers Celliers de Meknès: Merlot and Cabernet Sauvignon; Sémillant, a fruity, dry white wine, and two rosé wines – Gris de Guerrouane and Gris de Boulaouane. Also produced are Aït Soual, Vieux-Papes, Oustalet, Valpierre, Chaud-Soleil and Spécial Coquillages, which is best drunk with fish and seafood. Note that the

Vineyard near Boulaouane

quality of Moroccan wines can differ widely from year to year and sometimes even from bottle to bottle.

Red Amazir   Red Cabernet   Red Siroua   Red Guerrouâne   Red Oustalet   Rosé Guerrouane   Rosé Cabernet

Where to Eat and Drink

Rabat

AGDAL: Chez Paul
French **Map** C2
82 Av des Nations Unies
Tel *(0537) 67 20 00*
An excellent, chic eatery, great
for light lunches, tea and cake
as well as people-watching. The
home-made macaroons are
particularly good.

AGDAL: The Puzzle
Mediterranean **Map** C2
79 Av Ibn Sina Agdal
Tel *(0537) 67 00 30*
Bright and breezy little
restaurant with live music every
day. Mediterranean cuisine such
as chicken, kebabs, roast meats,
fish and stuffed vegetables, as
well as a good selection of fruit.

AGDAL: L'Entrecote
French **Map** C2
74 Charia Al-Amir-Fal-Ould-Oumeir
Tel *(0537) 67 11 08*
Beautifully presented; specializing
in classic French meat and
fish dishes in rich sauces.
Attracts a business clientele
as well as travellers.

CITY CENTRE: La Brasserie
French **Map** C2
*Hôtel Le Diwan Rabat, Place de
l'Unité Africaine*
Tel *(0537) 26 27 27*
A gourmet brasserie-style place,
with a good and extensive
French menu. Plush interiors
and intimate seating.

CITY CENTRE: Latium
Italian **Map** C2
16 Av Annakhil, Hay Riad
Tel *(0537) 71 77 16*
Much-frequented and family-
friendly spot that offers excellent
home-made pastas, salads and
wood-fired pizzas.

CITY CENTRE: Matsuri
Japanese **Map** C2
155 Av Mohamed VI, Rue des Zaer
Tel *(0537) 75 75 72*
Generally considered to be the
best conveyor-belt sushi place
in town, with a good choice of
wines, fresh fish and expert
waiting staff.

DK Choice

**CITY CENTRE: Le Grand
Comptoir**
French **Map** C2
279 Av Mohammed V
Tel *(0537) 20 15 14*
With its candelabras, sparkling
gilt mirrors and live piano music
in the background, Le Grand
Comptoir captures the essence
of a 1930s Parisian brasserie.
The food is classic French, with
a menu that features steaks,
grilled lobster and *crêpes
suzette* (pancakes). The bar
stays open to 1am and has live
music every Thursday, Friday
and Saturday.

CITY CENTRE: Le Ziryab
Fine Dining **Map** C2
Off Rue des Consuls
Tel *(0537) 73 36 36*
A heavy door and dimly
lit entrance hall lead to a lavish
dining area with elegant tables
and Moroccan fine dining at
its best. Serves delicious
home-made bread. Open for
dinner only.

**KASBAH DES OUDAIA:
Restaurant de la Plage**
Moroccan **Map** C2
Kasbah des Oudaïa Plage
Tel *(0537) 20 29 28*
Small, characterful eatery with
a sizeable following, drawn by
the great location on the beach
and its seafood specialities.

Price Guide
Prices are based on a three-course meal
for one, including tax and service (but
without wine).

up to 150 dirhams
150 to 450 dirhams
over 450 dirhams

MEDINA: La Koutoubia
Traditional **Map** C2
10 Pierre Parent
Tel *(0537) 70 10 75*
Excellent no-nonsense restaurant
with all the classics on the menu.
Lots of tilework and painted
panels. Good wine list.

**MEDINA: Cosmopolitan
Restaurant**
French **Map** C2
Av Ibn Toumert
Tel *(0537) 20 00 28*
Refreshingly uncluttered both in
menu and decor, this renovated
Art Deco villa offers seasonal
French dishes, with an emphasis
on the southwest.

MEDINA: Dinarjat
Traditional **Map** C2
6 Rue Belgnaoui
Tel *(0537) 70 42 39*
Housed in a former 17th-century
mansion-style residence, Dinarjat
serves superlative Moroccan
cuisine. Particularly known for
its *tajines* (rich stews).

SOUISSI: Relais de Paris
French **Map** C2
*173 Av Mohammed VI, ex John
Kennedy*
Tel *(0537) 65 56 56*
Highly trustworthy option for
good French bistro dishes such
as *magret de canard* and *tarte
tatin* with vanilla ice cream.
Good wine list and extensive
suggestions of the day.

**SOUISSI: La Villa
Mandarine**
International **Map** C2
19 Rue Ouled Bousbaa
Tel *(0537) 75 20 77* **Closed** *Sun*
Offers a haven of peace away
from the bustling city. Traditional
Moroccan decor and a varied
menu of international as well
as Moroccan dishes.

VILLE NOUVELLE: Zerda
Moroccan/Jewish **Map** C2
7 Rue Patrice Lumumba
Tel *(0537) 73 09 12*
The family-run Zerda generally
offers live music well into the
evening. There are extremely
good Moroccan and Jewish
specialities on the menu.

Wine bottles stocked at the bar at Le Grand Comptoir

Gently lit interiors at La Brasserie Bavaroise

VILLE NOUVELLE:
Le Goeland (Dh)(Dh)(Dh)
French Map C2
9 Rue Moulay Ali-Cherif
Tel *(0537) 76 88 85*
The influences here remain
largely French, with fresh fish and
seafood playing an important
role. Diners can enjoy their meals
in the pretty open-air courtyard.

Northern Atlantic Coast

ASILAH: Restaurant Al Alba (Dh)
Italian Map D1
Lot Nakhil, 35 Av Khalid Ibn Oualid
Tel *(0539) 41 69 23*
Pleasing, authentic, small
restaurant with a varied menu
of pastas, meats and – given the
location – very good seafood.

ASILAH: Casa Garcia (Dh)(Dh)
Spanish/Moroccan Map D1
51 Rue Moulay Hassan ben el-Mehdi
Tel *(0539) 41 74 65*
Noteworthy local institution
specializing in fish. Good grilled
options, as well as the more
exotic octopus, eels and barnacles.
Try the house *paella* and Spanish
shrimp. Book ahead.

ASILAH: La Perle (Dh)(Dh)
French Map D1
Rue Allal Ben Abd Allah
Tel *(0539) 41 87 58*
Hidden French restaurant
owned by a Moroccan chef and
his Irish wife. Surprisingly high
standards for such a tucked-away
location and a menu that offers a
welcome alternative to fried fish
and *paella*.

KENITRA: Restaurant Merzouga (Dh)
Traditional Map C2
1ére Rue front de mer, Nº84 Mehdia Plage
Tel *(0537) 38 89 71*
Efficient service and a no-
nonsense approach await

diners at this restaurant and café
favoured by locals. Try one of the
excellent fried-fish dishes.

DK Choice

LARACHE: Estrella del Mar (Dh)(Dh)
Mediterranean Map D1
68 Av Mohammed Zerktouni
Tel *(0539) 91 22 43*
Attractive Andalusian and
Arabian-styled, Estrella del Mar
is one of the best options in
town for grills, steaks and fish
dishes. The ground floor dining
room is more casual than the
smarter one upstairs.

Casablanca

AIN DIAB: La Scuderia da Flavio (Dh)(Dh)(Dh)
Italian Map C2
Av de la Cote d'Emeraude
Tel *(0522) 79 75 79*
Enjoy traditional Italian cuisine in
sleek, contemporary surrounds.
Only the freshest ingredients and
finest cured meats find their way
into the dishes served here.

CITY CENTRE: Au Petit Poucet (Dh)
Moroccan/French Map C2
86 Blvd Mohammed V
Tel *(0522) 27 54 20*
A 1920s landmark eatery with
pretentions of grandeur;
nevertheless, it does serve some
exceptionally good meals almost
round the clock.

CITY CENTRE: Chez Paul (Dh)
French Map C2
Villa Zevaco, Corner Blvd d'Anfa et Blvd Moulay Rachid
Tel *(0522) 36 60 00*
The former villa of Édith Piaf, this
lovely café and restaurant is the
place to be seen. Serves delicious
light meals, afternoon tea and ice
cream. Alcohol is served, except
on religious holidays. Has Wi-Fi.

CITY CENTRE: L'Etoile Centrale (Dh)
Traditional Map C2
107 Rue Allal ben Abdellah
Tel *(0522) 01 86 25*
Authentic home cooking done
to perfection. One of the best
spots to savour true Moroccan
food, such as the flavoursome
tajines and fabulous couscous
royale. No credit cards.

CITY CENTRE: La Bodéga de Casablanca (Dh)
Spanish Map C2
129 Rue Allal Ben Abdellah
Tel *(0522) 54 18 42*
Lively place that serves
delicious tapas, cocktails and
wine. The dance floor downstairs
hosts regular themed events,
including salsa, reggae, rock
and samba.

CITY CENTRE: The Irish Pub (Dh)
Irish Map C2
Av Hassan Souktani, Quartier Gauthier
Tel *(0522) 20 02 10*
A perfect match for those
pining for a Guinness, a trustworthy hamburger or wanting
to see a clothed, stuffed fox
and a dining table stuck to a
ceiling. Frequent live music
and rugby coverage.

CITY CENTRE: Al-Mounia (Dh)(Dh)
Moroccan Map C2
95 Rue du Prince Moulay Abdellah
Tel *(0522) 22 26 69*
With a beautifully planted
garden and an outdoor courtyard area, Al-Mounia is a great
option for alfresco dining, though
there is indoor seating as well.
The menu includes good
vegetarian specialities.

CITY CENTRE: La Brasserie Bavaroise (Dh)(Dh)
French Map C2
129 Rue Allal Ben Abdellah
Tel *(0522) 31 17 60*
Realistically styled, centrally
located French bistro, with daily
specials as well as an extensive
general menu. Particularly
favoured for its excellent meat
dishes and desserts.

CITY CENTRE: Taverne du Dauphin (Dh)(Dh)
Seafood Map C2
115 Blvd Houphouët Boigny
Tel *(0522) 22 12 00*
Easily one of the very best,
yet least pretentious, fish
restaurants in the city. It is
always bustling and for good
reason. All the dishes are
excellent but especially
notable is the baby squid.

For more information on types of restaurants *see page 315*

Intimate dining at the well-reviewed L'Atelier Oriental

CITY CENTRE: L'Atelier Oriental
Middle Eastern   **Map** C2
Sofitel Casablanca Tour Blanche, Rue Sidi Belyout
Tel *(0522) 45 62 00*
A welcome addition to the city's top destinations, this predictably dazzling restaurant in the Sofitel serves Asian, Persian and Arabian cuisine. Open for dinner only.

CITY CENTRE: La Maison du Gourmet
French   **Map** C2
159 Rue Taha Hussein
Tel *(0522) 48 48 46*
This discreet and elegant fine-dining French restaurant is a gastronomic delight and is easily one of the business capital's top venues. Try the excellent tasting menu.

CITY CENTRE: La Table du Retro
French   **Map** C2
22 Rue Abou Al Mahassine Royani
Tel *(0522) 94 05 55*
Known as the place where wealthier locals head to celebrate. Enjoy a range of French classics in particularly stylish surrounding.

CORNICHE: Boga Boga
Spanish   **Map** C2
7 Bis Rue La Tempete, off the Corniche
Tel *(0522) 79 79 60*
Unassuming restaurant that is a favourite with expats. Service may not always be the most attentive, but the food is of a consistently good standard, and the menu likely to appeal to even the choosiest customer.

CORNICHE: Morocco Mall Food Stalls
International   **Map** C2
Blvd de Biarritz
Tel *(0801) 00 12 30*
Over 40 eateries are scattered about this mammoth place,

ranging from Lebanese to sushi. No alcohol allowed, as the mall has a mosque on the upper floor. Instead, juice bars, café au lait and frozen yogurts abound.

CORNICHE: Morocco Mall Snail Sellers
Street Food   **Map** C2
Corner of Rue de Sidi Abderahmann, and Blvd de Barritz
Adventurous travellers will not want to miss sampling the piping hot snail soup from a cart outside Morocco Mall. At busy times, there can be over 50 carts lining the street.

CORNICHE: A Ma Bretagne
French   **Map** C2
Beside Morocco Mall, Blvd de la Corniche
Tel *(0522) 36 21 12*   **Closed** *Sun*
Looking slightly shabby next to the glistening Morocco Mall, this oceanfront institution is nevertheless a good option. Serves an à la carte menu with good vegetarian options.

CORNICHE: Relais de Paris
French   **Map** C2
Villa Blanca Hotel, Blvd de la Corniche
Tel *(0522) 39 25 10*
Excellent French bistro with various daily specials in addition to its regular menu. Fabulous fish, salads, steaks and desserts. Great views from its terrace.

CORNICHE: Le Cabestan
Mediterranean   **Map** C2
Blvd de la Corniche, Phare d'El Hank
Tel *(0522) 39 11 90*
The food and view at this chic Mediterranean restaurant, located near the lighthouse, has wowed locals and visitors for decades. Good choice of desserts. There is also a cocktail lounge and bar on site.

CORNICHE: Le Fibule
Moroccan/Lebanese   **Map** C2
Phare d'El Hank, Blvd de la Corniche
Tel *(0522) 36 06 41*
Dine at one of the best-known seafront restaurants in town. Try their legendary lamb couscous. The low tables offer astounding views of the rocks below. Book ahead.

CORNICHE: Le Mer
French   **Map** C2
Phare d'El-Hank, Blvd de la Corniche
Tel *(0522) 36 33 15*
Nautical-themed French restaurant with decades of experience, featuring crisp white linens and bone china. A variety of seafood and fish specialities on offer. Great views.

CORNICHE: Le Pilotis
French   **Map** C2
Tahiti Beach Club, Blvd de la Corniche
Tel *(0522) 79 84 27*
Chic establishment favoured by the city's elite. Delicious seafood and a range of Moroccan wines. Alfresco seating.

PORT QUARTER: Restaurant du Port
Seafood   **Map** C2
Port de Pêche
Tel *(0522) 31 85 61*
Bustling restaurant specializing in fresh fish and seafood dishes that keep the locals coming back for more. No credit cards.

PORT QUARTER: La Sqala
Traditional   **Map** C2
Blvd des Almohades
Tel *(0522) 26 09 60*
La Sqala is located in a stunning 18th-century saffron-stuccoed fort overlooking the ocean. Enjoy great food in calm, beautiful surroundings. No alcohol served.

DK Choice

PORT QUARTER: Rick's Café
American/Moroccan   **Map** C2
248 Blvd Sour Jdid, Place du Jardin Public
Tel *(0522) 27 42 07*
First-time visitors to Casablanca will not want to miss this popular themed restaurant. A tribute to the film *Casablanca*, Rick's is an American-owned *riad*-style establishment offering lunch and dinner menus. Featuring piano music, a tiny cocktail bar and the magic and romance of the Casablanca of another era.

Southern Atlantic Coast

EL-JADIDA: Mazagan Beach Resort (Dh) (Dh)
International **Map** B2
Mazagan Beach Resort
Tel *(0523) 38 80 00*
Overladen buffet tables offer a huge variety of international dishes. Good place to come for a day out with the kids. Pay a little extra to access the swimming pool.

ESSAOUIRA: Caravanne Café (Dh)
International **Map** B4
2 bis, Rue du Qadi Ayad
Tel *(0524) 78 31 11* **Closed** *Mon*
Bohemian and eclectic both in the menu and decor. Come for the vibe, live music and shows, the jumble of art on the walls and the rare opportunity to discuss vegetarian options.

ESSAOUIRA: Harbour (Dh)
Seafood **Map** B4
Essaouira Harbour
Just a stone's throw from the water, this is the perfect place to lazily savour dishes made with freshly caught fish.

ESSAOUIRA: La Licorne (Dh)
Traditional **Map** B4
26 Rue Scala
Tel *(0524) 47 36 26*
Excellent Moroccan eatery with an emphasis on seafood. Many vegetarian options and a good selection of wines. Cash only.

ESSAOUIRA: Restaurant Taros (Dh)
Moroccan/International **Map** B4
Pl Moulay Hassan
Tel *(0524) 47 64 07*
Café and restaurant with art on the walls, classical music playing in the background and live music in the evenings. Refined cooking.

ESSAOUIRA: Elizir (Dh) (Dh)
French/Moroccan **Map** B4
1 Derb Agadir
Tel *(0524) 47 21 03* **Closed** *Dinner*
Tiny retro diner much in demand. Delicious alternatives to classic Moroccan dishes, such as pumpkin and saffron soup and sirloin with balsamic sauce. Booking essential. Cash only.

ESSAOUIRA: Le Chalet de La Plage (Dh) (Dh)
French/Moroccan **Map** B4
Blvd Mohammed V
Tel *(0524) 47 59 72*
Smart beachside restaurant with lobster, shrimp, oysters and calamari on the menu, along with a selection of salads, soups and meats. Terrace seating with sea views.

ESSAOUIRA: Le Sirocco (Dh) (Dh)
French/Moroccan **Map** B4
15 Rue Ibn Rochd
Tel *(0524) 47 23 96* **Closed** *Tue*
Boisterous spot to dine, with loud live music. Local as well as international dishes served under the watchful eye of the French owner. Cash only.

ESSAOUIRA: Les Alizes (Dh) (Dh)
Traditional **Map** B4
26 Rue de la Sqala
Tel *(0524) 47 68 19*
Fancy, candlelit tables exude an elegant atmosphere at this restaurant, housed in a 19th-century building. Good classic Moroccan dishes at low prices.

ESSAOUIRA: Heure Bleue Palais (Dh) (Dh)
French/Moroccan **Map** B4
2 Rue Ibn Batouta
Tel *(0524) 78 34 34*
Sleek, ultra-fashionable gourmet establishment, extremely popular with the party crowd. Has an English lounge and a terrace grill.

OUALIDIA: L'Araignee Gormande (Dh) (Dh)
French **Map** B3
Oualidia Beach
Tel *(0523) 36 64 47*
Grab a table on the attractive terrace and gaze out to the breathtaking lagoon. Feast on delicious seafood or opt for one of a number of vegetarian dishes.

OUALIDIA: Ostrea II (Dh) (Dh)
Seafood **Map** B3
Oualidia Oyster Farm
Tel *(0523) 36 64 51*
This legendary restaurant sits right on the oyster farm which supplies this and other establishments. Enjoy delicious shellfish and grilled fish while looking out to the lagoon.

Beautiful Art Deco interiors at Cinema Rif

Tables prepared at the Mazagan Beach Resort, El-Jadida

Tangier

DK Choice

CITY CENTRE: Cinema Rif (Dh)
Café **Map** D1
Place 9 Avril, Grand Socco
Tel *(0539) 93 46 83*
Serves delicious tea, cake, coffee and juices in a truly unique Art Deco setting. The cinema was reopened in 2006 after painstaking renovation. Its location on a main square makes it an ideal place to watch the world go by.

CITY CENTRE: Le Coeur de Tanger and Café de Paris (Dh)
Traditional **Map** D1
1 Rue Annoual
Tel *(0539) 94 84 50*
A longtime Tangier landmark, the iconic Café de Paris may no longer serve food but head to Le Coeur de Tanger upstairs for classic Moroccan cuisine.

CITY CENTRE: Le Nabab (Dh) (Dh)
Traditional **Map** D1
4 Rue Al Kadiria
Tel *(0661) 44 22 20*
A large restaurant with arches, candlelight and a fireplace, Le Nebab is particularly welcoming in winter months. Can get noisy when crowded or when live music is playing.

CITY CENTRE: Le Relais de Paris (Dh) (Dh)
French **Map** D1
Complexe Dawliz, 42 Rue de Hollande
Tel *(0539) 33 18 19*
Excellent choice of fish, salads, daily specials and desserts at this reliable French-styled brasserie. Their home-made *foie gras* is a must-try.

For more information on types of restaurants *see page 315*

CITY CENTRE: Rif and Spa (Dh)(Dh)
Health Food   **Map** D1
Rif & Spa, 152 Av Mohammed VI
Tel *(0539) 34 93 00*
Juice bar and restaurant
frequented by healthy eaters –
tourists as well as guests – at
the hotel in which it is located.
Offers lighter dining choices
than most places in town.

CITY CENTRE: San Remo (Dh)(Dh)
Italian   **Map** D1
15 Rue Ahmed Chaouki
Tel *(0539) 93 84 51*
Well-established Italian
restaurant offering all the classic
dishes, many of them made
using imported ingredients.

CITY CENTRE: El Korsan (Dh)(Dh)(Dh)
French/Moroccan   **Map** D1
Hôtel El-Minzah, 85 Rue de la Liberté
Tel *(0539) 93 58 85*
A great way to experience
the legendary hotel without
paying for one of its luxurious
rooms. Stylish and lavishly
decorated, it is worthy of this
landmark locale.

CITY CENTRE:
La Fabrique (Dh)(Dh)(Dh)
French/Moroccan   **Map** D1
7 Rue d'Angleterre
Tel *(0539) 37 40 57*
New York loft-style, self-conscious
place that is very much in vogue.
Practically European prices but
one of the best meals in town.

CITY CENTRE:
Nord-Pinus (Dh)(Dh)(Dh)
Traditional   **Map** D1
11 Riad Sultan Kasbah
Tel *(0661) 22 81 40*
Dine in this hotel's rooftop
restaurant and drink in the
amazing view of the Spanish
coast. Highly recommended are
the filling soups, fresh fish and
wood-fired *tajines*.

CITY CENTRE: Riad Tanja (Dh)(Dh)(Dh)
Traditional   **Map** D1
Riad Tanja, Rue du Portugal
Tel *(0539) 33 35 38*
Historic *riad* restaurant offering
Moroccan dishes and wines in a
charming courtyard garden with
live music accompaniment.

Mediterranean Coast & the Rif

AL-HOCEIMA: Club Nautique (Dh)
International   **Map** E1
Port Gates, Port d' Al Hoceima
Tel *(0539) 81 14 61*
No-nonsense establishment
with sweeping views of the bay,

local wines – try the Guerrouane
Gris – and delicious grilled fish.
No credit cards.

CAP SPARTEL: Le Mirage
Restaurant (Dh)(Dh)(Dh)
French   **Map** D1
Le Mirage Hotel, Les Grottes d'Hercule
Tel *(0539) 33 33 32*
In the luxurious Le Mirage
Hotel this exquisite French
restaurant opens out into the
ocean and serves an à la carte
menu of both French and
international dishes, with a
slant on seafood.

CHEFCHAOUEN: Darcom (Dh)
Traditional   **Map** D1
*Rue Swika, Old Mellah (behind the
Great Mosque)*
Tel *(0661) 70 55 70*
The discerning traveller
need look no further than the
Moroccan speciality restaurant
Darcom. Opt for the set menu
and try some of the staple local
dishes. Offers panoramic views
of the medina and surrounding
hills. No credit cards.

CHEFCHAOUEN: Moulay Ali
Ben Rachid (Dh)
Traditional   **Map** D1
Tarik Ben Ziad   **Closed** *Fri lunch*
A favourite with locals, this
basement restaurant may look
unpromising from the outside
but is well worth a try thanks
to its excellent grilled fish and
salads. Cash only.

CHEFCHAOUEN: Tissemlal (Dh)
Traditional   **Map** D1
22 Rue Targui
Tel *(0539) 98 61 53*
Situated in the popular Casa
Hassan, Tissemlal serves grilled
meats, soups, desserts and most
Moroccan staples. Save room
for the sheep's milk yoghurt
with honey and walnuts.

OUJDA: Comme Chez Soi (Dh)
French   **Map** F2
Rue Sijilmassa
Tel *(0536) 68 60 79*
Smartly uniformed waiters
and fine table dressings at
Comme Chez Soi make it
the town's top dining choice.
Choose from a French menu
which includes wine options,
a rarity in Oujda.

OUJDA: Le Dauphin (Dh)
Seafood   **Map** F2
38 Rue Berkane
Tel *(0536) 68 61 45*
Le Dauphin is a seafood speciality
restaurant that also serves good
meat dishes. Popular with tourists
and locals. No credit cards.

OUJDA: La Table at the Ibis (Dh)
International   **Map** F2
*Ibis Moussafir Oujda, Blvd
Abdellah*
Tel *(0536) 68 82 02*
Hotel-restaurant that starts
serving breakfast very early, and
is open for lunch and dinner.
Reasonably priced, tasty food,
with terrace seating.

DK Choice

TETOUAN: Le Restinga (Dh)
Traditional   **Map** D1
21 Rue Mohammed V
Tel *(0539) 96 35 76*
La Restinga is one of
Tetouan's worst-kept secrets:
every visitor to the area is
sure to have paid it a visit,
and locals throng here as well.
Not a luxurious establishment
by any means, its reputation
for serving outstanding
Moroccan food at inexpensive
prices is well-founded. Call
ahead and check hours as
it sometimes closes early.
No credit cards.

Rooftop tables with an excellent view, Le Mirage Restaurant, Cap Spartel

**TETOUAN: Barcelo
Marina Smir** Ⓓⓗ Ⓓⓗ
International **Map** D1
Barceló Marina Smir, Rue de Sebta
Tel *(0539) 97 12 34*
Essentially serving the five-star hotel Barceló Marina Smir, the restaurant welcomes visiting diners as well. Attractively furnished and overlooking the hotel's gardens.

Fès

CITY CENTRE: Café Kortoba Ⓓⓗ
Café **Map** D2
Derb Boutouil
Next to the country's second largest mosque, the Karaouiyine, with its minaret soaring above, Café Kortoba is an excellent place to take a break for a mint tea, light snack, coffee or fresh juice. Cash only.

DK Choice

MEDINA: Café Clock Ⓓⓗ
Moroccan Fusion **Map** D2
7 Derb El Magana, Talaa Kbira
Tel *(0535) 63 78 55*
Home of the camel burger, Café Clock also provides light takes on traditional dishes and serves scrumptious salads. Offering cookery classes and food tours, this stylish but fun establishment manages to get it all just right at throw-away prices. Cash only.

MEDINA: Fes et Gestes Ⓓⓗ
French/Moroccan **Map** D2
39 Arsat El Hamoumi, Ziat
Tel *(0535) 63 85 32*
Good eatery in a restored Colonial house with a seasonal menu of French and Moroccan dishes. Hours tend to vary, so it is advisable to phone ahead.

MEDINA: Thammi's Ⓓⓗ
Traditional **Map** D2
Bab Boujloud, at the top of Talaa Sghira, between the barbershop and Hammam Mernissi
Hordes of expats and Moroccans head to Thammi's every day to sit at simple tables and tuck into dishes such as *kefta* (meatballs) and eggs and lamb with prunes. No credit cards.

**MEDINA: Le Palais
de Fes** Ⓓⓗ Ⓓⓗ
Traditional **Map** D2
15 Rue Makhfia
Tel *(0535) 76 15 90*
Gaze in amazement at the breathtaking view of the medina

Picturesque setting of the Fes et Gestes in Medina

while sampling the many excellent local dishes. Spacious spot, suited to groups.

**MEDINA: Restaurant
Numero 7** Ⓓⓗ Ⓓⓗ
Mediterranean/Moroccan **Map** D2
7 Zkak Rouah
Tel *(0535) 63 89 24*
Talk-of-the-town establishment, with its largely monochrome interior, has a very talented French chef at its helm. Offers light meals and vegetarian dishes as well as more hearty meats and fish. In the afternoons, the stunning gallery-style space opens as a *salon de thé*.

MEDINA: Al Jounaina Ⓓⓗ Ⓓⓗ Ⓓⓗ
Traditional **Map** D2
Sofitel Fès Palais Jamai, Bab Guissa
Tel *(0535) 63 43 31*
Dine like royalty while listening to live traditional music at dinner, or make the most of the lavish lunch buffet on the terrace earlier in the day. The salad bar alone is a sumptuous feast.

MEDINA: Al Firdaous Ⓓⓗ Ⓓⓗ Ⓓⓗ
Traditional **Map** D2
10 Rue Bab Zenjfour
Tel *(0535) 63 89 68*
No trip to Fès would be complete without a meal at this enchanting restaurant, where the food is authentic and the evening entertainment characterful. Call ahead to check opening hours. No credit cards.

**MEDINA: La Maison
Bleue** Ⓓⓗ Ⓓⓗ Ⓓⓗ
Traditional **Map** D2
2 Place de Batha
Tel *(0535) 74 18 43*
One of the most romantic places in town, La Maison Bleue offers signature Moroccan dishes in an elegant dining atmosphere. Begin with light snacks in the

courtyard and then sit on plump couches and enjoy live music. Open for dinner only.

**VILLE NOUVELLE:
Dar Roumana** Ⓓⓗ Ⓓⓗ
Traditional **Map** D2
30 Derb El Amer, Zkak Roumana
Tel *(0535) 74 16 37*
Dine at this lovely, intimate restaurant to truly 'feel' the magic of this ancient city. Book ahead and check dining times as these may vary.

**VILLE NOUVELLE:
L'Italien** Ⓓⓗ Ⓓⓗ
Italian **Map** D2
*Av Omar Ibn Khattab,
Champs de Courses*
Tel *(0535) 94 33 84*
Fresh, seasonal produce at this trendy pizzeria, with wood-fired pizzas, pastas and a range of superb sauces. The loft-style interior can get noisy late in the evenings. No credit cards.

**VILLE NOUVELLE:
Le Majestic** Ⓓⓗ Ⓓⓗ Ⓓⓗ
French **Map** D2
*Royal Tennis Club de Fès,
Route de Zwagha*
Tel *(0535) 72 99 99* **Closed** *Mon*
Elegant restaurant offering the best French and international dishes in a chic and modern atmosphere. High-quality wines complete the quality appeal.

**VILLE NOUVELLE: Les Trois
Sources** Ⓓⓗ Ⓓⓗ Ⓓⓗ
Traditional **Map** D2
Km 4, Rue d'Immouzer, 30000
Tel *(0535) 60 65 32*
Excellent daily specials, reasonably priced wines and delicious fish draw diners to Les Trois Sources. Although located outside of town, pick-ups can be arranged in advance. Live music at the weekends.

For more information on types of restaurants *see page 315*

VILLE NOUVELLE:
Maison Blanche Dh Dh Dh
Mediterranean **Map** D2
12 Rue Ahmed Chaouki
Tel *(0535) 62 27 27*
Sister restaurant of the famous
Parisian eatery of the same
name, this high-end
establishment offers a delectable
Mediterranean menu, along
with Moroccan and European
wines, a full bar menu and a
comprehensive cigar list.

Meknès and Volubilis

MEKNÈS: Zitouna Dh
Traditional **Map** D2
*44 Rue Jamaa Zitouna (close to the
Grand Mosque and the souks)*
Tel *(0535) 53 02 81*
Not the easiest to find, but
well worth the effort. Housed
in a beautiful old building, the
restaurant oozes character. The
Moroccan dishes are excellent
and the set menu options
good value. Cash only.

MEKNÈS: Le Dauphin Dh Dh
Seafood **Map** D2
5 Av Mohammed V
Tel *(0535) 52 34 23*
Popular with lovers of fresh fish,
Le Dauphin's menu offers a wide
selection of seafood dishes. The
decor is slightly faded but the
friendly service makes up for it.
A good option for groups.

MEKNÈS: Riad Meknes Dh Dh
Traditional **Map** D2
79 Ksar Chaacha
Tel *(0535) 53 05 42*
Part of the palace of the
17th-century ruler Moulay
Ismail, this restaurant serves up
mouthwatering Moroccan and
Continental dishes. Cash only.

Gorgeous interiors at Zitouna, Meknès

Key to Price Guide *see page 320*

MEKNÈS VILLE NOUVELLE:
Métropole Dh
Traditional **Map** D2
12 Av Hassan II
Tel *(0535) 52 25 76*
High ceilings and beautiful
ornate walls impart a sense
of space and elegance. The
outside dining area is perfect
for eating alfresco.

MEKNÈS VILLE NOUVELLE:
Gambrinus Dh
Traditional **Map** D2
Rue Omar Ibn Aïss
Tel *(0535) 52 02 58*
Do not be deterred by the
somewhat faded interior of
this popular budget eatery.
Knowledgeable locals flock here
for its tasty, cheap and whole-
some food, such as *tajines*,
couscous and brochettes.
No credit cards.

DK Choice

MEKNÈS VILLE NOUVELLE:
Le Collier de la Colombe Dh Dh
Traditional **Map** D2
67 Rue Driba
Tel *(0535) 55 50 41*
Panoramic views of the great
Wadi Boufekrane from the
main dining hall and terraces
ensure that Le Collier de la
Colombe stands out from the
rest. This restaurant is popular
for its family Sunday lunches
and with holidaying visitors.
The menu is wide and focuses
on traditional Moroccan and
international cuisine.

MEKNÈS VILLE NOUVELLE:
Le Relais de Paris Dh Dh
French **Map** D2
46 Rue Oqba, Ibn Nafia
Tel *(0535) 51 54 88*
Like its sister restaurants in
other major towns, this outlet

offers consistently high-
quality French brasserie-style
meals in pleasant surroundings
with great views.

MEKNÈS VILLE NOUVELLE:
Les Senteurs de la Mer Dh Dh Dh
Seafood **Map** D2
Rue Badr Al Kobra
Tel *(0535) 52 66 57*
Ultra-modern spot offering
Moroccan preparations of fish
and seafood in a matt black-and-
chrome interior. Phone ahead to
check opening times.

MOULAY IDRISS: Dyar Timnay Dh
Traditional **Map** D2
Rue LN7 Ain Rjal BP141
Tel *(0661) 10 43 18*
Delicious *tajines* and couscous
are available at this restaurant of
a small hotel of the same name.
The terrace seating offers lovely
views of Volubilis.

VOLUBILIS: La Corbeille
Fleurie Dh
Traditional **Map** D2
Ruins of Volubilis
Simple and straightforward as
far as the food goes, but the
view of the valley from its
terraces are simply outstanding
and worth the stop.

Middle Atlas

BENI MELLAL: SAT Agadir Dh
Traditional **Map** D3
155 Blvd el-Hansali
Tel *(0523) 48 14 48*
Modest eatery that does not
pretend to offer luxury decor or
fine dining, but just provides good
food at low prices and the chance
to meet other travellers.Cash only.

IFRANE: Café de Paix Dh
Traditional **Map** D2
Av de la Marché Verte
Tel *(0535) 56 66 75*
Small, atmospheric eatery
that offers some good local
dishes from a fairly limited
menu. The theme is largely
Moroccan, with the occasional
European dish.

IFRANE: Restaurant de
L'Hôtel des Perce-Neige Dh Dh
French **Map** D2
*Hôtel des Perce-Neige, Hay Riad,
Boulevard Mohammed VI*
Tel *(0535) 56 63 50*
The restaurant at the Hôtel
des Perce-Neige has earned
itself a reputation for good-
quality cuisine. Its lengthy menu
of classic French dishes attracts
locals as well as visitors.

DK Choice

IFRANE:
Michlifen Ifrane ⑩ ⑩ ⑩
French/Moroccan   Map D2
Av Hassan 2, BP 18
Tel *(0535) 86 40 00*
Michlifen Ifrane, a traditional
Swiss chalet, houses three
excellent restaurants and two
bars, including one dedicated
to cigars. This is the last word
in mountain luxury, and the
quality of the food and
attentiveness of the service lives
up to its stellar reputation.

KHENIFRA: Restaurant de
France ⑩
Traditional   Map D3
Quartier des Forces Armées Royales
Tel *(0535) 58 61 14*
Part of a small hotel on the road
linking Fès to Marrakech, this
small restaurant has good food
and great views from its terraces.

OUZOUD: Riad Des Cascades ⑩
Traditional   Map C3
Cascades d'Ouzoud Tanant Azilal
Tel *(0523) 42 91 73*
Dine overlooking Morocco's most
impressive waterfalls, and then
take a lovely walk down the path
alongside the falls. Lucky visitors
might even catch a glimpse of
the indigenous Barbary apes
while they eat. Bookings only.

OUZOUD: Riad Cascades
D'Ouzoud ⑩
Moroccan/French   Map C3
Riad Cascades D'Ouzoud
Tel *(0523) 42 91 73*
Dine in the traditional Moroccan
lounge or on the roof terrace at
Riad Cascades D'Ouzoud. Delicious
food. Book ahead.

Marrakech

GUELIZ: Café du Livre ⑩
International   Map C3
44 Rue Tarik Ben Ziad
Tel *(0524) 43 21 49*
The salads, desserts and fresh
juices at this popular café are
wonderful. Free Wi-Fi and a quiz
in English on Monday nights.

GUELIZ: Les Negotiants ⑩
Café   Map C3
Corner of Av Mohammed V and
Blvd Mohammed Zertouni
Offering thick black coffee,
snacks and the chance to shop
from street hawkers outside,
Les Negotiants promises a
memorable Marrakech
experience. Cash only.

Convivial atmosphere at the Le Comptoir Darna Marrakech, Hivernage

GUELIZ: Bab Restaurant ⑩ ⑩
Moroccan/French   Map C3
Corner of Blvd Mansour Eddahbi
and Rue Mohamed El Beqqal
Tel *(05240 43 52 50*
Featuring gleaming white
interiors with dashes of bold
colour, this restaurant could be
in any major European capital.
Offers tasty, light meals.

GUELIZ: Le Grand Café
de la Poste ⑩ ⑩
French/Mediterranean   Map C3
Corner of Blvd El Mansour Eddahbi
and Av Imam Malik
Tel *(0524) 43 30 38*
Wonderful Art Deco building with
a sweeping staircase. Come for
light lunch, dinner, afternoon tea
or cocktails. Service can be slow.

GUELIZ: L'Ultimo Bacio ⑩ ⑩
Italian   Map C3
Angle Rue Tarik Ibn Ziad & Moulay Ali
Tel *(0661) 11 26 09*
The chic exterior of this eatery
should not intimidate the casual
diner. L'Ultimo Bacio is a pasta
heaven for those tired of
traditional Moroccan dishes.

GUELIZ: Al Fassia ⑩ ⑩ ⑩
Traditional   Map C3
55 Blvd Zerktouni
Tel *(0524) 43 40 60*
Al Fassia is a popular restaurant
that continues to wow locals
and tourists with top-notch
Moroccan specialties. Run by
an all-female staff.

GUELIZ: La Trattoria ⑩ ⑩ ⑩
Italian   Map C3
179 Rue Mohammed el-Beqal
Tel *(0524) 43 26 41*
Set in a colonial-style *maison*
and beautifully decorated, this
upmarket eatery is a good
choice for special occasions.
The dessert trolley is especially
tempting. Open for dinner only.

HIVERNAGE: La Table
du Marche ⑩ ⑩ ⑩
International   Map C3
Corner Av Echouada & Rue des Temples
Tel *(0524) 42 41 00*
Light meals, juices and hot
drinks make a pleasant change
from heavy dishes in this chic
part of town. Good place to
recharge and unwind.

HIVERNAGE: Le Comptoir
Darna Marrakech ⑩ ⑩ ⑩
Moroccan/International   Map C3
Av Echouada
Tel *(0524) 43 77 02*
In one of the fanciest areas of
town, this upmarket and refined
spot promises immaculate design
and service plus top-quality
dishes from a varied French
bistro-style menu. Dinner only.

LA PALMERAIE: Flower Power
Alternative Café ⑩
Café   Map C3
Pépinière Casa Botanica, Rue de
Sidi Abdellah Ghiat
Tel *(0524) 48 40 87*   **Closed** *Mon &*
Tue
Eco-friendly family café that
runs regular activities for
the young and old. There is a
charming children's play area
as well as a small animal farm.
Call ahead for events. Cash only.

LA PALMERAIE: Manzil
la Tortue ⑩ ⑩
French/Moroccan   Map C3
Km 12 Rue de Ouarzazate, Douar
Gzoula, Commune Al Ouidane
Tel *(0525) 11 88 86*
Manzil la Tortue is situated amid
olive groves, in a lovely location
outside town. Diners here can
order from the menu or cook at
their own table on a griddle.
Known for its use of fresh, mostly
organic ingredients and its list of
fine wines. Charges extra to use
the pool.

DK Choice

LE MEDINA: Place Jamaa el-Fna Food Stalls
Traditional   Map C3
Place Jemaa el-Fna
Every visitor to Marrakech should visit the many food stalls in the medina jostling for attention come dusk each evening. The air fills with the aromas of spiced roasting meats, the stall lights dazzle and the whole square becomes the evening's entertainment. Unmissable, and to many, the city's greatest draw.

The spectacular Dar Moha in Le Medina

LE MEDINA: Dar Yacout
Traditional   Map C3
79 Sidi Ahmed Soussi, Bab Doukala
Tel *(0524) 38 29 29*   **Closed** *Mon*
Housed in a restored palace, in the heart of the medina, this is one of the top dining spots in which to experience the romance of Marrakech.

LE MEDINA: Dar Marjana
Traditional   Map C3
15 Derb Sidi Ali Tair Bab Doukkala
Tel *(0524) 38 51 10*   **Closed** *Tue*
Romantic and luxurious, this restaurant, in a former palace, is richly decorated and twinkles with lantern lights. Features regular music and dance shows.

LE MEDINA: Dar Moha
Traditional   Map C3
81 Rue Dar El Bacha
Tel *(0524) 38 64 00*
Located in the heart of the medina, in the former home of designer Pierre Balmain, Dar Moha serves delicacies and great Moroccan staple dishes, as well as more contemporary meals. Book ahead.

LE MEDINA: Gastro MK at Maison MK
French   Map C3
4 Derb Sebaai, Quartier Ksour
Tel *(0524) 37 61 73*   **Closed** *Wed*
Highly creative menu executed to perfection at this outstanding bistro-styled restaurant. It is wise to book well in advance.

LE MEDINA: La Maison Arabe
Traditional   Map C3
1 Derb Assehbé Bab Doukkala
Tel *(0524) 38 70 10*
Unabashedly romantic: dine under a hand-painted ceiling, surrounded by traditionally plastered *tadelakt*, tinkling fountains and candlelight.

LE MEDINA: La Mamounia
Moroccan/International   Map C3
Av Bab Jdid
Tel *(0524) 38 86 00*
Four resturants, two of them with Michelin stars, make this one of the most fashionable places to dine. Throw in Moorish opulence and an impressive history, and it is a guaranteed success.

LE MEDINA: Le Foundouk
Moroccan/Mediterranean   Map C3
55 Rue du Souk El Fassis
Tel *(0524) 37 81 90*   **Closed** *Mon*
Le Foundouk is located in a *riad*-style building that allows diners to look down into an inner courtyard. Luxurious decor and a tempting menu.

LE MEDINA: Le Tobsil
Moroccan/French   Map C3
22 Derb Moulay Abdellah ben Hessaien Bab Ksour
Tel *(0524) 44 40 52*   **Closed** *Tue*
Enjoy an intimate and romantic dinner in the central courtyard of this beautiful traditional house. The food is good but the main lure here is the chance to get a glimpse inside the building. Bookings essential.

MEDINA: Un Dejeuner a Marrakech
International   Map C3
2–4 Rue Kennaria
Tel *(0524) 37 83 87*
European-style bistro with salads and light lunches plus heartier options. Good children's options and delicious pastries. The climb to the roof terrace is well worth the effort. No alcohol or pork served. Cash only.

MEDINA: Pepe Nero
Italian/Moroccan   Map C3
17 Derb Cherkaou, Douar Graou
Tel *(0524) 38 90 67*   **Closed** *Mon*
Choose from the Italian or Moroccan menu and drink in the lovely ambience, complete with fountains, candles, pools and lush plants. May be a bit hard to find, so ask for directions.

High Atlas

DK Choice

ASNI: Kasbah Tamadot
International   Map C4
Asni 042150
Tel *(0524) 36 82 00.*
Owned by British entrepreneur Richard Branson; in a splendid location, perched on a mountain. Stunning views, great (and surprisingly affordable) food and the knowledge that some of the money spent here filters back into the local community makes it a great dining choice. Also offers cooking lessons and demonstrations. Reservations essential for dinner.

ASNI: Oliveraie de Marigha
Traditional   Map C4
Km 59 Douar Marigha, Taroudant Rd
Tel *(0524) 48 42 81*
Enjoys a magical setting, with a pool ringed by mountains and olive groves. Serves up standard Moroccan dishes, with a slant towards meat, rather than fish or vegetarian options. Phone ahead to reserve a table.

IMLIL: Kasbah du Toubkal
Traditional   Map C4
Toubkal National Park
Tel *(0524) 48 56 11*
This has to be one of the most striking places to eat in the Atlas region. Might be a bit of a climb or mule-ride to reach, but is worth it for the ambience and simple yet tasty Moroccan food. Book ahead. No credit cards.

Key to Price Guide *see page 320*

OUIRGANE: Auberge de Sanglier Qui Fume
French/Moroccan   Map C4
Km 61, 5 Rue Marrakech
Tel *(0524) 48 57 07*
The mainly meat-based menu offers hearty portions and thick, filling stews. Lighter options include salads and omelettes. After the meal, do take a tour of the characterful hotel.

OUIRGANE: Domaine Malika
French   Map C4
Douar Marigha, Rue d'Amizmiz par Asni, Imlil
Tel *(0661) 49 35 41*
Possibly one of the most relaxing and charming places to eat in the area. Choose between inside dining or the terrace by the pool. Fresh, locally sourced ingredients are used to make delicious food.

OUIRKA VALLEY: Bab Ourika
International   Map C4
Tnine Ourika
Tel *(0661) 63 42 34*
There can be few places in the area as beautiful as this hotel-restaurant, nor many menus as pleasing. Enjoy masterful food in a magical setting. Many of the ingredients are from the hotel's own garden. Booking essential.

OUKAÏMEDEN: Chez JuJu
Traditional   Map C4
Signposted from the village of Oukaïmeden
Tel *(0524) 31 90 05*
A ski-chalet hotel-restaurant that offers a European-style menu and simple, honest and delicious food to satisfy the skiers and mountain hikers who stop by.

OURIKA VALLEY: Nectarome Health Food   Map C4
Lot Pinatel, Tniine
Tel *(0524) 48 21 49*
Great lunch spot for a light meal or refreshments. Salads and snacks are served in the tranquil surroundings of a herb garden, encircled by mountain peaks.

OURIKA VALLEY: Le Maquis
Traditional   Map C4
Auberge Le Maquis, km 45 Aghbalou Ourika
Tel *(0524) 48 45 31*
Housed within the characterful hotel Auberge Le Maquis, this restaurant serves Moroccan dishes such as *harira* and *tajines*, lemon chicken and couscous. Children's menu also available.

TIZI-N-TEST PASS ROAD: La Belle Vue
Traditional   Map B4
Signposted from the Pass
Tel *(067) 59 57 58*
One of few places to eat in the area, La Belle Vue's dishes are simple but wholesome, and the valley views from the terrace are remarkable. Cash only.

Ouarzazate & the Southern Oases

AÏT BEN HADDOU: Auberge Restaurant Etoile Filante D'Or
Traditional   Map C4
Centre Aït Ben Haddou
Tel *(0524) 89 03 22*
The romantic terrace at this well-priced restaurant rewards evening visitors with spectacular views of the night sky, while the kitchen provides authentic Moroccan mains and desserts.

DK Choice
BOUMALNE DU DADÈS: Hôtel Xaluka Dades
Moroccan   Map D4
Rd Arfoud to Errachidia km 5
Tel *(0524) 57 84 50*
After the numerous hairpin bends of the passes, or a night in the desert, the overloaded buffet table at this restaurant can seem almost like a mirage. Amid the mountains of delicious Moroccan and Continental food and candles flickering by the pool, diners will find helpful waiters darting about in traditional dress – all of it making for a memorable, and filling, dining experience.

ERFOUD: Restaurant des Dunes
Moroccan/Italian   Map E4
142 Av Moulay Ismaïl, Opposite the ZIZ pretol station
Tel *(0535) 57 67 93*
Surprisingly good pizzas, in addition to other more classic Moroccan dishes at this restaurant. Located on the upper floor of a Moorish-inspired building complete with a terrace that overlooks the town.

ERFOUD: Restaurants of the Hôtel Bélère
International   Map E4
Hôtel Bélère, Route de Rissani
Tel *(0535) 87 81 90*
Choose from four excellent restaurants serving Italian, Asian, international and seafood dishes, housed within the Hôtel Bélère, one of the largest hotels in this relatively quiet desert town. Menus change regularly. There is also a bar on site.

ERFOUD: Restaurants of the Hôtel Xaluca
International   Map E4
Hôtel Xaluca, Rd Erfoud to Errachidia Km 5
Tel *(0535) 57 84 50*
Impressive air-conditioned restaurant in the Hôtel Xaluca packed with desert character. It caters well for large groups. Enjoy the blazing fire in the colder months.

OUARZAZATE: Chez Talout
Traditional   Map C4
Oulad Aarbiya
Tel *(0524) 85 26 66*
Overlooking Skoura's oasis is this charming inn-restaurant. Ask to dine on the terrace and enjoy magical desert views. Great for kids, with a pool and patio seating.

Outdoor seating at the Bab Ourika in the Ouirka Valley

For more information on types of restaurants *see page 315*

OUARZAZATE: Les Kasbahs des Sables (Dh)(Dh)
Traditional   Map C4
195 Hay Ait Ksif
Tel *(0524) 88 54 28*
Diners in search of a more authentic meal than that at their hotel might want to try this traditionally decorated, desert-style restaurant. The muted plasterwork is especially romantic by lantern light.

OUARZAZATE: Restaurant Chez Dimitri (Dh)(Dh)
International   Map C4
22 Av Mohammed V
Tel *(0524) 88 73 46*
Ask any local where Chez Dimitri is, and the chances are they would have dined there on several occasions. One of the first good restaurants to open in Ouarzazate and a popular spot for family parties and celebrations.

OUARZAZATE: Restaurant Douyria (Dh)(Dh)
Traditional   Map C4
Av Mohamed V, Taourirt
Tel *(0524) 88 52 88*
Enjoy lakeside and mountain views at this rammed earth lodge's restaurant. On the menu are traditional desert Moroccan dishes, including camel, pigeon and rabbit, served in colourful surroundings.

OUARZAZATE: Restaurant of the Berbere Palace (Dh)(Dh)
International   Map C4
Quartier Mansour Eddahbi 55
Tel *(0524) 88 31 05*
Dine like royalty for a fraction of European prices at Berbere Palace. Choose from one of three menus – Moroccan, French and Italian.

OUARZAZATE: Restaurant of the Hôtel Ibis Moussafir (Dh)(Dh)
Moroccan/International   Map C4
Av Moulay Rachid
Tel *(0524) 89 91 10*
Reliable hotel-restaurant popular with both hotel guests and other tourists. Several excellent Moroccan and international dishes on the menu.

OUARZAZATE: Restaurant Sultana Royal Golf (Dh)(Dh)(Dh)
International   Map C4
Golf Royal
Tel *(0524) 88 74 21*
Stunning lakeside views and a well-executed menu are the draws at this desert getaway restaurant, within a hotel of the same name. Lush gardens and modern, bright interiors.

RAMLIA: Auberge Aghbalou Ramlia (Dh)
Traditional   Map E4
Auberge Ramlia, Taouz Rissani
Those who make the trek to Auberge Aghbalou Ramlia will be rewarded with simple yet delicious food, which is served under a star-filled sky with a panoramic view of the mountains. Booking essential. Cash only.

SKOURA: Kasbah Ait Abou (Dh)(Dh)
Traditional   Map C4
Palmeraie de Skoura BP60
Tel *(0524) 85 22 34*
Partially tented desert kasbah with oasis and desert views. Breakfast, lunch, dinner and tea can be served outside in the carpet-strewn Berber tents. Simple yet delicious cooking on offer. Booking essential.

DK Choice

SKOURA: Dar Ahlam (Dh)(Dh)(Dh)
International   Map C4
Douar Oulad Cheikh Ali, Kasbah Madihi
Tel *(0524) 85 22 39*
The pure extravagance of this place might make visitors blink but relax in the knowledge that this is probably one of the world's most romantic picnic spots. Not cheap but then sheer luxury seldom is. Book ahead or check annual closings.

ZAGORA: Auberge Restaurant Chez Ali (Dh)
Traditional   Map D4
Avenue Atlas-Zaouite
Tel *(0524) 84 62 58*
Family-owned getaway that serves delicious traditional dishes in a flower-filled garden. Phone ahead to book a table. For those planning on staying overnight, note that the rooms are simple but comfortable.

Southern Morocco & Western Sahara

DK Choice

AGADIR: Harbour Stalls (Dh)
Seafood   Map B4
Agadir Harbour
Numerous little stalls line the street alongside the Agadir harbour, emitting tempting aromas that beg further investigation. Skewered meat and primarily fish, are the favourites of tourists and locals alike. This is a great place to enjoy the relaxed atmosphere of a balmy Moroccan evening and the proximity of the town to the ocean.

AGADIR: Jour et Nuit (Dh)
Traditional   Map B4
Av Tawada (formerly Rue de la Plage)
Tel *(0528) 82 23 47*
Duck into this air-conditioned restaurant, located on the promenade, especially for lunch, as the sun reaches its hottest. Also open for dinner.

AGADIR: Le Jazz (Dh)
European   Map B4
Blvd du 20 Août
Tel *(0528) 84 02 08*
Living up to its name, this eatery has become a popular venue for live jazz performances. Additionally, it offers European-style dishes and alcoholic drinks, making for a thoroughly enjoyable evening.

AGADIR: Little Norway (Dh)
French/Moroccan   Map B4
Complexe Tamlelt, Secteur Balnéaire
Tel *(0528) 84 08 48*
Oddly, there appears to be no link between Norway and this intimate French restaurant;

Unique interiors of Dar Ahlam, Skoura

Charming dining area at Hôtel La Gazelle D'Or, Taroudant

however, the portions are generous, tasty and well-priced, as are the wines and beers.

AGADIR: Mezzo Mezzo
Italian   ⓓⓗⓓⓗ   **Map** B4
19 Av Hassan II
Tel *(0528) 84 88 19*
Popular with locals and holiday-makers alike, this vibrant Italian restaurant offers classic Italian fare, along with delicious desserts and a range of alcoholic drinks.

AGADIR: Riad Villa Blanche
French/Moroccan   ⓓⓗⓓⓗ   **Map** B4
Baie des Palmiers secteur N°50 cité Founty
Tel *(0528) 21 13 13*
Find dishes befitting the fanciest Parisian tables. Choose from French or Moroccan delights, or opt for one of the impressive tasting menus. Snack menu available at the bar.

AGADIR: Jean Cocteau
European   ⓓⓗⓓⓗⓓⓗ   **Map** B4
Blvd Mohammed V
Tel *(0528) 82 11 11*
Ritzy place to dine in, located as it is inside Casino Shem's, but the menu is surprisingly simple. Serves mainly European fare, from salads to burgers.

AGADIR: Le Miramar
Italian   ⓓⓗⓓⓗⓓⓗ   **Map** B4
Blvd Mohammed V
Tel *(0528) 84 07 70*
High-end family-run restaurant that offers the usual Italian staples – pizzas, pastas and salads – and wines, many of which are imported from Italy.

AGADIR: Les Blancs
Spanish   ⓓⓗⓓⓗⓓⓗ   **Map** B4
Marina d'Agadir
Tel *(0528) 82 83 68*
The great view over Agadir's magnificent beach accompanies the truly superlative Spanish

food, a great change from the Moroccan and French cuisines offered elsewhere.

DAKHLA: Villa Dakhla
Moroccan/French   ⓓⓗⓓⓗ   **Map** A5
Blvd Mohammed V
Tel *(0648) 31 58 18*
Hungry travellers will be surprised to find a good restaurant in what could be described as 'the middle of nowhere'. Villa Dakhla may not be fine dining but they serve tasty food in pleasant surroundings.

MARINA D'AGADIR:
Le Parasol Bleue
French   ⓓⓗ   **Map** B4
7 Promenade Tawada
Tel *(0528) 84 87 44*   **Closed** *Mon*
Hidden away from the main promenade, this simple but pleasing French-owned restaurant offers good-value food, including a set lunch menu.

SIDI IFNI: Café Nomad
Traditional   ⓓⓗ   **Map** A5
5 Av Moulay Youseff
Tel *(0662) 17 33 08*
A welcome find in a small town, with a charming owner and a warm ambience. Service can be on the slow side. Bring your own wine.

SIDI IFNI: Restaurant of the
Hôtel Bellevue
Traditional   ⓓⓗ   **Map** A5
Hôtel Bellevue, Place Hassan II
Tel *(0528) 87 50 72*
Head here for well-presented Moroccan dishes made with fresh ingredients, good service and staggering clifftop views.

TAFRAOUTE: Chez Sabir
Traditional   ⓓⓗⓓⓗ   **Map** B5
Rue d'Amelne
Tel *(0528) 80 06 36*   **Closed** *Summer*
Miniscule but excellent eatery that offers fantastic home

cooking by a chef who is married to a Cornish writer. Phone ahead and make a booking well in advance. Cash only.

TAROUDANT: Jnane Soussia
Traditional   ⓓⓗ   **Map** B4
Rue de Marrakech
Tel *(0528) 85 49 80*
These Berber-style tents under the stars are very popular with groups, though lone travellers can stop by too. Copious amounts of food, plus music and dancing make for a good experience. Booking essential.

TAROUDANT: Restaurant
L'Agence
Traditional   ⓓⓗ   **Map** B4
Blvd Prince Heritier Sidi Mohamed
Tel *(0528) 55 02 70*   **Closed** *Sun*
The use of seasonal ingredients in the creation of some wonderful dishes and a very central location make this budget eatery one of the best eating options in town.

TAROUDANT: Hôtel La
Gazelle D'Or
French   ⓓⓗⓓⓗⓓⓗ   **Map** B4
Centre of Taroudannt
Tel *(0528) 85 20 39*
One way to experience the legendary hotel without staying in it is to dine at its excellent French restaurant, often populated by the rich and famous. Uses the freshest organic, home-grown produce. Bookings are essential.

TIZNIT: Riad Le Lieu
Traditional   ⓓⓗⓓⓗ   **Map** B5
273 Impasse Issaoui, Rue Haddada
Tel *(0528) 60 00 19*
Phone ahead to secure a table in the courtyard of this small riad and dine on French or Moroccan dishes cooked to perfection. Friendly service.

For more information on types of restaurants *see page 315*

SHOPPING IN MOROCCO

Every village in Morocco has its weekly souk. Lasting for a few hours, souks are busy, colourful places where agricultural produce and craft items brought by country people are sold alongside a range of other essential everyday items.

Large towns have several souks. These take place in the medinas and are laid out according to the type of goods that they sell. Traders are friendly and always ready to please their customers. The rich and diverse range of Moroccan crafts can be found in the country's souks and markets, as well as at cooperative craft outlets and specialist shops, and are also offered for sale by the roadside along tourist routes.

Slipper merchant with a colourful range of footwear in Tafraoute

Dates stacked in baskets and ready for sale, Ziz Gorge

Opening Hours

Country souks take place only in the morning. Grocers' shops, local supermarkets and butchers' shops are open every weekday from 8am to 9pm, although they close for about two hours in the middle of the day. Some may also open on Sundays, when different opening hours apply. Friday is theoretically a day of rest for Muslims; however, business goes on as normal, although some larger shops close in the middle of the day. During Ramadan, grocers' shops open late in the morning, close for part of the day and then open from the evening until very late. Shops run by Jews close on Saturdays (the Sabbath). In large towns and cities, clothes shops and fabric shops open from 9am to noon and from 3pm to 7pm. They do not open on Sundays. The hypermarkets that have sprung up in all large towns are open from 9am to 9pm seven days a week.

Methods of Payment

Credit cards are accepted only in large towns and cities and in modern shops. Some shopkeepers will add a percentage as tax onto the total automatically if you choose this form of payment. Also, credit card slips can be pre-dated or printed twice without your knowing. It is best, therefore, to carry sufficient amounts of cash before setting off on a shopping trip.

Food Stores

All towns are very well provided with grocers' shops. In villages, the grocer's is the only place, apart from the weekly souk, where people can buy provisions and essential items.

These shops are usually no bigger than a large cupboard. They are fitted with shelves from floor to ceiling, and offer all kinds of foods and household goods. It is wise to avoid buying perishable items such as yogurt and milk, since there is no guarantee that they are fresh. In butchers' shops, what is on offer is neither labelled nor priced. Fruit and vegetable shops, dairies and bakers are found only in large towns. Although French bread was introduced during the Protectorate, Moroccans prefer *kesra*, a round loaf baked at home or in the local communal oven.

A few *charcuteries*, selling cooked meats, have appeared in Casablanca, Rabat and Marrakech but they are geared

Semi-precious stones laid out for sale at the roadside, Middle Atlas

to an exclusively Western clientele, pork being forbidden to Muslims. By using a local supermarket, you can check the sell-by dates of fresh produce (when they are marked, that is). Imported foods can also be bought in supermarkets.

Hypermarket chains were set up in Morocco several years ago. There are supermarkets in all the major towns.

Markets

All large towns have several markets that supply fresh fruit and vegetables to the population every day of the year. In every market there is a fresh herb stall and a spice and olive stall. Household utensils, basketry and craft items are also on sale.

In the harbours along the Atlantic coast, particularly in the towns of Oualidia, Safi, Essaouira and Agadir, the fruits of the daily catch – such as sole, sardines, perch, shrimps, squid and oysters – can be eaten on the spot.

Souks

For foreign visitors, souks are lively and authentic expressions of rural life in Morocco (see p205), offering the opportunity to see a fascinating and genuine aspect of the country. Taking place once a week, souks are the focus of economic, social and administrative life in Morocco's rural areas. Country people come from miles around to stock up on supplies or to exchange agricultural produce (such as fruit, vegetables, eggs, butter and cereals) or craft items (such as pottery and carpets) for tea, oil, sugar and spices. Also on offer are plastic utensils

A brassware and copperware shop in the Quartier Habbous, Casablanca

and clothing made of synthetic fabrics, along with chickens, sheep and sometimes mules.

In the medinas of Rabat, Fès, Marrakech and Taroudannt, souks take place almost daily. Their location and layout are dictated by the nature of what they offer. More oriented towards tourists than are the country souks, they offer a huge range of craft items from all over Morocco.

Fassi glazed pottery is by no means identical to that made in Salé or Safi, and it differs from the Berber pottery of the Rif or that made in Tamegroute. Thuya wood (see p126) is a speciality of Essaouira; Ouaouzguite carpets are renowned in Tazenakht; and El-Kelaa M'Goun is famous for its daggers.

How to Bargain

In Morocco, bargaining is not so much a custom as a duty. Every self-respecting Moroccan uses this method, even when buying vegetables in the souk or renting a hotel room. In craft shops, no prices are marked and the shopkeeper considers it quite natural that potential clients should bargain over the price. When a potential customer shows an interest, the shop-owner will quote an initial price, which often bears no relation to the real price of the object in question but which tests the buyer's willingness to make a counter-offer. In order to bargain effectively, it

is important to know the value of what you wish to buy or at least to have a price in mind beyond which you will not go. By contrast, if you refuse to raise your offer sufficiently to allow the seller to make a profit, he will not pursue the transaction. The real purpose of bargaining is to obtain the desired object while feigning indifference. This is why bargaining takes time and should be a subtle game between buyer and seller.

Forgeries

Souks in medinas and in Morocco's major tourist centres offer "authentic" goods of dubious quality and origin, and for very inflated prices. You are advised to be on your guard against goods that, contrary to what the seller may assure you, are often no more than skilfully concocted and very convincing forgeries.

A bellows merchant in the souk in Marrakech

Produce stall at the Tahar el-Alaoui market in Casablanca

What to Buy in Morocco

Souks in Morocco present the visitor with a vast choice of jewellery, leather goods, wrought-iron work, brass and copper, pottery, carpets, basketry and fabrics. But the quantity, colours and sheer diversity of the items on offer can be bewildering and it can be difficult to distinguish quality pieces from inferior ones. Before deciding to buy, it is best to take some time to compare what is on offer in different shops. Country craft items offered for sale in markets are genuine and utilitarian, ranging from the baskets carried by donkeys and combs for carding wool to terracotta coolers for keeping milk or dried meat fresh.

Pouffe
Like other leather goods, this pouffe is made of good-quality goatskin or sheepskin, which, after tanning, is dyed and embroidered.

Ceramics

The place of origin of ceramics can be identified by their colours and decoration. Pottery from Fès is the most refined, that from Salé is glazed in pale colours, and that from Safi features polychrome colours and Berber motifs. Potters also devise new designs, such as that on the vase shown on the left.

Vase

Vase from Safi

Ashtray
This is an example of Fès blue-glazed ware. The Fassi pottery industry goes back to the 10th or 11th centuries.

Decorated *tajine* dish

Plate with a modern design

Wood and Stone Carving

Fès, Tetouan and Azrou are renowned for their carved cedar. In Essaouira, craftsmen work with thuya wood *(see p126)*, making boxes in various shapes, statues, trays, frames and other pieces. In Taroudannt, objects are carved from soft stone, and in Erfoud trinkets and other small items are fashioned from marble.

Thuya Camel
Small pieces like this figure of a camel are easier to make than larger items, since thuya wood tends to split as it dries out.

Inlaid Wood
Boxes and other objects made of thuya are decoratively inlaid with yellow citron wood and ebony or cedar.

Duck carved in stone

Metalware

Wrought iron, brown-hued copper, bright yellow brass (a mixture of copper and zinc) and nickel silver (a mixture of copper, zinc and nickel) are the main materials used in Moroccan metalware. The finest pieces are engraved or damascened (inlaid with contrasting metal).

Brass tray

Lantern

Teapot
A squat teapot with tapering lid, made of stainless steel or silver, is an essential piece of equipment for making mint tea.

Terracotta

Berber pottery features a combination of simple, sturdy shapes, ochre and brown colours and geometric motifs.

Terracotta kasbah

Berber pottery

Silver

Silver is the predominant material of Berber jewellery. The most common items are brooches, which Berber women wear in pairs, to secure their veils at each shoulder. The shape and decoration of brooches varies according to the region.

Hand of Fatima, a lucky charm

Anklet

Koumiya dagger

Silver and Coral Necklace
Berber women traditionally wear a lot of jewellery. Today, jewellery is made increasingly of synthetic resin that mimics the colour of coral.

Clothing

Jellabas, loose-fitting hooded cloaks with long sleeves, and gandouras, tunics with short sleeves, can be purchased in souks. Burnouses, hooded woollen cloaks, are seen in rural areas. Embroidered silk belts, traditionally made in Fès, are highly sought-after but are increasingly difficult to find.

Embroidery
Each city has its own traditions and styles of embroidery. It is used to adorn tablecloths, table napkins, cushions and other items, in a variety of patterns.

A child's *gandoura*

Babouches

Moroccan Carpets

There are as many different types of carpets in Morocco as there are tribal traditions. Moroccan carpets can, however, be divided into two main groups: Berber carpets and city carpets. The former are either knotted or woven; they are pleasingly unrefined and each one is unique. Their wool, which the women weave into simple or complex patterns, their harmonious colours, their shape and size, and also their patterns, vary from one region to another. City carpets, influenced by Oriental traditions, are finer. Symbols of luxury, they grace the living rooms of wealthy houses.

The fringe, at one end of the carpet, is part of the warp.

Berber Carpets

Most of the carpets made in Tazenaght and Taliouine, in the High Atlas, are made by the Ouaouzguite tribe. These carpets are typically long, narrow and supple, and thus well suited to use in the interiors of kasbahs in the Atlas.

Carpet Weaving

Carding wool

After the men have sheared the sheep in the spring, the women wash the wool and carefully pick over it. It is then carded, a process by which the strands are untangled by brushing with comb-like implements. Next, the wool is spun into yarn with a small spindle. Either in its natural colour or after it has been dyed, the wool is then ready to be woven. Berber women knot carpets on large, rudimentary looms consisting of two wooden vertical and two horizontal planks. The warp is set up by threading strands vertically on the loom. These determine the length and thickness of the carpet. The weft (the horizontal threads) are threaded by hand between the strands of the warp, the weaver working row by row, pressing the weave together with an iron comb.

A weaver in Abachkou

Carpet from the High Atlas, in which woven bands alternate with knotted bands. The well-ordered geometric motifs feature lozenges, triangles and broken lines.

Carpet made by the Zaïane of the Middle Atlas, featuring a combination of strict geometric and random motifs. These carpets are well suited to use in tents or for covering the beaten earth floors of houses.

City Carpets

Woven in Rabat, Salé and Casablanca, city carpets are perfectly symmetrical. They feature floral and geometric motifs and are edged with borders of differing widths.

A carpet seller in the Rue des Consuls in Rabat

Buying a Carpet

Colour and pattern are the primary considerations when buying a carpet. Then come the material, the carpet's softness, the density of the weave or knotting, and condition. A good-quality carpet has clearly defined motifs and perfectly straight edges. The value of a carpet is based on the number of knots per row and the density of the warp and weft. Some carpets have up to 380,000 knots per square metre (11 sq ft) and official price bands per square metre apply. Carpets checked by the Ministry of Crafts are hallmarked with the date that they were checked, their provenance and their quality. An orange label indicates extra-superior quality; a blue label, superior quality; a yellow label, medium quality, and green label, ordinary quality. Once the carpet has been unrolled in front of you, you can start to bargain (see p333).

Carpet shop in a crafts complex

Mediouna carpets, made in Casablanca, feature shades of brick red or soft pink, and always have a lozenge-shaped or star-shaped central motif.

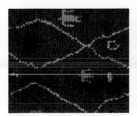

Haouz carpets, made in Marrakech, are knotted. They are characterized by a background scattered with naive motifs.

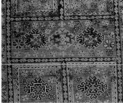

Middle Atlas carpets have a woollen pile. The exact outlines of the pattern can be seen only on their smooth side.

Dyes are traditionally obtained from vegetable extracts but are now very often supplemented by synthetic dyes.

ENTERTAINMENT IN MOROCCO

Most nightlife in Morocco takes place in the large towns and cities. International tourism and the desire for modernity on the part of the younger generation have both contributed to the development of centres of culture and entertainment. These are often the best places to meet young Moroccans. The number of fashionable bars and nightclubs is increasing, too, while Morocco's thriving cultural life ensures a wide variety of entertainment. Certain private art galleries showcase the country's artistic talent. The many feast days and *moussems* (pilgrimage festivals) provide opportunities to watch shows that are more authentically Moroccan than those aimed at tourists.

The Institut Français de Casablanca

Information Sources

Scanning the entertainment section of various newspapers (entitled *"Spectacles"* in Francophone publications) is the best way of checking what's on, even though they give such information only very irregularly.

The main daily newspapers are *El-Bayane*, *Le Matin du Sahara*, *L'Opinion* and *Libération*. Weeklies include *Le Magazine* and *TelQuel*. Monthly magazines, such as *Femmes du Maroc* and *Citadine*, or the fortnightly *Medina*, carry listings of cultural events. These publications are available from kiosks as well as in most tobacconists.

Unfortunately, there are no good sources of entertainment information available in English.

Cinemas

Taking up the threads of the movie culture that the country enjoyed in the 1950s, when Moroccans had the privilege of seeing early screenings of many American productions, Moroccan cinemas are enjoying a new lease of life as is, to a certain extent, the Moroccan film industry. Authentically restored auditoriums dating from the 1940s have reopened, particularly in Casablanca. The main cinemas in Rabat are the **Renaissance** and the **Salle du 7eme Art**. In Casablanca there are the **Rialto**, the **Lynx** and the **Megarama**; in Fès the **Empire** and the **Rex**; and, in Marrakech, the **Colisée** and the **Megarama**. In Tangier, the leading cinemas are **Le Paris** and the **Rif: Cinémathèque de Tange**; in Agadir, there is **Rialto**. But if you don't understand French or Arabic, this might not be your first choice of entertainment since almost all films are dubbed in French, or are in Arabic.

Daily local newspapers provide information on what is showing, or you can phone the cinemas themselves. The cultural institutes in various cities *(see p341)* are also good sources of information.

Theatres

Morocco is not well endowed with theatres. They are found only in the cities, and productions are usually limited and irregular. Nevertheless, foreign theatrical companies perform in Morocco, and efforts are being made to launch the Moroccan theatre, which is still in its infancy.

Although theatre listings are usually given in the daily press, it is best to obtain information directly from the theatres or from cultural institutions.

Throne Day, a highly colourful and popular event

Feast Days and Festivals

Prominent among the many feast days that punctuate the year *(see pp42–5)* are the *moussems*. These large popular gatherings usually focus on the tomb of a saint *(see pp202–203)*, and are spectacular shows with traditional dance performances.

Certain festivals, such as the Marrakech Folk Festival in June, draw dancers and musicians from all over Morocco, and the Gnaoua Music Festival in Essaouira, also in June, offers high-quality performances. Other festivals include the Sacred World Music Festival held in Fès in June and the Rabat Cultural Festival in July. Fantasias *(pp38–9)* are typically high-spirited Moroccan shows. They are performed most famously at the *moussem* of Moulay Abdallah, which takes place near El-Jadida in August.

The types of dances vary between the different Berber and rural tribes. Often performed are the *ahouach* of the High Atlas and Ouarzazate, and the *ahidou* of the Middle Atlas, in which men and women take part. The *guedra*, a dance from the Guelmim and Sahara, is performed by one woman within a circle of musicians.

A group performing at the Festival of Andalusian Music in Fès

Shows and Concerts

Large hotels often organize Moroccan evenings giving visitors a chance to see authentic popular performances of music and dance.

Certain restaurants also put on performances of folk dance in the evenings. At **Chez Ali** in Marrakech, on certain evenings guests are served their meal in a tent while a fantasia is performed. Those interested in hearing Moroccan music can choose between *raï*, which has roots in Bedouin music and whose star performer is Cheb Amrou; Gnaoua music, which Mustapha Baqbou has taken to many European jazz festivals; and the nostalgic chants of Andalusian music. Many such concerts are organized by various cultural institutes. Ask the local tourist office for information.

DIRECTORY

Cinemas

AGADIR

Rialto
Avenue des F.A.R.
Tel (0528) 84 10 12.

CASABLANCA

Lynx
150 Avenue Mers Sultan.
Tel (0522) 22 02 29.

Megarama
Boulevard de la Corniche.
Tel 0890 10 20 20.

Rialto
35 Rue Med Qorri.
Tel (0522) 26 26 32.

FÈS

Empire
60 Avenue Hassan II.
Tel (0535) 62 66 07.

Rex
Corner of Avenue Mohammed Es-Slaoui and Boulevard Mohammed V.
Tel (0535) 62 24 96.

MARRAKECH

Colisée
Boulevard M. Zerktouni.
Tel (0524) 44 88 93.

Megarama
Jardins de L'Aguedal.
Tel 0890 10 20 20.

RABAT

Renaissance
266 Avenue Mohammed V.
Tel (0537) 73 80 49.

Salle du 7eme Art
Avenue Allal Ben Abdellah.
Tel (0537) 73 38 87.

TANGIER

Le Paris
11 Rue de Fès.
Tel (0539) 32 43 30.
W leparis-tanger.com

Rif: Cinémathèque de Tanger
Grand Socco. Tel (0539) 93 46 83. W cinematheque detanger.com

Theatres

AGADIR

Théâtre Municipal de Plein Air
Avenue Mohammed V.

CASABLANCA

Complexe Culturel Moulay Rachid
Avenue Akid Allam.
Tel (0522) 70 47 48.

Complex Culturel de Sidi-Belyout
28 Rue Léon l'Africain.
Tel (0661) 05 32 38.

RABAT

Théâtre Mohammed V
Charia al Mansour Eddahbi.
Tel (0537) 70 73 00.

Salle Haj Mohammed Bahnini
1 Rue Gandhi.
Tel (0537) 70 80 37.

Shows

Chez Ali
After Pont de Tensift, Marrakech.
Tel (0524) 30 77 30.

The Villa des Arts in Casablanca

Cultural Centres

Among the most dynamic cultural centres in Morocco are the **French Cultural Institutes**, which are found in major cities. These organize a wide-ranging programme, including exhibitions, film festivals highlighting the work of particular directors, as well as concerts and theatrical performances. The remarkably well laid-out **Institut Français de Marrakech** even has an amphitheatre for open-air performances. The Spanish **Instituto Cervantes** and the German **Goethe Institut** also contribute to the promotion of the artistic activity of the multiple cultures that coexist in Morocco.

These centres are good places to meet Moroccans who have an interest in Europe. Programmes in the form of a bimonthly pamphlet are available on the premises. The **British Council** in Rabat also organizes an interesting range of events.

Art Galleries

Since the Dane **Frederic Damgaard** *(see p128)*, opened an art gallery in Essaouira in 1988, the artistic world in Morocco has enjoyed a new dynamism. Galleries exhibit the work of painters from far and wide, including, for example, that of the well-known "free artists of Essaouira" *(see p129)*.

Galleries in Casablanca include the **Villa des Arts**, an extensive showcase of Moroccan artistic creativity over the last 50 years,

and in Marrakech the **Matisse Arts Gallery** and **Dar Bellarj**.

Painting by Mohammed Tabal, one of Essaouira's "free artists"

Piano Bars

Places where traditional Moroccan music can be heard are relatively few. However, piano bars in large hotels and jazz clubs offer the opportunity to hear European and North American bands.

The **Amstrong Jazz Bar** and the **Villa Fandango** in Casablanca, for example, are very fashionable. Marrakech has several modish venues such as the huge **Al Anbar**, whose restaurant contains several hundred tables and has live orchestras, and the **Montecristo**, which is more intimate and is located in one

of Gueliz's villas. In Essaouira, Fès, Ouarzazate, Rabat and Tangier, it is mostly in hotel bars that music can be heard. The best approach is to obtain information directly from the various bars and hotels themselves.

Nightclubs

Except in Casablanca, Rabat and Marrakech, most nightclubs in Morocco are located within hotels. In Rabat, one of the most fashionable discos is **L'Amnesia**. In Casablanca, nightclubs are concentrated around Aïn-Diab. They include **La Bodega** and the **Carré Rouge**. **Theatro at Hôtel Essaadi** in Marrakech has a good reputation, as does **Le Flamingo** in Agadir.

While discos and night-clubs are relatively empty on weekday nights, all are filled to capacity at weekends and during school holidays.

Some close at about 3am or 4am. Others stay open until dawn, particularly in Marrakech, Agadir and other large tourist centres.

Casinos

Gambling is severely frowned on by Islam, so there are very few casinos in Morocco. The casino in **La Mamounia**, the famous hotel in Marrakech *(see p311)*, is easily the most prestigious.

If you decide to spend the evening in a casino, dress smartly. A jacket is essential, and jeans, track-suits and trainers are definitely not acceptable.

Nightclub in Agadir, with dancing beneath a replica of the Eiffel Tower

DIRECTORY

Cultural Centres

AGADIR

Institut Français d'Agadir
Rue Cheinguit,
Nouveau Talborjt.
Tel (0528) 84 13 13.

CASABLANCA

Dante Alighieri
23 Avenue Hassan
Souktani.
Tel (0522) 26 01 45.

Goethe Institut
11 Place du 16 Novembre.
Tel (0522) 20 77 35.

Instituto Cervantes
31 Rue d'Alger.
Tel (0522) 26 73 37.

Institut Français de Casablanca
121 Boulevard Zerktouni.
Tel (0522) 77 98 70.

FÈS

Institut Français de Fès
33 Rue Loukili.
Tel (0535) 62 39 21.

MARRAKECH

Institut Français de Marrakech
Route de Targa,
Jbel Gueliz.
Tel (0524) 44 69 30.

RABAT

British Council
11 Avenue Allal ben
Abdellah.
Tel (0537) 21 81 30.

Instituto Cervantes
5 Rue Madnine.
Tel (0537) 70 87 38.

Institut Français de Rabat
1 Rue Abou Inane.
Tel (0537) 68 96 50.

TANGIER

Instituto Cervantes
99 Avenue Sidi
Mohammed ben Abdellah.
Tel (0539) 93 20 01.

Institut Français de Tanger
2 Rue Hassan
Ibn Ouazzan
Tel (0539) 94 10 54.

Art Galleries

AGADIR

Artomania
El-Faïs Brahim estate (next
to the Ecole Pigier),
industrial quarter.
(0677) 21 46 33

CASABLANCA

Venise Cadre
25 Avenue
Moulay Rachid.
Tel (0522) 36 60 76.

Villa des Arts
30 Boulevard Roudani.
Tel (0522) 29 50 87.

ESSAOUIRA

Galerie Frederic Damgaard
Avenue Oqba Ibn Nafia.
Tel (0524) 78 44 46.

MARRAKECH

Dar Bellarj
9 Toualate Zaouiate Lahdar.
Tel (0524) 44 45 55.

Matisse Arts Gallery
61 Rue de Yougoslavie.
Tel (0524) 44 83 26.

RABAT

Villa des Arts
10 Rue Beni
Mellal Hassan.
Tel (0537) 66 85 82.

TANGIER

Lawrence Arnott Art Gallery
68 Rue Amra Ben Ass.

Piano Bars

CASABLANCA

Amstrong Jazz Bar
16 Rue de la Mer Noire,
Boulevard de la Corniche.
Tel (0522) 79 77 58.

Villa Fandango
Rue de la Mer Egée,
Boulevard de la Corniche.
Tel (0522) 79 74 77.

FÈS

Le Birdy
Jnan Palace Hotel, Avenue
Ahmed Chaouki.
Tel (0535) 65 22 30.

Oasis Bar
Hotel Royal Mirage,
Avenue des F.A.R.
Tel (0535) 93 09 09.

MARRAKECH

Al Anbar
47 Rue Jbel Lakhadar.
Tel (0524) 38 07 63.

Le Churchill
La Mamounia Hotel,
Bab el-Jedid.
Tel (0524) 38 86 00.

Le Montecristo
20 Rue Ibn Aïcha.
Tel (0524) 43 90 31.

OUARZAZATE

Le Piano Bar
Hôtel Kenzi Azghor.
Tel (0524) 88 65 01.

Zagora Bar
Hôtel Karam Palace,
Tel (0524) 88 22 25.

RABAT

Amber Bar
Sofitel Rabat Jardin des
Roses, Souissi quarter.
Tel (0537) 67 56 56.

Barrio Latino
61 Rue Oued Sebou,
Agdal. **Tel** (0663) 01 10 33.

Le Puzzle
79 Avenue Ibn
Sina, Agdal.
Tel (0537) 67 00 30.

TANGIER

El Carabo
Chellah Beach Club.
Tel (0539) 32 50 68.

Le Caïd's
Hôtel El-Minzah, 85 Rue
de la Liberté.
Tel (0539) 33 34 44.

Sable's Bar
Hôtel Tanjah-Flandria1,
Boulevard Med V.
Tel (0539) 93 30 00.

Nightclubs

AGADIR

Le Flamingo
Hôtel Beach Club.
Tel (0528) 84 43 43.

CASABLANCA

La Bodega
129–131 Rue Allal
Ibn Abdellah.
Tel (0522) 54 18 42.

Carré Rouge
Avenue Assa.
Tel (0522) 39 25 10.

MARRAKECH

Le Theatro Hotel Es Saadi
Rue Ibrahim el Mazini.
Tel (0524) 33 74 00.

RABAT

L'Amnesia
18 Rue Monastir.
Tel (0612) 99 11 90.

Casino

CASABLANCA

Mazagan Beach Resort
El Jadida.
Tel (0523) 38 80 00.

MARRAKECH

La Mamounia
Bab el-Jedid.
Tel (0524) 38 86 00.

SPORTS & OUTDOOR ACTIVITIES

Morocco's mostly warm climate and great topographical diversity make it suitable for all sorts of sports and outdoor activities. The natural environment, often on a majestic scale, readily lends itself to horse riding, trekking, bird-watching and, in winter, skiing. In areas suitably developed for the purpose, the Moroccan landscape is also a paradise for golfers. The Atlantic coast is internationally renowned for surfing and sailboarding. Thalassotherapy (therapeutic treatment using sea water and marine products) has also developed, and thalassotherapy centres continue to burgeon in the major tourist centres.

The beach at Agadir, where horse rides are available

Horse Riding

Thanks to the impulse provided by King Hassan II, horse riding has become very popular in Morocco. Many equestrian centres have been established, and an International Equestrian Week takes place every year in Dar es-Salam, near Rabat, where the **Fédération Royale Marocaine des Sports Equestres** is based.

Most horse riding is organized by clubs and large hotels, mainly those in Agadir, Marrakech and Ouarzazate. All equestrian centres are staffed by instructors with state-approved qualifications.

Skiing

Although not primarily a winter sports destination, Morocco has several high-altitude resorts, including Ifrane *(see p216)*, near Fès, and Oukaïmeden *(see p252)*, 60 km (37 miles) from Marrakech. Oukaïmeden can be reached by *grand taxi* for a one-way fare of about 400 dirhams. Although

the resort is small, it is equipped with all the necessary facilities, including ski-lifts located near where ski equipment is hired. Hiring equipment for a day costs about 250 dirhams. Skiers can sleep in one of several gîtes. These elegant rest-houses are built in a combined European and traditional Moroccan style. There are not many areas of the country that are suitable for skiing, so this remains a marginal activity in Morocco. Mountain resorts offer a diverse range of

activities, however, including hang gliding, hiking and trekking *(see pp344–5)*. **Fédération Royale Marocaine de Ski et Montagne** can provide further information.

Golf

Many overseas travel agents offer packaged golfing holidays to Morocco. There are over 20 golf links in the country. Many are pleasant and popular. In addtion, there are the royal golf courses (which are open to the public) and numerous private courses, often forming part of hotel complexes, particularly in Agadir and Marrakech.

In April, the height of the holiday season, visitors are advised to book in advance to avoid a long wait. A handicap is theoretically required although in practice this is always overlooked.

There are some excellent golf coaches in Morocco, and their services can be hired for much less than in Europe and the US. The low cost of tuition,

Oukaïmeden *(see p252)*, renowned for its pistes

One of the many fine golf courses in Morocco

combined with an often outstanding natural environment, are ideal conditions for an introduction to the sport. Further information can be obtained from the **Fédération Royale Marocaine de Golf**.

Tennis

Almost all the large hotels have tennis courts. The major towns and cities are also well provided with tennis clubs. Most of them have beaten earth courts, the condition of which can vary. Around the courts it is not unusual to see young Moroccans, who readily offer their services as ball boys or tennis partners. Many are good players.

Bird-Watching

Morocco offers many excellent opportunities for bird-watching, and many travellers, particularly Britons and Americans, tailor their visit around this interest.

The country has a small number of bird sanctuaries, the most important of them at Souss Massa, south of Agadir *(see p296)*, and at Moulay Bousselham, north of Rabat *(see p94)*. The latter attracts large numbers of migratory birds, including some rare species.

Unfortunately, these areas are being threatened by the massive urban development that is spreading along the Moroccan coastline, despite the efforts of associations for the protection of birds.

Off-Road Driving

Morocco is an excellent country for off-road activities, either in a four-wheel-drive vehicle or on a motorbike. The good network of tracks, even near large towns, means that the hinterland is always within easy reach.

It is, however, advisable to check your route thoroughly and preferable to travel in groups of two or more vehicles, since breaking down in a remote spot can be a real problem. Some areas, particularly in southern Morocco, near the border with Mauritania, are patrolled by the army and may be set with land mines. It is unwise to venture into this territory without the help of a reliable guide.

In Marrakech and Ouarzazate quad bikes and go-karts can be hired and **Wilderness Wheels** *(see p345)* organizes all-inclusive motorcycle excursions into the High Atlas mountains and the desert.

Sailing, a popular sport off the Mediterranean coast

Watersports

For surfers, certain spots along Morocco's Atlantic coast are among the best in the world. Essaouira and its environs are the best-known locations, and these are Morocco's windsurfing and surfing centres, particularly in summer. Dakhla has also become very popular for kite-surfing. Most of these places are, however, suitable only for experienced surfers. Strong winds, currents and high waves are not safe for beginners.

The best surfing beaches are also on the Atlantic coast. In summer, the beaches between Agadir and Essaouira are overrun by surfers from all over the world. A particularly popular beach is La Madrague, near Taghazout, 20 km (12 miles) north of Agadir. There is also a surfing centre, **Club Mistral**, in Essaouira.

For less strenuous watersports, there are also some very fine beaches all along the Atlantic and Mediterranean coasts. Sailing boats and jet-skis can be hired on the latter.

Information on water-skiing, which is also available, can be obtained from the **Fédération Royale Marocaine de Jet Ski et Ski Nautique**.

Hiking and Trekking

In the space of a few years, Morocco has become a paradise for hikers. The country's spectacular and varied landscape offers great scope for hikers and trekkers of all abilities. However, any hiking or trekking expedition requires preparation. It is essential to take proper equipment, and basic safety precautions must be observed. Options are many – whether to go on an organized or an independent trek, and whether or not to have porters: luggage carried by mule, camel or vehicle. The most important decision is the choice of route through Morocco's numerous and highly diverse geographical regions.

A hike in the South, with luggage carried by camels

Mountain biking, an increasingly popular activity in Morocco

Basic Safety Precautions

The first consideration is your physical condition. You must be able to withstand the sometimes arduous demands of a long trek. Do not venture even a little way off the beaten track without a reliable guide, or unless you are on a well-organized trek. Never set off alone, and if you are not part of an organized party, inform your next of kin or your country's embassy of your intended date of return so that emergency aid can be sent if necessary. The cost of mountain rescue in the more remote regions of Morocco is very high. Check your personal insurance to see whether it will cover you for this type of risk.

By far the best option is to let a specialist agency arrange your hike or trek. This may be a Western tour operator or one of the specialist agencies in Morocco. Using their infrastructure and logistics will give you peace of mind.

Equipment

The most important piece of equipment is a good pair of walking boots. Even though ordinary trainers may be quite adequate for a short walk on even ground, a strong pair of walking boots is essential for longer and more demanding walking over rough ground.

As for clothing, strong, lightweight fabrics are the best choice. Although it rarely rains in Morocco, it is prudent to pack a rainproof garment as well as a few warm clothes, since temperatures drop quickly at high altitudes. Finally, even for a short walk, always take enough water, and something to eat.

A first-aid kit is also necessary. The minimum that it should contain is treatment for minor cuts and blisters. More adequate first-aid equipment will also include anti-venom treatment, insect repellent, antihistamine for allergies, aspirins and sunblock cream.

For nights in a tent or in the open air, a good-quality body-hugging sleeping bag is recommended. Check carefully its insulating properties, but bear in mind that you will still need a light mattress to insulate you from cold or wet ground.

Finally, it is the small things that can be the most useful. Head lamps, for example, give you light while

also leaving your hands free. Also remember to pack water-purifying tablets, so that you can drink from springs and refreshing mountain streams along the way.

Types of Hiking

Some hikes are organized with the advantage of using animals to carry equipment. Hikes with mules take place in the Atlas, a region where this animal is particularly at home. Further south, camels are used to carry luggage and food supplies. Caravans of camels are a common sight here, particularly south of Zagora.

It is also possible to go on combined treks, alternating walking with mountain biking, or with canoeing or rafting. Vehicle-assisted treks allow greater distances to be covered. More luggage can also be carried, which means that camping can be much more comfortable.

Participants in the Marathon des Sables

Four-wheel-drive vehicles, essential for negotiating rough tracks

Popular Routes

The main regions of Morocco that are most suitable for trekking and hiking are the Atlantic coast; the Middle Atlas, High Atlas and Atlantic slopes of the Atlas; Jbel Sirwa and Jbel Sarhro; the valleys of Wadi Draa, Wadi Dadès and Wadi Tafilalet; and the Saharan provinces of the South.

In the High Atlas, Jbel Toubkal, which reaches a height of 4,167 m (13,676 ft), is the highest point in North Africa *(see p253)*. The mountain offers great scope for hikes. The summit can be reached in two days and climbing it does not require a high level of experience as a mountaineer. The only disadvantage is the fact that this is where most hikers come in the high season, so you will not be alone. The **Club Alpin Français** manages five refuges on Jbel Toubkal.

In the central High Atlas, the Aït Bouguemez valley *(see pp258–61)* offers a very fine itinerary. The route is not very demanding and passes through a striking variety of different landscapes. This expedition to the deep heart of Berber country takes five to six days, and the starting point is Demnate, four hours' drive from Marrakech.

On the other side of the Atlas, there are hikes that combine Jbel Sarhro, the foothills at the edge of the Sahara, and the sublime Dadès gorge *(see p277)*, one of the great attractions of the Moroccan South.

Many camel treks take place southwest of Zagora, their ultimate destination being Mhamid and Iriki, where the first dunes of the immense Sahara can be seen.

Further east, towards Erfoud *(see p284)*, the spectacular Merzouga dunes *(see p285)* offer many possibilities for hikes and camel rides through unforgettable scenery.

Marathon des Sables

This long-distance race takes place in the Ouarzazate region every year. About 700 competitors from all over the world take part. The route covers 230 km (143 miles) and the race lasts seven days. Each competitor carries his or her own food and equipment. The Marathon des Sables is considered to be the most demanding race of its kind in the world.

Jbel Toubkal, to which large numbers of hikers are drawn

DIRECTORY

Specialist Tour Operators

Adam Travel
5146 Leesburgh Pike, Alexandria, VA 22302, USA.
Tel 1-703 379 2428.

Backroads
801 Cedar Street, Berkeley, CA 94710-1800, USA.
Tel 1-800 462 2848.
w backroads.com

Discover
Timbers, Oxted Road, Godstone, Surrey RH9 8AD, UK.
Tel 01883 744 392.
w kasbahdutoubkal.com

Exodus
9 Weir Road, London ONE, UK. **Tel** 020 8772 3942.
w exodus.co.uk

Overseas Adventure Travel
625 Mount Auburn Street, Cambridge, MA 02138, USA.
Tel 1-800 955 1925.

Ramblers Holidays
Lemsford Mill, Lemsford Village, Welwyn Garden City, Herts, AL8 7TR UK.
Tel 01707 331 133.
w ramblersholidays.co.uk

Sherpa Expeditions
81 Craven Gardens, Wimbledon, London SW19 8LU, UK.
Tel 020 8577 2717.
w sherpaexpeditions.com

Agencies in Morocco

Atlas Sahara Trek
6 bis Rue Houdhoud, Majorelle Quarter, Marrakech.
Tel (0524) 31 39 01.

Club Alpin Français
50 Sidi Abderrahmane, Casablanca.
Tel (0522) 99 01 41.

Sport Travel
154 Avenue Mohammed V, Gueliz, Marrakech. **Tel** (0524) 43 63 69. **w** sporttravel-maroc. com

Wilderness Wheels
61 Hay Al-Qods, Ouarzazate.
Tel (0524) 88 81 28 (Ouarzazate).
w wildernesswheels.com

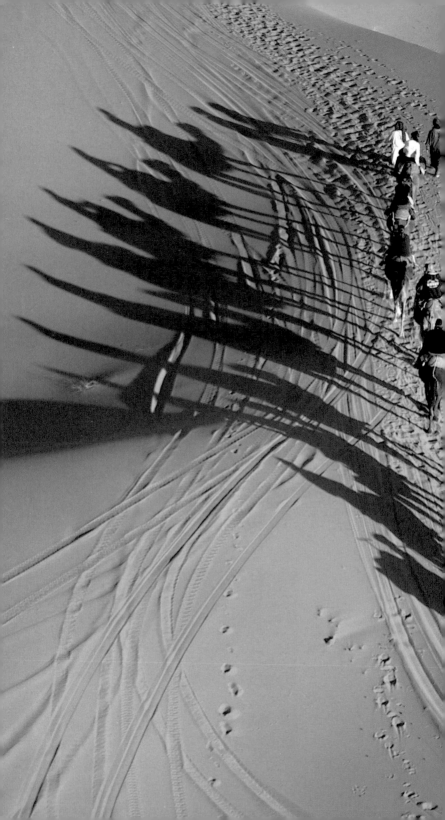

SURVIVAL GUIDE

PRACTICAL INFORMATION

Morocco, a country with a wide range of attractions, receives a large number of visitors. Much of its economic success is due to tourism. The country has a good tourism infrastructure and tourist offices, both at home and abroad. Moroccan hotels have undergone major restructuring and many regions have significantly increased their capacity to accommodate visitors.

The major museums and historic monuments have been reorganized so as to be seen to their best advantage by the maximum number of visitors. Customs formalities are minimal and while French is the most widely spoken foreign language, at least the bigger hotels and restaurants and all tourist offices have English-speaking staff.

Summer crowds on the beach at Casablanca

When to Go

Morocco is a relatively large country with a varied climate, ranging from the arid, desert conditions of the south to the Mediterranean climate of the north (see pp46–7).

The peak of the tourist season in the South, is in spring, from March to mid-May, and, to a lesser extent, in the early autumn, in September and October. At those times, visitors can enjoy many hours of sunshine and almost no rain.

Summer is the best time to visit the Mediterranean and Atlantic coasts. The South and the Centre, where the heat is then intense, are best avoided. Even when the winters are mild they are still very cold, and snowfall at high altitude, which can close passes, may interfere with your itinerary.

Reservations

Morocco is a fashionable tourist destination, and the publicity campaigns that are mounted to advertise its attractions are effective in attracting large numbers of visitors. Around 10 million tourists visit Morocco each year.

Most months are busy and hotel reservations have become essential. It is best to arrange your visit several months in advance, so as to be able to use the most direct flights and the most convenient schedules, and particularly if you want to reserve a room in smaller hotels and guesthouses, which have more character and which get booked up quickly.

Tourist Information

All the major tourist centres in Morocco have a branch of the Office National Marocain du Tourisme (ONMT), which often goes under the name "Délégation Générale du Tourisme". Smaller towns have a Syndicat d'Initiative (tourist bureau). These bureaux provide information on the town's principal features of interest, and the addresses of hotels and restaurants. Official guides are also usually available. The Délégations Générales and Syndicats d'Initiative are open from 8:30am to noon and from 2:30 to 6:30pm. During Ramadan and in summer, in the busiest towns and cities they are open continuously from 9am to 5pm. Before leaving home, you may also wish to contact the Moroccan tourist office in your own country.

Entry Charges and Opening Hours

Tourist brochure

An entry charge (usually about 10 to 20 dirhams) is made for museums and historic sites and buildings. When entry is free, it is customary to give the caretaker a tip equal to the average value of an entry ticket.

Opening hours can be irregular. Tourist sites are generally open from 9am to 6pm, with some closing for up to three hours midday. However, these times may change during Ramadan and at times of the year when the heat is very intense. The opening of smaller sites sometimes depends on the goodwill of the caretaker.

Passports and Visas

Citizens of the European Union, Swiss nationals and citizens of some other countries, including the

Entrance to the Dar Si Saïd Museum in Marrakech

United States, Canada, Australia and New Zealand need a valid passport to visit Morocco. A passport, which should be valid for at least six months after the date of your arrival, allows you to stay in Morocco for three months. If this period is exceeded, the authorities react strictly and at the very least will escort you back to the frontier.

If you intend to stay in Morocco for more than three months, you will need to obtain a resident's permit. Travellers from some countries will need a visa to cover the whole duration of their stay. Information on entry formalities is available from the Moroccan Consulate in your home country.

The border with Algeria is closed, but visas for Mauritania can be obtained quickly in Casablanca.

Customs

During your flight to Morocco, or when you arrive at the border, you will be handed a customs declaration form which you should fill in and hand over at passport control. You are legally entitled to bring into the country 200 cigarettes, 75 cl of alcohol and small quantities of photographic material and video equipment.

Drugs, firearms and pornographic material are strictly prohibited. Permission must be obtained to bring in hunting weapons.

Importing a vehicle for a limited period is possible but the formalities are lengthy. The vehicle should be registered in your first name and surname.

Language

The official language is Arabic, which is spoken by almost all Moroccans. French, a vestige of the Protectorate, is also very widely used, at least in large towns. It is less current in country areas, except among older people. In the South, Berber is widely spoken, especially in rural and mountainous areas.

Because of the city's proximity to Spain, Spanish is widely understood in Tangier, and is spoken in the Spanish enclaves. German is most often heard in Agadir, which attracts large numbers of Germans. English is spoken only by those closely involved in the tourist industry, such as guides and certain staff in the larger hotels.

Trekkers following a high mountain trail in an arid region of Morocco

Etiquette

Moroccans are very friendly people. You will have many opportunities to talk to them, and may even be invited into their homes. However, Morocco is a Muslim country, and certain conventions must be observed to avoid inadvertently causing offence. It is especially important to dress appropriately, not to take photographs of Moroccans without their permission, and to avoid certain sensitive subjects in conversation. If you are invited into the home of a Moroccan family, it is as well to be aware of certain points of etiquette. Respecting a few simple rules will be appreciated by your naturally hospitable hosts.

Mint tea served to guests, one aspect of Moroccan hospitality

Hospitality

Among Moroccans, hospitality is more than a tradition; it is an honour. After just a few minutes of conversation, traders in the souks and country people in the remotest regions of the Atlas may well invite you into their homes to drink a glass of tea or share a meal. It is difficult to decline these invitations, and a refusal may cause offence.

When you enter a house, take your shoes off if shoes have already been left near the door; this is a sign of respect towards your host. It is often the men who will invite you in, although you are sure to see the women of the house as well, in which case avoid being over-familiar. Accepting an invitation from a trader in a souk puts you under no obligation to buy anything from him. Finally, even if you are invited in by Moroccans of very modest means, never offer to pay for your meal. Offering a small gift is a far better and more acceptable way of thanking your hosts.

Sharing a Meal

If you are invited to share a meal in the home of a Moroccan family, be prepared to be plied with copious helpings of food.

Moroccans customarily eat with their right hand

As with other invitations, it is difficult to refuse first, let alone second, helpings of food.

People usually eat with their fingers, with the additional aid of a piece of bread. If you cannot master the technique, you will be given eating implements. When eating, you should use your right hand since the left hand, used for personal hygiene, is traditionally considered to be impure.

A Moroccan meal invariably ends with mint tea. It is not unusual to drink three or four glasses of this very sweet infusion. Again, the offer is very hard to refuse.

Photography

You can take photographs almost anywhere in Morocco. In some museums, a supplementary fee is charged if you want to take photographs, and in others photography is forbidden.

Avoid taking pictures of military or official buildings since this may result in your film being confiscated and you being questioned at length about what you were trying to photograph.

Before turning the lens on anyone, always ask the person's permission, since Moroccans have an ingrained suspicion of any type of image. Bear in mind that anyone who agrees to your photographing them may ask you for a little money, especially in the major tourist spots.

Muslim Customs

Islam is a state religion, and the king of Morocco is the leader of the faithful. It is thus considered very bad form to criticize religion. It is also ill-mannered to disturb someone while they are at prayer, whether by speaking to them or by taking a photograph of them.

It is above all during Ramadan that certain rules must be obeyed. The fast of Ramadan is strictly observed in Morocco. Although non-Muslims may eat, drink and smoke whenever they please, they should avoid

The Grand Mosque in Casablanca, open to non-Muslims

doing so in public. Lastly, couples in the street must behave with decorum; they should not kiss in public, for example.

Visiting Mosques

All mosques, except the Grand Mosque in Casablanca and the old Tin Mal Mosque, are closed to non-Muslims. When visiting these mosques, remove your shoes and behave in a respectful manner, appropriate to the holy nature of the building.

Never insist on being admitted to a mosque and do not try to see inside it by peeping through the door. Acting like this is likely to be considered sacrilegious.

Dress

Attitudes towards dress have changed significantly in Morocco, so that, in large towns and cities, it is far from unusual to see Moroccan women in Western-style dress. Even so, scanty clothing should not be worn when exploring traditional quarters of towns or venturing into the country. Very short skirts, shorts and clothes that leave the shoulders or chest bare are likely to cause deep offence to Moroccans. For women, wearing a headscarf may help avoid unwanted attention. Women going topless, on the beach or in the swimming pool, is severely frowned on. Nudity is strictly forbidden in Morocco, and nudists run the risk of being arrested.

The Monarchy

Since the accession of Mohammed VI, attitudes towards the monarchy are much more relaxed. You may even hear Moroccans openly criticizing the king. Even so, the subject of the monarchy is surrounded by a great deal of taboo in Morocco. As a general rule, do not express too trenchant an opinion on the subject and never show disrespect towards the king's image, which can be seen hanging

in all shops and public places. Lastly, be aware that the Moroccans are very patriotic and that any discussion of their country can quickly become heated.

Bargaining

You may bitterly disappoint a trader if you do not show a willingness to indulge in the ritual of bargaining, another Moroccan custom.

Bargaining revolves around the considerable difference between the price quoted by the buyer and that offered by the seller and the slow process by which both sides arrive at a mutually fair figure.

When bargaining, you should keep smiling since the whole process is treated as a game.

Moroccan women, customarily fully dressed, on the beach

Smoking

Public places very rarely have no-smoking areas. However, smoking is now prohibited in most buses and modern cinemas.

Except in large towns and cities, where attitudes have changed, it may still be considered shocking for women to smoke in public. Smoking *kif* (marijuana) is technically illegal, and it is best to avoid any contact with dealers.

Tourist negotiating the price of a camel ride

Health and Security

Crime in Morocco is no worse than elsewhere and most visitors will experience no serious problems. The fact that the police have a high-profile presence contributes to this degree of personal safety. As in any other country, a few basic precautions should be taken so as to avoid the attention of pickpockets. Visitors should also be aware that drug-taking, especially in the north of the country, is one of the prime threats to personal safety. The best policy is to have nothing whatsoever to do with drugs, however mild. While the standard of Morocco's public hospitals is uneven, private clinics are very expensive. It is advisable to take out health insurance in your own country before you leave.

SAMU ambulance

Vaccinations and Minor Health Risks

No vaccinations are required for visitors entering Morocco, except for those coming from a country where yellow fever exists. However, vaccination against hepatitis A and B and typhoid is advised. Visiting certain regions of southern Morocco in summer carries a slight risk of exposure to malaria; anti-malaria pills are available locally.

However long you plan to stay in Morocco, and wherever you intend to go, take a first-aid kit with you. It should include gauze, bandages, antiseptic and syringes, particularly if you intend to spend any time in sparsely inhabited rural areas.

To prevent sunstroke, drink plenty of water, wear a hat and use a sunblock with a high UV-protection factor.

Medical Care

Although most public hospitals in Morocco have excellent specialist doctors, they are underfunded and lacking in equipment. Standards of hygiene are also unsatisfactory.

If you have the option, choose a private clinic. Although these are expensive, standards of care are close to European ones. Your country's embassy or consulate will provide a list of approved doctors and hospitals.

Emergencies

In the case of accidents that occur in the home or on the public highway, the fire brigade is the first to attend the scene. Its ambulances are usually run by the Moroccan Red Crescent and they are marked "ambulance".

In the case of medical emergencies that occur in the street, SAMU ambulances will take you to the nearest hospital. Tell the ambulance or taxi driver to which (private) hospital or clinic you wish to go, otherwise you will be taken automatically to the nearest public hospital. In remote regions, the only way of reaching a hospital is to hire a taxi.

Pharmacies

All pharmacies in Morocco are denoted by a sign in the form of a crescent. Duty pharmacies are open on Sundays, and their address is posted in the window of pharmacies that are closed. In large towns and cities, duty pharmacies stay open round the clock.

Pharmacies have helpful, knowledgeable staff who are able to give advice on minor health problems. Certain medicines that can only be obtained on prescription in Europe are available over the counter in Morocco.

Food and Water

Many visitors to Morocco suffer from stomach upsets, which are often caused by the change of diet. Avoid drinking tap water, especially in rural areas, and keep to bottled mineral water (see p319). Make sure that the bottle is opened in front of you. Do not add ice to any drink and avoid diluted fruit juices.

On hikes and treks take water-purifying tablets to make spring water safe to drink. Alternatively, boil the water for 20 minutes.

Pharmacy sign

Be wary of salads and raw vegetables, and of peeled fruit and vegetables. They should be washed carefully. Food prepared at street stalls is another potential hazard. Although it is usually safe, as long as it is freshly cooked,

A fire brigade vehicle

A pharmacy in Essaouira

people with delicate stomachs are advised to resist it.

Fortunately, Moroccans like their meat well cooked. This destroys such parasites as tapeworms, which are rampant in Morocco.

Insects

There are no particularly harmful insects in Morocco, but scorpions, snakes, cockroaches and spiders are common in the countryside. Check your clothes and shoes before dressing, particularly when camping in rural areas.

If you are bitten by a snake or spider or stung by a scorpion, apply a suction pump to the wound. These devices are sold in pharmacies all over the country.

Mosquitoes can be particularly bad in desert oases. An effective mosquito repellent is essential, especially in summer.

Serious Illness

Being careful about what you eat should stop you contracting cholera. In case of serious diarrhoea that persists after taking ordinary medication,

consult a doctor without delay. Stray animals – especially dogs, which roam the streets of large towns during the night – may carry rabies. If you are bitten, it is essential to seek first aid immediately.

Although the authorities deny it, sexually transmitted diseases such as AIDS are spreading in Morocco. The use of condoms (which are available in all pharmacies) is strongly advised.

Personal Safety

Violence is rare throughout Morocco, and it is safe to go anywhere with no great risk to personal safety. Serious theft and burglary are not a widespread problem; this is because of the large number of caretakers who supplement the work of the police and act as an effective deterrent.

However, pickpockets with finely honed techniques are likely to patrol the souks, and unwary tourists are the most likely targets. If you are the victim of theft, report it immediately at the nearest

police station. If you intend to make an insurance claim, ask to be given a copy of the police record of the incident; this should be written in French rather than Arabic.

Police

Policemen are omnipresent both in towns and cities and on the roads in Morocco, and they have considerable powers. Uniformed police officers, traffic police on the roads and numerous plain-clothes officers are present everywhere.

The Moroccan police, who once had a reputation for corruption, have adopted a very courteous attitude in their dealings with tourists.

In the case of more serious problems, you should contact your country's consulate (see p349) as soon as possible. The consulate will give you advice and assistance in dealing with the finer details of the Moroccan legal system.

DIRECTORY

Hospitals and Clinics

Rabat
Centre Hospitalier Ibn Sina
Tel (0537) 67 64 64.

Marrakech
Polyclinique du Sud
Tel (0524) 44 79 99.

Casablanca
Centre Hospitalier Ibn Rochd
Tel (0522) 48 20 20.

Emergencies

SAMU Casablanca
Tel (0522) 25 25 25.

SOS Médecins Casablanca
Tel (0522) 38 73 87.

SOS Médecins Rabat
Tel (0537) 20 20 20.

SOS Médecins Marrakech
Tel (0524) 40 14 01.

Police
Tel 177, 19.

Fire Brigade & Ambulance
Tel 15.

Entrance to the Hôpital Ibn Rochd in Casablanca

Banking and Currency

Moroccan currency cannot be obtained abroad. On your arrival in the country, you will find many exchange offices where you can easily obtain dirhams. With an international banker's card you will also be able to draw money from automatic cash dispensers, as well as over the counter in banks that do not have ATMs. In country areas it can sometimes be difficult to change foreign currency, and shopkeepers and traders are seldom able to give change for high-denomination banknotes. It is also useful to keep a collection of coins for small purchases.

A branch of the French bank Société Générale

Banks

Morocco's main banks are Banque Marocaine du Commerce Extérieur (**BMCE**), Banque Marocaine du Commerce et de l'Industrie (**BMCI**), **Attijariwafa Bank** and **Crédit du Maroc**. Most of them either have agreements with certain large international banks, such as **Citibank** and the French bank **Société Générale**, or are their subsidiaries. There are branches throughout the country. Small towns usually have only one bank, and there are no banks at all in rural areas.

Banks are open continuously from 8am to about 4pm, Monday to Friday including Ramadan.

Automatic cash dispenser

Automatic Cash Dispensers

In large towns, automatic cash dispensers (ATMs) are becoming increasingly easy to find. Most have instructions in several languages, and a notice or sticker lists those cards – Visa, Eurocard and MasterCard – that are accepted.

Some dispensers give cash only against accounts that are held in Morocco and may swallow your international card if you insert it by mistake. Cash dispensers give out dirhams, and there is often an upper limit to individual withdrawals. The machines do not always work properly, and it is advisable to withdraw money during bank opening hours so that you can retrieve your card immediately in the event of any problems arising.

Banks in Morocco charge commission for foreign cash withdrawals, usually between 4.50 and 7 dirhams, regardless of how much is withdrawn. Obtain information on charges from your bank and avoid making frequent withdrawals of small amounts. If the cash dispenser fails to work, most banks will issue cash over the counter to holders of a banker's card.

Bureaux De Change

Bureaux de change can be found in almost all banks, in hotels with a grading of three stars and upwards, and at airports. The exchange rate is uniform and variations in the commission charged are unusual. To avoid queueing, it is best to change money at a hotel. While exchange offices in hotels and airports are open almost permanently, those attached to a bank have the same opening hours as the bank's.

When changing money, you will usually be asked to show your passport. All foreign currencies are accepted, but the euro and the dollar are the preferred currencies. Worn and torn banknotes are not accepted as a matter of policy. In the major tourist centres, money-changers may offer you their services in the street at a preferential rate, but it is best to decline the offer.

You can change back any dirhams that you have left at the end of your stay, although the exchange rate will be poor and, unlike dollars and euros, pounds sterling are not always available.

Credit Cards

Most reasonably comfortable hotels (usually those with a rating of three stars and above), as well as mainstream restaurants in large towns, and certain stores (usually those in the most upmarket bracket) accept credit cards for payments.

Traveller's Cheques

The safest way of carrying money when travelling is still in the form of traveller's cheques (in sterling, euros or dollars). Traveller's cheques are accepted at almost all exchange offices and in most large hotels.

Currency

The Moroccan unit of currency is the dirham (Dh in its abbreviated form), which is divided into 100 centimes. Banknotes are issued in the following denominations: 20, 50, 100 and 200 dirhams. Coins are issued in denominations of 5, 10, 20 and 50 centimes, and of 1, 2, 5 and 10 dirhams.

Notes and coins are inscribed in French and Arabic. In rural areas and in souks it is very difficult to obtain change for large-denomination notes. Always carry small change to cover ordinary purchases.

Both banknotes and coins bear the likeness of King Mohammed VI or of his father Hassan II. It is considered sacrilegious to tear or damage them. Any coin or banknote where the sovereign's portrait is defaced in any way may even be refused.

In some areas, especially in the countryside, prices are given in riales (or reales) instead of in centimes. One rial equals 5 centimes, but it is a purely conceptual unit: there are no rial coins.

Coins

Coins come in denominatons of 5, 10, 20 and 50 centimes and of 1, 2, 5 and 10 dirhams. While centime coins are not widely used, 1-dirham coins are handy, especially for paying someone to guard your car and for occasional tips.

10 dirhams   5 dirhams   2 dirhams

1 dirham   50 centimes   20 centimes   10 centimes   5 centimes

Banknotes

Banknotes are issued in denominations of 20 dirhams, 50 dirhams, 100 dirhams and 200 dirhams.

20-dirham note

50-dirham note

100-dirham note

200-dirham note

Communications

Morocco's telephone network is run by national operators Maroc Télécom, Meditel and Wana. The network has developed significantly and provides an efficient service, despite occasional problems. The use of mobile telephones is widespread. Postal services are generally reliable, although deliveries can be subject to long delays. Moroccan television is fighting a losing battle against satellite channels and foreign programmes. Newspapers, many of which are in French, cover current affairs both in Morocco and on the international stage.

A *téléboutique*, where telephone calls can be made and faxes sent

A typical yellow postbox seen on the street in Morocco

Public Telephones

Public phone boxes, which are relatively rare, are usually located outside post offices, markets and bus stations. Coin-operated telephones are still relatively common, and they take coins up to a denomination of 5 dirhams. Because of the number of coins needed, it is not practical to make international calls from a coin-operated telephone. Such calls are best made from a card-operated telephone. Phonecards are available at post offices and in tobacconists, which are indicated by a blue and white sign with three interlinked rings.

With some telephones, an illegal card rental system applies. The cardholder inserts the phonecard for you, noting the number of existing units on the

Moroccan phonecard

card. You make the call, and then pay the cost (based on the difference between the number of units on the card before and after your call). Calls made by this method are more expensive but obviate the need to buy a whole card.

Public Telephone Centres

The number of small public telephone centres, known as *téléboutiques*, has mush-roomed in Morocco. These centres are run either by private operators or by one of the three national operators. They house plastic phone boxes or kiosks (which are usually a sandy colour) with card-operated, coin-operated or metered telephones. The cards that are sold here often only work in telephones in the centre from which the card was bought or in telephones owned by the relevant operator. Faxes can also usually be sent and received in these public telephone centres.

Mobile Phones

Almost everyone, it seems, has a mobile phone in Morocco. The three competing network operators – Méditel, Maroc Télécom and Wana – are locked in a fierce price war. The network is excellent and mobile phones can be used in

even the most remote regions of the country.

Most European network operators have arrangements with one or other of the three Moroccan network operators, so that visitors can use their mobile phones in Morocco (but bear in mind that calls will be expensive).

Mobile-phone users may also buy a prepaid SIM card from either of the Moroccan network operators. For a modest charge (no more than about 200 dirhams), you are provided with a Moroccan number through which national and international calls can be made at more favourable rates.

Useful Dialling Codes

- Telephone numbers consist of ten digits, and the country is divided into two zones (052 and 053).
  – Casablanca zone: 0522 + 6 digits
  – Rabat zone: 0537 + 6 digits
  – Marrakech zone: 0524 + 6 digits
  – Fès zone: 0535 + 6 digits.
- Always dial ten digits, whether calling from one zone to another or within a single zone.
- To call Morocco from abroad: dial 00 212 + nine digits (the ten-digit number minus the initial 0).
- To dial internationally: dial 00 + country code + telephone number.

An Internet café in a large town in Morocco

Internet Cafés

In large towns, it is increasingly common to find Internet cafés. Here, you can pick up and send e-mail and surf the Internet. Charges vary widely between different cybercafés, and are calculated according to the time spent on line.

Moroccan postage stamps

Postal Service

Morocco's postal service has a reputation for being very slow. This is often borne out by reality, especially in the case of international mail.

There are post offices in all sizeable towns. Here, you can buy stamps, send letters and parcels and cash or, send postal orders. Stamps are also available in tobacconists and at the reception desk of large hotels. Central post offices are open from 8.30am to 4pm. Sub-post offices close at lunchtime; precise times vary according to location.

A newspaper vendor's display showing several daily publications

Post offices also provide an express mail delivery service. However, if you have something urgent to send, it is better to use a private company such as **DHL Worldwide Express** or **Globex (Federal Express)**. It is also best to post letters at a central post office rather than use one of the yellow street postboxes as collections can be unreliable.

Poste Restante

Most post offices provide a poste restante service, and this system works well in Morocco. Mail should bear the first name and surname of the recipient, as well as the name of the town. You will need some form of identification when collecting mail from a poste restante. The service is free of charge.

Newspapers

Morocco has many daily newspapers in Arabic and in French. The major leading newspapers in French are *Le Matin*, *Libération* and *TelQuel*. Several weekly magazines, such as *Maroc Hebdo*, *TelQuel's Le Mag and Le Temps*, or the quarterly publications such as *Medina*, *Femmes du Maroc* and *Citadine* have given a new voice to the Moroccan press, which is usually quite conservative.

French newspapers like *Le Monde* and *Le Figaro* are printed in Casablanca at the same time as in France. English-language newspapers are available in Tangier, Agadir, Casablanca and Marrakech. Outside large towns

DIRECTORY

DHL Worldwide Express
52 Boulevard Abdelmoumen, Casablanca.
Tel (0522) 97 20 20.

Globex (Federal Express)
313 Boulevard Mohammed V, Casablanca.
Tel (0522) 54 12 12

Internet Cafés
Marrakech: Cyber Behja, 27 Rue Bani Marine (in the medina); Cybercafé Hivernage, 106 bis Rue Yougoslavie (in Gueliz).
Rabat: Student Cyber, 83 Avenue Hassan II.
Tangier: Futurescope, 8 Rue Youssoufia.

you often find outdated daily newspapers on sale.

Television and Radio

Morocco has two television channels: Radio Télévision Marocaine (RTM), the public national channel that broadcasts in Arabic and in French, and 2M, a privately run channel that also broadcasts in both languages, although programmes in French predominate.

Both the Moroccan television channels are, however, severely rivalled by the spread of satellite dishes, which provide access to a huge number of international channels. Most households, as well as upmarket hotels, have satellite dishes.

Medina, the quarterly magazine

Broadcasts in English are obtainable only via satellite (mostly CNN and BBC). Around Tangier, it is also possible to tune in to broadcasts in English from Gibraltar.

After many years of state monopoly (by RTM and Médi 1), Moroccan radio has been liberalised and private stations such as Aswat and Radio Atlantic have been set up. It is also possible to tune into some European stations, including BBC World Service (on MHz 15,070) and Voice of America.

TRAVEL INFORMATION

The easiest way to reach Morocco is by air. The country is served by many regular flights from most major European cities and less frequent flights from North America. Internal flights link Morocco's major cities. During the high tourist season, many charter flights are also available. Getting to Morocco by train or bus can be cheaper than travelling by air, but for most visitors the journey overland by these means is far too long to be practicable. It is also possible to reach Morocco by car and ship. Using your own car also saves the cost of hiring one on arrival in Morocco, which can be quite expensive.

A Royal Air Maroc aircraft taking off from Ouarzazate airport

Arriving by Air

Morocco has 14 international airports. The busiest are those at Casablanca, Marrakech and Agadir. **Royal Air Maroc** (RAM), the national carrier, provides many links between Morocco and Europe, including departures from provincial cities, and a less frequent service between North America and Casablanca.

RAM provides flights from London Heathrow to Casablanca, Marrakech, Ouarzazate and Agadir, and from London Gatwick to Marrakech. **EasyJet** serves Tangier, Marrakech and Agadir from London Gatwick. **Ryanair** flies to Marrakech, Rabat and Fès from London and, Agadir, Essaouira, Nador, Tangier and Oujda from European cities. **British Airways** operates flights to Marrakech from Gatwick.

From North America, RAM flies most days from Montreal and New York JFK to Casablanca. From other North American cities, the best links are via London or Paris. There are no direct flights to Morocco from Australia or New Zealand. Connections can be made either via Singapore to Casablanca or via Dubai to Casablanca, or by flying to London.

During the high tourist season, many charter flights supplement scheduled services. Most charter flights serve Marrakech, Agadir and Ouarzazate. As part of the "Open Sky" agreement, low cost airlines can now fly to Marrakech. As well as Ryanair, these include EasyJet, Aigle Azur and Corsair.

Many tour operators offer economical package deals including flights and accommodation in hotels, villas or resorts. The deals may also include guided tours, desert trips, activity and sporting holidays, and trekking. Specialist tour operators offer all this and can provide tailor-made arrangements.

Casablanca Airport

Mohammed V Airport in Casablanca is Morocco's main airport, both in terms of its size and of the volume of traffic that it handles. Most international flights arrive in and depart from Casablanca, and many flights serving other cities in Morocco touch down here. Internal flights to smaller airports – at Agadir, Marrakech, Ouarzazate, Fès, Oujda and Essaouira – also depart from Mohammed V Airport. The airport is located about 30 km (19 miles) south of the city centre, and is served by efficient bus and train services.

Marrakech Airport

Rebuilt and considerably enlarged, Marrakech-Ménara Airport is now able to handle a large volume of flights and passengers. Located not more than a few kilometres southwest of the city centre, it is very easy to reach by bus or taxi. Charter flights make up most of its traffic, although it also handles many scheduled flights.

Airport Links

Mohammed V Airport, outside Casablanca, is served by bus and train links (there is one train service every hour). By contrast,

Ferry in the Straits of Gibraltar

the only way of reaching certain other airports is by taxi from the town centre. Only

Sign for Casablanca's
Mohammed V Airport

the *grands taxis* are permitted to wait for passengers at airports. The fact that they hold a monopoly allows them to charge relatively high fares, and they are unwilling to bargain. Airports are well provided with car-hire companies, and if you plan to travel around during your stay, you can hire a car upon arrival at the airport.

To reach an airport from a city centre, you can hire a *grand taxi*.

Arriving by Car and Ferry

Several ferry companies provide various sea links between Spain and Morocco, including the Spanish Transmediterrànea and the Moroccan Comarit. Their UK agent **Southern Ferries** has schedules and prices. The crossing from Algeciras, in Spain, to Tangier or Ceuta (the Spanish enclave in Morocco) takes about two hours but boarding can be very slow, especially in summer, when Moroccans working abroad return home.

Ferry tickets can be purchased in advance or at the time of travel. In either case, the time spent queuing is the same. The adult fare is about €40. Taking a car across costs between about €100 and €210 depending on its size. Most travellers take the ferry from Algeciras to Tangier,

since services from here are more frequent, but there are also ferry links to Tangier and to Melilla from Málaga and Almerìa; to Ceuta from Málaga; and to Tangier from Gibraltar.

In Spain, you need to collect an exit form before boarding. On leaving Morocco, you need to fill in an embarkation form and have this and your passport stamped before boarding the ferry.

Arriving by Train

Travelling by train means a long but scenic journey. From London, take the Eurostar to Paris, from where there is a daily TGV service to Algeciras, in Spain, changing at Irún, on the Spanish border. This is run by the French SNCF, but tickets (including Eurostar) can be bought at **European Rail Ltd** and **Rail Europe**. Holders of an InterRail card, which allows travel in 29 European countries (Spain, Portugal and Morocco are treated as a single zone), can break their journey anywhere they wish.

The fare from Paris to Algeciras is about 155 euros (£97). Avoid train services that go via Barcelona, as links between Catalonia and Algeciras are poor. It is better to use a service that goes via Madrid. From Algeciras, there are ferry services to Tangier and to Ceuta (*see Arriving by Car and Ferry, left*).

DIRECTORY

Airlines

British Airways
w britishairways.com

EasyJet
w easyjet.com

Royal Air Maroc (RAM)
w royalairmaroc.com

Ryanair
w ryanair.com

Ferry Companies

Southern Ferries
22 Sussex Street, London
SW1V 4RW.
Tel (0844) 815 7785.
w southernferries.com

Railways

European Rail Ltd.
Tel (020) 7619 1083.
w europeanrail.com

Voyages-Sncf.com
Tel (0870) 848 5848.
w voyages-sncf.com

Tour Operators

Naturally Morocco
29 Parc Hafan, Newcastle
Emlyn, Carmarthenshire
SA38 9AR.
Tel (01239) 710 814.
w naturallymorocco.co.uk

The Ultimate Travel Company
25–27 Vanston Place,
London SW6 1AZ.
Tel (020) 3582 2653.
w theultimatetravelcompany.co.uk

The interior of Agadir's airport

Travelling by Car in Morocco

The best way of travelling around Morocco, and of exploring the country's historic sites and natural environment in areas not served by local public transport, is by car. The imperfect road network is constantly under improvement, and the number of metalled roads means that a four-wheel-drive vehicle is not essential, even in the South. A greater hazard is Moroccan driving standards. There are a number of car-hire companies in Morocco with varying standards of service. Satellite navigation is also available in Morocco for driving around major towns.

Traffic in town, where other cars are not the only obstacles

Rules of the Road

The Moroccan highway code is based on the one that is used in France, so you must usually give way to the right. At roundabouts, you should give way to cars already on the roundabout.

In general, Moroccan drivers obey traffic lights, perhaps because most junctions are patrolled by a gendarme or policeman.

The speed limits are 40 or 60 kmh (25 or 37 mph) in built-up areas, 100 kmh (60 mph) on the open road and 120 kmh (74 mph) on the motorway. In the approach to towns, drivers will sometimes see signs giving different speed limits; when in doubt, keep to 40 kmh (25 mph), since speed traps are common on these stretches of road. Fines for speeding and other traffic offences range from 300 to 600 dirhams.

Road Signs

The international system applies to road signs in Morocco, most of which have wording in Arabic and French. In large towns, direction signs are sparse, so that it is inadvisable to set out without a map or reliable instructions. Signage on motorways and major roads is usually good. Lighting, however, is normally non-existent, except on the approaches to large towns.

الحزام السلامة
CEINTURE : SECURITE

Road sign in French and Arabic

Traffic Hazards

Negotiating local traffic is difficult mainly because of the great variety of vehicles that use the roads. As a general rule, avoid driving at night, when carts and bicycles with no lights are a real hazard. In towns, the rules of the road are not meticulously observed at night. Be particularly careful about pedestrians crossing roads and even motorways.

Indicator lights are rarely used, and you will find that you must try to anticipate the changes of direction of the vehicles in your vicinity. Many major roads often have two carriageways, which can make overtaking hazardous. On mountain roads, taxis and buses are often driven somewhat dangerously. Sound your horn when driving into a blind bend.

Roads and Tracks

Morocco's relatively dense road network is undergoing constant improvements. So as to reap the benefit of the latest new stretches of road, buy the most up-to-date road map.

The well-developed road network in northern Morocco is gradually being supplemented by motorways, which are very pleasant to use as they do not carry many trucks. The road network in southern Morocco is less dense and the few minor roads in the region are often in a bad state of repair.

In the South and in the Atlas mountains, metalled roads serve most places of interest to tourists, and they are complemented by a relatively good network of tracks. A four-wheel-drive vehicle is essential for journeys in these regions.

Driving in Towns

The volume of traffic in large towns and cities can be considerable, and the increasing number of vehicles on the roads leads to multiple jams and bottlenecks, which are aggravated by the flotilla of bicycles and mopeds that also impede traffic flow.

Although it is possible to drive into most medinas (the old areas of towns), their narrow streets and

Parking attendant wearing a badge

many dead ends can make circulation difficult. It is usually far more pleasurable to explore them on foot.

Driving in the Country

When driving on minor roads in rural areas, you should look out for animals, such as donkeys and flocks of sheep or goats. Wandering freely without human supervision, they may step into the road without warning.

The many trucks and buses that use the roads may slow your progress considerably, and overtaking, particularly in the mountains, is difficult. Passing on narrow roads is often hazardous. Slow down and hug the hard shoulder so as to reduce the risk of collision.

A "Stop" sign in Arabic

Fuel

Service stations are found at fairly frequent intervals along roads in Morocco, even in the most remote areas. Although four-star petrol (gas) and diesel are widely available, unleaded petrol is rarely sold outside large towns. Irregular deliveries to service stations in rural areas may mean that they run out of fuel. Wherever you are, you should fill up before starting a long journey.

Self-service is uncommon; you should wait for the attendant to arrive and then pay him in cash, including a tip.

Parking

In large towns and cities, an attendant wearing a small brass badge is assigned to every pavement. He will help you to park, will watch your car in your absence and will help you manoeuvre out of your parking place.

Payment for this service varies according to how long the car is parked, and is at the driver's discretion; allow 1 to 2 dirhams for a short stay (even lasting no more than a few minutes) and 5 dirhams for several hours' parking. If you want to park for a longer period (overnight, for example), it is advisable to come to an agreement with the attendant before leaving your vehicle. The advantage of this system is that car theft and break-ins are virtually non-existent. Parking meters are common in major cities.

Car Hire

Large towns and airports are well provided with car-hire companies, not all of which offer the same service. When hiring a car for an extended period, it is best to use an international car-hire company (such as **Hertz**, **Avis** or Europcar) or a Moroccan firm (such as Thrifty or First-Car) with an extensive network and reliable insurance and breakdown assistance. On payment of a supplement, the hire vehicle may be dropped off at a different place from where it was picked up. Check the terms of the agreement, especially clauses relating to insurance and cover in case of accident or theft. Also check the state of the vehicle and ask for any damage to be noted before you drive off.

Car hire in Morocco is quite expensive. Charges (excluding collision damage waiver) are about 900 dirhams per day for a Class A car (such as a Renault Logan) and 1,800 dirhams for a four-wheel-drive vehicle. There is usually a wide range of cars to choose from.

In Case of Accident

If you are involved in a road accident, you should wait for the police to arrive. They will usually arrive quickly and will arbitrate in case of any disagreement. Official statement forms similar to those used in Europe are available at tobacconists.

DIRECTORY

Car-Hire Companies

Avis
w avis.com

Agadir
Al Massira Airport.
Tel (0528) 82 92 44.

Casablanca
19 Avenue de l'Armée Royale.
Tel (0522) 31 24 24.

Marrakech
Marrakech-Menara Airport.
Tel (0524) 43 31 69.

Hertz
w hertz.com

Agadir
Bungalow Marhaba, Boulevard Mohammed V.
Tel (0528) 84 09 39.

Casablanca
25 Rue Al-Oraibi Jilali.
Tel (0522) 48 47 10.

Marrakech
154 Avenue Mohammed V.
Tel (0524) 43 99 84.

Driving in the desert, where a four-wheel-drive is essential

Getting Around in Towns

The most important historic sites in Morocco's towns and cities are often located in the medinas, where, in a maze of narrow streets and frequent dead-ends, the only practical way of getting around is on foot. But because many hotels are located in the modern quarters of towns, visitors will frequently need to takes buses or taxis. Although buses are an inexpensive means of getting around in town, visitors may be baffled by the way that they work and the routes that they follow. *Petits taxis* offer a greater degree of flexibility at relatively little cost. In some towns the services of a guide are virtually indispensable to save spending too much time working out a route, but others are much more straightforward to navigate.

By Bus

All large towns in Morocco are served by a wide network of bus lines linking their various districts. It can, however, be difficult to find the bus that you need since the destination is often given only in Arabic. For visitors, the most useful routes are those running between the new town *(ville nouvelle)* and the medina. Bus fares are cheap (3 to 4 dirhams) and tickets are purchased on board from the driver. Be sure to carry some small change.

By Tram

The Rabat-Salé tramway began operating in 2011. The service links the towns of Rabat and Salé, which are separated by the Wadi Bou Regreg. The network has two lines with a total of 32 stations and is 19.5 km (12 m) long. Line 1 connects Hay Karima in Salé to the district of Agdal in Rabat while Line 2

serves the densely populated quarter known as L'Ocean in Rabat. It extends to the bus station in Salé passing through the Yacoub el Mansour locality and Bettana.

Tickets for the Rabat-Salé, tramway are available from the driver for 6 dirhams. The service operates between 6am to 11pm daily. The tram stations have been designed to be accessible to disabled travellers, as well as for pushchairs. In Casablanca, the first tramline is due to open in December 2012. It will link the town centre with outlying residential areas.

By Grand Taxi

The most frequent journeys made by *grands taxis*, many of which are Mercedes and which seat up to six passengers, are those between towns and cities *(see p365)*. They are also useful if you are a large party, are weighed down with luggage

or want to explore the countryside beyond the town, although they won't leave until they are full.

Grands taxis are not fitted with meters, so the fare for your journey must be agreed according to mileage and the length of the hire. The charge for hiring a *grand taxi* for a whole day will be about 500 dirhams.

Grands taxis often wait outside large hotels, and they should not be mistaken for *petits taxis*, which are cheaper and which are used for shorter runs.

By Petit Taxi

These vehicles are identifiable by their colour, which is different in every town, and by the words *"petit taxi"* on the roof. They are prohibited by law from going beyond built-up areas and can only be hired for short trips.

The use of meters is becoming more common. You should always ask for the meter to be switched on, and be prepared to round up the usually modest amount that is shown at the end of your journey. The usual fare for a short journey by *petit taxi* during the day is about 10–20 dirhams. At night a 50 per cent surcharge is added to the amount shown on the meter. Taxi fares are paid in cash, and it is important to have a good supply of small change as drivers are rarely able to give change for a 100- or 200-dirham banknote.

Petits taxis usually take up to three people (two in the back and one in front). They make frequent stops along the way to pick up other passengers going in the same direction. This should reduce the cost of the journey.

It is better to ask to be taken to a specific restaurant, hotel or historic building, rather than name the relevant street. Although most drivers have a good knowledge of the town in which they work, they navigate by landmarks rather than street names.

Local bus, a cheap but not always easy way of getting around in town

A cyclist in Rahba Kedima, Marrakech

Taxi ranks are marked by white rectangular signs saying "taxi". You can also hail a taxi in the street by waving your hand. Because of the large number of taxis circulating in towns, it is unusual to wait for very long. There are no radio taxi firms, but some drivers have mobile phones and will give you their card.

If your journey entails driving along a track, the fare will automatically increase. In this case, the full amount should be agreed with the driver beforehand.

On Foot

Moroccan towns, and their medinas in particular, are typically very poorly signposted for pedestrians. A street map is therefore useful. You can also ask your way, in return for a few words of thanks in French or, if the person takes you there, a few dirhams. Town centres are easy to explore on foot and best appreciated at a relaxed pace, especially if you have time to enjoy the maze of narrow streets. Cars, mopeds and bicycles take little heed of pedestrians, and you should take special care when crossing the street.

Streets in towns throughout Morocco are very safe. There are, of course, insalubrious quarters, although these are rarely frequented by tourists. In tourist spots, an obvious

police presence together with large numbers of people (both Moroccans and visitors) is the best guarantee of safety. In small crowded streets where pickpockets may operate, take special care of personal possessions.

By Bicycle or Moped

In the major tourist centres, particularly Marrakech and Agadir, bicycles and mopeds can be hired. The level terrain in these two cities makes cycling here quite easy. Mopeds and bicycles are an ideal means of getting around the old quarters, where the streets are narrow. However, a degree of caution is called for, since car drivers show little consideration to other road-users.

Bicycle attendants, who can be found where there is a concentration of parked cycles and mopeds, are worth using. Charges range from 1 to 2 dirhams for a few hours to 10 dirhams for a night. Lock your bicycle or moped even if an attendant is guarding it.

By Carriage

Horse-drawn carriages are found mainly in Marrakech. Hiring one costs more than a *petit taxi*, but they can be a fun way of getting

Bus stop in
a town

around town. In Marrakech, the largest carriage "rank" is at the foot of the Koutoubia Mosque.

Guides

The bogus guides who were once so ubiquitous in tourist spots have become more discreet since measures were taken to clamp down on anyone acting as a guide without an official card.

Even if you have a street map, you will find some towns very confusing to explore. The services of a guide may be necessary on your first day in a certain town or city, particularly in the largest medinas, like that of Fès.

Official guides are identifiable by the cards that they carry, almost always pinned to their clothing. These cards are issued by the Ministry of Tourism and bear an identity photograph of the holder. Official guides can be requested at tourist information offices, and also by hotels (in which case make sure they carry the card). They also often wait near hotels and major historic buildings. Specify which buildings and other features you wish to see, and whether or not you wish to be taken into shops. The fees are fixed by the government, but always agree the fee with the guide beforehand.

A horse-drawn carriage, a popular form of transport in Marrakech

Travelling Around in Morocco

The Moroccan rail network (ONCF) links the towns and cities of northern Morocco, the southernmost town with a rail link being Marrakech. Trains are clean and reliable, and journey times depend on the number of stops along the route. The rail network is complemented by long-distance bus services, which are run either by public or by private companies, and which are cheaper than the train. Whatever your chosen means of transport, you should check the various timetables beforehand and note any stops that may seriously lengthen your journey. *Grands taxis (see p362)* are a swift means of travelling from one town to another, but their fares are not fixed and bargaining is a matter of course. The best way to travel between principal cities is often on a domestic flight.

Grand entrance of the train station in Marrakech

Train drawing into the station at Mohammedia, near Casablanca

The Rail Network

Run by the Office National des Chemins de Fer (**ONCF**), the Moroccan rail network, while very good, is not very extensive. It covers just 1,700 km (1,056 miles) and serves mainly the northern part of the country, linking Tangier, Oujda, Rabat, Casablanca, Fès, Marrakech and El-Jadida. Plans to extend the railways southwards, particularly to Agadir, are under way. The Atlas, however, is an insuperable barrier.

Services are frequent, since trains are the preferred means of transport for ordinary people. A separate rail network is used for transporting phosphates,

of which Morocco is the world's largest producer.

Casablanca and Rabat have several railway stations, located in different districts but served by the same line.

Trains

With a few exceptions, Moroccan trains are relatively modern. Those known as Trains Navettes Rapides, or TNR (express shuttles), and referred to as "Aouita" after a famous Moroccan Olympic runner, link Casablanca and Rabat in 50 minutes, Mohammed V Airport and Casablanca in 40 minutes, and Rabat and Kenitra in 30 minutes. The service is frequent at peak times.

Trains known as Trains Rapides Climatisés (air-conditioned express trains) cover the longer distances

A *grand taxi*, used for longer journeys

between Casablanca, Fès, Oujda, Tangier and Marrakech, and are identified by names such as Koutoubia and Hassan. They are air-conditioned and soundproofed and have proper toilets. On the most heavily used route (from Casablanca to Marrakech, Fès and Tangier), there is a service at least every two hours, and it is possible to make the round trip from Casablanca to Tangier and back again in a single day.

For long journeys, the compartments on night trains can be converted into couchettes. Second class, which is air-conditioned, is very comfortable. The toilets are located at the end of the coach and are reasonably clean. On-board catering services are rather basic. Vendors walk up and down the coaches offering cakes, confectionery, drinks and sometimes sandwiches.

Train Tickets and Fares

The cheapest way to buy a train ticket is at a railway station. Passengers must have a ticket valid for the relevant class of seat and type of train. If you reserve a couchette or a bed in a sleeper, you must be able to show the ticket for the relevant supplement.

You can purchase a ticket without booking a seat six days in advance, a combined train and bus ticket one month in advance, and a ticket with a bed booked on a sleeper two months in advance. You can break your journey so long as you collect a form (bulletin d'arrêt) at the station where you alighted. This form makes your ticket valid for an extra five days.

If you have to board a train without having bought a ticket at the station ticket office, ask for a boarding ticket (ticket d'accès), which is issued free of charge at the entrance to the platform, or tell the inspector before you board the train. A ticket bought on the train is always more expensive than one bought from a station ticket office before boarding.

The train is a relatively inexpensive means of getting around. A second-class ticket on an express train from Casablanca to Marrakech or Fès costs about 125 dirhams, and from Marrakech to Tangier about 250 dirhams. There are various concessions for families, young people and groups, and season tickets are also available, although these are economical only for regular travel on a particular route.

Coaches

Many coach (bus) companies operate in Morocco. The best known is **CTM**, the national company that runs services between towns in Morocco and also abroad. Two private companies, **SATCOMA SATAS** and **Supratours**, also cover long-distance routes. Coaches are comfortable and air-conditioned, and are very convenient, especially in the South. They depart from bus stations, which are usually well signposted. A combined train and Supratours coach will take you from Casablanca to Dakhla in the far south.

It is advisable to buy your ticket, and thus reserve a seat, at least 24 hours in advance since coaches are often fully booked at time of departure. Luggage is checked in ahead of departure and is carried in the hold. Make sure that yours has been loaded.

Many small local coach companies also operate in Morocco, although the

comfort of their buses is often minimal and journey times painfully long.

Grands Taxis

This is the most flexible way of travelling from one town to another. Grands taxis are mostly found at bus stations, parked according to their destination.

Grands taxis are not fitted with meters, and fares must be agreed by bargaining. The main factors involved are the length of the journey and how many people are to be carried. If the taxi is full (with seven or perhaps eight people), each person's fare will be only slightly higher than for the same journey made by bus.

If you do not wish to share the taxi, expect to pay the equivalent that the driver would receive for a fully loaded car. This allows you the option of a tailor-made route. Any stops along the way, to visit places of interest, should be agreed beforehand, since they will lengthen the journey time and add to the fare.

Domestic Flights

The most economical way of making longer journeys between Morocco's largest cities is often on one of the internal flights provided by **Royal Air Maroc**, especially to Agadir or Ouarzazate, neither

DIRECTORY

Railway Company

ONCF
8 bis Rue Abderrahmane El-Ghafiki, Agdal, Rabat.
Tel (0890) 20 30 40.
W oncf.ma

Bus Companies

CTM
Tel (0522) 54 10 10 (for travel in Morocco). **W** ctm.ma

Supratours
65 Avenue Fal Ould Oumeir, Bureau No.1. **Tel** (0537) 68 62 97 (for travel in Morocco).
W supratourstravel.com

Airlines

Air Arabia
Mohammed V Airport, Casablanca. **Tel** (0523) 94 48 30.
W airarabia.com

Royal Air Maroc
Casablanca-Anfa Airport, Casablanca. **Tel** (0522) 48 97 97 or (0890) 00 08 00 (for travel in Morocco).
W royalairmaroc.com

of which has a rail link. The one-way fare to either place is about 700 dirhams, although prices may vary according to the time of year. **Air Arabia** also operates internal flights.

An air-conditioned CTM coach parked near a fuel station

General Index

Acknowledgments

Dorling Kindersley and Hachette Livre would like to thank the following people whose contributions and assistance have made the preparation of this guide possible. Special thanks are extended to the staff of the Institut du Monde Arabe in Paris.

Publishing Manager
Jane Ewart.

Managing Editor
Anna Streiffert.

Publisher
Douglas Amrine.

Cartography
Dave Pugh.

Senior DTP Designer
Jason Little.

Consultant
Christine Osborne.

Translator & Editor, UK Edition
Lucilla Watson.

Revisions & Relaunch Team
Shruti Bahl, Younès Cherkaoui Jaouad, Karen Faye D'Souza, Caroline Elliker, Mariana Evmolpidou, Carole French, Emily Hatchwell, Jacky Jackson, Jude Ledger, Carly Madden, Nicola Malone, Alison McGill, Rebecca Milner, Casper Morris, Scarlett O'Hara, Jane Oliver-Jedrzejak, Rada Radojicic, Ellen Root, Sands Publishing Solutions, Dawn Schwartz, Safiya Shah, Beverly Smart, Leah Tether, Ian Thomas, Conrad van Dyk, Vinita Venugopal, Nikhil Verma, Karen Villabona, Tanvir Zaidi.

Proofreader
Stewart J. Wild.

Indexer
Helen Peters.

Main Contributors

Rachida Alaoui
Rachida Alaoui was born in Morocco. She lives and works in Paris. After studying the history of art in France, she specialized in Moroccan fashion, and in Arab fashion in particular.

Jean Brignon
A history teacher, Jean Brignon has taught Muslim history for 12 years at the University of Rabat. He was the general editor of *Histoire du Maroc*, published by Hatier, and has written many academic works. He is president of Rives Sud, the cultural tours organizer and leads cultural and other thematic tours in Morocco.

Nathalie Campodonico
A literary translator, Nathalie Campodonico has lived in Casablanca for about ten years. She is a contributor to various periodicals.

Fabien Cazenave
After having lived in Morocco for many years, Fabien Cazenave now heads the Arabic world division of the specialist travel agency Voyageurs dans le Monde Arabe. He thus has an extensive knowledge of Morocco and its facilities for foreign visitors.

Gaëtan du Chatenet
An entomologist, ornithologist, corresponding member of the Musée National d'Histoire Naturelle in Paris, draughtsman and painter, Gaëtan du Chatenet is the author of many works published by Delachaux et Niestlé and Gallimard.

Alain Chenal
A specialist in international relations and in the Arab world, Alain Chenal teaches law and political science at the Université de Paris X-Nanterre. He is also Director of the Institut du Monde Arabe in Paris.

Emmanuelle Honorin
An ethnologist and freelance journalist who contributes to *Géo* and *Le Monde de la Musique*, Emmanuelle Honorin has special knowledge of Morocco, a country on which she has written extensively.

Maati Kabbal
Maati Kabbal teaches philosophy at the Faculty of Humanities in Marrakech. He is also a translator and journalist, and head of cultural activities at the Institut du Monde Arabe.

Mohamed Métalsi
Specializing in town planning and music, Mohamed Métalsi is director of cultural affairs at the Institut du Monde Arabe in Paris. He is the author of many articles and of a book on the imperial cities of Morocco (published by Terrail).

Marie-Pascale Rauzier
The historian and journalist Marie-Pascale Rauzier lived in Morocco for nine years, during which time she explored the Atlas and the Moroccan desert. Besides writing on Morocco, she contributed to the launch of Morocco's first large-circulation weekly publication. She is also the author of three books and a CD-Rom on Morocco.

Additional Contributors
Sophie Berger, Carole French, Delphine Pont, Sonia Rocton, Sarah Thurin, Sébastien Tomasi, Richard Williams.

Picture Research
Marie-Christine Petit.

Cartography
Fabrice Le Goff.

Additional Cartography
Quadrature Créations.

Illustrations
François Brosse
Architectural drawings, Street-by-Street maps and drawings on pp72–3, 80–81, 106–7, 118, 176–7, 180–1, 198–9, 206–7, 208, 240–1, 270–1 and 280–1.

Gaëtan du Chatenet
Drawing on pp222–23.

Éric Geoffroy
Illustrations on "Exploring" and "At a Glance" maps, on small town and city maps and tour maps on pp66–7, 88–9, 114–5, 125, 130–1, 148–9, 155, 164–65, 185, 212–3, 217, 250–1, 253, 266–7, 288–9 and 291.

Emmanuel Guillon
Architectural drawings on pp28–9, 30–1, 52–3 and 105.

Photography
Anne Chopin, Ian O'Leary, Jean-Michel Ruiz and Cécile Tréal.

Additional Photography
Jean-Michel Ruiz and Cécile Tréal, Rough Guides/Roger Norum, Suzanne Porter.

Special Assistance
Taoufiq Agoumy, Babette and François Aillot, A. Akouad (tourist officer, Ifrane), Jamal Atbir (Hôtel des Cascades, Imouzzer), Amina Bouabid (Office National Marocain du Tourisme, Paris), Ahmed Derouch (tourist officer, Beni Mellal), Soraya Eyles, Kadiri Fakir (Ministère des Affaires Culturelles, Rabat), M. Hassani, Hôtel Tombouctou (Tinerhir), Ali Lemnaouar (Boumalne du Dadès), Sisi Mohamed (Hôtel Asmaa, Zagora), M. Mokthari (Fujifilm Maroc), Natasha, Georges Philippe (Académie d'Architecture de Paris), Joël Poitevin (Météo France), Marie-José Taube (Ministère des Affaires étrangères, Paris), Mohammed Temsamani, Abdelaziz Touri (Ministère des Affaires Culturelles, Rabat), Adolfo de Velasco, Eric Vo Toan (architect of Mausoleum of Mohammed V), Oulya Zwitten.

Photography Permissions
Franciscan sisters' weaving workshop (Midelt), Askaoum inn (Taliouine), Kahina inn (Imessouane), André Azoulay (royal chamber), Banque d'État du Maroc, M. Belghazi (Musée Belghazi), M. Bennani, Pierre Berger (Villa Majorelle Gardens), M. Binbin (library of the Palais Royal), M. Bruno (rose-distillation factory, El-Kelaa M'Gouna), Amastou campsite (Tazarine), CTM, Frederic Damgaard (Galerie Damgaard, Essaouira), 2M Télévision, Fibule du Draa (Zagora), M. Gérard and Françoise (Ksar Sania, Merzouga), Mahmoud Guinea, M. Hamid (royal stud at Bouznika); Hôtel Salam (Taroudannt), M. Jeannot (Chalet de la Plage restaurant, Essaouira), M. Lahcen, M. Larossi (Ministère de la Communication in Rabat), Marrakech Médina, M'Barek Bouguemoun (Kasba Dadès), M. Michel (Derkaoua kasbah-inn, Merzouga), Ministère d'Affaires Etrangères in Rabat, Ministère des Eaux et Forêts in Rabat, Ministère des Habbous, M. Ibrahimi (Office National de Pêche), Ministère de l'Intérieur in Rabat, M. Laforêt (Les Sablons royal stud), Ministère des Postes et Télécommunications in Rabat, Ministère de Santé in Rabat, Ministère de Tourisme in Rabat, Ministère des Transports in Rabat, M. Lahcen, Office National des Aéroports au Maroc, Office National des Chemins de Fer in Morocco, Office National d'Exploitation des Ports in Morocco, M. Oulhaj (Mosque of Hassan II), M. Painclou (oyster farm No. 7, Oualidia), Liliane Phan (Gallimard), Madame Michel Pinseau and her children, Coco Polizzi (medina of Agadir), Radio Télévision Marocaine, M. Ribi (Sous Massa Nature Reserve), Royal Air Maroc, M. Saf (Ministère de l'Information in Rabat), Commandant Skali (Mausoleum of Mohammed V), M. Tarik (Hôtel Anezi, Agadir), M. Tazi (Palais de Fès restaurant, Fès), Baudouin de Witte (Élan-Sud, a society for the protection of the architectural heritage of the Atlas and the Moroccan South).

Picture Credits
The page number (in bold) is followed, where necessary, by a letter referring to the position of the photograph on the relevant page; a-above; b-below/bottom; c-centre; f-far; l-left; r-right; t-top.

1 **Dreamstime.com**/Sean Pavone.
2-3 **Dreamstime.com**/Roberto Marinello.
8–9 **Réunion des Musées Nationaux**/Arnaudet, *Fête Marocaine*, André Suréda (1872–1930). Musée des Arts d'Afrique et d'Océanie, Paris.
10cl **Dreamstime.com**/Ghm Meuffels.
11bl **Dreamstime.com**/Rechitan Sorin.
12tl **Dreamstime.com**/Danmir12; 12bc **Dreamstime.com**/Ed Francissen.
13b **Dreamstime.com**/Hel080808; 13tr **Dreamstime.com**/Tatjana Keisa.
14t **Dreamstime.com**/Harald Biebel; 14bc **Dreamstime.com**/Karol Kozlowski.
15br **Dreamstime.com**/Daniel Schreiber; 15tr **Dreamstime.com**/Witr
16tr Dreamstime.com/Javarman.
17t Dreamstime.com/Gunter Hoffmann;17br Dreamstime.com/Karol Kozlowski.

20 **Alamy Images**/Travelwide.

24a Corbis Sygma/J. Langevin.
26bl **Jacana**/PHR/D. Nigel; 26bc **Jacana**/PHR/ Mc. T. Hugh; 26bcl **Jacana**/C. Pissavini; 26br **Jacana**/M. Willemeit; 26bcr**Jacana**/ J.-L. Dubois.
27cbl **Jacana**/J.-L. Dubois; 27cra **Jacana**/Th. Dressler; 27clbl **Jacana**/P. Jaunet; 27bc **Jacana**/C. Nardin; 27br **Jacana**/A. Brosset.
34tr Corbis Sygma/M. Attar; 34-5c: **A.K.G.**/J.-L. Nou. 34bl **Arthephot**/Oronoz/J.-C. Varga Musée des Arts d'Afrique et d'Océanie, Paris; 34br **Réunion des Musées**

Nationaux/Arnaudet. Musée des Arts d'Afrique et d'Océanie, Paris.
40–1c **Paris Musées**/K. Maucotel. Musée des Oudaïas, Rabat.
48J.-L. Josse; *Mulay Abd Ar-Rahman, Sultan du Maroc, Sortant de son Palais de Meknès* (1845). Musée des Augustins, Toulouse.
49br **G. Dagli Orti**/Musée Leone, Vercelli (Italy).
50tl **Philippe Maillard**.
51b Réunion des Musées Nationaux/Arnaudet. Musée des Arts d'Afrique et d'Océanie, Paris.
52tr **G. Dagli Orti**/Bibliothèque Marciana, Venice; 52cral **Arthephot**/Oronoz/Biblioteca Apostolica, Vatican; 52bl **G. Dagli Orti** *The Triumph of St Thomas Aquinas* Gozzoli (v.1420/2-1497). Musée du Louvre, Paris.
53tr Réunion des Musées Nationaux/J. G. Berizzi, Th. Le Mage. Musée des Arts d'Afrique et d'Océanie, Paris; 53cr **Rapho**/R. S. Michaud. Escorial, Madrid; 53br Réunion des Musées Nationaux/G. Blot, *King Boabdil's Farewell to Granada*, Alfred Dehodencq (1822–82). Musée d'Orsay, Paris.
54cr Réunion des Musées Nationaux/Arnaudet. Musée des Arts d'Afrique et d'Océanie, Paris; 54br **Arthephot**/Oronoz, monastery of Las Huelgas, Burgos; 54clb **Arthephot**/Oronoz. Diputación Foral, Pamplona.
55tr **Bibliothèque Nationale, Paris** Eldressi's map; 55cb **G. Dagli Orti** Azulero Portimao (Portugal); 55br **Photothèque Hachette**. Army Museum, Lisbon.
56br **Roger-Viollet**; 56tc **Philippe Maillard**/Musée Numismatique de la Banque du Maroc, Marrakech; 56c **Arthephot**/Oronoz/Descalzas Reales, Madrid.
57tc **J.-L. Charmet**/Archives of the Ministry of Foreign Affairs; 57cb **J.-L. Josse**/ *Battle of Isly* (1844), E. Vernet, known as Horace (1789–1867). Musée du Château, Versailles.; 57br **Photothèque Hachette**/Meurisse.
58–9c Réunion des Musées Nationaux/G. Blot; *Audience Given in Meknès by the Moroccan Sultan Moulay Ismaïl to François Pidou, Chevalier de Saint-Olon, Ambassador of Louis XIV, on 11 June 1693,* Martin Pierre Denis (1663–1742). Château de Versailles and Château du Trianon; 58tr **Photothèque Hachette**/Bibliothèque Nationale, Paris; 58cl **J.-L. Josse**/*The Moroccan Ambassador Mohammed Temin, at the Commedia dell' Arte in Paris* (1682), Antoine Coypel (1661–1722). Musée du Château, Versailles; 58bl Réunion des Musées Nationaux/F. Raux; *The Moroccan Emperor's Ambassadors.* Château de Versailles and Château du Trianon.
59tc **Bridgeman Art Library**/Giraudon; *Portrait of Anne Marie de Bourbon, Mademoiselle de Blois (1666–1739).* Coll. Lobkowicz, Nelahozeves Castle (Czech Republic).
60tl **Roger-Viollet**; .60c **Photothèque Hachette**; 60bcl **Photothèque Hachette**; 60br **Photothèque Hachette**/Meurisse.
61crb **Roger-Viollet**.
62tl **Magnum**/B. Barbey; 62crb **Roger-Viollet**; 62bl **Corbis Sygma**/M. Attar.
63tl Corbis Sygma/A. Nogues; 63crb **Corbis Sygma**/J. Langevin. 63bl; **Corbis Sygma**/P. Robert.
64-5 **Dreamstime.com**/Iryna Sosnytska.

68 **Robert Harding Picture Library**/Tristan Deschamps.
69b**Hemispheres Images**/Stéphane Frances.
76-7 **Robert Harding Picture Library**/Vincenzo Lombardo.
86 **Dreamstime.com**/Rechitan Sorin.
87b **Alamy Images**/Marek Zuk.
92-3 **Corbis**/Design Pics.
97clal Réunion des Musées Nationaux/Popovitch. Musée du Louvre, Paris; 97ca Réunion des Musées Nationaux/H. Lewandowski. Musée du Louvre, Paris.
98 **Robert Harding Picture Library**/Dave Stamboulis.
108-9 **Robert Harding Picture Library**/Gavin Hellier.
112 **Robert Harding Picture Library**/Dave Stamboulis.
117tr **Anne Chopin**; 117b Réunion des Musées Nationaux/Musée des Arts d'Afrique et d'Océanie, Paris.
120-1 **Corbis**/Neil Farrin.
126br **Horizon Features**/A. Lehalle.
132 **Robert Harding Picture Library**/Yadid Levy.
133b **Robert Harding Picture Library**/Tony Gervis.
139cla **Photothèque Hachette** *Seated Arab,* Eugène Delacroix (1798–1863). Musée du Louvre, Paris; 139cra Réunion des Musées Nationaux/C. Jean. *Odalisque à la Culotte Grise* Henri Matisse (1869–1954). Musée de l'Orangerie, Paris © Succession Matisse/DACS, London 2011; 139crb **Magnum**/D. Stock; 139bl **G. Rondeau**.
139br © **Flammarion**. *Hécate et ses Chiens* Paul Morand, Gallimard coll. Folio, 1974 (cover illustration by H.P.G. Berthier).
140-1 **Robert Harding Picture Library**/Bruno Morandi.
146 **Robert Harding Picture Library**/Bruno Morandi.
153br Réunion des Musées Nationaux/J.G. Berizzi; *Jewish Festival in Tetouan* (c.1848), Alfred Dehodencq (1822–82). Musée du Judaïsme, Paris.
156bc **Alamy Images**/dave stamboulis.
157tr **Alamy Images**/Chris Hellier.
160-1 **Getty Images**/Dave Stamboulis Travel.
166 **Dreamstime.com**/Javarman.
172b **Arthephot**/Oronoz. Musée Dar Batha, Fès.
174b **Philippe Maillard**.
182-3 **Robert Harding Picture Library**/Sylvain Grandadam.
185cl © **Actes Sud** rights reserved.
188 **Dreamstime.com**/Vladislav Gajic.
193br **Gamma**/Hadjih.
195bl/br Réunion des Musées Nationaux. Musée des Arts d'Afrique et d'Océanie, Paris.
200-1 **Dreamstime.com**/Anibal Trejo.
202c **ACR Éditions** *Les Aïssaouas,* Georges Clairin (1843–1919) private collection.
210 **SuperStock**/Hemis.fr.
217tr **Jacana**/S. Cordier.
218–219 **Photoshot**: NHPA/Jordi Bas Cas.
220br Réunion des Musées Nationaux/R.G. Ojeda; *Reclining Lion with Prey,* Eugène Delacroix (1798–1863). Musée Bonnat, Bayonne.
223cbl **Jacana**/M. Bahr. 223crb **Jacana**/S. Cordier.
223br **Jacana**/J. and P. Wegner.
226 **Dreamstime.com**/Kemaltaner.
235tr **G. Dagli Orti**/Islamic Museum, Cairo, pharaonic village.

236-7 **Robert Harding Picture Library**/Matthew Williams-Ellis.
248 **Getty Images**/Christian Aslund.
254-5 **Robert Harding Picture Library**/Wigbert Roth.
264 **Dreamstime.com**/Madd.
274-5 **Alamy Images**/blickwinkel.
281bc **Jacana**/J.-L. Dubois; 281br **Jacana**/PHR/S. J. Collins; 281fbr **Jacana**/Frédéric.
286 **Robert Harding Picture Library**/Vincent Leduc
291tll **Photothèque Hachette**/ *L'Illustration* (11 September 1911).
294-5 **Robert Harding Picture Library**/Bruno Morandi.
297tr **Jacana**/J. Trotignon.
299bl **Photothèque Hachette**.
300-1 **Corbis**/Bernados.
302cl **Be Live Hotels & Luabay Hotels**; 302br **Sofitel Rabat Jardin des Roses**.
303br **Dar Attamani**.
304br **Riad d'Or**; 304tl **The Repose Luxury Riad**.
305tr **La Sultana Hotels**.
306bl **Sofitel Rabat Jardin des Roses**.
307tr **The Repose Luxury Riad**.
308tr **Mazagan Beach and Golf Resort**.
309bl **Be Live Hotels & Luabay Hotels**.
310bc **Sofitel Palais Jamai**.
311tr **Michlifen Ifrane**.
312tl **La Sultana Hotels**.
313br **Sofitel Royal Bay Resort**.
314br **Le Mirage Restaurant**; 314cl **Nord-Pinus Restaurant**.
315tl **Mazagan Beach and Golf Resort**.
316cla **Alamy Images**/Danita Delimont Collection/John and Lisa Merrill.
317tl **Alamy Images**/Kevin Foy;317c **PunchStock**/PhotoAlto/Jean-Blaise Hall.

320bl **Le Grand Comptoir**.
321tl **La Brasserie Bavaroise**.
322tl **L'Atelier Restaurant**.
323bc **Cinema Rif Restaurant**; 323tr **Mazagan Beach and Golf Resort**.
324br **Le Mirage Restaurant**.
325tr **Fes et Gestes Restaurant**.
326bl **Alamy Images**/Tibor Bognar.
329bl **Bab Ourika**.
330br **Relais & Châteaux Morocco**.
331t **La Gazelle D'Or Morocco**.
337bl **Réunion des Musées Nationaux**/Arnaudet. Musée des Arts d'Afrique et d'Océanie, Paris.
346-7 **Robert Harding Picture Library**/Steve Brockett.
364tr Alamy Images/Rob Crandall.
365br Alamy Images/Peter Erik Forsberg.
Front End papers Lbc **Dreamstime.com**/Kemaltaner; Ltc **Dreamstime.com**/Rechitan Sorin; Lbr **Robert Harding Picture Library**/Vincent Leduc; Ltr **Robert Harding Picture Library**/Dave Stamboulis; Rcr **Dreamstime.com**/Vladislav Gajic; Rbr **Dreamstime.com**/Javarman; Rbc **Dreamstime.com**/Madd; Rbl **Getty Images**/Christian Aslund; Rtl **Robert Harding Picture Library**/Tristan Deschamps; Rcl **Robert Harding Picture Library**/Dave Stamboulis; Rt **Robert Harding Picture Library**/Yadid Levy; Rc **Robert Harding Picture Library**/Bruno Morandi; Rclb **SuperStock**/Hemis.fr.
Jacket
Front and spine top: **Corbis**/Wolfgang Kaehler.
All other images © Dorling Kindersley. For further information see: www.dkimages.com

Further Reading

History and Society

David Hart, *Tribe and Society in Rural Morocco*, Frank Cass, UK and US. Essays on Moroccan tribes and the Berbers.

Donna Lee Bowen and Evelyn A. Early (eds), *Everyday Life in the Muslim Middle East*, Indiana University Press, US. Focusing on Morocco.

Peter Mansfield, *The Arabs*, Penguin, UK and US. General history, with a section on Morocco.

Gavin Maxwell, *Lords of the Atlas, The Rise and Fall of the House of Glaoui 1893–1956*, Cassell, UK.

Susan Raven, *Rome in Africa*, Routledge, US and UK. North Africa in Roman times.

Barnaby Rogerson, *A Traveller's History of North Africa*, Windrush, UK; Interlink, US. Readable general history, from the Roman period to the present day.

Natural and Urban Landscapes

Ann and Yan Arthus-Bertrand, *Morocco Seen from the Air*, Vendome Press, UK and US, 1994. Stunning aerial photographs of Morocco.

Jean-Marc Tingaud and Tahar Ben Jelloun, *Medinas: Morocco's Hidden Cities*, Thames & Hudson, UK and US. An intimate glimpse into the palaces of the imperial cities.

Hugues Demeude, Jacques Bravo and Xavier Richer, *Morocco*, Taschen, Germany. Lavish photographic survey.

Art and Architecture

Titus Burkhardt, *Art of Islam, Language and Meaning*.

Lisl and Landt Dennis, *Living in Morocco*, Thames & Hudson, UK. Lavishly illustrated portrait of the domestic environment.

James F. Jereb, *Arts and Crafts of Morocco*, Thames & Hudson, UK; Chronicle Books, US. Well-illustrated survey, including a guide to major museums in Morocco.

A. Khatabi and M. Sigilmassa, *The Splendours of Islamic Calligraphy*, Thames & Hudson, UK.

Richard Parker, *A Practical Guide to Islamic Monuments in Morocco*, Baraka Press, US.

Flora and Fauna

T. Haltenorth and H. Diller, Heinzel, BA, *Field Guide to the Mammals of Africa*, Collins, UK.

Fitter and Parslow, *The Birds of Britain and Europe with North Africa and the Middle East*, Collins, UK.

Cuisine

Robert Carrier, *Taste of Morocco*, Arrow, London.

Anissa Helou, *Café Morocco*, Conran Octopus, UK and US.

Paula Wolfert, *Couscous and Other Good Foods from Morocco*, HarperCollins, US.

Travel, Biography and Fiction

Paul Bowles, *The Sheltering Sky*, Penguin, UK; Ecco Press, US. *Let It Come Down*, Penguin, UK; Black Sparrow Press, US. *Collected Stories of Paul Bowles 1939–76*, Black Sparrow Press, US. *Midnight Mass*, Peter Owen, UK; Black Sparrow Press, US. On the theme of Westerners in a foreign land, from the best-known writer on Morocco. *Their Heads are Green*, Peter Owen, UK. Travel essays. *Without Stopping*, Peter Owen, UK; Ecco Press, US. Bowles' autobiography.

William Burroughs, *Naked Lunch*, Flamingo, Harper Collins UK; Grove Press, US. Revolutionary novel of sexuality and drug addiction, set in Tangier.

Anthony Burgess, *Earthly Powers*, Penguin, UK; Carroll & Graf, US. *The Complete Enderby*, Carroll & Graf, US. Tangier in the 1950s.

Elias Canetti, *The Voices of Marrakesh*, Marion Boyars, UK. Marrakech near the end of the Protectorate.

Esther Freud, *Hideous Kinky*, Penguin UK, WW Norton, US. An English hippy in Marrakech.

Walter Harris, *Morocco That Was*, Eland Books, UK. Observations by *The Times* correspondent, 1890s–1933.

Richard Hughes, *In the Lap of Atlas*, Chatto, UK. Moroccan tales.

Amin Malouf, *Leo the African*, Abacus, UK; *Leo Africanus*, New Amsterdam, US. Historical novel about the 15th-century geographer.

Moroccan Writing in English

Tahar Ben Jalloun, *The Sand Child*, Hamish Hamilton UK, Johns Hopkins UP, US. Novel of childhood in southern Morocco.

Mohammed Choukri, *For Bread Alone*, I.B. Tauris, UK. Volume I of the Rif-born Choukri's autobiography.

Five Eyes, Black Sparrow Press, US. Stories by five Moroccan writers.

Driss Chraibi, *Heirs to the Past*, Heinemann, UK and US. Semi-autobiographical novel set in post-colonial times.

Glossary

adrar: mountain.

agadir: collective granary in the western Atlas.

agdal: large garden, orchard.

aguelmane: permanent natural lake.

ahidou: collective dance performed by the Berber tribes of the Middle Atlas and eastern High Atlas.

ahwach: collective dance performed by villagers of the western High Atlas and the Anti-Atlas.

aïd: festival.

aït: "son of", referring to a tribe or the region occupied by this tribe.

Ammeln: Berber tribe of the Anti-Atlas whose language is Chleuh (qv).

assif: river or watercourse.

bab: city gate.

baraka: divine blessing, which is passed down from parent to child. *Baraka* is also obtained by making a pilgrimage to a holy shrine.

bendir: drum consisting of a goatskin stretched over a frame.

bled: countryside, village.

borj: bastion or tower set at the corners of the defensive walls of fortified houses.

burnous: voluminous woollen hooded cloak worn by men.

cadi: religious judge, once having the power to impose *sharia* law.

caid: chief of a defined territory, subordinate to the governor of a province.

caliph: title held by a Muslim chief, designating Mohammed's successor.

chergui: hot, dry southeasterly wind.

Chikhate: female dancer from the Middle Atlas.

Chleuh: Berber tribe of the Atlas and Anti-Atlas. Also the language spoken by the tribes of these regions.

dahir: decree having the force of law in Morocco.

dar: house.

dayet: natural lake formed by underground water.

diffa: feast-day meal.

dirham: Moroccan unit of currency.

douar: hamlet.

emir: personal title meaning "he who commands".

erg: expanse of sand or ridge of dunes.

Fassi: inhabitant of Fès.

fiqh: Islamic legal code.

fondouk: in the past, hostelry for travelling merchants, their beasts of burden and their merchandise.

gebs: plaster that can be decoratively carved. Also known as stucco.

gurbi: house of semi-nomadic people, built with mud and branches.

Gnaoua: religious brotherhood of popular belief originating in black Africa. Followers consider themselves to be the spiritual descendants of Bilal, an Ethiopian slave, whom the Prophet Mohammed set free before making him his muezzin (qv).

guedra: dance characteristic of the Goulimine region of Morocco, performed by kneeling women. Also the large drum that is played to accompany the dancers.

Hadith: collection of legends relating to the life, words and deeds of the Prophet Mohammed.

Hadj: pilgrimage to Mecca.

haik: long woman's wrap made from a single piece of fabric, worn draped around the body.

hamada: stony, arid plateau in the Sahara.

hammam: Turkish bath.

hanbel: carpet or blanket woven by Berbers.

Hegira: starting point of the Muslim era, on 16 July 622.

henna: shrub grown for its leaves, which, among other things, are used in the manufacture of cosmetics.

igherm: communal fortified granary typical of the central High Atlas.

imam: Islamic leader of congregational prayer.

jbel: mountain.

jellaba: wide-sleeved, hooded garment worn by both men and women.

jemaa: village assembly of the heads of families in Berber tribes.

kaftan: long woman's garment secured at the front and decorated with passementerie and embroidery.

kasbah: fortified house with a single crenellated tower, or four crenellated towers, one at each corner of the walls.

khoubz: bread (usually a circular loaf).

khaima: tent made of woven goat-hair or camel-hair, used by the nomads of the Sahara and the semi-nomadic people of the Atlas.

khettara: underground channels for the provision of water, along whose course wells are sunk. Synonymous with foggara.

koubba: cube-like building crowned by a dome and housing the tomb of a venerated individual.

ksar (pl. *ksour***):** fortified village surrounded by solid walls set with towers at the angles.

Lalla: title of respect given to women.

maalem: master-craftsman.

makhzen: central power, royal authority.

marabout: prestigious head of a religious brotherhood. By extension, the term also refers to the tomb of such a holy man.

mashrabiyya: wooden latticework panel used as a screen in front of balconies and in the windows of mosques and houses, to hide those within from view.

méchouar: parade ground at the entrance to a royal palace.

medersa: Koranic school with resident students.

medina: traditional Arab town enclosed by ramparts; from Medina, the city where the Prophet Mohammed found refuge from persecution.

mellah: Jewish quarter of a medina.

menzah: pavilion in a palace garden.

mihrab: niche in a mosque, indicating the direction of Mecca.

minaret: tower of a mosque from the top of which the muezzin (qv), or an electric recording, calls the faithful to prayer.

minbar: pulpit in a mosque, from which the imam (qv) leads Friday prayers.

moqqade: head of a village or of a religious brotherhood.

Mouloud: birthday of the Prophet Mohammed.

moussem: important annual festival involving a pilgrimage to the tomb of a saint, a commercial fair and popular entertainment.

muezzin: religious official who calls the faithful to prayer.

muqarna: decorative elements in the form of stalactites, made of stucco or wood and suspended from the ceiling.

nisrani: "Nazarene"– a Christian, or European.

pisé: mixture of sun-baked earth, grit and sometimes straw used as a building material in rural areas.

qibla: direction of Mecca, indicated in mosques by a wall in the centre of which is the mihrab (qv).

Ramadan: ninth month of the Muslim (lunar) year, during which

Muslims are required to fast from sunrise to sunset.

reg: stony desert.

riad: traditional residence organized around a courtyard planted with trees and flowers.

ribat: fortified monastery from where Muslim warrior monks set out to spread the Islamic faith.

seguia: irrigation canal for crops.

serdal: brightly coloured scarf worn by Berber women, decorated with coins.

seroual: loose, calf-length trousers fastened at the waist and the knees, worn under the *jellaba* (qv).

shamir: long, wide-sleeved man's shirt worn under another garment.

sharia: religious law based on the teachings of the Koran.

sheikh: chief of a tribal subdivision or the leader of a religious brotherhood.

sherif (pl. shorfa)**:** descendant of the Prophet Mohammed.

shorfa: *see sherif.*

souk: market, laid out according to the various goods and services that the stallholders offer.

sura: verse of the Koran.

tighremt: Berber word for a kasbah (qv). A fortified patriarchal house several storeys high with towers at the corners.

tizi: mountain pass.

wadi: river bed that is dry or semi-dry except in rainy season; river; river valley. Anglicized form of *oued.*

zakat: obligatory almsgiving. One of the five pillars of Islam.

zaouia: seat of a religious brotherhood that gives religious instruction, the shrine where a *marabout* (qv) is buried.

zellij: geometric tilework, typically arranged in intricate, colourful patterns.

French Phrase Book

In Emergency

Help!	Au secours!	oh se**koor**
Stop!	Arrêtez!	aret-**ay**
Call a doctor!	Appelez un médecin!	apuh-**lay** uñ med**sañ**
Call an ambulance!	Appelez une ambulance!	apuh-**lay** oon oñboo-**loñs**
Call the police!	Appelez la police!	apuh-**lay** lah poh-**lees**
Call the fire department!	Appelez les pompiers!	apuh-lay leh poñ-**peeyay**
Where is the nearest hospital?	Où est l'hôpital le plus proche?	oo ay l'ope**etal** luh ploo **prosh**

Communication Essentials

Yes	Oui	wee
No	Non	noñ
Please	S'il vous plaît	seel voo **play**
Thank you	Merci	mer-**see**
Excuse me	Excusez-moi	exkoo-**zay** mwah
Hello	Bonjour	boñ**zhoor**
Goodbye	Au revoir	oh ruh-**vwar**
Good night	Bonsoir	boñ-**swar**
Morning	Le matin	ma**tañ**
Afternoon	L'après-midi	l'apreh-**meedee**
Evening	Le soir	swar
Yesterday	Hier	ee**yehr**
Today	Aujourd'hui	oh-zhoor-**dwee**
Tomorrow	Demain	duh**mañ**
Here	Ici	ee-**see**
There	Là	lah
What?	Quel, quelle?	kel, kel
When?	Quand?	koñ
Why?	Pourquoi?	poor-**kwah**
Where?	Où?	oo

Useful Phrases

How are you?	Comment allez-vous?	kom-moñ tal**ay** voo
Very well, thank you.	Très bien, merci.	treh byañ, mer-**see**
Pleased to meet you.	Enchanté de faire votre connaissance.	oñshoñ-**tay** duh fehr votr kon-ay-**sans**
See you soon.	A bientôt.	byañ-**toh**
Where is/are…?	Où est/sont…?	oo ay/soñ
How far is it to…?	Combien de kilomètres d'ici à…?	kom-**byañ** duh keelo-metr d'ee-see ah
Which way to…?	Quelle est la direction pour…?	kel ay lah deer-ek-**syoñ** poor
Do you speak English?	Parlez-vous anglais?	par-**lay** voo oñg-**lay**
I don't understand.	Je ne comprends pas.	zhuh nuh kom-**proñ** pah
Could you speak slowly please?	Pouvez-vous parler moins vite s'il vous plaît?	poo-**vay** voo par-**lay** mwañ veet seel voo play
I'm sorry.	Excusez-moi.	exkoo-**zay** mwah

Useful Words

big	grand	groñ
small	petit	puh-**tee**
hot	chaud	show
cold	froid	frwah
good	bon	boñ
bad	mauvais	moh-**veh**
enough	assez	assay
open	ouvert	oo-**ver**
closed	fermé	fer-**meh**
left	gauche	gohsh
right	droite	drwaht
straight ahead	tout droit	too drwah
near	près	preh
far	loin	lwañ
early	de bonne heure	duh bon urr
late	en retard	oñ ruh-**tar**
entrance	l'entrée	l'on-**tray**
exit	la sortie	sor-**tee**
toilet	les toilettes, les WC	twah-**let**, vay-**see**
free, no charge	gratuit	grah-**twee**
Monday	lundi	luñ-**dee**
Tuesday	mardi	mar-**dee**
Wednesday	mercredi	mehrkruh-**dee**
Thursday	jeudi	zhuh-**dee**
Friday	vendredi	voñdruh-**dee**
Saturday	samedi	sam-**dee**
Sunday	dimanche	dee-**moñsh**

Making a Telephone Call

I'd like to place a long-distance call.	Je voudrais télé-phoner a l'etranger.	zhuh voo-dreh fehr uñ añter-oorbañ
I'll try again later.	Je rappelerai plus tard.	zhuh rapel-**eray** ploo tar
Hold on.	Ne quittez pas, s'il vous plaît.	nuh kee-**tay** pah seel voo play
Could you speak up a little please?	Pouvez-vous parler un peu plus fort?	poo-**vay** voo par-**lay** uñ puh ploo for
local call	la communication locale	komoonikah-**syoñ** low-**kal**

Shopping

How much does this cost?	C'est combien s'il vous plaît?	say kom-**byañ** seel voo play
I would like …	je voudrais…	zhuh voo-**dray**
Do you have?	Est-ce que vous avez?	es-kuh voo zavay
I'm just looking.	Je regarde seulement.	zhuh ruh**gar** suh**moñ**
Do you take credit cards?	Est-ce que vous acceptez les cartes de crédit?	es-kuh voo zaksept-**ay** leh kart duh kreh-**dee**
This one.	Celui-ci.	suhl-wee-**see**
That one.	Celui-là.	suhl-wee-**lah**
expensive	cher	shehr
cheap	pas cher, bon marché	pah shehr, boñ mar-**shay**
size, clothes	la taille	tye

Sightseeing

art gallery	la galerie d'art	galer-**ree** dart
bus station	la gare routière	gahr roo-tee-**yehr**
garden	le jardin	zhar-**dañ**
mosque	la mosquée	mos-**qay**
museum	le musée	moo-**zay**
tourist information office	les renseignements touristiques, le syndicat d'initiative	roñsayn-**moñ** too-rees-teek, sandee-ka d'eenee-sya**teev**
train station	la gare	gahr

Staying in a Hotel

Do you have a vacant room?	Est-ce que vous avez une chambre?	es-kuh voo-**zavay** oon shambr
double room, with double bed	la chambre à deux personnes, avec un grand lit	shambr ah duh pehr-**son** avek un groññ lee
twin room	la chambre à deux lits	shambr ah duh lee
single room	la chambre à une personne	shambr ah oon pehr-**son**
room with a bath, shower	la chambre avec salle de bains, une douche	shambr avek sal duh bañ, oon doosh
I have a reservation.	J'ai fait une réservation.	zhay fay oon rayzehrva-**syoñ**

Eating Out

Have you got a table?	Avez-vous une table de libre?	avay-**voo** oon tahbl duh leebr
I want to reserve a table.	Je voudrais réserver une table.	zhuh voo-**dray** rayzehr-**vay** oon tahbl
The check please.	L'addition s'il vous plaît.	l'adee-**syoñ** seel voo play
I am a vegetarian.	Je suis végétarien.	zhuh swee vezhay-**tehryañ**
menu	le menu, la carte	men--**oo**, karto
breakfast	le petit déjeuner	puh-**tee** deh-**zhuh-nay**
lunch	le déjeuner	deh-**zhuh-nay**
dinner	le dîner	dee-**nay**

Numbers

1	un, une	uñ, oon
2	deux	duh
3	trois	trwah
4	quatre	katr
5	cinq	sañk
6	six	sees
7	sept	set
8	huit	weet
9	neuf	nerf
10	dix	dees

Moroccan Arabic Phrase Book

Moroccan Arabic is unique to Morocco and is not understood by other Arabic speakers. Moroccans speak faster and abbreviate words. Pronunciation is gentler due to the influence of French.

In Emergency

Help!	**aa**we**noo**oni
Stop!	**ow**kof!
Can you call a doctor?	momkin **kellem** el ta**beeb**?
Call an ambulance!	**aa**ye**to** aala el isaaf
Can you call the police?	mom**kin** kel**lem** el po**lees**?
Call the fire department!	**aa**ye**to** aala el matafie
Where is the nearest hospital?	fin **kayn akrab** mos**tash**fa

Communication Essentials

Yes	**na**-am
No	laa
Please	min **fad**lak
Thank you	se'hha / **shuk**ran
Excuse me	is**mah**lee
Hello /	selaam
Peace be upon you	
Goodbye	ma'eel sa**laa**ma
Good evening	ma**saal** kheer
Good morning	es**be'h** el**kheer**
Yesterday	**el** baareh
Today	el yoom
Tomorrow	gha**dan**
Here	hina
There	hinak
What?	shnoo?
When?	**im**ta?
Why?	alash?
Where?	fayn?

Useful Phrases

How are you?	wash**raak**?
I'm fine.	**laa**bas
Pleased to meet you.	metshar-fin
Where is/are…?	fayn…?
Which way to…?	ina te**rik…** ?
Do you speak English?	**tat**kalam engleeze-ya?
I don't understand.	**a**na mafhim**taksh**
I'm sorry.	es**me'h**lee

Useful Words

big	k**beer**
small	s**geer**
hot	so**khoon**
cold	**baa**red
good	m**lee**'ha
bad	mashem**lee**'ha
open	maf**too**'h
closed	magh**look**
left	li**seer**
right	li**meen**
straight ahead	**nee**shan
near	qu**rayab**
far	ba**eed**
entrance	do**khool**
exit	khrooj
toilet	towa**lett**
tonight	fel**leel**
day	ne**haar**
hour	**sa**'aa
week	se**maa**na
Monday	el et**neen**
Tuesday	el t**laa**ta
Wednesday	el ar**be**'aa
Thursday	el kha**mee**s
Friday	el **jo**mo'aa
Saturday	el sabet
…day	el a'**had**

Shopping

How much is it?	kam else'**er**?
I would like…	**a**na 'hab**bayt** …
Do you have?	**an**dak…?
This one	haazi
expensive	**ghaa**lya
cheap	re**khee**sa

Sightseeing

art gallery	gali**ree** daar
bus station	stas**yon** do boos
garden	el**jo**nayna
mosque	mas**jid**
museum	**moo**zi
tourist office	mek**tab** so**yaa**'h
train station	ma**hat**tat el tren
beach	b**har**
guide	geed
map	kaart
park	baark
ticket	**te**kee

Staying in a Hotel

Do you have a room?	en**ta** '**an**dak **ghor**fa?
double room,	**ghor**fa le shakh**sayn**
with double bed	joj bioot
single room	**ghor**fa le shakhs **waa**'hid
with bathroom / shower	ma'al '**ham-maam** / **doosh**
I have a reservation.	**a**na me**reser**ve hna

Eating Out/Food

Have you got a table for…?	en**ta** '**an**dak **tow**la le…?
I want to reserve a table.	brit **re**serve wahd tabla
The check please.	te'e**tee**ni elfa**too**ra min **fad**lak?
I am a vegetarian.	**a**na na**bat**i wa la a**ku**lu lehoum **wala** hout
breakfast	if**tar**
lunch	reda
dinner	**aa**sha
steamed pot of vegetables with meat, etc.	ta**jeen**
hand-made couscous	**kus**kus
pastry filled with vegetables and meat, etc.	elbas**tee**la
soup	'**hree**ra
meatballs with herbs	**kef**ta
fish	el'**hoot**
chicken	djaaj
meat	l'hem
vegetables	le**goom**/**kho**dra
water	**maa**'a

Numbers

1	**waa**'hid
2	zooj
3	t**laa**ta
4	ara**ba**'aa
5	**kham**sa
6	**set**-ta
7	**seb**a'a
8	t**maan**ya
9	**tes**'aa
10	'**ash**ra
20	esh**reen**
50	kham**seen**
100	me**ya**